Erzählen und Recht

Narrative and Law

Herausgegeben von

Monika Fludernik

Frank L. Schäfer

FAKTUALES UND FIKTIONALES ERZÄHLEN

Schriftenreihe des Graduiertenkollegs 1767

Herausgegeben von
Monika Fludernik

Band 12

ERGON VERLAG

Erzählen und Recht

Narrative and Law

Herausgegeben von

Monika Fludernik
Frank L. Schäfer

ERGON VERLAG

Umschlagabbildung:
© CanStockPhoto.com – csp 16487225

Bibliografische Information der Deutschen Nationalbibliothek:
Die Deutsche Nationalbibliothek verzeichnet diese Publikation in der Deutschen Nationalbibliografie; detaillierte bibliografische Daten sind im Internet über http://dnb.d-nb.de abrufbar.

Gedruckt auf alterungsbeständigem Papier.
Gesamtverantwortung für Druck und Herstellung bei der Nomos Verlagsgesellschaft mbH & Co. KG
Umschlaggestaltung: Jan von Hugo

www.ergon-verlag.de

ISSN 2365-8851
ISBN 978-3-95650-963-6 (Print)
ISBN 978-3-95650-964-3 (ePDF)

Inhalt

Einleitung

Frank L. Schäfer und Monika Fludernik

Der vorliegende Sammelband geht auf die Tagung „Law and Literature from a Narratological Perspective / Recht und Literatur aus narratologischer Sicht" zurück, die im Rahmen des von der DFG geförderten Graduiertenkollegs „Faktuales und fiktionales Erzählen" (GRK 1767) vom 6. bis 8. Mai 2021 in Freiburg stattfand. Dabei sollte die Arbeit des Graduiertenkollegs im Bereich des faktualen Erzählens interdisziplinär auf das Erzählen im Recht und das Erzählen über das Recht ausgedehnt werden. Innerhalb des Graduiertenkollegs wird so mit dem Recht ein weiterer Bereich neben der Geschichte (bzw. Geschichtswissenschaft), den Kommunikations- und Medienwissenschaften, der Ökonomie, der linguistischen Diskursanalyse, der Kunstgeschichte, der Medizin, der Philosophie, Psychologie und Theologie sowie den Literaturwissenschaften aufgegriffen, in dem faktuales und manchmal auch fiktionales Erzählen eine wichtige Rolle spielt.

Wenn die Narratologie auf das Recht trifft, dann trifft sie auf einen überaus weitverzweigten Gegenstand. Das Recht stellt in dieser Konstellation die Universalität narratologischer Begriffe und Methoden auf die Probe. Als Textkorpus der Narratologie umfasst das Recht alle Rechtsnormen und die dazugehörige Rechtsliteratur. Zu den Rechtsnormen zählen nicht nur Parlamentsgesetze, exekutive Rechtsverordnungen, Satzungen öffentlich-rechtlicher Körperschaften, Gewohnheitsrecht und interne Verwaltungsanweisungen, sondern auch Verwaltungsakte und Gerichtsentscheidungen sowie individuelle Verträge und Allgemeine Geschäftsbedingungen, d.h. alle Stufen der Rechtsanwendung von der abstrakten Rechtsgrundlage bis hin zum konkreten Einzelfall bzw. bis hin zu privaten Vereinbarungen. Daneben bietet der vorgelagerte Akt der Rechtsquellenschöpfung der Narratologie reiches Material. Zu denken ist hier nicht allein an die Entstehungsgeschichte von Gesetzen, sondern an jeden Normschöpfungsakt bis hin zu Vertragsverhandlungen. Förmliche staatliche und nichtstaatliche Entscheidungsverfahren wie Gerichts- und Schiedsverfahren bieten eine Schnittmenge von Rechtsanwendung und Rechtsquellenschöpfung, da solche Verfahren einerseits auf prozeduralen Normen basieren (z.B. die Zeugenbefragung), andererseits aber eine juristische Entscheidung vorbereiten. Rechtsordnungen in der modernen Welt müssen sich ausdifferenzieren und spezialisieren, um sich den schnell ändernden gesellschaftlichen, ökonomischen und technischen Rahmenbedingungen anzupassen. Das steigert die Vielfalt zusätzlich. Ebenso divergieren die Normadressaten. Im Zivilrecht dominieren Gesetze mit einer für Rechtslaien kryptischen und voraussetzungsvollen, an Rechtsanwälte gerichteten Terminologie; im Verfassungsrecht erzählen Präambeln den Bürgern mit Pathos Bruchstücke der Nationalgeschichte; das Strafrecht wiederum nimmt die Bürger in den Blick, an welche sich die in den Strafrechtsnormen enthaltenen Verbote unmittelbar richten.

Hinzu kommt auch noch die Rechtsliteratur, die sich (vereinfacht gesprochen) in die Literatur zum geltenden Recht und die Literatur der Grundlagenfächer wie Rechtsphilosophie und Rechtsgeschichte unterteilt. Die Literatur zum geltenden Recht orientiert sich in Aufbau und Sprache an Gesetzbüchern und bietet daher ungeachtet des Grades wissenschaftlicher Originalität nur wenige Erzählungen. Aus Sicht der Narratologie ist also kein Unterschied zwischen Gebrauchsliteratur für die Rechtspraxis und wissenschaftlicher Literatur für das akademische Publikum festzustellen. Anschlussfähiger ist die Literatur zu den Grundlagenfächern, die keinem strengen Formzwang unterliegt und wie im Fall der Rechtsgeschichte oft chronologisch aufgebaut ist.

Die der wissenschaftlichen Rechtsliteratur zugrundeliegenden akademischen Fächer befinden sich in unterschiedlicher Distanz zu den Literaturwissenschaften als intellektueller Basis der Narratologie. Während beispielsweise die Rechtsgeschichte bereits auf den ersten Blick als Teil der Geschichtswissenschaft im Lager der Geisteswissenschaften steht und somit für die Narratologie taugliche Korpora generieren kann, liegen die Dinge bei den Fächern des geltenden Rechts nicht so einfach. Diese Fächer basieren auf Texten in Form von Lehrbüchern, Kommentaren usw., doch sind sie weitaus stärker als die Grundlagenfächer an die spezifischen Eigenschaften des Rechts gebunden. Rechtsnormen stellen eine Sollensordnung auf. Normen ordnen Verbote oder Gebote an, erlauben Handlungen oder stellen von einer Handlungspflicht frei. Alle Rechtsnormen eint ihre Verbindlichkeit, d.h. sie sind auch gegen den Willen des Normadressaten vollstreckbar. Das unterscheidet sie von sozialen Normen, aber auch von einer normativen Übereinkunft in der Narratologie, z.B. über den faktualen oder fiktionalen Gehalt einer Erzählung. Dementsprechend können die Fächer des geltenden Rechts Erzählungen grundsätzlich nur generieren, soweit die zugrundeliegenden Normen Erzählungen enthalten oder diese voraussetzen.

Weitaus seltener als die Literaturwissenschaften bedient sich die Rechtswissenschaft der Narratologie, genauer gesagt, die deutsche Rechtswissenschaft, der die folgenden Anmerkungen gewidmet sind. Die moderne Rechtswissenschaft hat bereits seit ihren Anfängen um 1800 Recht und Literatur im Sinne des Oberbegriffs Law and Literature verbunden. Die Germanistik als Disziplin nimmt ihren Ausgangspunkt nicht in der Literaturwissenschaft, sondern in der juristischen Germanistik, d.h. in der Deutschen Rechtsgeschichte. Davon zeugen die Brüder Jacob (1785–1863) und Wilhelm Grimm (1786–1859) mit ihrem Deutschen Rechtswörterbuch und ihrer Märchensammlung sowie Dichterjuristen wie Felix Dahn (1834–1912). Teils werden Recht und Literatur im Werk synthetisiert, teils stehen beide Sparten in einer Person nebeneinander. Die Synthese hat zwei Gesichter (zur Unterscheidung im Folgenden Schramm 2007): Nicht wenige juristische Studien in den vergangenen 200 Jahren widmeten sich der Literatur, benutzten diese als Steinbruch für Rechtstexte und Rechtsfälle. Insofern ist auch der Begriff Law in Literature (vgl. Weisberg 1984, 1992) der Sache nach für die deutsche Rechtswissenschaft eine altbekannte Konstante. Weitaus seltener betrachtet die Rechtswissenschaft ihren Forschungsgegenstand Recht allerdings *als Literatur* (Law as Literature – Levinson 1988, Hyde1997). Denn für einen solchen Blickwechsel müsste die Rechtswissenschaft nicht nur auf interdisziplinäre Instrumentarien zurückgreifen, sondern ihren Gegenstand selbst als Subsystem anderer Wissenschaften begreifen und somit die vertraute Perspektive auf das Rechtssystem *als normative Ordnung* verlassen.

Innerhalb des kleinen Bereichs Law as Literature finden sich im Bereich der deutschen Rechtswissenschaft nur wenige Studien über Narratologie oder Studien, welche mit narratologischen Instrumentarien im Sinne von Law as Narrative arbeiten. Das erstaunt auf einen ersten unbefangenen Blick, weil sich auch in der Rechtswissenschaft, insbesondere in der Rechtsgeschichte, in den vergangenen zwanzig Jahren die Begriffe Meistererzählung und Narrativ eingebürgert haben. Zumeist fehlt allerdings ein wissenschaftlicher Bezug zur Narratologie. Als Ausnahmen sind vor allem Lüderssen (2002), Arnauld (2009, 2017), Arnauld und Martini (2015) sowie Stolleis (2008, 2015) und in jüngerer Zeit umfassend Blufarb (2017) zu nennen. Blufarb untersucht darüber hinaus, inwiefern sich die Narratologie für spezifisch juristische Zwecke bei der Gesetzgebung und Urteilsfindung einsetzen lässt, in anderen Worten, ob die Narratologie sich in den Kanon der juristischen Methodenlehre und in den Rahmen der Sollensordnung des Rechts integrieren lässt.

Die Gründe für die Zurückhaltung der Rechtswissenschaft gegenüber der Narratologie liegen nicht offen zutage, sondern sind nur zu vermuten. Die deutsche Rechtswissenschaft übt in Europa aufgrund der herausragenden ökonomischen Stellung der Bundesrepublik und durch die vergleichsweise gewaltige Masse an juristischer Literatur eine enorme Gravitationskraft aus. Umgekehrt ist der Blick der deutschen Rechtswissenschaft oft nach innen gekehrt und auf die Rechtsdogmatik, das heißt auf Systeme, Begriffe und Lehrsätze des Rechts, sowie auf den nationalen Diskurs fokussiert. Komparative und interdisziplinäre Ansätze wie solche, die die Narratologie einbinden, stehen an der Peripherie. Unser Tagungsband will daher nicht nur den internationalen Diskurs an der Schnittstelle von Narratologie und Recht fördern. Vielmehr wollen Herausgeberin und Herausgeber auch einen Beitrag zum interdisziplinären Diskurs innerhalb der deutschen Rechtswissenschaft und der deutschen Rechtswissenschaft mit den Literaturwissenschaften leisten.

Im Gegensatz zur noch relativ seltenen Berücksichtigung der Erzählforschung in der deutschen Rechtswissenschaft (mit den oben genannten Ausnahmen) hat sich, aus Amerika kommend, Law and Literature bereits stärker etabliert, was auch der unter anglistischer Leitung stehende Sonderforschungsbereich 1385 in Münster zeigt,[1] aus dem auch zwei der Autoren dieses Bandes stammen. Insofern die Mehrzahl von Beiträgen im Bereich Law and Literature sich mit Romanen oder Filmen befassen, ist die Narratologie in dieser Forschung zwar allseits präsent, aber die Fragestellungen sind nicht konkret narratologisch, bzw. die Narratologie spielt neben vielen anderen literaturtheoretischen Ansätzen eine untergeordnete Rolle. In den USA, wo die Law and Literature-Bewegung ihren Ausgangspunkt genommen hat, ist diese mittlerweile Teil der Law and Humanities-Bewegung (Sarat et al., 2010). In Deutschland aber auch in Europa hat sich die Law and Literature-Bewegung vorrangig in der anglistischen Literaturwissenschaft etabliert, wie auch die Beiträge in diesem Band zeigen.

Der Band beginnt mit dem Aufsatz von **Ruth Blufarb**, der die wesentlichen Ergebnisse ihrer Dissertation (Blufarb 2017) zusammenfasst und die Chancen und Grenzen der Analyse von Recht(-stexten) mit narratologischen Instrumenten diskutiert. Dazu verortet sie Law as Narrative im weiteren Kontext von Law as Literature und prüft, inwiefern sich Ergebnisse der angloamerikanisch geprägten Diskussion über Law as Narrative vom Fallrecht des Common Law auf die vom Kodifikationsprinzip geprägte deutsche Rechtsordnung übertragen lassen. Anschließend umreißt Blufarb die Narrativität in Bezug auf deutsche Rechtstexte und stellt die wichtigsten Konzepte des Law as Narrative-Ansatzes vor. Zum Abschluss überprüft sie auf zahlreichen Feldern, von *narrative competition* über *stock stories* bis hin zum *outsider scholarship*, die Tragfähigkeit dieser Konzepte für die deutsche Rechtsordnung.

Die beiden folgenden Beiträge befassen sich aus juristischer und danach literaturwissenschaftlicher Sicht mit dem Copyright bzw. mit auktorialen Ansprüchen auf literarische Rechtstitel. Dabei skizziert **Robert Spoo** die Institution der sog. *trade courtesy* im amerikanischen Verlagswesen, d.h. eines unverbindlichen Handelsbrauchs zwischen Verlegern. Dahinter verbirgt sich das Problem, dass das US-amerikanische Urheberrecht im 19. Jahrhundert ausländischen Autoren bzw. deren amerikanischen Verlegern keinen Urheberschutz bzw. keine gegen Dritte wirkenden Nutzungsrechte gewährte. Die amerikanischen Verleger schlossen sich daher zu einem Kartell zusammen, das für solche Fälle einen Schutz vergleichbar mit dem Urheberrecht für inländische amerikanische Autoren fingierte. Spoo untersucht am Beispiel des englischen Autors Charles Dickens und dessen Verhalten gegenüber amerikanischen Verlegern die Grenzen dieser Fiktion. **Peter Schneck** geht von der Frage aus, wie der Autor

[1] Siehe https://www.uni-muenster.de/SFB1385/.

für seine Erfindung Anspruch auf geistiges Eigentum erheben kann und wie sich die Diskurse solcher Eigentumsansprüche mit rechtlichen Diskursen über Landnahme und Landeinnahme überschneiden. In der Folge weist Schneck anhand von drei Fallbeispielen nach, dass das Verhältnis von Eigentum und Identität im Rechtssystem sich in den drei gewählten Romanen (James Fenimore Coopers *The Pioneers*, dt. *Die Ansiedler*; Charles Chesnutts *The House Behind the Cedars* und Kaui Hart Hemmings *The Descendants*) symptomatisch und pointiert repräsentiert findet. So kann Coopers wegweisender historischer Roman als *romance of property*, als Besitz-Romanze, gelesen werden, während Chesnutts *The House Behind the Cedars* die Grundannahmen Coopers im Lichte der rassistischen Diskriminierung und Enteignung afroamerikanischer Subjekte dekonstruiert. Der postkoloniale Text von Hart Hemmings hingegen restituiert Besitzansprüche der indigenen Bevölkerung im Rahmen einer Rekonzeptualisierung von Eigentumsrechten.

Hans J. Lind greift die gegenseitige Beeinflussung von Recht und Literatur anhand der Frage der juristischen Verhandlung fiktionaler Literatur auf. Er untersucht amerikanische und deutsche Urteile darauf hin, ob die darin getroffenen Schlüsse von der fiktionalen auf die faktuale Ebene einem narratologischen Test standhalten und welche juristischen Implikationen daraus folgen.

Die beiden folgenden Beiträge befassen sich mit den Geschichten, die im Rechtsverfahren erzählt werden. **Jeanne Gaakeer** weist mit zahlreichen Beispielen nach, dass in Rechtsverfahren die Konstruktion des Geschehens durch narratologisch wohl bekannte Interpretationsverfahren von der Wahrheitsfindung ablenken kann und dass die Gefahr der Typisierung von Motiven und daher Schuldzuschreibungen allgegenwärtig ist. **Frode Helmich Pedersen** verfolgt eine ähnliche Argumentation. Er konzentriert sich auf ein norwegisches Fallbeispiel und zeigt auf, dass eine Verurteilung bei einem Indizienprozess auch auf stereotypen Motivationszuschreibungen basieren kann.

Mit **Dominique Hipps** Beitrag wird ein zentrales Thema des Graduiertenkollegs, nämlich die Unterscheidung von Faktualität und Fiktionalität, die bereits in den zwei vorangegangenen Aufsätzen eine tragende Rolle spielte, noch einmal radikaler aufgegriffen. Hipp wählt in Abgrenzung zu ihrer Dissertation (Hipp 2020) über Tätererzählungen von Angeklagten in Prozessen zu nationalsozialistischen Konzentrationslagern in ihrem Beitrag für den vorliegenden Sammelband das Zeugnis des überlebenden Opfers Maryla Rosenthal aus dem ersten Frankfurter Auschwitz- Prozess als ihr Fallbeispiel. Hipp wechselt damit von der prozessualen zur narratologischen Sichtweise auf Zeugenaussagen und arbeitet den Wert solcher Aussagen als historische und erzählende Dokumente heraus. Damit stehen nicht mehr die Glaubwürdigkeit der Zeugin und die Glaubhaftigkeit ihrer Aussage (wie das bei den Täternarrativen der Fall war), sondern Subjektivität und repräsentativer Charakter der Erzählung im Mittelpunkt. Mit anderen Worten: Die Erzähltheorie transformiert einen Tatsachenbericht zu einem Erfahrungsbericht.

Mit dem Beitrag von **Arild Linneberg** kommen philosophische Fragen zum Zuge. In Vorwegnahme einiger Ideen, die Hayden White popularisiert hat, wurde bereits von Siegfried Kracauer beobachtet, dass die erzählende Gestaltung im juristischen (bei White im historischen) Text fundamentale Auswirkung auf die Interpretation hat. Linnebergs Darstellung konzentriert sich darauf, den Beitrag von Siegfried Kracauer zu Fragen der Verbindung von Recht und Literatur wieder in Erinnerung zu rufen, nachdem dieser lange Zeit aus dem Blickfeld geraten war.

Die folgenden drei Beiträge konzentrieren sich auf literaturwissenschaftliche Fragestellungen bzw. auf Probleme, die aus literaturwissenschaftlicher Sicht erörtert werden. **Claudia Lieb** sucht nach dem Ursprung der Einteilung der Geschichtsschreibung in eine äußere und in eine innere Geschichte. Im Anschluss zeichnet sie nach, wie sich diese Unterteilung in Romanen, in der Romantheorie, der Geschichtswissenschaft und in der Deutschen Rechtsgeschichte verbreitete. Damit schlägt Lieb den Bogen von der philologischen zur juristischen Germanistik.

Claire Wrobel befasst sich mit dem Panoptikon-Schema des britischen Utilitariers Jeremy Bentham, das in den Studien Foucaults aufgegriffen und weithin bekannt gemacht wurde. Sie vergleicht und kontrastiert die Strafjustizvorstellungen Benthams in seinen Panoptikon-Schriften mit den dystopischen Praktiken, welche in Margaret Atwoods Roman *The Heart Goes Last* dargestellt sind. Hierbei spielt weniger die Architektur des Benthamschen Panoptikons als vielmehr die Sozialpolitik des Philosophen eine Rolle. Analysiert wird daher, wie sich diese in der fiktionalen Welt Atwoods reflektiert, aber auch radikal verfälscht findet.

Klaus Stierstorfer wendet sich Mahatma Gandhi und seiner Biografie zu. Er skizziert die eminente Bedeutung des Rechts und der (britischen) Rechtsauffassung im Leben Gandhis und diskutiert, wie diese auf die Selbstkonstruktion der Lebensgeschichte des Politikers einwirkte.

Über Erzählstrategien hinaus wird im Beitrag von **Ulrike Tabbert** die visuelle Darstellung von Kriminalität in Gemälden diskutiert, womit auch die Frage nach der Beeinflussung der breiten Öffentlichkeit durch juristische Fälle angesprochen ist. Neben der Sensationspresse sind es neben der Literatur auch der Film sowie andere bildliche Darstellungen, die die öffentliche Meinung in Bezug auf das Verbrechen und seine moralische und politische Aushandlung instruieren.

Der vorliegende Sammelband sollte für die deutsche Rechtswissenschaft die breite Palette von Fragestellungen und Diskussionen innerhalb der Law and Literature-Bewegung mit einem Schwerpunkt auf der Narratologie Revue passieren lassen, aber auch für ein internationales Publikum europäische Forschung zugänglich machen. Dieses doppelte Ziel hat zur Wahl einer zweisprachigen Publikation geführt. Die Sprachbarrieren zwischen den zwei Zielgruppen werden dadurch ausgeglichen, dass hier nun eine englischsprachige auf die deutschsprachige Einleitung folgt.

Zu danken haben die Herausgeberin und der Herausgeber vor allem Tanja Haferkorn, Sophia Zschache und Franca Leitner, die ihnen in Formatierungsbelangen und bei der Lektorierung der Beiträge zur Hand gingen. Darüber hinaus wird der DFG für die großzügige finanzielle Unterstützung der Tagung und der Publikation dieses Sammelbandes gedankt.

Zitierte Literatur

Arnauld, Andreas von (2009) „Was war, was ist – und was sein soll. Erzählen im juristischen Diskurs." *Wirklichkeitserzählungen: Felder, Formen und Funktionen nicht-literarischen Erzählens*. Hg. Christian Klein und Matías Martínez. Stuttgart: Metzler. 14–50.

Arnauld, Andreas von, und Stefan Martini (2015) „Unreliable Narration in Law Courts." in *Unreliable Narration and Trustworthiness: Intermedial and Interdisciplinary Perspectives*. Hg. Vera Nünning. Berlin: de Gruyter. 347–370.

Arnauld, Andreas von (2017) Hg. *Völkerrechtsgeschichte(n): Historische Narrative und Konzepte im Wandel*. Berlin: Duncker und Humblot.

Blufarb, Ruth (2017) *Geschichten im Recht: Übertragbarkeit von „Law as Narrative" auf die deutsche Rechtsordnung*. Baden-Baden: Nomos.

Hipp, Dominique (2020) *Von NS-Konzentrationslagern erzählen: Angeklagte vor Gericht über Dachau, Mauthausen, Ravensbrück und Neuengamme*. Bielefeld: transcript.

Hyde, Alan (1997) *Bodies of Law*. Princeton, NJ: Princeton Univ. Press.

Levinson, Sanford (1988) "Law as Literature." *Interpreting Law and Literature. A Hermeneutic Reader*. Ed. Sanford Levinson and Steven Mailloux. Evanston, IL: Northwestern Univ. Press. 155–173.

Lüderssen, Klaus (2002) „Das Narrative in der Jurisprudenz." *Produktive Spiegelungen: Recht in Literatur, Theater und Film* [1991]. Hg. Klaus Lüderssen. Baden-Baden: Nomos: 66–78.

Sarat, Austin, Matthew Anderson, and Cathrine O. Frank (2010) Ed. *Law and the Humanities. An Introduction*. Cambridge: Cambridge Univ. Press.

Schramm, Edward (2007) "Law and Literature." *Juristische Ausbildung*: 581–585.

Stolleis, Michael (2008) *Rechtsgeschichte schreiben: Rekonstruktion, Erzählung, Fiktion?* Basel: Schwabe.

Stolleis, Michael (2015) *Margarethe und der Mönch: Rechtsgeschichte in Geschichten*. München: Beck.

Weisberg, Richard H. (1984) *The Failure of the Word. The Protagonist as Lawyer in Modern Fiction*. New Haven, CT: Yale Univ. Press.

Weisberg, Richard H. (1992) *Poethics and Other Strategies of Law and Literature*. New York: Columbia Univ. Press.

Introduction

Monika Fludernik and Frank L. Schäfer

The subject of narrative in and in relation to the law has been one of the facets that occupied the graduate school "Factual and Fictional Narration" (GRK 1767), funded by the German Research Foundation (DFG) between 2012 and 2022. DFG-financed graduate schools run for two four-and-a-half-year periods. The interdisciplinary graduate school GRK 1767 arose from a previous graduate institution on "History and Narrative" and was designed to extend work done on narrative and history to other areas of factual narration. The director of the graduate school, Monika Fludernik, is a narratologist, and PIs from other disciplines are also working with a narratological methodology. Since the original set of PhD students were majoritatively based in literary studies, narratology being mainly a philological approach, the first cohort concentrated on the distinctions between fiction(ality) and fact(uality). At the mid-term evaluation of the graduate school, we engaged to concentrate more widely with factual narratives from a broader number of disciplines. Hence, the GRK 1767, which had already included PhD projects from history, psychology and philosophy in its first cohort, accepted and supervised also projects from media studies, linguistics, pedagogics, art history, ethnology and legal studies, besides continuing research in German medieval and modern studies, Romance literature, English medieval and modern studies, Russian literature and ancient and modern history.[1] The inclusion of narration in legal texts and narrative in the law was therefore a key aspect of the graduate school.

In May 2021, the graduate school organized an online conference with the title "Law and Literature from a Narratological Perspective," and this book is the proceedings volume of that conference. The major aim of the meeting and of this collection of essays was to cater to two quite different audiences. On the one hand, the volume introduces major tendencies of Law and Literature (based on models geared towards the British and American common law) to German legal scholars, focusing especially on the importance of narrative in law and illustrating the use of narratological concepts and categories. One of the major questions is the applicability of the common law analyses to the European legal system(s). It is for this reason that German papers were solicited to extend the reach of the volume to an audience of German legal scholars. On the other hand, the collection contains English-language essays from the

[1] See www.grk-erzaehlen.uni-freiburg.de.

anglophone tradition of Law and Literature, mostly though not exclusively from scholars working in English-language literature, where the approach has been current for several decades. It is hoped that the volume will therefore also convey some European perspectives of Law and Literature to an anglophone audience. In particular, the illustrations of how narrative 'works' in Dutch and Norwegian trials can help to broaden the understanding of narrative in the law beyond the anglophone world. Though we do not provide translations of the German essays, we have decided to offer two introductions, one in German and one in English, in order to address the two audiences, i.e. German legal scholars and anglophone colleagues working on Law and Literature.

Law and Literature has stereotypically been categorized as either 'law in literature' (i.e. the representation of law in literary texts, films and the other arts) or, as 'law as literature,' i.e. the analysis of literary aspects (e.g. metaphor) in legal texts and procedures (Ward 1995, 3–27).[2] As for law and narrative, there has in fact already been quite some work on narratives in law, not merely on the prominent fact of storytelling in jury trials by prosecutors and defense counsels in the framework of common law (Yovel & Mertz 2005, Farmer 2010, Burns 2012, Hjorth 2021), but also on the use of narrative in a variety of legal texts (Brooks & Gewirtz 1996, Sternberg 2008, Fludernik 2014, Olson 2014). Nevertheless, practitioners still see the need for more extensive analysis:

> Academic study sympathetic to "law and literature" has by now given considerable attention to narrative and its uses throughout the law, as institution and as praxis. Still, one looks in vain within legal doctrine, and in judicial opinions, for any explicit

[2] Law in Literature consists mostly in what Dolin (2007, 10) describes as "literary representations of legal trials, practitioners and language, and of those caught up in the law"; the approach is linked to the work of James Boyd White's *The Legal Imagination* (1973), Weisberg (1984) and Thomas (1987). Law as Literature, i.e. "the role played by narrative, metaphor and other rhetorical devices in legal speech and writing, including judgments" (Dolin 2007, 10), is represented by Hyde (1997), one of the early key texts in that vein. Many scholars also now propose a triple typology, adding "law of" to "law in" and "law as." "Law of" "typically investigates the dynamics of laws that regulate the production and circulation of literature, whether obscenity laws or copyright restrictions" (Anker & Meyler 2017, 8). Representative of this strain are Saint-Amour (2003) and Spoo (2013). Another tripartite division is undertaken by Jane Baron (1999) and Julie Peters (2005), who distinguish a "humanist" strand (e.g. represented by work by Martha Nussbaum), a "hermeneutic" strain, "study[ing] the techniques for meaning making within law" (Anker & Meyler 2017, 7), and, third, a "narrative" strand, which "emerged in part out of feminist legal studies and critical race theory's efforts to expose the historical subject of Anglo-American law as white, male, straight, and economically entitled" (7). Dolin (2007), on the other hand, presents nine types of analyses typical of law and literature. Her third category, "how the supposed freedom of literary expression is contained and regulated by the law" (2007, 10) corresponds to "law of", but she also adds types of research that focus on philosophical and sociological issues ("the circulation of legal ideas in literary culture, and vice versa in various periods and societies"; "the effects of social ideologies such as race and gender in legal language" – categories iv and v) and the performativity of the law ("the use of theatricality and spectacle in the creation of legal authority" – category vii) (10–11).

> recognition that "narrative" is a category for adjudication, that it is something that needs to be talked about and brought to bear analytically; that rules of evidence, for instance, implicate questions of how stories can and should be told. (Brooks 2017, 93)

Recent research on law and narrative has not only focused on metaphor (Hanne & Weisberg 2018, Fludernik 2019, Douthwaite & Tabbert 2022), but has in addition started to analyze and distinguish between a large range of different legal texts (Kayman 2002, Stern et al. 2020). Thus, the existence and use of literary strategies, fiction(ality) or fictivity[3] and narrative in legal writings needs to be examined separately for law codes, legal norms or private contracts.

In fact, legal texts pose a huge challenge for a narratological analysis since they contain so many different subgenres, for each of which narratological analysis is bound to arrive at distinct results. Besides law codes and case law, one can here additionally list executive ordinances, by-laws of public corporations, consuetudinary law and internal administrative directions as well as administrative deeds, individual contracts and general terms and conditions. The range of legal documents therefore includes all phases of the application of the law from the abstract level of statutes to that of concrete cases and of private agreements. By the same token, the initiative process of law creation offers rich material for narratological analysis. Thus, one can, for instance, analyze the history of particular law, as well as examine all types of processes that create new norms including contract negotiation papers. Moreover, one will have to analyze public and private decision-making processes such as trial procedures or arbitral tribunals; these combine the application of law with the creation of new laws since such procedures follow procedural norms but also prepare the way for legal decisions.

In addition to these sources, one could moreover include literature and criticism discussing the law from a present-day legal perspective but also such areas of fundamental thinking about the law as the philosophy of law or the history of law. Since the literature on the law that is currently in force focuses on law codes, it is rarely narrative and linguistically imitates the language, style and structure of these texts. Hence, in this respect there is little difference in narrative quality between legal texts that are in pragmatic use and scholarly legal literature. For texts in the areas of legal philosophy and history, on the other hand, their often chronological structure makes them more susceptible to narratological analysis.

It is quite obvious that the history of law generates texts that, belonging to history in the wider sense, allow themselves to be treated from a narratological perspective as does history in general. Like many other areas of the humanities,

---

3 In German research on fiction(ality), a major distinction is draw between the ontological category of inventedness, i.e. non-existence (*fictivity*), and the authorial intention of producing a text that is to be read as 'fiction' (*fictionality*). For this kind of question in Law and Literature studies see, for instance, Stern (2017).

history provides a fertile ground for narratology, originally an approach that arose within literary studies or philosophy. Areas of the law that concern current law are much more difficult to approach from a narratological perspective since they are based on documents like textbooks, commentaries or judgments. These are bound up with peculiar qualities of the law, namely its normativity and deontic aspects. Legal norms impose obligations or prohibitions (commands or interdictions), they license particular actions, activities or operations or release from certain obligations. Legal norms share the property of being legally binding, which is as much as to say that they can be enforced against the will of the subject targeted by these norms. Legal norms thus differ from norms in society, which are negotiable and consensual, but also from norms and rules in narratology, for instance interpretative norms that allow one to pronounce on the fictionality or factuality of a text. One can therefore see that legal subdisciplines dealing with current law are able to generate narratives only to the extent to which their underlying norms already contain narratives or presuppose a narrative.

While literary studies regularly have recourse to narratology, this has so far not been the case within law. This is particularly true for German law, on which we will concentrate in what follows. However, German legal studies from early on were interested in the connection between law and literature. Modern law as an academic discipline started around 1800. In fact, German studies (*Germanistik*) as an academic discipline originated not in the literary studies but in the studies of German law. Thus, one can point to the work of Jacob Grimm (1785–1863) and his brother Wilhelm (1786–1859), especially their *Lexicon of German Law* and their famous collection of fairytales, as well as to the poet jurist Felix Dahn (1834–1912). In the approach of these proponents of German law, law and literature are either synthesized in their work, or the two perspectives come to stand side by side. Those who operated a synthesis of law and literature did so in two ways (see Schramm 2007). One group of authors focused on literary texts in order to gather material on legal cases and legal texts from the past. The category "law in literature" (Weisberg 1984, 1992; Posner 1988) has therefore been a familiar practice in the history of German legal writing since the nineteenth century. At the same time, German legal practice is much more rarely given to the category of "law as literature" (Levinson 1988, Hyde 1997), i.e. the analysis of law texts from a literary, stylistic or rhetorical perspective. This type of analysis requires a willingness to work in an interdisciplinary manner, having recourse to categories and analytical tools from other disciplines, and it would tend to reduce law to a subdiscipline of the humanities – a situation running much against the grain of traditional legal self-understanding of the law as imposing a normative order and therefore superior to other more variable disciplines.

Within German legal studies, only very little research has so far focused on law as narrative. This may seem surprising since the narrative turn has also affected law research and given rise to the frequent use of concepts like *master narrative* and *Narrativik* (a German quasi-synonym for narratology). Despite this, a concrete methodological application of the narratological approach and of narratological terminology has been rare. Among the few scholars who have been inspired by narratology one can point to Lüderssen (2002), Arnauld (2009, 2017; Arnauld & Martini 2015) and Stolleis (2008, 2015). More recently, Ruth Blufarb (2017) has integrated narratology into her work. Her research additionally tries to determine whether the narratological approach is suitable also for an application to legal purposes in the context of jurisdiction and judgments, which is as much as to say that narratology can be incorporated into juridical methodology and the deontic framework of law.

The comparative reticence of German legal studies towards narratology is not easily explained. One might surmise that this is due to the peculiar position of German legal science in Europe. Thanks to Germany's strong economic situation and owing to the sheer bulk of German law which is being generated, Germany's legal system and its case law have a disproportionally strong impact on neighboring European judicial contexts. At the same time, German legal studies are often focused on vernacular Germany and methodologically on the dogmatics of law, i.e. on the systems, concepts and doctrines of the law, and they are concerned mostly with contexts and discourses relevant to Germany alone. Comparative and interdisciplinary approaches (such as narratology would provide) are peripheral to German law's main business. It is therefore one of the aims of this collection of essays to not merely support the international discussions taking place between narratology and legal studies but to provide in addition a contribution to an interdisciplinary dialogue between law and literary studies within German legal research.

Internationally, Law and Literature has been a well-established subdiscipline within law schools and an interdisciplinary tendency in the humanities, especially in English studies. This trend has now found its way to Germany in the institutional setting of the SFB 1385 in Münster, a collaborative research center funded by the German Research Foundation. Two members of this center are contributors in this volume. While narrative (in the form of novels and films) is the most popular genre for Law and Literature analysis of literary texts (law in literature; see, for instance, Heinzelman 2010), specifically narratological approaches have been rare even in the United States. Particularly within law and literature work within the humanities, it is more common for narratology to be applied in tandem with other theoretical perspectives, a situation that is also mirrored in the development of what is now called Law and Humanities (Sarat et al., 2010 and Stern et al., 2020).

As for law as narrative, the anglophone tradition of Law and Literature[4] has for a long time recognized the centrality of narration to law. As Bruner already opined in 1990: "To sum up, law stories are narrative in structure, adversarial in spirit, inherently rhetorical in aim, and justifiably open to suspicion" (1990, 41). Previous reluctance to deal with narrative in the legal system were swept away by the "narrative turn in legal studies, whereby what was once considered a problematic quality of narrative, its potential to fictionalize, has now been recognized as a basic part of legal discourse and legal interpretation" (Olson 2018, 19; see also Brooks 2005). Olson cites Robert Cover's classic statement that "[n]o set of legal institutions or prescriptions exists apart from the narratives that locate it and give it meaning" (Cover 1992, 95; qtd. Olson 19), highlighting the "ubiquity" of narrative in law and foregrounding what one could call "the literary dimensions of legal life" (Sarat et al. 2010, 3). Narrative thus takes a central position both in the representation of law in literature and in the analysis of legal life:

> Where studies of law in literature focus on literary (typically narrative, novelistic) representations of legal professionals, the use of legal forms and documents, legal settings or, more fundamentally, the pervasiveness of legal culture that literature both helps to constitute and critique, law as literature reads the law for its own narrative procedures and rhetorical functions. (Sarat et al. 2010, 3, fn. 6)

Law and Literature's focus on narrative has in fact raised a number of very different perspectives that include sociological, linguistic and cognitive facets. As Binder & Weisberg (2000) propose, narrative legal scholarship (or what Dolin 2007, 11 calls "legal storytelling or narrative jurisprudence"; her category ix) includes the following ten claims:

1. That human perception and thought inevitably rely on narrative.
2. That competing narratives may be told about the same events [...].
3. That legal argument and decision rely on the selective rendition of events in narrative form.
4. But that in this very selectivity, legal argument represses competing stories.
5. That the stories most often repressed may be those reflecting perspectives of subordinated groups.
6. That legal discourse denies that it "privileges" some stories over others.
7. That legal decision-making purports to achieve impartiality by applying rules that abstract away the very particularities of human experience that narrative emphasizes.
8. That by suppressing the concrete human consequences and meanings of legal decisions, rules make law morally obtuse.

---

[4] For surveys of the Law and Literature movement see, for instance, Ward (1995), Binder & Weisberg (2000), Dolin (2007) and Anker & Meyler (2017), especially Thomas (2017).

9. That the authority of rules depends upon implicit narratives linking them to the will of authoritative decision-makers and explaining how those decision-makers came to be authoritative.
10. That the inclusion of narratives, whether fictional or factual, in legal scholarship can morally improve the law, subvert its claims to impartiality, and advance the interests of subordinated groups.

(Binder & Weisberg 2000, 201)

Many of these claims will be recognized in the essays that follow. For instance, claims (2) to (4) are central to the arguments of Jeanne Gaakeer and Frode Pedersen in their contributions. Claims (8) and (9) surface in Peter Schneck's essay, while (10) correlates with the arguments of Dominique Hipp in her contribution. This takes us to a brief introduction to the papers that follow. The contributions in this volume reflect the strong presence of Law and Literature in German English Studies (*Anglistik*), where the approach has had its widest impact via the influence from American Studies (*Amerikanistik*) and of course through the omnipresence of American law in popular culture.

Essays in this Volume

This volume starts with the contribution of **Ruth Blufarb**, who summarizes some of the major results of her PhD dissertation (for the resulting study see Blufarb 2017). She focuses on a discussion of the chances for an application of the narratological method in law studies and points out the limits of such an application. Situating Law and Narrative in the larger context of Law as Literature, Blufarb scrutinizes the possible transfer of the American Law as Literature research, based on the case law of American Common Law, to German culture which is based on the codification of law. In what follows, Blufarb sketches aspects of narrativity in German law and introduces the reader to major tenets of the Law as Narrative approach. She concludes by testing the validity of Law and Literature for the German legal system by discussing a number of facets and arguments such as those connected with the terms *narrative competition*, *stock stories* and *outsider scholarship*.

The following two contributions discuss ownership and copyright issues from both a legal and a literary perspective. **Robert Spoo** explains that the so-called *trade courtesy* in United States publishing is a nonbinding convention which in nineteenth-century America responded to the lack of copyright protection for foreign authors and their publishers. Publishers in the United States agreed to form a trust that would afford protection similar to copyright law, a protection that was however fictitious. Taking Charles Dickens as an example, Spoo shows how American publishers engaged with the fiction of the trade courtesy. **Peter Schneck** considers the question how authors could claim intellectual property, and how such claims find a parallel in discourses on the occupation and settlement of land. Schneck's three case studies further demonstrate that the relation of property and identity, which is so pivotal in the American legal system, is poignantly represented in the novels he analyzes. Fenimore Cooper's seminal historical novel *The Pioneers* can be read as a *romance of property*, Schneck asserts, while Chesnutt's *The House Behind the Cedars* deconstructs Cooper's premise in the light of racial discrimination and the dispossession of African Americans. Finally, the postcolonial novel *The Descendants* by Hart Hemmings shows the restoration of indigenous peoples' property claims as it reconceptualizes the right to ownership.

Hans J. Lind explores the mutual interdependence of law and literature in that he charts how fictional literature has been discussed in British, American and German legal discourse since the trials of Oscar Wilde. Lind demonstrates that, although problematic moral content in literary works is now less frequently treated in court as evidence of an author's immorality, certain misconceptions regarding the way in which fiction should be assessed have lingered on in the legal sphere. Taking *drill* and other rap genres with their performative strategy of *realness* as his example, Lind shows that three aspects in particular – the assumption of unproblematic referentiality, the conception that the author is identical with the narrator or character, and the ignorance of legal representatives regarding intertextual allusions as a key feature of fiction – continue to persist in court rulings to this day.

The following two chapters are concerned with storytelling in trial procedures. Relying on a large number of examples, **Jeanne Gaakeer** demonstrates that the reconstruction of events in the reconstruction of a crime is based on interpretations that rely on widespread narratological conventions of storytelling. As a result, this narrative 'prejudice' can impede the establishment of the truth by involving assumptions that are stereotypical but not true to the facts. Gaakeer thus tries to alert legal professionals to the danger of stereotyping and easy recrimination. **Frode Helmich Pedersen** reasons along similar lines. His focus is on a Norwegian case study which shows that a conviction in a trial based on circumstantial evidence may easily be the result of stereotyping. Both essays speak to the issue of fictionalization arising from the use of narratives and from the need to employ narratives in order to comprehend events and the motives of the defendants.

The contribution by **Dominique Hipp** goes beyond the distinction between factuality and fictionality, a key concern of the graduate school. While Hipp's dissertation (Hipp 2020) explored offender narratives of defendants in trials concerned with crimes committed in concentration camps during World War II, her contribution to this volume examines the testimony of the Holocaust survivor Maryla Rosenthal in the first Auschwitz trial in Frankfurt. Taking a narratological rather than a procedural perspective on witness testimonies, she demonstrates the narrative and historical value of testimonial evidence. Thus, it is no longer the credibility and plausibility of witness testimony that is of interest (as was the case for the offender narratives) but the subjectivity and representational character of the narrative. In other words, on the basis of her narratological approach Hipp now treats the testimony not as a documentary report but as an experiential rendering of suffering.

The contribution by **Arild Linneberg** extends the narrative approach by considering larger philosophical questions. As Linneberg demonstrates, Siegfried Kracauer at the beginning of the twentieth century already anticipated the idea later popularized by Hayden White that the narrative structuring of a legal (or, in the case of White, a historiographical) text has considerable impact on its interpretation. Linneberg revisits Kracauer's discussion of the relation between law and literature that had unaccountably disappeared from view among scholars of Law and Literature.

The following three contributions are concerned with questions of literary criticism in particular or approach problems from the perspective of literary studies. **Claudia Lieb** argues that nineteenth-century authors of literary and legal history elaborated on a notion of biography or life narrative that Christoph Martin Wieland and other novelists had placed at the center of their poetics. In the course of her chapter, Lieb delineates how the distinction between external and internal history was disseminated in interdisciplinary fashion, moving into the theory of the novel, historical scholarship and legal history. She is thus able to show that this key distinction defined both philological disciplines and legal German studies.

Claire Wrobel discusses Jeremy Bentham's concept of the panopticon, which features prominently in the studies of Michel Foucault and has therefore been widely disseminated. Wrobel compares and contrasts Bentham's utilitarian conception of criminal justice with the dystopian practices depicted in Margaret Atwood's novel *The Heart Goes Last*. Here it is less the specific architecture of Bentham's panopticon and more his social politics that take center stage. The chapter analyzes how Benthamite philosophy is reflected and radically distorted in Atwood's fictional world.

The contribution by **Klaus Stierstorfer** turns to Mahatma Gandhi, his life and his autobiography. Stierstorfer points to the crucial significance of the law and the (British) legal system for Gandhi's life and self-understanding and how they impacted on his autobiographical narrative. The chapter thus highlights how Gandhi as the dominant figure in Indian politics relied on a legal framework and saw himself as doing so.

Looking beyond narrative strategies, the contribution by **Ulrike Tabbert** discusses the visual representation of crime in painting and so addresses the question of how the wider public is influenced by legal cases and issues of the law. Apart from tabloid journalism and literature, it is especially movies that have an effect on the public debate about the moral and political implications of crime.

The editors would like to thank Tanja Haferkorn, Sophia Zschache and Franca Leitner who at various stages of the project have been involved in formatting and copy-editing the contributions of this volume. In addition, we would like to thank the German Research Foundation for their financial support both of the conference and the costs of publication.

Works Cited

Anker, Elizabeth S., and Bernadette Meyler (2017) Ed. *New Directions in Law and Literature*. Oxford: Oxford Univ. Press.

Arnauld, Andreas von (2009) „Was war, was ist – und was sein soll. Erzählen im juristischen Diskurs.“ *Wirklichkeitserzählungen: Felder, Formen und Funktionen nicht-literarischen Erzählens*. Ed. Christian Klein and Matías Martínez. Stuttgart: Metzler. 14–50.

Arnauld, Andreas von, und Stefan Martini (2015) “Unreliable Narration in Law Courts.” *Unreliable Narration and Trustworthiness: Intermedial and Interdisciplinary Perspectives*. Ed. Vera Nünning. Berlin: de Gruyter: Berlin. 347–370.

Arnauld, Andreas von (2017) Ed. *Völkerrechtsgeschichte(n): Historische Narrative und Konzepte im Wandel*. Berlin: Duncker und Humblot.

Baron, Jane B. (1999) “Law, Literature and the Problem of Interdisciplinarity.” *Yale Law Journal* 108: 1059–1085.

Binder, Guyora, and Robert Weisberg (2000) *Literary Criticisms of Law*. Princeton, NJ: Princeton Univ. Press.

Blufarb, Ruth (2017) *Geschichten im Recht: Übertragbarkeit von „Law as Narrative“ auf die deutsche Rechtsordnung*. Baden-Baden: Nomos.

Brooks, Peter (2005) “Narrative in and of the Law.” *A Companion to Narrative Theory*. Ed. James Phelan and Peter Rabinowitz. Oxford: Blackwell. 415–426.

Brooks, Peter (2017) “Retrospective Prophecies: Legal Narrative Constructions.” *New Directions in Law and Literature*. Ed. Elizabeth S. Anker and Bernadette Meyler. Oxford: Oxford Univ. Press. 92–108.

Brooks, Peter, and Paul Gewirtz (1996) Ed. *Law's Stories: Narrative and Rhetoric in the Law*. New Haven, CT: Yale Univ. Press.

Bruner, Jerome (1990) *Making Stories. Law, Literature, Life*. Cambridge, MA: Harvard Univ. Press.

Burns, Robert P. (2012) “Narrative and Drama in the American Trial.” *Faculty Working Papers*. Paper 201. Web. http://scholarlycommons.law.northwestern.edu/facultyworkingpapers/201.

Cover, Robert (1992) "*Nomos* and Narrative" [1983]. *Narrative, Violence and the Law*. Ed. Robert Cover et al. Ann Arbor, MI: Michigan Univ. Press. 95–172.

Dolin, Kieran (2007) *A Critical Introduction to Law and Literature*. Cambridge: Cambridge Univ. Press.

Douthwaite, John, and Ulrike Tabbert (2022) Ed. *The Linguistics of Crime: A Linguistic Contribution to the Study of Crime*. Cambridge: Cambridge Univ. Press.

Farmer, Lindsay (2010) "Trials." *Law and the Humanities. An Introduction*. Ed. Sarat et al. Cambridge: Cambridge Univ. Press. 455–477.

Fludernik, Monika (2014) "A Narratology of the Law? Narratives in Legal Discourse." *CAL: Analysis of Law: An International & Interdisciplinary Law Review* 1.1: 87–109. Web. http://cal.library.utoronto.ca/index.php/cal/article/view/21024/17173.

Fludernik, Monika (2019) *Metaphors of Confinement. The Prison in Fact, Fiction and Fantasy*. Oxford: Oxford Univ. Press.

Hanne, Michael, and Robert Weisberg (2018) Ed. *Narrative and Metaphor in the Law*. Cambridge: Cambridge Univ. Press.

Heinzelman, Susan Sage (2010) "Imagining the Law: The Novel." *Law and the Humanities. An Introduction*. Ed. Austin Sarat et al. Cambridge: Cambridge Univ. Press. 213–240.

Hipp, Dominique (2020) *Von NS-Konzentrationslagern erzählen: Angeklagte vor Gericht über Dachau, Mauthausen, Ravensbrück und Neuengamme*. Bielefeld: transcript.

Hjorth, Line N. (2021) "Underlying Narratives in Courtroom Exchanges." *Narratives in the Criminal Process*. Ed. Frode Helmich Pedersen, Espen Ingebrigtsen and Werner Gephart. Frankfurt: Klostermann. 139–154.

Hyde, Alan (1997) *Bodies of Law*. Princeton, NJ: Princeton Univ. Press.

Kayman, Martin A. (2002) "Law-and-Literature: Questions of Jurisdiction." *REAL: Yearbook of Research in English and American Literature 18: Law and Literature*. Ed. Brook Thomas. Tübingen: Narr. 1–20.

Levinson, Sanford (1988) "Law as Literature." *Interpreting Law and Literature. A Hermeneutic Reader*. Ed. Sanford Levinson and Steven Mailloux. Evanston, IL: Northwestern Univ. Press. 155–173.

Lüderssen, Klaus (2002) „Das Narrative in der Jurisprudenz." *Produktive Spiegelungen: Recht in Literatur, Theater und Film* [1991]. Ed. Klaus Lüderssen. Baden-Baden: Nomos. 66–78.

Olson, Greta (2014) "Narration and Narrative in Legal Discourse." *The Living Handbook of Narratology*. Web. https://www.lhn.uni-hamburg.de/node/113.html.

Olson, Greta (2018) "On Narrating and Troping the Law: The Conjoined Use of Narrative and Metaphor in Legal Discourse." *Narrative and Metaphor in the Law*. Ed. Michael Hanne and Robert Weisberg. Cambridge: Cambridge Univ. Press. 19–36.

Peters, Julie Stone (2005) "Law, Literature, and the Vanishing Real: On the Future of an Interdisciplinary Illusion." *PMLA* 120: 442–453.

Posner, Richard A. (1998) *Law and Literature* [1988]. Revised and enlarged edition. Cambridge, MA: Harvard Univ. Press.

Saint-Amour, Paul K. (2003) *The Copywrights: Intellectual Property and the Literary Imagination*. Ithaca, NY: Cornell Univ. Press.

Sarat, Austin, Matthew Anderson, and Cathrine O. Frank (2010) "Introduction: On the Origins and Prospects of the Humanistic Study of Law." *Law and the Humanities. An Introduction*. Ed. Austin Sarat et al. Cambridge: Cambridge Univ. Press. 1–46.

Sarat, Austin, Matthew Anderson, and Cathrine O. Frank (2010) Ed. *Law and the Humanities. An Introduction*. Cambridge: Cambridge Univ. Press.

Schramm, Edward (2007) "Law and Literature." *Juristische Ausbildung*: 581–585.

Spoo, Robert (2013) *Without Copyrights: Piracy, Publishing, and the Public Domain*. New York: Oxford Univ. Press.

Stern, Simon (2017) "Legal and Literary Fictions." *New Directions in Law and Literature*. Ed. Elizabeth S. Anker and Bernadette Meyler. Oxford: Oxford Univ. Press. 313–326.

Stern, Simon, Maksymilian Del Mar, and Bernadette Meyler (2020) Ed. *The Oxford Handbook of Law and Humanities*. Oxford: Oxford Univ. Press.

Sternberg, Meir (2008) "If-Plots: Narrativity and the Law-Code." *Theorizing Narrativity*. Ed. John Pier and José Àngel García Landa. Narratologia 12. Berlin: De Gruyter. 29–107.

Stolleis, Michael (2008) *Rechtsgeschichte schreiben: Rekonstruktion, Erzählung, Fiktion?* Basel: Schwabe.

Stolleis, Michael (2015) *Margarethe und der Mönch: Rechtsgeschichte in Geschichten*. München: Beck.

Thomas, Brook (1987) *Cross-Examinations of Law and Literature: Cooper, Hawthorne, Stowe, and Melville*. Cambridge: Cambridge Univ. Press.

Thomas, Brook (2017) "Minding Previous Steps Taken." *New Directions in Law and Literature*. Ed. Elizabeth S. Anker and Bernadette Meyler. Oxford: Oxford Univ. Press. 33–45.

Ward, Ian (1995) "Law and Literature: A Continuing Debate." *Law and Literature: Possibilities and Perspectives*. Ed. Ian Ward. Cambridge: Cambridge Univ. Press. 3–27.

Weisberg, Richard H. (1984) *The Failure of the Word. The Protagonist as Lawyer in Modern Fiction*. New Haven, CT: Yale Univ. Press.

Weisberg, Richard H. (1992) *Poethics and Other Strategies of Law and Literature*. New York: Columbia Univ. Press.

White, James Boyd (1973) *The Legal Imagination. Studies in the Nature of Legal Thought and Expression*. Boston: Little & Brown.

Yovel, Jonathan, and Elizabeth Ellen Mertz (2005) "Courtroom Narration: A Capsule Essay." Web. https://www.researchgate.net/publication/46417903_Courtroom_Narration_A_Capsule_Essay.

Law as Narrative und das deutsche Recht – Chancen und Grenzen

Ruth Blufarb

Aus rechtswissenschaftlicher Perspektive ist von besonderem Interesse, welche Chancen das *Law as Narrative* für die deutsche Rechtswissenschaft bietet und inwiefern diese im US-amerikanischen Rechtssystem entstandene Bewegung auf die deutsche Rechtsordnung übertragbar ist (dazu ausführlich Blufarb 2017).

Zunächst soll das *Law as Narrative* in der *Law as Literature*-Bewegung verortet werden. Dabei sollen einerseits die wesentlichen Unterschiede zwischen dem *Common Law* und dem deutschen Recht dargestellt und andererseits das rechtswissenschaftlich geprägte *Law as Narrative* zu erzähltheoretischen Konzepten in Bezug gesetzt werden. Anschließend soll ein Vorschlag für eine Definition von Narrativität für deutsche Rechtstexte entwickelt werden. Narrative Strukturen im Recht sollen identifiziert und die wesentlichen Untersuchungsansätze, Ideen und Forderungen des *Law as Narrative* vorgestellt werden. Abschließend wird geprüft, wie die Ansätze gewinnbringend auf die deutsche Rechtsordnung übertragen werden können und wo Grenzen der Übertragbarkeit liegen.

1. Law as Narrative – *eine Einordnung*

1.1 *Law as Literature* und *Law as Narrative*

Das *Law as Literature*, ein Teil der *Law and Literature*-Bewegung, entstand Ende der 1970er Jahre in den USA und wurde vor allem von Juristen entwickelt. James Boyd White begründete mit seinem Werk *The Legal Imagination* dessen Strömungen inhaltlich (White 1973). Binder und Weisberg (Binder & Weisberg 2000) differenzieren fünf Perspektiven der Betrachtung des Rechts als Literatur:

1. Die hermeneutische,
2. die dekonstruktivistische,
3. die rhetorische,
4. die kulturelle
5. und die narratologische Perspektive bzw. das *Law as Narrative.*[1]

Die narratologische Perspektive des Rechts etabliert das Recht als narratologischen Untersuchungsgegenstand und zeichnet sich durch eine Vielzahl sehr unterschiedlicher Ansätze aus (Lachenmaier 2008, 146–147; Arnauld 2009, 45–47).

Vertreter des *Law as Literature* betonen die Gemeinsamkeiten von Recht und Literatur. Recht und Literatur teilen, nicht zuletzt angesichts ihres gemeinsamen Ursprungs, wesentliche strukturelle Merkmale. Sie basieren auf Sprache, vermitteln Informationen durch Texte und haben Textwissenschaften hervorgebracht, die diese Texte interpretieren. Beide Disziplinen verbindet das Ziel größtmöglicher Angemessenheit von Gegenstand und Aussage, das Bedürfnis nach Objektadäquanz (Müller-Dietz 1990a, 167). Dworkin sieht das Interpretieren in beiden Disziplinen als eine von ästhetischen Erwägungen geleitete Tätigkeit, die den Text möglichst in seiner Gesamtheit erfasst und als Kunstwerk erscheinen lässt (Dworkin 1985, 149–158).[2] Recht und Literatur verfügen zudem über zahlreiche verschiedene Textformen, die kontextabhängig sind und menschliche Erfahrungen und Absichten beschreiben.

Kritiker des *Law as Literature* lehnen eine Übertragbarkeit literaturwissenschaftlicher Konzepte auf das Recht ab und heben deren Unterschiede hervor (Posner 2009, 308–315). Beide Materien haben sich während der Neuzeit zunehmend auseinanderentwickelt, sodass sie nunmehr prinzipiell unterschiedliche Lebensbereiche ausfüllen (Müller-Dietz 1990b, 17). Die Objektadäquanz führt dazu, dass die Sprache beider Disziplinen sich wesentlich unterscheidet. Juristische Texte, insbesondere Gesetze, haben den Anspruch, rational, transparent, objektiv und eindeutig zu sein. Gesetzen kommen bestimmte Funktionen zu wie die politische Gestaltungsfunktion oder die Legitimationsfunktion. In der Literatur hat die Sprache oft mehrdimensionalen Charakter und ist mehrdeutig (Polysemie). Das Recht muss anwendbar sein, als Ergebnis rechtlicher Textproduktion muss in der realen Welt ein Problem gelöst, ein Streit befriedet, Situationen geregelt werden. Die Literatur hat jedoch nicht zum Ziel, erschöpfend, problemlösend oder streitentscheidend zu sein. Der Leser oder Interpret von Literatur muss keine Lücken füllen und die Literatur nicht fortbilden. Literatur darf unterhalten, Recht muss Zwang ausüben (Gewirtz 1996b, 5). Gesetze und Urteile sind verbindlich, ein verbindlicher Literaturkanon existiert nicht (Wagner 1965, 533). Die Ästhetik bildet einen wesentlichen inhaltlichen und formellen Charakterzug von Literatur, spielt in der Jurisprudenz aber eine untergeordnete Rolle (Bleich 1989, 3199).[3] Literarische Auslegung ist in Text-

[1] Die narratologische Perspektive des Rechts wird in dieser Arbeit in Anlehnung an Binder & Weisberg sowie Brooks auch mit *Law as Narrative* bezeichnet. Manche Autoren bezweifeln, dass die Bewegung überhaupt eine gemeinsame narratologische Perspektive beinhaltet (Gewirtz 1996b, 4).

[2] Er folgert, dass der Rechtsfindungsvorgang mit einem Fortsetzungsroman vergleichbar sei. Jeder zur Entscheidung berufene Richter binde die nachfolgenden „Autoren“.

[3] Anderer Ansicht sind indes einige Vertreter des *Law and Literature*.

und Methodenwahl und den Fragen, mit denen sie an Texte herantritt, relativ frei, während die rechtswissenschaftliche Auslegung auf die Bestimmtheit von Normtexten und die praktische Falllösung hinarbeiten muss (Pieroth 2015, XII).

1.2 *Common Law* und Deutsches Recht

Fraglich ist, wie sich die Unterschiede zwischen dem US-amerikanischen und dem deutschen Rechtssystem hinsichtlich der Übertragbarkeit auswirken (siehe Blufarb 2017, 350–379).

1.2.1 *Common Law* (USA)

Die Rechtsordnung(en) der USA sind geprägt vom englischen *Common Law* und bilden damit einen Gegensatz zum kontinentaleuropäischen *Civil Law* (Bernstorff 2011, 7–9). Basis des US-amerikanischen Rechts ist im Wesentlichen das Richterrecht. Das richterliche Fallrecht hat im *Common Law* einen anderen Stellenwert als im kontinentaleuropäischen Recht, denn es enthält allgemeingültige Rechtssätze (Hay 2020, 8–9). Nach der Lehre von der *stare decisis* sind Untergerichte an die Rechtsgrundsätze früherer Entscheidungen der Obergerichte, die Präjudizien, gebunden. Diese stellen für niedrigere Instanzen höherrangiges, allgemeingültiges Recht dar. Allerdings ist nicht der gesamte Präjudizienfall bindend, sondern nur die Rechtssätze, die zur Entscheidung des jeweiligen Sachverhaltes notwendig waren (*ratio decidenci*) (Youngs 2007, 71).

Diese Sachverhaltsbezogenheit der bindenden Rechtssätze von Präzedenzfällen setzt eine tiefgehende Beschäftigung mit deren Sachverhalt voraus. Denn die Anwendung eines Rechtssatzes auf einen anderen Sachverhalt erfordert eine Vergleichbarkeit der Sachverhalte. Rechtliche Argumentation ist damit vor allem vergleichende Sachverhaltsanalyse mit dem Ziel, ein bestimmtes Präjudiz aufgrund der Vergleichbarkeit der Sachverhalte für anwendbar zu erklären bzw. ein anderes, für die Partei ungünstiges Präjudiz aufgrund der Nichtvergleichbarkeit der Sachverhalte auszusortieren (Hay 2020, 9).

Die Wahrheitsfindung in US-amerikanischen Prozessen verläuft vor allem mündlich und adversarial, als ein Widerstreit zwischen den „Wahrheiten“ der Parteien, Verfahrensbeteiligten, Zeugen und Anwälte. Zwar gilt der Mündlichkeitsgrundsatz in den Prozessordnungen des *Common Law* und in Deutschland gleichermaßen,[4] doch kommt dem Haupttermin und dem, was darin mündlich vorgetragen wird, im *Common Law* in der Praxis eine höhere Bedeutung zu als in Deutschland (Kötz 2003, 84).

[4] Für den deutschen Zivilprozess ergibt sich dies z.B. aus § 128 Abs. 1 ZPO.

Grund dafür ist unter anderem die Rolle der Richterschaft. Die Gerichte haben im Gegensatz zum deutschen Verfahren eine weniger prozessentscheidende Rolle inne. In Juryprozessen obliegt den Geschworenen die Feststellung der entscheidungsrelevanten Tatsachen und in Verfahren ohne Jurybeteiligung wird die Sachverhaltserforschung stärker als Aufgabe der Prozessparteien und ihrer Vertreter verstanden denn als richterliche Tätigkeit. Während die deutschen Gerichte selbst im Zivilrecht, wo der Beibringungsgrundsatz gilt, aktiv auf Sachverhaltsaufklärung hinwirken und beispielsweise von Amts wegen Beweiserhebungen anordnen können, gehen die Prozessordnungen des *Common Law* davon aus, dass die Wahrheit durch eine offensiv vorgetragene Zeugenbefragung durch die Anwälte zutage tritt.[5] Die Gerichte fungieren als Zuhörer und Zuschauer und greifen nicht aktiv in die Sachverhaltsermittlung ein. In Geschworenenprozessen passt sich die Rhetorik der adversarialen Wahrheitsfindung in vielen Fällen den Vorkenntnissen und Erwartungen der Geschworenen an (Kötz 2003, 83–85).

Während die Staatsanwaltschaft im deutschen Strafprozess mit Verlesung der sachlich und kurz formulierten Anklageschrift beginnt, soll das *opening statement* die Sichtweise der Staatsanwaltschaft zu den Fakten und zur Beweislage darstellen und vermitteln, dass der Angeklagte schuldig ist. Das Eröffnungsplädoyer ist umfassender und emotionaler als in Deutschland, es stimmt die Geschworenen und das Gericht ein, es handelt sich um die erste prägende Geschichte des Prozesses. Anschließend folgt die Gegengeschichte der Verteidigung. Es schließt sich die Beweisaufnahme an, die von Zeugenaussagen und Kreuzverhören geprägt ist. Die Verhandlung schließt mit den Schlussplädoyers der Parteien, wiederum zwei sich widersprechenden Geschichten (Hay 2020, 325–327; Kötz 2003, 84).

Die Institution des Geschworenenprozesses ist in der US-amerikanischen Verfassung garantiert, sowohl für das Zivilrecht als auch für das Strafrecht. In Strafprozessen ist die Einberufung einer Jury, die im Allgemeinen einen Querschnitt der Bevölkerung repräsentieren soll, bei schweren Verbrechen der Regelfall. Die Geschworenen entscheiden nicht nur über Tatsachen, sondern auch über Schuld und Unschuld der Angeklagten. Das Gericht entscheidet – in den meisten Bundesstaaten – lediglich über das Strafmaß und wacht über die Einhaltung von Verfahrens- und Beweisregeln (Hay 2020, 323–328).

Bei Urteilen von Kollegialorganen sind Sondervoten grundsätzlich zulässig. Die Persönlichkeit der Richterin bzw. des Richters spiegelt sich in Inhalt, Stil und Sprache des Sondervotums wider, insbesondere bei Urteilen des Supreme Court (Kötz 2003, 86). Die sprachlichen und stilistischen Gestaltungsmöglichkeiten US-amerikanischer Richter sind damit weitreichender als in Deutschland.

---

[5] Zum englischen Zivilprozess Bernstorff (2011, 154–155).

1.2.2 Deutsche Rechtsordnung

Während die induktive Methode des *Common Law* auf vergleichender Sachverhaltsanalyse basiert, setzt das deutsche Recht auf das Prinzip der Deduktion. Kern des positivistischen, vom römischen Recht geprägten deutschen Rechtssystems ist ein Korpus von Rechtsnormen, die das menschliche Verhalten regeln. Das menschliche Verhalten, das sich tatsächlich ereignet hat, verkörpert der zu entscheidende Sachverhalt. Die Rechtsanwendung versucht den Gegensatz zwischen diesem Sein und dem gesetzlich normierten Sollen zu vereinen.[6] Der Denkweg hin zur Lösung des Falles setzt mehrere methodische Schritte voraus: Herausarbeiten der einschlägigen Rechtsnorm, gegebenenfalls Deutung der Rechtsnorm mit den Methoden der Auslegung und Anwendung auf den konkreten Fall (Subsumption). Hierbei prägend ist der Syllogismus, ein logisches Schlussverfahren, bestehend aus Obersatz, Untersatz und Schlusssatz. Der Schlusssatz stellt die Anwendung des Gesetzes auf den konkreten Sachverhalt dar (Schellhammer 2019, 2–3; Bleich 1989, 3200). Diesem methodischen Verfahren liegt die positivistische Überzeugung zugrunde, dass die Lebenswirklichkeit unter abstrakte Begriffe subsumiert werden kann. Verschiedene Theorien haben diese Überzeugung jedoch erschüttert. Die Lehre vom Pendelblick geht davon aus, dass die Rechtsanwendung sich nicht in begrifflichen Operationen und logischen Schlussfolgerungen erschöpft, sondern dass der Blick der Rechtsanwender hin- und herwandert zwischen der Rechtsnorm und dem Sachverhalt, bis der Sachverhalt der Rechtsnorm so weit angenähert ist, dass beide miteinander verbunden werden können (siehe Lüderssen 1996, 286). Die Rechtsanwendung ist damit ein Suchprozess, bei dem Rechtsnorm und Sachverhalt sich wechselseitig beeinflussen (Schellhammer 2019, 6). Nach der Theorie vom Vorverständnis hängt die rechtliche Wertung der Richter maßgeblich von ihrem Vorverständnis ab. Niemand könne Prozessakten wertfrei lesen: Die juristische Vorbildung, individuelle außerrechtliche Kenntnisse und Erfahrungen prägen die rechtliche Bewertung (Esser 1970, 9–12). Theoretiker aus dem Bereich „Recht und Sprache" plädieren für ein Konflikts- anstelle eines Ordnungsdenkens in der Rechtswissenschaft (Haft 2009, 34).

Von der Rechtsanwendung im engeren Sinne zu unterscheiden ist die Arbeit am Sachverhalt, die erfolgt, bevor Richter mit der Rechtsanwendung beginnen. Hierfür existiert keine feste wissenschaftliche Methode, und die Prozessordnungen geben nur unvollständige Hinweise darauf, wie der konkrete, für das Urteil relevante Sachverhalt zu konstruieren ist (Schellhammer 2019, 25–27; Nichterlein 1982, 244). Für den Zivilprozess geht die Zivilprozessordnung davon aus, dass die Parteien die Tatsachen liefern und das Gericht daraus die rechtlichen Schlüsse zieht (Beibringungsgrundsatz). Das Gericht erhebt Beweis nur über

---

[6] Maunz & Dürig (2016), Art. 95 Grundgesetz, Rdnr. 19: „Rechtsanwendung bedeutet Anwendung eines abstrakten Prüfungsmaßstabes auf den konkreten Sachverhalt."

streitige erhebliche Tatsachen, während unstreitige Tatsachen als feststehend betrachtet werden, §§ 138 Abs. 3, 288 ZPO. Die Beweiswürdigung, § 286 ZPO, und die Rechtsanwendung sind entsprechend dem Grundsatz *iura novit curia*[7] [„das Gericht kennt das Recht"] Sache des Gerichts, während die Beibringung des Sachverhalts unter Parteiherrschaft steht (Schellhammer 2019, 10–13). Der Sachverhalt, der zur Grundlage der rechtlichen Bewertung wird, entsteht also im Regelfall aus den widerstreitenden Tatsachenvorträgen der Parteien, und Richter konstruieren nach der Beweiswürdigung einen Sachverhalt, ein Masternarrativ. Bei der Beweiswürdigung ist die persönliche Überzeugung der Richterin oder des Richters mitentscheidend: Rechtsgefühl, berufliche Routine, die eigenen Erfahrungen und wirtschaftlichen, kulturellen oder gesellschaftlichen Hintergründe wirken maßgeblich an der Konstruktion des Sachverhaltes mit (Schellhammer 2019, 21–25). Im Strafprozess, in der Verwaltungs-, der Sozial- oder der Finanzgerichtsbarkeit hingegen gilt der Amtsermittlungsgrundsatz. Dem Gericht obliegt es, die Wahrheit zu ermitteln und im Masternarrativ verbindlich abzubilden.

Das Bundesverfassungsgericht versteht die Aufgabe der Rechtsprechung im Sinne einer Interessen- und Wertungsjurisprudenz. Ziel richterlicher Tätigkeit ist es danach, den im Einzelfall bestehenden Interessenkonflikt zu erkennen, ihn mit den gesetzlichen Vorgaben abzugleichen und die dabei sich offenbarenden Lücken anhand gesetzgeberischer Wertvorstellungen zu füllen bzw. nach den „Maßstäben der praktischen Vernunft und den fundierten allgemeinen Gerechtigkeitsvorstellungen der Gemeinschaft" (Bundesverfassungsgericht, BVerfGE 34, 269, 286–287). Die Gerichte sind demnach zur Rechtsfortbildung befugt, wobei die Grenzen dieser Befugnis umstritten sind.[8] Es gibt verschiedene Formen richterlicher Rechtsfortbildung (z.B. Rechtsfindung *praeter legem*, Gesetzeskonkretisierung) (Wülfing 1995, 12–13).

Gerichtsentscheidungen erwachsen in Rechtskraft. Die materielle Rechtskraft hindert abweichende Entscheidungen desselben oder eines anderen Gerichts innerhalb bestimmter objektiver, subjektiver und zeitlicher Grenzen. Die materielle Rechtskraft erstreckt sich im Zivilprozess nur auf denselben Streitgegenstand und wirkt zwischen den Parteien. Die Gründe der Entscheidung erwachsen nicht in Rechtskraft, lediglich deren Tenor. Formell rechtskräftig ist eine Entscheidung, wenn sie unanfechtbar geworden ist.[9] Ein Urteil deutscher Gerichte kann – anders als im US-amerikanischen Recht – unter anderem aufgrund seiner begrenzten Rechtskraft nicht unmittelbar auf ein anderes Urteil mit einem anderen Streitgegenstand einwirken (vgl. Youngs 2007, 73–74). Eine

---

[7] Im *Common Law* gilt dieser römisch-rechtliche Grundsatz nicht.

[8] Die freie richterliche „Rechtsfortbildung", bei der die Richter unter Missachtung des Gewaltenteilungsprinzips an die Stelle des Gesetzgebers treten, wird zumeist abgelehnt, siehe Kaufmann (2011, 134–135).

[9] Zum zivilprozessualen Urteil siehe Zöller (2002), ZPO, vor § 322 Rdnr. 7–9.

Bindungswirkung höchstrichterlicher Rechtsprechung ist zwar vorhanden, sie ist allerdings faktischer und nicht rechtlicher Natur (Hassemer 2011, 263–264).

Beim Bundesverfassungsgericht gibt es gemäß § 30 Abs. 2 BVerfGG die Möglichkeit, abweichende Meinungen in einem Sondervotum niederzulegen, das der Entscheidung angefügt wird. An den meisten übrigen Gerichten verbietet der Schutz des Beratungsgeheimnisses nach § 43 DRiG eine Offenbarung abweichender Meinungen.

Der Stil juristischer Entscheidungen deutscher Gerichte ist grundsätzlich unpersönlich und sachlich sowie gekennzeichnet durch den Gebrauch feststehender Formeln. Urteile ergehen im Namen des Volkes und stellen die verbindliche Anwendung allgemeingültiger Normen auf einen konkreten Einzelfall dar. Durch die nüchterne, unpersönliche Sprache soll erreicht werden, dass persönliche Akzente unterbleiben, damit das Urteil wie ein Akt einer anonymen, von den Talenten und Anschauungen ihres Personals unabhängigen Einrichtung erscheint (Kötz 2003, 85). Auch hier ist ein deutlicher Unterschied zum *Common Law* erkennbar.

Das deutsche Verfahren ist, verglichen mit dem *Common Law*, verschriftlicht (Seibert 1989, 242). Die meisten deutschen Prozessordnungen schreiben vor, dass das Gericht seine Überzeugung aus dem Inbegriff der mündlichen Verhandlung schöpft, und der Mündlichkeitsgrundsatz bildet eine wichtige Prozessmaxime. Doch sind Bezugnahmen auf Schriftsätze möglich, und regelmäßig wird in der mündlichen Verhandlung darauf verwiesen. Zudem sehen die Prozessordnungen Durchbrechungen des Mündlichkeitsgrundsatzes vor.

Das Rechtsinstitut einer Jury kennt das deutsche Verfahrensrecht nicht. Beim Arbeitsgericht etwa werden jedoch ehrenamtliche Richter aus Kreisen der Arbeitgeber und der Arbeitnehmer berufen, §§ 20–23 ArbGG, und auch im Strafverfahren sind ehrenamtliche Richter als Schöffenrichter beim Amtsgericht und Landgericht zugelassen, §§ 29, 76 GVG. Im Unterschied zu den Geschworenen haben die ehrenamtlichen Richter in Deutschland formal dieselbe Position wie die Berufsrichter, eine klare Aufgabenverteilung zwischen Laienrichtern und Berufsjuristen wie im Geschworenenprozess gibt es nicht. Auch die exklusive Aufgabenzuweisung an die Geschworenen führt neben der hohen praktischen und gesellschaftlichen Bedeutung der Juryprozesse in den USA zu der herausragenden Position der Geschworenen bei der Rechtsfindung.

Die mündlichen Verhandlungen in Deutschland sind im Allgemeinen schriftlicher, sachlicher und weniger adversarial als in den USA. Nichtsdestotrotz produzieren auch in Deutschland die Verfahrensbeteiligten und Zeugen mündliche Erzählungen. Raum für Geschichten bieten auch die Schriftsätze. Adressat dieser Geschichten ist – abgesehen von den ehrenamtlichen Richtern – stets ein juristisch geschultes Gericht.

1.2.3 Auswirkungen der Unterschiede

In beiden Rechtsordnungen werden vor Gericht unterschiedliche, sich widersprechende Geschichten erzählt (vgl. Schellhammer 2019, 5), die um die Aufnahme in ein Masternarrativ konkurrieren, das Urteil. Richterinnen und Richter konstruieren in Deutschland dieses Masternarrativ, das hinsichtlich der Tatsachenschilderung und auch hinsichtlich der rechtlichen Bewertung narrative Züge aufweist. Das erfolgt sowohl im Zivilprozess als auch in Rechtsbereichen, in denen der Amtsermittlungsgrundsatz gilt. Die konkrete Reichweite der Bindungswirkung der im Urteil festgestellten Narrative ist dabei nicht ausschlaggebend – zumindest nicht für die Beteiligten, denn für diese entfaltet das Urteilsnarrativ sowohl in Deutschland als auch in den USA eine Bindungswirkung.[10] Daher ist auch in Deutschland von Interesse, wie Gerichtserzählungen narratologisch gestaltet sind und welche Mechanismen die Aufnahme in das Masternarrativ begünstigen. Die Art und Weise der Darstellung der konkurrierenden Geschichten (mündlich oder schriftlich, emotional oder sachlich, sprachlich formalisiert oder freier) ist hinsichtlich der Frage, ob ein Narrativ vorliegt, dabei nicht entscheidend. Denn hierbei kommt es vor allem auf strukturelle Aspekte an. Die Merkmale der jeweiligen Gerichtsgeschichten können mit Blick auf die unterschiedlichen Eigenschaften der Rechtstexte im *Common Law* und in der deutschen Rechtsordnung freilich divergieren.

Adressaten der Gerichtsgeschichten vor deutschen und europäischen Gerichten sind überwiegend Juristen. Wie dargelegt sind deutsche Rechtsanwendende stärker an Gesetze und logische Schlussverfahren gebunden als US-amerikanische. Doch die geltenden Gesetze, die Rechtsprechung und das Schrifttum räumen den deutschen Rechtsanwendern Spielräume bei der Sachverhaltserstellung, Rechtsanwendung und Rechtsfortbildung ein. Bei der Wahrnehmung dieser Spielräume sind das Vorverständnis, das Rechtsgefühl, eigene Erfahrungen oder allgemeine Gerechtigkeitsvorstellungen relevant. Wenn man davon ausgeht, dass menschliches Wissen grundsätzlich narrativ strukturiert ist[11], dann müsste das Vorverständnis deutscher Rechtsanwender gleichermaßen narrativ sein wie die Wissens- und Erfahrungsbasis von Geschworenen. Über erzähltheoretische Vorkenntnisse verfügen Berufsjuristen – ebenso wie Geschworene – im Regelfall nicht. Daher ist es denkbar, dass auch in Deutschland Richterinnen und Richter bzw. andere Rechtsanwender ungeachtet ihrer fundierten juristischen Ausbildung durch narrative Strukturen oder Wirkungsweisen – je nachdem, welche spezifischen Wirkungen dem Narrativen zugeschrieben

[10] Dworkins Idee von Gerichtsentscheidungen als Fortsetzungsroman kann angesichts der abweichenden Bindungswirkung indes nicht auf die deutsche Rechtsordnung übertragen werden.

[11] Hierzu s.u.

werden[12] – beeinflusst werden und dass diese, bewusst sowie unbewusst, mit dem juristischen Wahrheits- und Entscheidungsfindungsprozess interferieren können.

Zudem ist es nicht nur im fallrechtlich geprägten *Common Law*, sondern auch im von Gesetzen dominierten deutschen Rechtssystem möglich, bei der Rechtsanwendung im Wege des Hin- und Herwanderns des Blicks zwischen der Rechtsnorm und dem Lebenssachverhalt die jeweilige Sachverhaltsgeschichte zu berücksichtigen und Geschichtenvergleiche zwischen Sachverhalt und allgemeingültigen Rechtsnormen durchzuführen, die den sachverhaltsbezogenen Methoden des *Case Law* vergleichbar sind.

Insgesamt zeigt sich, dass die Unterschiede zwischen den Rechtsordnungen einer Übertragbarkeit des *Law as Narrative* nicht grundsätzlich entgegenstehen.

1.3 *Law as Narrative* und Erzähltheorie

Zu den Vorläufern des *Law as Narrative* gehören die *Critical Legal Studies*, die feministische Rechtskritik oder die *Critical Race Theory*. Das Geschichtenerzählen (*Legal Storytelling*) wurde als taugliches Medium erachtet, um Standpunkte von Minderheiten in das Recht einzubringen. Zudem wurde ein Weg gesucht, um Emotionen und Erfahrungen in das Recht zu integrieren. Einige Vertreter des *Law as Narrative* nutzen daher die narratologische Perspektive des Rechts, um ideologische und politische Ziele durchzusetzen sowie Machtungleichgewichte aufzudecken. Begriffe der strukturellen Narratologie werden verwendet – mitunter jedoch ohne Definition. Andere Autoren nähern sich Rechtstexten analytisch.

Demgegenüber verfolgt die strukturalistische Narratologie einen formalistischen Ansatz, der unabhängig von ideologischen Zielen steht. Poststrukturalistische Narratologien stehen vielen Ansätzen des *Law as Narrative* näher, da sie stärker auf ideologische Hintergründe, Wirkungen, Bewertungen oder den Interpretationsprozess abstellen.[13]

1.3.1 Narrativitätsbegriffe

Die meisten Arbeiten des *Law as Narrative* legen keinen spezifischen Begriff der Erzählung zugrunde (Arnauld 2009, 47). Das Narrative wird als Gegenstück

[12] Die rhetorische Narratologie etwa untersucht die Überzeugungswirkung narratologischer Konzepte und deren Rezeption durch die Lese- bzw. Zuhörerschaft, die postkoloniale Erzähltheorie versteht Narrativität als Mittel der Identitätserhaltung, -bildung, -festigung. Zu den Wirkungen narrativer Texte im Recht: Blufarb (2017, 207).

[13] Zum Unterschied zwischen strukturalistischen und poststrukturalistischen Narratologien siehe Nünning (2003, 243–244).

zum traditionellen juristischen Denken verstanden, als Ausdruck des Konkreten im Gegensatz zum Abstrakten, des Emotionalen im Gegensatz zum Fach-lich-Sachlichen, des Fließenden im Gegensatz zum Starren (Binder 1999, 73). Mitunter wird das Narrative metaphorisch verwendet als „Synonym jeglicher kultureller Sinnproduktion" (Arnauld 2009, 47). Für White ist das Erzählen strukturell von der Ausdrucksweise des analytischen Denkens zu unterscheiden (White 1973, 245–246). Verbreitet ist zudem das Verständnis, dass Narrativität ein grundlegendes kognitives Muster darstellt (Turner 1996, 4–5).[14]

> Narrative imagining – story – is the fundamental instrument of thought. Rational capacities depend upon it. It is our chief means of looking into the future, of predicting, of planning, and of explaining. It is a literary capacity indispensable to human cognition generally. (Turner 1996, 4–5)

Legal Storytelling und *Outsider Scholarship* verzichten auf eine Definition. Allerdings hält Delgado, zugleich führender Vertreter der *Critical Race Theory*, Geschichten für „powerful means for destroying mindset – the bundle of presuppositions, received wisdoms, and shared understandings against a background of which legal and political discourse takes place" (Delgado 1989, 2413). Das die Mehrheitsgesellschaft prägende „mindset" müsste demnach ebenfalls narrative Aspekte aufweisen.

Auch in der Narratologie besteht kein Konsens bezüglich der Begrifflichkeiten. Schmid fordert eine Zeitstruktur mit mindestens zwei Stadien, Veränderung zwischen den Situationen dieser Stadien und einen gemeinsamen gleichbleibenden Bezugspunkt der Veränderung (Schmid 2003, 19–20). Fludernik bezeichnet in der Lehre von der „natürlichen Narratologie" Narrativität als eine Funktion narrativer Texte, das Hervorrufen von „Erfahrungshaftigkeit" (Fludernik 1996, 12).

1.3.2 Faktuale und fiktionale Erzählungen

Die Narratologie unterscheidet zwischen faktualen und fiktionalen Erzählungen. Faktuale Texte erheben den Anspruch, auf eine Alltagsrealität bzw. auf reale, räumlich und zeitlich konkrete Sachverhalte und Ereignisse[15] zu referenzieren, die sowohl konstruiert als auch verschiedenen Perspektiven unterworfen ist (Breitenwischer et al. 2020, 8).

Diese Dichotomie ist für das *Law as Narrative* untypisch. Viele Autoren streben gerade eine Gleichbehandlung fiktional-literarischer und faktual-rechtlicher Texte an. Hintergrund sind unter anderem Hayden Whites Ideen zur Perspektivenabhängigkeit und Fiktionalität von Geschichtsschreibung. White war

---

[14] Vgl. auch das Konzept der „Protonarrativität" bei Schaeffer (2020, 266).

[15] Klein & Martínez (2009, 6), die Wirklichkeitserzählungen als besondere faktuale Erzählungen verstehen.

Historiker und der Ansicht, dass jede Geschichtsschreibung eine subjektive und mittelbare Sicht des jeweiligen Historikers auf vergangene Ereignisse darstelle und daher wie ein fiktives Werk der Literatur zu behandeln sei (White 1986, 74–92). Dies wurde auch auf das Recht bezogen. Daraus erwuchs die Überzeugung, dass das Recht subjektiv und die Prozesswahrheit nur eine Geschichte unter vielen sei. Das Ergebnis juristischer Prozesse wurde als Konstrukt der vorgetragenen Geschichten enttarnt. Nur eine narratologische Analyse könne zur Aufdeckung der unbewussten Mechanismen führen, durch die die Geschichten der Prozessbeteiligten bei Geschworenen, Gericht und Publikum den Eindruck von Wahrheit vermitteln (Binder & Weisberg 2000, 261–264; Jackson 1988, 161–174).

Bereits im Jahr 1949 hatte Frank festgestellt, dass es vor Gericht keine Fakten gibt. Recht baue auf den Tatsachenfeststellungen eines Gerichts auf, das die Ereignisse niemals miterlebt und seine Informationen aus zweiter Hand habe. Die Rekonstruktion mittels Beweiserhebung habe Schwächen. Die „im Namen des Volkes" festgestellte Geschichte, der Sachverhalt, werde als Wahrheit angesehen, obwohl es keine objektive Wahrheit gäbe (Frank 1949, 14–20).

Bedeutsam für das *Law as Narrative* wurde das Konzept der multiplen Realitäten und der Multiperspektivität, das von einer grundsätzlichen Gleichwertigkeit aller Perspektiven ausgeht (Baron & Epstein 1998, 669–670).

2. *Vorschlag einer Definition für deutsche Rechtstexte*

Vorgeschlagen wird eine Definition von Narrativität, die sich auf den Kontext der deutschen Rechtsordnung beschränkt und nur für das textliche Medium Geltung beansprucht. Es müssen mindestens zwei Ereignisse vorliegen, die zeitlich, aber nicht notwendigerweise kausal oder final miteinander verbunden sind und menschliche Erfahrungen in den Mittelpunkt stellen bzw. eine Art „Erfahrungshaftigkeit" vermitteln. Das Vorhandensein von Darstellung („*discours/narration*") einerseits und der Ebene des Dargestellten („*histoire*") andererseits ist charakteristisch für juristische Geschichten. Kausalität kommt vor (z.B. im Strafrecht und Schadensersatzrecht), ist aber nicht zwingend. Regelungsgegenstand des Rechts ist menschliches Verhalten. Daher ist „Erfahrungshaftigkeit" treffend. Die Zustandsveränderungen müssen nicht tatsächlich geschehen sein, es genügt, wenn sie versucht oder gedacht sind (Blufarb 2017, 383).

Diese Definition soll dazu dienen, Narrativität im Recht prinzipiell abgrenzbar und für strukturalistische Methoden handhabbar zu machen. Die Konzepte von Narrativität als grundlegendem kognitivem Muster sowie als bedeutungskonstituierendem Aspekt bestehen daneben. Auch die zielgerichteten Ansätze, die ohne Definition arbeiten, sind anwendbar.

3. Narrative Strukturen im deutschen Recht

Anhand dieser Definition lassen sich narrative Strukturen im Recht identifizieren.

Der Bereich der Gerichtserzählungen umfasst die mündlichen und schriftlichen Geschichten, die vor Gericht erzählt werden, wie etwa die Anklageschrift der Staatsanwaltschaft, den Schlussvortrag des Strafverteidigers, den Parteienvortrag im Zivilrecht, Geständnisse, Zeugenaussagen oder Urteile. Ebenfalls zu den *courtroom narratives* gehören narratologische Prozessstrategien. Das gesamte Strafverfahren mit den dazugehörigen Figuren einschließlich der Öffentlichkeit stellt ebenfalls eine Erzählung dar.

Rechtsnormen sind zwar abstrakt-generell formuliert, doch Jackson hat gezeigt, dass in Rechtsnomen narrative Fallmuster eingeschlossen sind.

> Although we increasingly use abstract terminology to express our general rules of law, this has certainly not been a universal phenomenon in the history of law and there is reason to believe that the understanding of abstract legal propositions and conceptions, even amongst the most sophisticated, is informed by subconcious narrative models, of typifications of action, and our reactions to them. (Jackson 1988, 58)

Cover interpretiert Rechtsnormen als Relikte des historischen und kasuistischen Rechts einschließlich der jeweiligen Gerechtigkeitsvorstellungen (Cover 1983, 39). Für Sternberg sind Rechtsnormen narrativ, weil sie mögliche, noch nicht aktualisierte Realitäten, zukünftige Möglichkeiten erfassen, ähnlich den Erzähluniversen im Sinne der *possible worlds theory*. Er stellt ab auf die Gesamtgeschichte der Norm, d.h. ihre Entstehungsgeschichte, den in der Norm eingeschlossenen *if-plot* und die potentiellen Folgen der Normanwendung (Sternberg 2008, 32–33). Auch Schapp hat gezeigt, dass das Gesetz „in eine, zu einer Geschichte gehört und selbst wieder eine Geschichte ist“, die sich „auf viele Geschichten bezieht“ und „ebenso konkret“ ist wie diese Geschichten (Schapp 2012, 110).

Gründungsmythen bzw. Legitimationsgeschichten für die Gründung eines Gemeinwesens weisen gleichfalls narrative Strukturen auf. Ihnen wird legitimierende und identitätsbildende Wirkung zugesprochen. Sie klingen in vielen Präambeln von Gründungstexten wie Verfassungen an. Cover zufolge ist Recht ein System der Bedeutungsgebung, und die normative Kraft wird wesentlich von der Akzeptanz und interpretativen Kraft der jeweiligen Gemeinschaft bestimmt. Jede Rechtsordnung sei dabei aus einem aus ihrer Sicht unrechtmäßigen Zustand erwachsen. Die Geschichten über Revolutionen, Katastrophen, etc. erklären und begründen den Neuanfang. Ein Mythos, der dem Gründungsmythos ähnelt, eine Gegengeschichte, sei indes in der Lage, die Rechtsordnung und Gesellschaft wieder zurückzuführen (Cover 1983, 21–23). „[T]he sacred beginning always provides the typology for a dangerous return“ (Cover 1983, 23).

Narrative Strukturen finden sich auch in juristischen Lehrbüchern oder Vorlesungen, denn Rechtsgrundsätze werden Studenten oft anhand von konkreten Fällen anschaulich vermittelt.

Delgado hat den Begriff der „stock stories" geprägt. Er versteht darunter diejenigen Geschichten, die Menschen in dominanten Positionen bzw. Gruppen („ingroups") auswählen und über sich selbst, identitäts- und realitätsbildend, erzählen und die ihre eigene Machtposition stützen (Delgado 1989, 2421; Martinez 2014, 38). Als „stock story" wird dabei die Mehrheitsgeschichte und als „counterstory" die Minderheitsgeschichte, die den Standpunkt gesellschaftlicher Minderheiten vermittelt, bezeichnet (Martinez 2014, 51). Delgado ist der Ansicht, dass juristische Entscheidungen zugleich moralische und politische Werturteile enthalten, die wiederum auf Geschichten beruhen, da Menschen ihre soziale Realität mittels Geschichten konstruieren (Delgado 1989, 2441). Scheppele geht davon aus, dass es auf individueller sowie kollektiver Ebene akzeptierte und nicht akzeptierte Geschichten gebe und dass Richter oftmals diejenige Geschichte vorziehen, die sie aufgrund ihrer eigenen Erfahrungen und Weltsicht für wahr halten (Scheppele 1989, 2081–2083). Beide dürften Narrativität auch als grundlegendes kognitives Muster verstehen. Individuen und Kollektive verfügen danach über einen Fundus von Erzählungen, die eine bestimmte Bedeutung produzieren, und neue Informationen bzw. Narrative werden mit dem vorhandenen Grundstock an Erzählungen abgeglichen. Dieser Abgleich erfolgt auch im juristischen Kontext. Im *Law as Narrative* kann der Begriff „stock story" – teilweise losgelöst von den im Rahmen der *Critical Race Theory* oder des *Outsider Scholarship* behandelten Themen – auch im Sinne einer die Sicht der Mehrheit in einer bestimmten Gruppe prägenden Erzählung, verstanden werden (Blufarb 2017, 445–452).[16]

4. *Untersuchungsansätze des* Law as Narrative *und deren Übertragbarkeit*

4.1 Analyse von Gerichtserzählungen

Unter dem Oberbegriff *narrative competition* werden die miteinander konkurrierenden Gerichtsgeschichten einander gegenübergestellt, auf ihren narrativen Gehalt und ihre Wirkung untersucht, und es wird gefragt, welche Geschichten aus welchen – narratologischen – Gründen bei Gerichten und Geschworenen erfolgreich sind (siehe Blufarb 2017, 232–237). Richter erstellen ein „Masternarrativ" mindestens hinsichtlich des Sachverhalts. Sie gleichen die Vorträge der Prozessbeteiligten mit anderen Geschichten wie beispielsweise Zeugenaussagen

[16] Der Begriff „stock story" wird im *Law as Narrative* auch anders verwendet, z.B. als Synonym für Masternarrativ (Paskey 2014, 52, FN 7 m.w.N.).

oder anderen Beweismitteln ab. Narrative Aspekte werden dabei ähnlich wie rhetorische Mittel als Überzeugungsinstrumente im juristischen Wahrheitsfindungsprozess verstanden.

> It is not, to be sure, morally neutral, for it always seeks to induce a point of view. Storytelling, one can conclude, is never innocent. If you listen with attention to a story well told, you are implicated by it and in it. (Brooks 1996, 16)

Zu den Parametern, die die Wahl einer Geschichte begünstigen, gehören die interne Kohärenz und Vollständigkeit der Geschichte (darunter fallen z.B. Szenen, Akte, handelnde Personen, Handlungen, Objekte, Zielrichtung, Symbolik, Vollständigkeit, Detailtiefe, Konsistenz) und ihre externe Plausibilität, d.h. die Übereinstimmung des Erzählten mit der externen Realität oder dem, was die Geschworenen oder Gerichte als solche ansehen (Burns 1999, 164–176). Narrative Kohärenz wird auch durch Wiederholungen und die Wortwahl hergestellt, wobei die Wortszenarien von Anklage und Verteidigung sich oft unterscheiden und den Angeklagten unterschiedlich charakterisieren. Manche Autoren (z.B. Goodwin 1999) betonen, dass die Jury – um überzeugt zu werden – sich mit dem Angeklagten identifizieren müsse.

Schäfer geht unter anderem der Frage nach, inwiefern der Angeklagte Erzähler bzw. Autor seiner Geschichte ist (Schäfer 2020, 205–208). Im Bereich narratologischer Prozessstrategien werden die Strategien von Anklage und Verteidigung gegenübergestellt, etwa im O. J. Simpson-Fall (Dershowitz 1996). Bei der Betrachtung des Strafverfahrens insgesamt stehen die Protagonisten (Opfer, Täter, Öffentlichkeit, Geschworene) und Handlungsstränge im Fokus (Gewirtz 1996a). Zudem gehört dazu die Urteilsanalyse, bei der die Verwendung narratologischer und rhetorischer Stilmittel, die Stimme, die narrative Kohärenz, die Handlungsstränge, die ideologischen Hintergründe, die Multiperspektivität oder „histoire“, „discours“ und „narration“ insgesamt untersucht werden (z.B. Levinson 1996, Yovel 2004). Häufig werden die Mehrheitsmeinungen mit den dazu ergangenen Minderheitsmeinungen verglichen.

> Multiple opinions are also reminders that the sources of law at hand are far richer than any one account exhausts, that each account contains the shaping mind of its describer, and that judges come to different understandings about what the law means. (Gewirtz 1996b, 12)

Für die Untersuchung von Gerichtsgeschichten in Deutschland sind Urteile des Bundesverfassungsgerichts, die komplexe gesellschaftliche Themen behandeln und eine Mindermeinung enthalten, besonders geeignet. Zudem werden sie in der amtlichen Sammlung veröffentlicht.

Dementsprechend wurde das Erste Kopftuchurteil des Bundesverfassungsgerichts und die dazu ergangene Mindermeinung untersucht (Blufarb 2017, 388–425).

Im Ergebnis lassen das Urteil des Bundesverfassungsgerichts[17] und das Sondervotum deutliche Unterschiede hinsichtlich ihrer „histoire", aber auch hinsichtlich des „discours" und der „narration" erkennen.

Während die Beschwerdeführerin im Urteil das Opfer ist, das für Gerechtigkeit kämpft, will sie in der abweichenden Meinung ihre Grundrechte auf Kosten der schwächeren Kinder und Eltern ausleben und hält sich nicht an die grundgesetzlich verankerte Vereinbarung, dass Beamte auf Seiten des Staates stehen und als solche den Bürgern gegenüber gemäßigt auftreten müssen. Der Beamte ist in der abweichenden Meinung Hauptfigur, während er im Urteil nur am Rande in Erscheinung tritt. Die Positionierung von Staat, Beamten und Bürgern unterscheidet sich. Während die abweichende Meinung die Fronten und die Distanz zwischen Bürgern und Staat betont und die Grundrechte als Abstandswahrer einsetzt, versteht das Urteil den Staat als vereinende Heimstatt aller Staatsbürger, die eine Grundrechtsausübung erst ermöglicht.

Insgesamt arbeitet die abweichende Meinung viel mit Gegensätzen, Widersprüchen und bildet Fronten. Sie greift das Urteil an, indem sie dessen narrative Kohärenz, die Regeln der „histoire" zerstört, die Autorität des Autors hinterfragt und neue narratologische Prinzipien etabliert. Die kopftuchtragende Lehrerin greift ihr zufolge verschiedene Werte an: die Gleichberechtigung zwischen Mann und Frau, das Mäßigungsgebot des Beamten oder das Vertrauen der Eltern in eine positive, gewaltfreie Erziehung ihrer Kinder durch den Staat. Dies geschieht sowohl inhaltlich als auch durch die sprachliche Darstellung mit polarisierenden Bildern, die auf Mythen wie den der Vollverschleierung der Frauen im Islam Bezug nehmen. Die abweichende Meinung übt auf diese Weise scharfe Kritik an der Senatsmehrheit hinsichtlich der im Urteil dargestellten „histoire".

Interessant ist, dass es im Ersten Kopftuchurteil das Bundesverfassungsgericht und nicht die Mindermeinung war, das die althergebrachten gesellschaftlichen Verhältnisse infrage stellte und der Stimme der gesellschaftlichen Minderheit, verkörpert durch die kopftuchtragende Klägerin, Gehör verschaffte. In diesem Fall nicht zutreffend ist die These, dass Mehrheitsmeinungen die bestehenden gesellschaftlichen Rollenverhältnisse manifestieren, während Mindermeinungen sich durch Einnehmen der Opferperspektive und externe Kohärenz zu Mythen, die Momente von Gewalt und Unterdrückung beinhalten, in die Situation gesellschaftlicher Minderheiten hineinversetzen (siehe Yovel 2004, 136).

Die *Law as Narrative*-Analyse von Urteilen verdeutlicht, wie die narratologische Gestaltung das rechtliche Ergebnis plausibilisiert und auf welche Symbole und Erzählungen der Urteilstext verweist.

---

[17] Urteil des Bundesverfassungsgerichts v. 24. September 2003, 2 BvR 1436/02, BVerfGE 108, 282–282.

4.2 Analyse von Rechtsnormen

Nach Jacksons *Pattern*-Methode wird der zu entscheidende Fall bei der Rechtsanwendung in loser Analogie mit dem im Gesetz eingeschlossenen Musterfall verglichen. Je ähnlicher er diesem ist, desto leichter falle es, eine rechtliche Entscheidung zu treffen (Jackson 1988, 101–106). Dieser Ansatz wurde auf die deutsche Rechtsordnung übertragen (Arnauld 2009, 28–31). Grasnick hat darauf hingewiesen, dass die rechtspraktische Arbeit mit Gesetzen trotz begrifflicher Einheitlichkeiten ein Bewusstsein für die Differenz unterschiedlicher Fallgeschichten erfordert, eine hohe „Fallgeschichtensensibilität" (Grasnick 2010, 210). Bereits Kaufmann hat die enge Verbindung von Sollen und Sein demonstriert (Kaufmann 1982, 18–20).

Bei Gesetzen ist besonders die Untersuchung der „histoire" ergiebig. Wenn man die narrativen Grundfälle herausarbeitet, die einer Vorschrift zugrunde liegen, und dabei deren historische Entwicklung, die Vorstellungen des Gesetzgebers und die in der Gesellschaft existenten „stock stories" der Mehrheit sowie vorhandene abweichende Gegengeschichten berücksichtigt und den vorliegenden Fall (einschließlich der Vorgeschichte, Motive, Charakterisierung, etc.) als eine Geschichte versteht, die mit den im Gesetz eingeschlossenen Fallgeschichten abgeglichen wird, kann das zu einzelfallgerechteren Lösungen beitragen, indem Aspekte einbezogen werden, die sonst vielleicht unberücksichtigt geblieben wären. Allerdings ist es erforderlich, sich eng am Gesetz zu bewegen und die Methode dieses Geschichtenvergleichs nur ergänzend zu den etablierten Methoden anzuwenden – insbesondere dort, wo Entscheidungs- und Bewertungsspielräume bestehen. Interessante Ergebnisse kann dieser Ansatz bei Normtexten zutage fördern, die den gesellschaftlichen Wandel widerspiegeln, wie beispielsweise § 177 StGB[18], dem Anhang zu § 3 Abs. 3 UWG (Blufarb 2017, 441–442) oder dem Vierten Gesetz zum Schutz der Bevölkerung bei einer epidemischen Lage von nationaler Tragweite.[19] Das Gesetz war die vierte Änderung des Infektionsschutzgesetzes seit März 2020 und reihte sich in die Erzählung der Coronagesetzgebung in Deutschland ein, die wiederum – beispielsweise durch Verwendung des Begriffs des „seuchenrechtlichen Notfalls" (Begründung zum Ersten „Bevölkerungsschutzgesetz", Bundestagsdrucksache 19/18111 v. 24. März 2020, 14) – auf bekannte historische und literarische Narrative verweist.

[18] Zu § 177 Abs. 1 StGB a.F. (vor Änderung durch das Fünfzigste Gesetz zur Änderung des Strafgesetzbuches vom 4. November 2016) siehe Blufarb (2017, 445–452).

[19] Viertes Gesetz zum Schutz der Bevölkerung bei einer epidemischen Lage von nationaler Tragweite, BGBl. Jahrgang 2021 Teil I Nr. 18, 22. April 2021.

4.3 Analyse von Gründungsmythen / Legitimationsgeschichten

Mehrere Autoren betrachten die Funktionen von Gründungsmythen und gehen z.B. der Frage nach, inwiefern sie einem Gemeinwesen Generationengerechtigkeit oder Identität vermitteln (siehe Blufarb 2017, 266–282). Untersuchungsobjekte sind häufig Verfassungen. Auch das Erzählen und die Analyse kollektiver Gegengeschichten sind hier zu verorten.

In der Präambel des EU-Vertrags beispielsweise sind mehrere Gründungsmythen erkennbar, darunter etwa der Mythos von der gemeinsamen Friedenssicherung als Lehre aus der blutigen Vergangenheit Europas. In nationalen Gesellschaften kursieren Gegengeschichten dazu, die nach den Ideen Covers und Bhabas (siehe Blufarb 2017, 278, 459–467) die Europäische Union schwächen könnten.

Reinhardt betont, dass sich hinter dem „Friedensnarrativ“ oder dem „Narrativ einer immer enger werdenden Union“ mehr verberge als Narrativität, nämlich komplexe politische Konzeptionen, Rechtsbegriffe und Begründungsmuster, deren Bedeutung über Erzählstrukturen nicht vollumfänglich erschlossen werden könne (Reinhardt 2019, 36). Lübbe-Wolff wendet sich gegen die Suche nach einem Narrativ für die EU und legt dar, dass die Erwartungen der Mitgliedstaaten an die EU ebenso heterogen sind wie die Probleme, die sie mit ihr haben (Lübbe-Wolff 2019, 204–206). Narrativität kann in der Tat nur eine zusätzliche Kategorie der Beschreibung und Untersuchung anbieten und keine rechtswissenschaftlichen oder politischen Methoden ersetzen. Zudem bedürfen Narrative einer offenen Zuhörerschaft. Im EU-Kontext wäre daher, unabhängig davon, ob ein einheitliches Narrativ der EU existiert bzw. geschaffen werden sollte, eine verständliche und werbende Vermittlung bereits bestehender, gewachsener Narrative hilfreich. Im Sinne der *narrative competition* gegen anti-europäische Erzählungen wäre es zu begrüßen, wenn die überzeugende Kraft von Geschichten genutzt werden könnte, um mehr Begeisterung der EU-Bürger für die EU zu wecken.

4.4 *Outsider Scholarship*

Das *Outsider Scholarship* untersucht Rechtstexte unter Bezugnahme auf die Annahme, dass das Recht nicht objektiv sei, sondern Werte und Ideologien der Mehrheitsgesellschaft verkörpere, um die dahinterstehenden Machtstrukturen aufzudecken (z.B. Coughlin 1995, 1229; siehe Blufarb 2017, 298–321). Das Recht und die juristische Sprache würden gesellschaftlich benachteiligte Gruppen unterdrücken und ihnen im Rechtssystem weniger Erfolgsaussichten zugestehen als der Mehrheit. Ausgehend vom Konzept der multiplen Realitäten untersucht das *Outsider Scholarship*, warum bestimmte Geschichten von der Mehrheit der Gerichte und der Rechtswissenschaft akzeptiert werden, während andere, insbesondere die Geschichten gesellschaftlich unterdrückter Minderheiten, als unwahr abgetan werden (Scheppele 1989, 2082–2084). Hintergrund sei unter anderem das „mindset" (Delgado 1989, 2413) der gesellschaftlichen Mehrheit, das die Grundlage ihrer Weltsicht bilde, sich wie ein Filter vor die Interpretation der Welt durch die Mehrheit lege, im Recht aber nicht kenntlich gemacht werde. Zudem würden rechtliche Ungerechtigkeiten unbemerkt durch Ideologien gerechtfertigt (Delgado 1989, 2414). Delgado sieht das *Legal Storytelling* durch Minderheiten als wirksamstes Mittel an, diese „stock stories" der Mehrheit zu erweitern. Die identitätsstiftende Wirkung der Gegengeschichten gesellschaftlicher Minderheiten beruhe ebenso wie bei den Mehrheitsgeschichten darauf, dass sie an die Vergangenheit und Herkunft der Minderheitengruppierung erinnere (Delgado 1989, 2412). Damit verbunden werden politische Forderungen nach einem bewussten Umgang mit Geschichten im Recht, nach der Einfügung von individuellen und kollektiven Minderheitsnarrativen und nach mehr Geschichtenpluralismus. Dem Narrativen wird dabei die Fähigkeit zugesprochen, außerhalb des juristischen Diskurses zu stehen und für alle Gesellschaftsschichten zugänglich zu sein.

Die Blickrichtung und die Forderungen des *Outsider Scholarship* sind auch für die deutsche Rechtswissenschaft von Interesse. Ob das deutsche Recht und die Rechtssprache Stimmen von Minderheiten und gesellschaftlichen Außenseitern systematisch ausgrenzt, ist anhand von Analysen von Rechtstexten zu bestimmen und kann nicht pauschal festgestellt werden.

4.5 Mehr Empathie durch Geschichten im Recht

Einige Autoren plädieren für mehr Empathie im Recht durch Erzählungen (Henderson 1987). Mehr Menschlichkeit und Empathie könnten durch Geschichten auch in der deutschen Rechtsordnung erreicht werden. Individuelle Geschichten, z.B. über Schmerz und Leid wegen des Rechts, könnten den Rechtsdiskurs bereichern. Damit diese das „mindset"[20] der Mehrheitsgesellschaft erweitern, wäre indes mitfühlendes Zuhören seitens der Rechtsanwender erforderlich. Zu berücksichtigen ist dabei, dass Empathie keinen Rechtsbegriff darstellt und nicht erzwungen werden kann. Es kann sich nur um eine Einladung zum empathischen bzw. sympathischen Zuhören handeln.

4.6 *Legal Storytelling*

Legal Storytelling erschöpft sich nicht im Erzählen von Minderheitsgeschichten. Jede Art der Vermittlung individueller und kollektiver Erfahrungen mit

[20] Zum Begriff s.o.

rechtlichem Bezug im rechtswissenschaftlichen Diskurs und in der Rechtsausbildung (Geschichten, Gegengeschichten, Emotionen als Folgen von Gesetzen, etc.) kann hier verortet werden. *Legal Storytelling* wirkt insbesondere im Vorfeld durch Aufzeigen von Regelbedarfen und gegebenenfalls einer Erweiterung des Erfahrungshorizonts. Pieroth fordert die Einführung von *Law and Literature* als Grundlagenfach im deutschen Jurastudium (Pieroth 2015, XV). In diesem Rahmen könnte auch *Legal Storytelling* praktiziert werden.

4.7 Mehr Moral durch Geschichten im Recht

Einige Autoren betonen die Korrelation zwischen literarischer und rechtlich-moralischer Hochwertigkeit von Urteilen (Weisberg 1992, 16). Dass Narrative moralisch hochwertiger sind als andere Textformen, überzeugt zumindest für die deutsche Rechtswissenschaft jedoch nicht. Wie Brooks zutreffend feststellt, sind Geschichten ein „moralisches Chamäleon" (Brooks 2002, 2). Sie können zu mehr Einzelfallgerechtigkeit beitragen, wenn sie einem Rechtsstreit eine neue Perspektive hinzufügen, und sie können aufgrund ihrer selbstheilenden Wirkung unter Umständen Opfern im Recht helfen. Aber zu mehr Moral im Recht dürften sie – ungeachtet der Diskussion, wie Moral und Recht sich zueinander verhalten – deshalb nicht zwingend führen. Zudem bieten formalisierte deutsche Urteile wenig Möglichkeiten zu einem literarisch hochwertigen Schreibstil.

4.8 Bewusster Umgang mit Geschichten im Recht / Geschichtenpluralismus

Ein bewusster Umgang mit narrativen Strukturen im Recht ist zu befürworten. Denn es wäre von Vorteil, wenn sich die Rechtsanwender, die Autoren juristischer Texte sowie deren Adressaten der Wirkungen bewusst wären, die narrative Strukturen im Recht auslösen können.

Die Forderung nach einem stärkeren Geschichtenpluralismus im deutschen Recht ist angesichts gesellschaftlicher Heterogenität auch in Deutschland nachvollziehbar. Individuelle und kollektive Narrative, die für das Recht relevante Erfahrungen veranschaulichen, könnten zunächst in den bestehenden rechtlichen Rahmen eingefügt werden. Den Rechtsdiskurs könnten sie z.B. durch Veröffentlichungen in Rechtszeitschriften bereichern und die Rechtsausbildung durch entsprechende Lehrveranstaltungen. Gegengeschichten zu den herrschenden Gründungsmythen, „stock stories" bzw. kursierende Mehrheits- und Minderheitsnarrative sowie Geschichten hinter Gesetzen könnten auch in Kommentaren bereitgestellt werden. Darüber hinaus könnten die bestehenden Spielräume im materiellen Recht, das subjektive Geschichten oft voraussetzt, z.B. beim Abstellen auf den Empfängerhorizont oder der Anknüpfung an individuelle Schuld, im Sinne des *Law as Narrative* genutzt werden. Fallorientierte Methoden wie Jacksons *Pattern*-Methode können der deutschen Rechtsordnung von Nutzen sein, soweit sie die etablierten Auslegungs- und Rechtsanwendungsmethoden ergänzen und etwa den Zweck, den eine Regel verfolgt, konkretisieren.

Eine Abkehr von den Grundstrukturen der deutschen Rechtsordnung und von der Methodik der Subsumption des Einzelfalls unter abstrakte Regeln zugunsten einzelfallorientierter Methoden, die manche fordern, würde hingegen gegen die Grundsätze der Rechtssicherheit und Rechtsgleichheit verstoßen und ist abzulehnen. Zudem würde dadurch kein Mehr an Einzelfallgerechtigkeit oder ein menschlicheres Recht garantiert. Ebenso wahrscheinlich wäre ein Zuwachs an Willkür und Rechtsunsicherheit (siehe Lüderssen 1996, 337–338). Zudem stellt sich die Legitimationsfrage.

5. Chancen und Grenzen

Insgesamt hat das *Law as Narrative* viele interessante Ansätze zu bieten, die das deutsche Recht bereichern können, von denen einige in diesem Beitrag vorgestellt wurden (im Einzelnen siehe Blufarb 2017, 501–548). Grenzen der Übertragbarkeit dürften sich vor allem aufgrund der Unterschiede zwischen Recht und Literatur und aus den Zielen, Funktionen und Maßstäben des deutschen Rechts und der Rechtswissenschaft ergeben. Soweit diese bei der Übertragung berücksichtigt werden, bestehen Chancen, den *narrative turn* zur interdisziplinären Zusammenarbeit und Modernisierung zu nutzen, neue Perspektiven einzubeziehen und das Rechtssystem kommunikativer, kreativer, pluralistischer und menschlicher zu gestalten.

Zitierte Literatur

Arnauld, Andreas von (2009) „Was war, was ist – und was sein soll: Erzählen im juristischen Diskurs.“ *Wirklichkeitserzählungen – Felder, Formen und Funktionen nicht-literarischen Erzählens*. Hg. Christian Klein und Matías Martínez. Stuttgart/Weimar: Metzler. 14–50.

Baron, Jane B. und Julia Epstein (1998) „Language and the Law: Literature, Narrative, and Legal Theory.“ *The Politics of Law. A Progressive Critique*. Hg. David Kairys. 3. Auflage. New York: Basic Books. 662–679.

Begründung zum Ersten „Bevölkerungsschutzgesetz“, Bundestagsdrucksache 19/18111 v. 24. März 2020, 14.

Bernstorff, Christoph Graf von (2011) *Einführung in das englische Recht*. 4. Auflage. München: C.H. Beck.

Binder, Guyora (1999) „The Law-as-Literature Trope." *Law and Literature*. Hg. Michael Freeman und Andrew Lewis. Band 2. Oxford: Oxford Univ. Press. 65–89.

Binder, Guyora und Robert Weisberg (2000) *Literary Criticisms of Law*. Princeton: Princeton Univ. Press.

Burns, Robert P. (1999) *A Theory of the Trial.* Princeton: Princeton Univ. Press.

Bleich, Susanne (1989) „Die literarische und die juristische Hermeneutik – Ein Vergleich." *Neue Juristische Wochenschrift* 42: 3197–3202.

Blufarb, Ruth (2017) *Geschichten im Recht – Übertragbarkeit von „Law as Narrative" auf die deutsche Rechtsordnung*. Baden-Baden: Nomos.

Breitenwischer, Dustin, Hanna-Myriam Häger und Julian Menninger (2020) „Zur Geschichte und Medialität faktualer und fiktionaler Erzählpraktiken: Eine Einleitung." *Faktuales und Fiktionales Erzählen II*. Hg. dies. Baden-Baden: Ergon. 7–29.

Brooks, Peter (1996) „The Law as Narrative and Rhetoric." *Law's Stories: Narrative and Rhetoric in the Law*. Hg. ders. und Paul Gewirtz. New Haven/London: Yale Univ. Press. 14–22.

Brooks, Peter (2002) „Narrativity of the Law." *Cardozo School of Law: Law and Literature*. Band 14. 1–10.

Coughlin, Anne M. (1995) „Regulating the Self: Autobiographical Performances in Outsider Scholarship." *Virginia Law Review* 81: 1229–1340.

Cover, Robert M. (1983) „The Supreme Court 1982 Term, Foreword: Nomos and Narrative." *Harvard Law Review* 97: 4–68.

Delgado, Richard (1989) „Storytelling for Oppositionists and Others: A Plea for Narrative." *Michigan Law Review* 87.8: 2411–2441.

Dershowitz, Alan M. (1996) „Life is not a Dramatic Narrative." *Law's Stories: Narrative and Rhetoric in the Law*. Hg. Peter Brooks und Paul Gewirtz. New Haven/London: Yale Univ. Press. 99–105.

Dworkin, Ronald (1985) *A Matter of Principle*. Cambridge/London: Harvard Univ. Press.

Esser, Josef (1970) *Vorverständnis und Methodenwahl in der Rechtsfindung*. Frankfurt a.M.: Athenäums-Verlag.

Fludernik, Monika (1996) *Towards a ‚Natural' Narratology*. London: Routledge.

Frank, Jerome (1949) *Courts on Trial, Myth and Reality in American Justice*. Princeton: Princeton Univ. Press.

Gewirtz, Paul (1996a) „Victims and Voyeurs: Two Narrative Problems at the Criminal Trial." *Law's Stories: Narrative and Rhetoric in the Law*. Hg. Peter Brooks und ders. New Haven/London: Yale Univ. Press. 135–161.

Gewirtz, Paul (1996b) „Narrative and Rhetoric in the Law.“ *Law's Stories: Narrative and Rhetoric in the Law.* Hg. Peter Brooks und ders. New Haven/London: Yale Univ. Press. 2–13.

Goodwin, Jill Tomasson (1999) „The ‚Final Struggle‘: A Discoursal, Rhetorical, and Social Analysis of Two Closing Arguments.“ *Law and Literature.* Hg. Michael Freeman und Andrew Lewis. Band 2. Oxford: Oxford Univ. Press. 301–322.

Grasnick, Walter (2010) „Die Erzählbarkeit des Rechts.“ *Festschrift für Jan Schapp zum siebzigsten Geburtstag.* Hg. Patrick Gödicke. Tübingen: Mohr Siebeck. 195–212.

Haft, Fritjof (2009) *Juristische Rhetorik.* 8. Auflage. Freiburg: Alber.

Hassemer, Winfried (2011) „Rechtssystem und Kodifikation: Die Bindung des Richters an das Gesetz.“ *Einführung in Rechtsphilosophie und Rechtstheorie der Gegenwart.* Hg. Arthur Kaufmann, Winfried Hassemer und Ulfrid Neumann. 8. Auflage. Heidelberg u.a.: Müller. 251–269.

Hay, Peter (2020) *US-Amerikanisches Recht.* 7. Auflage. München: C.H. Beck.

Henderson, Lynne N. (1987) „Legality and Empathy.“ *Michigan Law Review* 85.7: 1574–1653.

Jackson, Bernard S. (1988) *Law, Fact and Narrative Coherence.* Liverpool: Deborah Charles Publications.

Kaufmann, Arthur (1982) „Analogie und Natur der Sache: Zugleich ein Beitrag zur Lehre vom Typus.“ *Heidelberger Forum* 12. 2. Auflage. Heidelberg: Müller.

Kaufmann, Arthur (2011) „Problemgeschichte der Rechtsphilosophie.“ *Einführung in Rechtsphilosophie und Rechtstheorie der Gegenwart.* Hg. ders., Winfried Hassemer und Ulfrid Neumann. 8. Auflage. Heidelberg u.a.: Müller. 26–147.

Klein, Christian und Matías Martínez (2009) *Wirklichkeitserzählungen – Felder, Formen und Funktionen nicht-literarischen Erzählens.* Stuttgart/Weimar: Metzler. 1–13.

Kötz, Hein (2003) „Rhetorik und Jurisprudenz im deutschen Recht und im Common Law.“ *Festschrift für Peter Schlechtriem zum 70. Geburtstag.* Hg. Ingeborg Schwenzer und Günter Hager. Tübingen: Mohr Siebeck. 79–90.

Lachenmaier, Maria (2008) *Die Law as Literature-Bewegung – Entstehung, Entwicklung und Nutzen.* Berlin: wvb.

Levinson, Sanford (1996) „The Rhetoric of the Judicial Opinion.“ *Law's Stories: Narrative and Rhetoric in the Law.* Hg. Peter Brooks und ders. New Haven/London: Yale Univ. Press. 187–205.

Lübbe-Wolff, Gertrude (2019), „Narrativkur für die EU? Forget it.“ *Die Neuerfindung Europas.* Hg. Claudio Franzius, Franz C. Mayer und Jürgen Neyer. Baden-Baden: Nomos. 195–206.

Lüderssen, Klaus (1996) *Genesis und Geltung in der Jurisprudenz*. Frankfurt a.M.: Suhrkamp.

Martinez, Aja Y. (2014) „A Plea for Critical Race Theory Counterstory: Stock Story versus Counterstory Dialogues Concerning Alejandra's ‚Fit' in the Academy." *Composition Studies* 42.2: 33–55.

Maunz, Theodor und Günther Dürig (2016) *Grundgesetz, Kommentar*. 78. Auflage. München: C.H. Beck.

Müller-Dietz, Heinz (1990a) „Zur literarischen und juristischen Hermeneutik." *Essais zur Theorie von Recht und Verfassung*. Hg. Friedrich Müller und Ralph Christensen. Berlin: Duncker und Humblot. 157–171.

Müller-Dietz, Heinz (1990b) *Grenzüberschreitungen: Beiträge zur Beziehung zwischen Literatur und Recht*. Baden-Baden: Nomos.

Nichterlein, Reiner (1982) „Recht und Sprache – Versuch zur Verbesserung der richterlichen Schriftsprache im Zivilprozeß." *Deutsche Richterzeitung* 7: 241–246.

Nünning, Ansgar (2003) „Narratology or Narratologies? Taking Stock of Recent Developments, Critique and Modest Proposals for Future Usages of the Term. " *What is Narratology? Questions and Answers Regarding the Status of a Theory*. Hg. Tom Kindt und Hans-Harald Müller. Berlin/New York: De Gruyter. 239–275.

Paskey, Steven (2014) „The Law is Made of Stories: Erasing the False Dichotomy Between Stories and Legal Rules." *Legal Communications & Rhetoric: JALWD* 51: 51–82.

Pieroth, Bodo (2015) *Recht und Literatur. Von Friedrich Schiller bis Martin Walser*. München: C.H. Beck.

Posner, Richard A. (2009) *Law and Literature*. 3. Auflage. Cambridge: Harvard Univ. Press.

Reinhardt, Jörn (2019) „Wozu Narrativität? Interventionen der Erzählforschung in Recht und Politik." *Die Neuerfindung Europas*. Hg. Claudio Franzius, Franz C. Mayer und Jürgen Neyer. Baden-Baden: Nomos. 33–44.

Schäfer, Frank L. (2020) „Theater des Schreckens: Eine diachrone Narratologie des Strafprozesses." *Faktuales und fiktionales Erzählen II*. Hg. Dustin Breitenwischer, Hanna-Myriam Häger und Julian Menninger. Baden-Baden: Ergon.193–223.

Schaeffer, Jean-Marie (2020) „Grenzsituationen des Erzählens." *Faktuales und fiktionales Erzählen II*. Hg. Dustin Breitenwischer, Hanna-Myriam Häger und Julian Menninger. Baden-Baden: Ergon. 263–282.

Schapp, Wilhelm (2012) *In Geschichten verstrickt: Zum Sein von Mensch und Ding*. 5. Auflage. Frankfurt a.M.: Klostermann.

Schellhammer, Kurt (2019) *Die Arbeitsmethode des Zivilrichters für Rechtsreferendare und junge Praktiker mit Fällen und einer Musterakte*. 18. Auflage. Heidelberg: Müller.

Scheppele, Kim Lane (1989) „Foreword: Telling Stories." *Michigan Law Review* 87.8: 2073–2098.

Schmid, Wolf (2003) „Narrativity and Eventfulness." *What is Narratology? Questions and Answers Regarding the Status of a Theory*. Hg. Tom Kindt und Hans-Harald Müller. Berlin/New York: De Gruyter. 17–31.

Seibert, Thomas-Michael (1989) „Schriftform und Mündlichkeitsprinzip im Rechtsdiskurs." *Rechtsdiskurse. Untersuchungen zur Kommunikation im Gerichtsverfahren*. Hg. Ludger Hoffmann. Tübingen: Narr. 217–250.

Sternberg, Meir (2008) „If-Plots: Narrativity and the Law-Code." *Theorizing Narrativity*. Hg. John Pier. Berlin/New York: De Gruyter. 29–108.

Turner, Mark (1996) *The Literary Mind: The Origins of Thought and Language*. Oxford: Oxford Univ. Press.

Wagner, Heinz (1965) „Interpretation in Literatur- und Rechtswissenschaft." *Archiv für die civilistische Praxis* 165: 520–557.

Weisberg, Richard (1992) *Poethics, and Other Strategies of Law and Literature*. New York: Columbia Univ. Press.

White, Hayden (1986) *Auch Klio dichtet oder Die Fiktion des Faktischen, Studien zur Tropologie des historischen Diskurses*. Stuttgart: Klett-Cotta.

White, James Boyd (1973) *The Legal Imagination. Studies in the Nature of Legal Thought and Expression*. Boston: Little, Brown.

Wülfing, Max (1995) „Richtermacht und Rechtsgestaltung." *Verfassungsrichter: Rechtsfindung am U.S. Supreme Court und am Bundesverfassungsgericht*. Hg. Bernhard Großfeld und Herbert Roth. Münster/Hamburg: Lit. 1–26.

Youngs, Raymond (2007) *English, French and German Comparative Law*. 2. Auflage. London: Routledge.

Yovel, Jonathan (2004) „Running Backs, Wolves, and Other Fatalities: How Manipulations of Narrative Coherence in Legal Opinions Marginalize Violent Death." *Cardozo School of Law: Law and Literature*. Band 16.1. 127–159.

Zöller, Richard (2002) *Zivilprozessordnung, Kommentar*. 23. Auflage. Köln: Verlag Dr. Otto Schmidt.

Urteilsverzeichnis

Urteil des Bundesverfassungsgerichts v. 24. September 2003, 2 BvR 1436/02, BVerfGE 108, 282–340.

Abkürzungsverzeichnis

ArbGG	Arbeitsgerichtsgesetz (Deutschland) in der Fassung der Bekanntmachung vom 2. Juli 1979 (BGBl. I S. 853, 1036), zuletzt geändert durch Artikel 10 des Gesetzes vom 5. Oktober 2021 (BGBl. I S. 4607)
BGBl.	Bundesgesetzblatt
BVerfGE	Entscheidungen des Bundesverfassungsgerichts
BVerfGG	Gesetz über das Bundesverfassungsgericht (Deutschland)
DRiG	Deutsches Richtergesetz in der Fassung der Bekanntmachung vom 19. April 1972 (BGBl. I S. 713), zuletzt geändert durch Artikel 4 des Gesetzes vom 25. Juni 2021 (BGBl. I S. 2154)
GVG	Gerichtsverfassungsgesetz (Deutschland) in der Fassung der Bekanntmachung vom 9. Mai 1975 (BGBl. I S. 1077), zuletzt geändert durch Artikel 8 des Gesetzes vom 7. Juli 2021 (BGBl. I S. 2363)
Rdnr.	Randnummer
StGB	Strafgesetzbuch (Deutschland) in der Fassung der Bekanntmachung vom 13. November 1998 (BGBl. I S. 3322), zuletzt geändert durch Artikel 2 des Gesetzes vom 22. November 2021
UWG	Gesetz gegen den unlauteren Wettbewerb (Deutschland) in der Fassung der Bekanntmachung vom 3. März 2010 (BGBl. I S. 254), zuletzt geändert durch Artikel 1 des Gesetzes vom 10. August 2021 (BGBl. I S. 3504)
ZPO	Zivilprozessordnung (Deutschland) in der Fassung der Bekanntmachung vom 5. Dezember 2005 (BGBl. I S. 3202; 2006 I S. 431; 2007 I S. 1781), zuletzt geändert durch Artikel 3 des Gesetzes vom 5. Oktober 2021 (BGBl. I S. 4607)

Fictions of Copyright: Charles Dickens and American Trade Courtesy

Robert Spoo

This essay may seem somewhat anomalous in a volume on narrative and law, since my subject is really neither law, legally speaking, nor narratology, theoretically speaking.[1] Rather, it concerns a system of informal norms by which American publishers fashioned a rough approximation of copyright law during the nineteenth century, to compensate for the legislatively decreed lack of U.S. copyright protection for non-U.S. authors that extended from 1790 into the 1890s, and long afterward in less overt forms.[2] This system of professional norms, called *courtesy of the trade* or *trade courtesy*, was a loosely cartelized agreement among publishers to treat each other's foreign books as if they enjoyed actual legal protection. The practice of courtesy became so cohesive and reliable that it allowed publishing houses, with fair regularity, to pay reprinted foreign authors or their publishers honoraria, royalties, or other sums.

There were two dimensions to trade courtesy: a horizontal axis on which publishers recognized each other's informal claims to foreign works, cooperat-

---

[1] This essay incorporates brief portions, substantially revised, of two earlier pieces: Spoo (2017) and Spoo (2020). I wish to thank Mike Everton, Dirk Hartog, Richard Hix, and Simon Stern for their very helpful ideas and suggestions. Portions of this essay were presented at the conference, Law and Literature from a Narratological Perspective / Recht und Literatur aus narratologischer Sicht, University of Freiburg; at a Law and Public Affairs (LAPA) Seminar, Princeton University; and in the Faculty Works in Progress Series, University of Minnesota Law School. I wish to thank the participants in those events for their valuable insights and comments. I am especially grateful to Hanna Häger, Monika Fludernik, and Frank L. Schäfer for hosting the conference at University of Freiburg and inviting me to speak there. I am also grateful to Princeton University for a Law and Public Affairs (LAPA) Fellowship in 2020–2021.

[2] The text of the 1790 U.S. copyright act – the first federal copyright statute in the United States – expressly excluded foreign authors' works from protection. See Act of 31 May 1790, ch. 15, § 5, 1 Stat. 124, 125. The 1790 act did this in two ways, by providing a strict definition of qualified rights-holders and by openly immunizing American piracy. First, copyrights were available only to "a citizen or citizens of these United States, or residents therein" (Act of 31 May 1790, ch. 15, § 5, 1 Stat. 124, 124). Second, the statute provided that "nothing in this act shall be construed to extend to prohibit the importation or vending, reprinting or publishing within the United States, of any map, chart, book or books, written, printed, or published by any person not a citizen of the United States, in foreign parts or places without the jurisdiction of the United States" (Act of 31 May 1790, ch. 15, § 5, 1 Stat. 124, 125). Later U.S. copyright acts perpetuated these legal disabilities for foreign authors. See Act of 3 February 1831, ch. 16, § 8, 4 Stat. 436, 438; Act of 8 July 1870, ch. 230, § 103, 16 Stat. 198, 215.

ed with each other, sometimes disputed each other's claims, and punished misbehaving publishers; and a vertical axis on which publishers negotiated with foreign authors, acquired reprint rights to desirable titles, and, when possible, remunerated foreign authors or their publishers. Courtesy was a shared fiction that was crafted over several decades to fill the copyright vacuum for foreign works in nineteenth-century America.

Thus, this essay is about a "legal fiction" in a sense quite different from the way Stern (2017) and others use that term. Courtesy claims were "as-if copyrights," agreed fictions of literary property with which publishers sought to fill a negative space within U.S. intellectual-property law (Rosenblatt 2013). That these fictions were self-conscious and sometimes unstable was a natural consequence of their extralegal, purely customary status in a property-less space created and condoned by U.S. law. Temptations to reprint popular, unprotected books by Charles Dickens, George Eliot, Alfred Tennyson, and many other British writers were just too great to be consistently resisted in favor of such a fragile, consensual fiction of property. Courtesy's narrators – advocates such as publishers Henry Holt and the Harpers – were unreliable ones, not because they did not promote and adhere to courtesy, but because courtesy norms could never command the degree of obedience paid to adjacent copyright laws. Formal copyrights – existing only for citizens or permanent residents of the United States – operated alongside the informal norms of courtesy, authorizing legal monopoly practices that the adherents of courtesy strove to imitate in their private ordering.

1. *A Brief History of Trade Courtesy*

The aggressive reprint trade in America, fed by foreign works that were daily entering the premature public domain created by U.S. law, threatened to destroy a sustainable market for those works. If one publisher could reprint an uncopyrighted novel, so could another, and houses often undercut each other's prices in a scrimmage that one historian likened to a "Hobbes-like State of nature" (Barnes 1966, 36). Realizing that a code of self-regulation would be more profitable than unrestrained competition, publishing firms began to work together to stabilize the public domain through a communal fiction that was variously called the "usage of the trade," "etiquette," "good faith," or the "laws of honor." Most often, however, these practices were referred to as "courtesy of the trade," "trade courtesy," or simply "courtesy."[3]

[3] For contemporaneous names for courtesy, see Harper (1912, 358) ("law of courtesy"); "Note Respecting Harper & Brothers' Edition of Reminiscences by Thomas Carlyle" (316) ("trade usage"); "Charles Scribner's Sons Publish the Authorized Edition of Reminiscences. By Thomas Carlyle" (322) ("the courtesy of the trade"). Trade courtesy was

In its most basic form, courtesy was premised on an intuitive prior-rights logic: the first firm to announce (often in a trade journal) its plans to publish a foreign book had a monopoly claim to that book and sometimes also to later books by the same author (Spoo 2013, 37–38). In time, this custom grew along with the field of American publishing. For example, Publisher A would publicly claim the latest novel by Charles Dickens; Publisher B would recognize that claim so long as its own association with Wilkie Collins was respected; and Publisher C would, ideally, acknowledge the claims of both A and B if its entitlement to the sole reprinting of George Eliot went unchallenged. By means of such horizontal arrangements and understandings, publishers, within and between the publishing centers of Philadelphia, New York City, and Boston, averted a public-goods problem and resultant market failure for this lucrative foreign resource (30–32). With courtesy, one hand washed the other. Rivals became *pro tanto* partners, and earnings on reprints of foreign titles climbed.

Publishers could also acquire courtesy title to a foreign work by making a contract with the author or his or her publisher, or by paying the author for early proof sheets of the work, or by engaging in some combination of these acts. As courtesy took firmer root, publishers adopted procedures for securing options on a foreign author's subsequent writings and for associating authors with their firms on an exclusive basis (37–42). These practices became so widely shared that publishers were able to pay honoraria or even royalties to foreign authors; many authors benefited from payments, large or small, solicited or unsolicited, from courtesy-abiding houses. Payments were typically modest (£10 or £15), but some publishers paid their British authors handsome sums, even though no law (and perhaps no enforceable contract) compelled them to do so. Sir Walter Scott received £75 for advance proof sheets of each of the *Waverley* novels, and £300 for his *Life of Napoleon Bonaparte* (Sheehan 1952, 62). Harper & Brothers paid Dickens £360 for magazine rights to *Bleak House*, £250 for *Little Dorrit*, £1000 each for *A Tale of Two Cities* and *Our Mutual Friend*, £1250 for *Great Expectations*, and (probably) £2000 for the never-finished *The Mystery of Edwin Drood* (Madison 1966, 26).[4] One publisher in 1876 reported that courtesy payments for proof sheets ranged on average between £25 and £100; and dutiful publishers sometimes even turned sums over to deceased authors' estates.[5]

---

sometimes called the "Harper Rule," from the role that the powerful New York firm Harper & Brothers played in establishing courtesy rules (Johns 2009, 300–301).

[4] According to the U.K. National Archives' currency converter, £2000 in 1870 (the year in which magazine serialization of *The Mystery of Edwin Drood* began) would have the buying power of £125,218 in 2017 (https://www.nationalarchives.gov.uk/currency-converter/, visited 7 October 2021).

[5] For a discussion of courtesy payments, see *Minutes of the Evidence Taken Before the Royal Commission on Copyright Together with an Appendix* (1878, 63, 91).

To enforce courtesy's rules, participating houses fashioned penalties for reprinters who trespassed on other houses' recognized claims. These escalating sanctions ranged from a private protest lodged with the trespasser, to public shaming in trade journals or newspapers, to predatory pricing to match or undersell the trespasser, and climaxed, as a last and most dangerous resort, in retaliatory reprinting of one of the trespasser's own books.[6] Publishers only reluctantly employed this latter tit-for-tat strategy because it threatened a return of the disorder that courtesy had been forged to replace: an unregulated scramble for copyright-free works that often drove book prices down so far that no one could turn a profit. Courts were useless in courtesy disputes; they did not recognize these unfamiliar claims as literary property or business assets.[7] Publishers' concessions often made courtesy sanctions unnecessary, however. A publisher might cede a profitable British title to a rival, not so much out of fear of reprisal as because he had not secured the work under courtesy principles, and pursuing his claim would be, quite simply, discourteous.[8] Courtesy was to be earned, not stolen.

Thus, publishers responded in one of two ways to the American commons of foreign works: by engaging in lawful piracies or by observing informal, extralegal courtesies. Here were two distinct business ethics. One claimed justification under the letter of U.S. copyright law; the other operated according to a spirit of fairness in publishing, a moral imperative described by one Philadelphia publisher in the 1830s as the "rules that govern gentlemen."[9] Courtesy required interpersonal trust, seemly behavior, and voluntary forbearance. Without formal law to restrain appetites, there was always the possibility of a return of the savage scrum. Courtesy practices were a frail barrier against renegade houses or unpledged newcomers, even at the best of times.

Though there is evidence of proto-courtesy arrangements as early as the 1820s (Groves 2007, 141), and the rules of the courtesy game were systematically laid down, it is believed, in the mid-1830s during a series of clashes between two powerful firms, courtesy's golden age was probably between the 1850s and 1870s (Johns 2009, 295–302; Spoo 2013, 32–36). The system was, in essence, an improvised monopoly for sustaining prices at profitable levels and for inducing the type of artificial scarcity that copyrights create as a matter of legal right.

6 For overviews of trade courtesy, see Everton (2011, 44–47, 125–127); Harper (1912, 110–11); Johns (2009, 295–302); Sheehan (1952, 61–62); Vaidhyanathan (2001, 52–55); Groves (2007, 139–148); Holt (1888, 27–32).

7 See *Sheldon v. Houghton*, 21 F. Cas. 1239, 1241–1242 (C.C.S.D.N.Y. 1865) ("[Courtesy can] hardly be called property at all – certainly not in any sense known to the law.").

8 For a discussion of the moral, religious, and customary underpinnings of nineteenth-century American publishing, see generally Everton (2011).

9 Letter from Carey, Lea, & Blanchard to Harrison Gray, 27 April 1835, Lea & Febiger Records, ms. 227B, Letterbook, Carey, Lea, & Blanchard, 17 June 1834 to 2 September 1835, 336–337, Historical Society of Pennsylvania.

Courtesy was a carefully wrought communal fiction that substituted self-serving monopoly for self-destructive competition.[10]

By the late 1870s, changes in the publishing world shifted the ground on which courtesy had stood. The expansion of book manufacturing; the vogue for cheap fiction; the influx of new publishers lacking allegiance to the older houses; competition from Canadian publishers to whom the ethic did not apply; and the rise of literary agents who encouraged friction rather than cooperation among publishers, thus undermining the paternal treatment of authors which courtesy boasted – all these developments sapped the stability of the system of trade courtesy (Spoo 2013, 53–64). Changes in the legal landscape also disrupted courtesy practices. By the 1890s, with calls for trust-busting growing more strident, insurgent publishers outside the courtesy comity began accusing its adherents of engaging in anticompetitive practices and erecting barriers that prevented newcomers from entering the trade (53–58). Finally, Congress's passage of the 1891 Chace Act gave foreign authors a path to obtaining U.S. copyright, but only if they could comply with stringent statutory requirements. Not all authors could, and courtesy would continue into the twentieth century as an implicit code, a quiet doctrine of amity, observed by respectable houses (59–64).

2. *Trade Courtesy as Relational Copyright*

Trade courtesy might be thought of as a system of *relational copyright.* I model this concept in part on the theory of *relational contract* advanced by Ian Macneil, Stewart Macaulay, and others, who noticed that many businesspersons treat legal contracts as little more than a basis for "creating good exchange relationships," a vehicle for sustaining and nurturing long-term economic interactions, rather than as formal documents for defining and enforcing discrete bargains (Macaulay 1963, 64). A business contract, on this view, is a ground for a relationship, a context for the fluid pursuit of mutual opportunities, and only in extreme, irretrievable disputes the basis for a lawsuit, "since a contract action is likely to carry charges with at least overtones of bad faith" (65). A relational contract is not an isolated agreement that is treated by the parties as something "formed once and for all"; rather, it is "more like an ongoing motion picture," a medium for supporting change and flexibility (Macaulay 2000, 778). Such relationships promote solidarity, joint effort, and future collaboration; they are little concerned with full, punctual performance followed by a termination of relations. Relational contract is cohesive, not divisive; it envisions cooperation,

[10] The foregoing aspects of the courtesy system, as well as others, are described in considerable detail in Spoo (2013, 13–64).

not stand-your-ground legalism or zero-sum gamesmanship (Macneil 1980, 14–20).

Relational contracts are oriented towards futurity rather than endgames, towards ongoing, evolving obligations instead of specified rights and duties. Such contracts are supplemented and sustained by norms that shape and motivate business behavior, "intricate interlinkings of habits, custom, internal rules, social exchange, expectations respecting the future, and the like" (65). As Macneil shows, relational norms enhance role integrity, preservation of relations, and harmonization of relational conflict. As contractual relations grow, they "take on more and more the characteristics of minisocieties and ministates" (70). Relational contracts thus foster complex cohabitation within a structure of expectations, and encourage participants to imagine their interactions as a product of ethical choices and acts, rather than as merely commanded by enforceable promises exchanged at a particular moment in time, induced by legal consideration, and insusceptible of modification without a fresh exchange of definite, consideration-backed promises. Relational contract reflects mutual need. Even litigation does not necessarily destroy relationality. Longtime business partners who have sued each other sometimes resolve their dispute after lengthy litigation; they might even do so in ways that surprise their attorneys, who are accustomed to pursuing zero-sum victories for their clients. All the while that the attorneys were competing, their clients were quietly seeking a return to the *status quo*.[11]

Courtesy practices among American publishers in the nineteenth century also thrived on norms of relationality, what we might call relational copyrights.[12] Ordinary copyright law is a field for unplanned encounters between strangers – a copyright owner and an unauthorized user. Strict liability is the standard, so that intent to infringe a copyright, or reasons for the unauthorized

11 Richard Hix, an experienced business litigator in Oklahoma, has observed this phenomenon of unexpected cooperation between litigants on several occasions. If a lawsuit has not irreparably damaged a business relationship, it can serve as a sort of "lovers' quarrel" that ends in reunion, in some cases even after one of the parties has been assured of legal victory in the case (interview, 30 September 2021).

12 My use of the term "relational copyright" differs from that of other scholars. I do not employ it here to suggest some alternative to the traditional possessive-individualist model of copyright ownership, or to offer an imagined restructuring of "relationships between authors and users, allocating powers and responsibilities amongst members of cultural communities, and establishing the rules of communication and exchange" (Craig 2007, 263). Nor do I employ "relational copyright" to redefine the rights and responsibilities of authors and users of intellectual property, or to reframe the interests of the various contributors to creativity (Shi & Fitzgerald 2011). Rather, I use "relational copyright" to characterize a set of norms shared by competing American publishers and sometimes extended by them to the foreign authors whose otherwise unprotected foreign works they reprinted. The relational copyrights of trade courtesy were different from ordinary copyrights, but they did not redefine traditional notions of authorship. Publishers recognized them as a means of promoting self-interest and private ordering.

use of a protected work, are usually irrelevant.[13] Of course, copyright combatants sometimes know each other – a songwriter might sue her record label; a screenwriter might threaten his movie company – but copyright law presupposes mostly unsought encounters, discrete disputes, and adjudicated endgames, as much of tort law does (Radin 2013, 197). In relational copyright as practiced by courtesy publishers, however, a close-knit community employed its shared fiction to form business relationships and to grow them over time, rather than to meet and clash in brief, single combats. Courtesy sought to make pacts between rival houses, sustain those alliances, and keep the publishing peace.

Moreover, the relational copyrights of trade courtesy inaugurated business alliances that would not have existed if foreign titles had been treated as public-domain works available for unchecked appropriation. The shared norms of courtesy were the opposite of the self-maximizing impulses of piracy. When publishers ignored or defied courtesy, they were regarded by participating publishers as "cheap Ishmaelites of the trade" (Kellogg 1897, 914). Ishmaelite, renegade, outlaw – the pirate was a thing to be pitied or scorned, an "outside barbarian" whom Holt (1908) contrasted with those "men of exceptional character" who operated within the rules of courtesy (523). The publishing firm of Ticknor & Fields once referred to pirates as "keen-scented rascals, our friends in the *Craft*" (quoted in Groves 2007, 143 [original emphasis]).

Courtesy's relational copyrights allowed publishers to treat foreign works as the basis of a kind of idealized community of better businessmen. It is difficult to think of ordinary copyrights in quite this way, as giving rise to voluntary associations of competitors. Statutory copyrights typically preexist business relationships and form the basis of hierarchized licensing arrangements. Instead of encouraging cooperative equilibrium, statutory copyrights preserve order among publishers by threatening mutual assured litigation. Although the threat of courtesy sanctions played an important role in maintaining order among publishers, relational copyrights achieved, in their heyday, what Holt (1908) referred to as "a brief realization of the ideals of philosophical anarchism – self-regulation without law" (522–523).

Courtesy differed from ordinary copyright in a number of other ways. For example, courtesy gave its monopoly right initially to publishers, not to authors, as copyright statutes did. In that regard, courtesy turned back the clock by recreating the type of guild privilege enjoyed by the booksellers of the Stationers' Company of London prior to the Statute of Anne of 1710. Statutes in Britain and the United States had dealt a blow to such publishing monopolies

[13] Although many courts and commentators treat copyright infringement as a strict-liability tort, some scholars have questioned whether this is, or should be, the case, particularly in light of the doctrine of fair use, which allows accused infringers to show that the character of their unauthorized use, in some cases, serves social or other productive purposes and therefore relieves them of legal liability (Hetcher 2013).

by recognizing authors as possible proprietors of their own works (Patterson 1968, 147; Rose 1992, 4, 47–48). Moreover, courtesy rights had no set duration; they endured just as long as they were practically needed, or remembered, in the book trade. Copyrights, in contrast, had fixed statutory terms which applied equally to many types of works.[14] This one-size-fits-all approach continues today in many countries and has been criticized as leading to excessively long copyrights and to the problem of "orphan works" – copyrighted works whose owners are impossible to identify or contact (Lessig 2004, 248–253). Courtesy had no orphans. Publishers adopted foreign works and held them out as their filiated property for as long as necessary to exploit their economic potential. When these works no longer had a market value, they did not remain in a limbo of putative protection, as many copyrighted works do today. Instead, they returned, after the *de facto* lapse of their relational copyrights, to the familiar public domain, from which they had been claimed originally.

3. The Dickens Controversy of 1867

The subject of Charles Dickens, copyright, and American piracy is a familiar one. This essay concerns the less familiar story of Dickens and American trade courtesy – specifically, a controversy in which he scandalized the book trade by declaring his loyalty to the Boston firm of Ticknor & Fields and slighting Harper and other houses that had dealt courteously with him in the past. The controversy clarified certain assumptions of courtesy as they had evolved over the decades, and showed that publishers had come to expect courteous, faithful treatment from authors they had paid, no less than from fellow publishers who were part of the courtesy league. Thus, courtesy could be demanded, though not always successfully so, on the vertical as well as the horizontal axis. Where the Dickens of 1842 had offended Americans by his strident calls for copyright justice (Seville 2006, 165–166; O'Sullivan 1843, 120), the Dickens of 1867 offended them by his casual disregard for the voluntary rough justice of trade courtesy.

Trade courtesy could not fully protect an author as prolific and popular as Dickens from the flood of unauthorized reprints in the American market. By 1864, at least twelve publishers were issuing his writings in book form (Ballou 1970, 53, 591 n.17). Several of these firms competed to place collected editions of Dickens in homes. For years, Harper & Brothers of New York had claimed,

[14] For example, the 1870 U.S. copyright act provided an initial copyright term of 28 years, with a possible renewal term of 14 years, to books, maps, charts, dramatic or musical compositions, engravings, cuts, prints, or photographs or negatives thereof, paintings, drawings, chromos, statues, statuary, and models or designs intended to be perfected as works of fine arts. Act of 8 July 1870, ch. 230, §§ 86-88, 16 Stat. 198, 212–213.

by courtesy, exclusive magazine rights in Dickens's novels. The Philadelphia publishing firm of T.B. Peterson & Brothers asserted, also by courtesy, the exclusive right to issue those novels in book form.[15] The Harpers and the Petersons recognized each other's informal claims by mutual arrangement. Their concurrent entitlements were based on payments the two firms had made to Dickens or his English publisher. As noted above, the Harpers had sometimes paid more than £1000 for early sheets of Dickens's novels; the Petersons had contributed to the Harpers' purchase money and had bought the Harpers' printing plates after serializations had ended (Ballou 1970, 52–53; Lea 1867, 36; Bracher 1976, 325 n.23; "The Dickens' [*sic*] Controversy", 69). Even though the Harpers were the ones who dealt directly for early proof sheets, the Petersons considered that their payments gave them a derivative courtesy title to the completed books (Bracher 1976, 324–325). In treating their respective courtesy entitlements as applying to different publishing media – serials and books – the Harper and Peterson firms in effect constituted themselves beneficiaries of a sublicensing arrangement. The dividing up of Dickens in America – a fragile, provisional undertaking at the best of times – was accomplished through such mutual understandings and adjustments of dominant courtesy publishers.

The salient features of trade courtesy can be observed in the dispute that broke out in 1867 over Dickens's alleged disloyalty to his American courtesy publishers. The furor arose when Dickens appeared to turn his back on the Harper and Peterson firms by negotiating a deal to make Ticknor & Fields the exclusively authorized American reprinter of his collected works. Ticknor's offer had been irresistible: a £200 advance on a ten-percent royalty on future book sales, coupled with an arranged speaking tour of America (Ballou 1970, 82–85; Tebbel 1987, 89). A gratified but impolitic Dickens was quoted in the press as saying that this arrangement would make him, for the first time in his experience of America, "retrospectively and prospectively – a sharer in the profits of [an] [...] Edition of my books" (Ticknor & Fields 1867, 84).

The practice of paying authors a royalty on copies sold came later than other forms of remuneration, under both copyright and courtesy systems. Dickens himself had not accepted a royalty arrangement from his English publishers, "precisely because it deferred payments too long" (Patten 1978, 389 n.10). He had resisted royalties from American courtesy publishers as well. The gray, uncertain prospect of actually receiving a percentage of book sales was worrisome enough in any publishing relationship, quite apart from the special insecurities of transatlantic dealings. But when Ticknor offered Dickens an ongoing royalty on sales, a £200 advance, and other financial prospects, Dickens succumbed to the blend of present and future incentives (Ballou 1970, 80–81).

---

15 See letter of T.B. Peterson & Brothers reproduced in "The Dickens' [*sic*] Controversy" (69).

Dickens's invidious commendation of Ticknor's "manhood, delicacy, and honor" was bad enough in the eyes of the trade (quoted in "Dickens's Dealings with Americans", 348). In another letter widely circulated in the press, he rubbed salt in the wounds of his earlier courtesy publishers by stating that "[i]n America the occupation of my life for thirty years is, unless it bears [the Ticknor] imprint, utterly worthless and profitless to me" (quoted in "The Dickens' [*sic*] Controversy", 68). The American book trade was stunned by Dickens's amnesia. Had he forgotten the houses that had paid him hundreds or thousands for serial fictions, the newspapers that had paid £1000 for a single story, the small publishers who had risked insolvency by promising him sums for reprinting his periodicals? Was this the Dickens whose fictions celebrated magnanimity, fidelity, and reward for past kindnesses? Or was this evidence of a spirit as "[h]ard and sharp as flint, from which no steel had ever struck out generous fire" (Dickens 1843, 3)?

The snub was felt keenly by the Harper and Peterson firms. Trade journals rushed to their defense. The *American Literary Gazette and Publishers' Circular* called Dickens "ungenerous, illiberal, and ungentlemanlike" in his failure to acknowledge the "voluntary liberality" of the courtesy arrangements from which he had benefited in the past ("The Dickens' [*sic*] Controversy", 69). Dickens, the *American Literary Gazette* charged, was "a flagrant violator of usage, for he or his publisher having sold advance-sheets of his latest novels to one firm, and received good pay therefor, he now seeks to transfer to another house an exclusive interest in those very works!" (69). Here, the publishing trade was turning the tables on Dickens, who had assailed American reprinters' lawful piracies during and after his visit to the United States in 1842. He had then talked of blackguards, buccaneers, and bandits. Now he himself had become a kind of pirate; he was a transatlantic Ishmaelite, a deviant from courtesy norms, and was being treated to the sanction of public shaming. If Dickens could demand copyright from Congress, American publishers could at least expect him to honor copyright's homely approximation, the friendly fiction of trade courtesy.

Dickens plainly had attained a level of celebrity that allowed him to dictate the terms of courtesy rather than remain a passive, grateful recipient of publishers' largesse. He now treated the Harpers' payments as a thing of the past, mere compensation for serial rights that imposed no further obligation after he had shipped the early sheets off to New York; he scarcely acknowledged the Petersons' claim that they enjoyed a courtesy relationship by virtue of having assisted the Harpers with their payments. These dealings among publishers were their own affair, he seemed to say; he would not allow an exclusive association to be permanently imposed on him just because it benefited publishers in their self-serving efforts to repair the defects of an unjust copyright law. In Dickens we see the restlessness of a bold free agent, a literary giant who had outgrown courtesy's paternalism towards its authors, and now rejected a collusive practice that had sometimes excluded him from the bargaining table.

Dickens felt bound by no sentimental ties to old business partners; he had often treated contracts as ephemeral inconveniences.[16] Moreover, he evidently viewed Ticknor's collected edition of his works as a third medium of publication – different from serializations and single editions – which justified a new courtesy relationship. He now enjoyed the celebrity clout to choose his own forms of sublicensing, rather than have sublicensing thrust upon him.

In its censure of Dickens, the book trade was instinctively reaching for the remedial norms of public shaming and negative gossip.[17] These rebukes were aimed more at Dickens than at Ticknor & Fields. Dickens was the faithless and ungrateful one, even if the Boston firm had worked to alienate his affections. Meanwhile, the Petersons, who continued to issue Dickens, took out full-page advertisements with banner headings in the trade journals: "GREAT REDUCTION ON DICKENS' WORKS" ("Great Reduction on Dickens' Works", 86). The Petersons were employing price-slashing to match the Dickens editions offered by Ticknor.[18] Though courtesy's precepts had been flouted, its sanctions – predatory pricing and public shaming – survived as reminders that a great author and a prestigious publisher had behaved badly.

4. *Conclusion*

Scholars have estimated that direct payments to Dickens or his publishers from American firms over the years amounted to nearly £10,000.[19] This number does not include annual sums he received for reprints of his periodicals or the £20,000 he earned from packed readings and appearances during his 1867 visit to the United States (McParland 2010, 212 n.1; Patten 1978, 314, 342–343).

---

16 Dickens's friend, William Charles Macready, wrote in his diary that Dickens "makes a contract, which he considers advantageous at the time, but subsequently finding his talent more lucrative than he had supposed, he refused to fulfil the contract" (quoted in Patten 1978, 85).

17 On the normative use of public shaming, see Ellickson (1991, 214–215).

18 For details and prices of the Ticknor editions of Dickens, see Ticknor & Fields (1867, 84–85). In 1865, the Petersons were selling their Illustrated Duodecimo Edition of Dickens for $4.00 a copy; the Illustrated Octavo Edition for $2.50; the People's Duodecimo Edition for $2.50; and a cheap buff paper edition for 75 cents per copy (Denison 1865, advertising pages 1–2). Two years later, the Petersons reduced their Illustrated Duodecimo Edition to $3.00 per volume; the Illustrated Octavo Edition to $2.00; the People's Duodecimo Edition to $1.50; and kept the cheap paper edition at 75 cents per copy ("Great Reduction on Dickens' Works", 86).

19 According to the U.K. National Archives' currency converter, £10,000 in 1860 (when Dickens was regularly receiving courtesy payments from America) would have the buying power of £591,292 in 2017 (https://www.nationalarchives.gov.uk/currency-converter/, visited 7 October 2021).

America's public domain, deplored by Dickens as the nation's great moral failing, had prepared these successes through cheap reprints and mammoth newspapers "circulated," as one historian put it, "in every possible format from Maine to the banks of the Mississippi" (Patten 1978, 343). The premature public domain was an asset waiting for Dickens to monetize it. His large revenues from America are almost unimaginable without the previous cheap dissemination of his works under copyright-free or courtesy-managed conditions.

The Dickens controversy of 1867 shows that the carefully evolved fiction of trade courtesy could not consistently stabilize the American public domain for an author as popular as Dickens. Temptations to cast courtesy aside for easy profits infected all parties: respectable houses, non-courtesy firms, Dickens himself. In the years after his death in 1870, collected editions of his works proliferated. Numerous publishers – D. Appleton & Co.; Harper & Brothers; Fields, Osgood & Co.; Lea & Shepherd of Boston, and others – were marketing "Household Editions."[20] The Petersons, their claim to courtesy long forgotten, continued to sell Dickens for years in their "Cheap Edition for the Million" (Lippard 1876, unnumbered advertising page). Trade courtesy proved a fragile contrivance in the face of massive sales and authorial celebrity; the close-knit community that usually upheld its norms fell into unruly skeins. The Dickens craze revealed the power and the limitations of courtesy as a communal fiction.

Works Cited

Ballou, Ellen B. (1970) *The Building of the House: Houghton Mifflin's Formative Years*. Boston: Houghton Mifflin.

Barnes, James J. (1966) "Edward Lytton Bulwer and the Publishing Firm of Harper & Brothers." *American Literature* 38.1: 35–48.

Bracher, Peter S. (1976) "Harper & Brothers: Publishers of Dickens." *Bulletin of the New York Public Library* 79.3: 315–335.

Carey, Lea, & Blanchard, Letterbook, 17 June 1834 to 2 September 1835, Historical Society of Pennsylvania.

"Charles Scribner's Sons Publish the Authorized Edition of Reminiscences. By Thomas Carlyle." *Publishers' Weekly* 19.13 (26 March 1881): 322.

Chicago Tribune (31 October 1870): 3.

Craig, Carys J. (2007) "Reconstructing the Author-Self: Some Feminist Lessons for Copyright Law." *American University Journal of Gender, Social Policy and the Law* 15.2: 207–268.

[20] For example, anonymous notices of Household Editions of Dickens appeared in *Chicago Tribune* (31 October 1870): 3 (Fields, Osgood & Co.); *The Tennessean* (Nashville) (16 December 1871): 4 (D. Appleton & Co.).

Denison, C.W. (1865) *Illustrated Life, Campaigns and Public Services of Philip H. Sheridan*. Philadelphia: T.B. Peterson & Brothers.

Dickens, Charles (1843) *A Christmas Carol*. London: Chapman and Hall.

"Dickens's Dealings with Americans." *American Literary Gazette and Publishers' Circular* 8.12 (15 April 1867): 348–349.

Ellickson, Robert C. (1991) *Order Without Law: How Neighbors Settle Disputes*. Cambridge: Harvard Univ. Press.

Everton, Michael J. (2011) *The Grand Chorus of Complaint: Authors and the Business Ethics of American Publishing*. New York: Oxford Univ. Press.

"Great Reduction on Dickens' Works." *American Literary Gazette and Publishers' Circular* 9.3 (1 June 1867): 86.

Groves, Jeffrey D. (2007) "Courtesy of the Trade." *The Industrial Book, 1840–1880*. Ed. Scott E. Casper. A History of the Book in America 3. Chapel Hill: Univ. of North Carolina Press. 139–147.

Harper, J. Henry (1912) *The House of Harper: A Century of Publishing in Franklin Square*. New York: Harper & Brothers.

Hetcher, Steven (2013) "The Immorality of Strict Liability in Copyright." *Marquette Intellectual Property Law Review* 17.1: 1–26.

Hix, Richard, interview, 30 September 2021.

Holt, Henry (1888) "The Recoil of Piracy." *Forum* 5 (March 1888): 27–46.

Holt, Henry (1908) "Competition." *Atlantic Monthly* 102 (October 1908): 516–526.

Johns, Adrian (2009) *Piracy: The Intellectual Property Wars from Gutenberg to Gates*. Chicago: Univ. of Chicago Press.

Kellogg, D.O. (1897) "Copyright." *New American Supplement to the Latest Edition of the Encyclopædia Britannica*. Ed. D.O. Kellogg. Vol. 2. New York: Werner. 913–915.

Lea, Henry C. (1867) "American Editions of Dickens." *American Literary Gazette and Publishers' Circular* 9.2 (15 May 1867): 36–37.

Lessig, Lawrence (2004) *Free Culture: How Big Media Uses Technology and the Law to Lock Down Culture and Control Creativity*. New York: Penguin.

Lippard, George (1876) *Washington and His Men*. Philadelphia: T.B. Peterson & Brothers.

Macaulay, Stewart (1963) "Non-Contractual Relations in Business: A Preliminary Study." *American Sociological Review* 28.1: 55–67.

Macaulay, Stewart (2000) "Relational Contracts Floating on a Sea of Custom? Thoughts About the Ideas of Ian Macneil and Lisa Bernstein." *Northwestern University Law Review* 94.3: 775–804.

Macneil, Ian (1980) *The New Social Contract: An Inquiry into Modern Contractual Relations*. New Haven: Yale Univ. Press.

Madison, Charles A. (1966) *Book Publishing in America*. New York: McGraw-Hill.

McParland, Robert (2010) *Charles Dickens's American Audience*. Lanham: Lexington Books.

Minutes of the Evidence Taken Before the Royal Commission on Copyright Together with an Appendix [1878]. London: Eyre & Spottiswoode.

"Note Respecting Harper & Brothers' Edition of Reminiscences by Thomas Carlyle." *Publishers' Weekly* 19.12 (19 March 1881): 316.

O'Sullivan, John (1843) "The International Copyright Question." *United States Magazine and Democratic Review* 12.46 (February 1843): 113–122.

Patten, Robert L. (1978) *Charles Dickens and His Publishers*. Oxford: Clarendon Press.

Patterson, Lyman Ray (1968) *Copyright in Historical Perspective*. Nashville: Vanderbilt Univ. Press.

Radin, Margaret Jane (2013) *Boilerplate: The Fine Print, Vanishing Rights, and the Rule of Law*. Princeton: Princeton Univ. Press.

Rose, Mark (1992) *Authors and Owners: The Invention of Copyright*. Cambridge: Harvard Univ. Press.

Rosenblatt, Elizabeth (2013) "Intellectual Property's Negative Space: Beyond the Utilitarian." *Florida State University Law Review* 40.3: 441–486.

Seville, Catherine (2006) *The Internationalisation of Copyright Law: Books, Buccaneers and the Black Flag in the Nineteenth Century*. Cambridge: Cambridge Univ. Press.

Sheehan, Donald (1952) *This Was Publishing: A Chronicle of the Book Trade in the Gilded Age*. Bloomington: Indiana Univ. Press.

Shi, Sampsung Xiaoxiang, and Brian Fitzgerald (2011) "A Relational Theory of Authorship." *Knowledge Policy for the 21st Century: A Legal Perspective*. Ed. Mark Perry and Brian Fitzgerald. Toronto: Irwin Law. 291–312.

Spoo, Robert (2013) *Without Copyrights: Piracy, Publishing, and the Public Domain*. New York: Oxford Univ. Press.

Spoo, Robert (2017) "Courtesy Paratexts: Informal Publishing Norms and the Copyright Vacuum in Nineteenth-Century America." *Stanford Law Review* 69.3: 637–710.

Spoo, Robert (2020) "The Lawful Piracy of James Joyce's Poems." *Forgotten Intellectual Property Lore: Creativity, Entrepreneurship and Intellectual Property*. Ed. Shubha Ghosh. Cheltenham: Edward Elgar. 31–53.

Stern, Simon (2017) "Legal and Literary Fictions." *New Directions in Law and Literature*. Ed. Elizabeth Anker and Bernadette Meyler. New York: Oxford Univ. Press. 313–326.

Tebbel, John (1987) *Between Covers: The Rise and Transformation of Book Publishing in America*. New York: Oxford Univ. Press.

The Tennessean (Nashville) (16 December 1871): 4.

"The Dickens' [*sic*] Controversy." *American Literary Gazette and Publishers' Circular* 9.3 (1 June 1867): 68–69.

Ticknor & Fields (1867) "Important Announcement from Charles Dickens." *American Literary Gazette and Publishers' Circular* 9.3 (1 June 1867): 84–85.

Vaidhyanathan, Siva (2001) *Copyrights and Copywrongs: The Rise of Intellectual Property and How It Threatens Creativity*. New York: New York Univ. Press.

Cases Cited

Sheldon v. Houghton, 21 F. Cas. 1239 (C.C.S.D.N.Y. 1865).

Online Resources

Https://www.nationalarchives.gov.uk/currency-converter/.

Abbreviations

Stat. Statutes et Large (United States of America).

Narrative Claims: Literary Ownership and the Question of Property

Peter Schneck

1. Narrative Claims: History, Literature and Property

The following discussion tries to productively align two rather different perspectives on the question of how literary narratives engage with property: as a legal institution or as a cultural practice. Since these two perspectives at first sight may appear to be too dissimilar to be aligned productively at all, it may be necessary to say a few words on behalf of their specific relation and, in fact, interdependence.

The first perspective which informs my readings is fairly straightforward and focuses on the ways in which U.S.-American literature has been engaged in central debates about property, possession and ownership throughout its history. Questions of possession and ownership may be said to form a central problematic 'core' in U.S.-American prose writing since the early republic and until today. One could even argue that there is something of a literary history of property at the heart of American letters. While this observation has been readily acknowledged and discussed by various scholars and critics in regard to specific, canonical woks, a more systematic investigation and a more thorough critical assessment are still pending.[1]

Obviously such a discussion lies far beyond the scope of my observations here, but nevertheless the discussion will be driven both by an interest in the individual works at hand and an attempt at a systematic understanding of certain patterns and elements which inform narratives of property in the U.S.-American context – by which I mean both *literary* and *legal* narratives. This latter point is important for the initial focus of interest, for the questions of property that U.S.-American literature engages with are social, cultural, and political, but most of all they are legal: whenever a literary text is concerned with property it is also, and inevitably so, concerned with the legal institution of property, its dominant concepts as well as its dominant practices. My leading hypothesis in this respect will be that literary narratives about property are by necessity deeply engaged with legal narratives about property; more precisely, literary narratives are fundamentally shaped by the specific way in which the

1 For some excellent examples see Luck (2014), Clymer (2013) and Holloway (2014).

law's understanding of property – meaning both its legal definition and form – relies on and generates specific narratives: precisely, *narratives of property*.

As will become clear in the discussion of my examples, what is of central interest in regard to these 'narratives of property' is their normative charge and function. At the basis of these narratives lies a *normative* understanding of property and property rights; they are, thus, what Rainer Forst has called *Rechtfertigungsnarrative* (justification narratives), i.e. basic cultural plots and narrative schemata that help to legitimize, stabilize and expand the ideological principles and functions attached to the legal and cultural institution of property. While Forst does not explicitly address property or property narratives in his discussion of the important foundational relation between normative social orders (*Rechtfertigungsordungen*) and their specific justification narratives, he indeed singles out the U.S. and its foundational narratives as one of his prime examples for the historical emergence of political justification narratives during the eighteenth century, showing their mutual affirmation, as well the specific counter-narratives they did, and continue to, engender (Forst 2018). Given the central significance of property and property rights for the political, cultural and legal justification narratives in the U.S., Forst's observations about the basic structure and internal dynamic or tension of such narratives may also serve as points of reference for my discussion of the dominant narratives and basic plot structures which characterize the U.S.-American 'culture of property' (Stolzenberg 2000).

The 'normative force' of justification narratives, Forst argues, is due, on the one hand, to the specific way in which they are able to combine and bring into focus the specific experience and the aspirations of human agents but also, on the other hand, how – by way of referencing more abstract and general principles and notions of universal rights and values – they are able to transcend these specific contexts, thus claiming their general universal validity and truth.[2] This 'narrative construction' however, is never finished and never complete because the dominant narratives constantly engender, and are challenged by, counter-narratives, which then over time become part of the larger narratives of legitimacy:

---

[2] "Let us note here that the justification narratives briefly sketched here gain their normative force, on the one hand, from the specific way in which they bundle human experiences and expectations and shape them into ideals; but that they also, on the other hand, essentially aim at relative, abstract principles such as justice, freedom, or collective self-determination, whose validity constitutes the quality of justification and transcends specific contexts." ("Halten wir an dieser Stelle fest, dass die hier kurz skizzierten Rechtfertigungsnarrative ihre normative Kraft einerseits aus der spezifischen Art gewinnen, wie sie menschliche Erfahrungen und Erwartungen bündeln und zu Idealen formen – dass sie andererseits aber im Kern auf relative abstrakte Prinzipien wie solche der Gerechtigkeit, der Freiheit oder der kollektiven Selbstbestimmung abzielen, deren Geltung die Rechtfertigungsqualität ausmacht und spezifische Kontexte transzendiert.") (Forst 2018, 93; my translation).

> Again, this reveals the unfinished and contested narrative construction of the 'true America(n)', and the extent to which different justificatory narratives and counter-narratives overlap. [...] These larger stories form the indispensable reservoir for the narrative construction of the legitimation of American politics – not only in inauguration speeches of American presidents, but also in everyday culture and in the aesthetic negotiation of the past or present. (Forst 2018, 95–96; my translation)[3]

My argument moves beyond Forst's general observations in focusing on both law and literature as specific and rather significant contexts in which the dominant cultural justification narratives are negotiated, made explicit, but also may be interrogated and challenged. The term *narratives of property* thus refers to the specific manner in which both legal and literary discourses participate and intervene in the larger justification narratives by addressing property, property rights and proprietary relations and how they do so in specific cases or stories, but, at the same time, in reference to a more universal 'plot' or 'narrative' about legitimate ownership.

To this rather straightforward approach to narratives of property in law and in literature, I would like to join a second, less obvious and probably even more vexing perspective. This alternative perspective on literature's engagement with the law and with property foregrounds questions about *literature's own status as literary property* and the interests of writers and readers connected with this status. My leading hypothesis here is similar to the one which informs my initial perspective on property in literature and in law – only here the question is about literature as property in its own right.

What connects the two approaches in my discussion is a dominant notion of property as a *claim*, instead of a thing (that is owned) or a right (which is granted or protected). 'Property' from this perspective (shared by law and literature) denotes a specific way of connecting a potential object of possession with a subject of ownership in the form of a claim. To look at property as a claim also insists on its inevitably *intersubjective* nature since a claim is only valid in relation to other claims by other (potential or factual) owners. This is why narratives of property in law and literature are ways of grounding conflicting claims in contesting versions of historical facts and 'truths'; each one claiming legitimate ownership by claiming both historical truth and narrative authority.

The legitimacy of ownership is thus bound up with questions of narrative authority and legitimate authorship – this is where the various perspectives on

---

[3] Original: "Wieder zeigt sich, dass die narrative Konstruktion des 'true America(n)' unabgeschlossen und umstritten ist und wie sehr unterschiedliche Rechtfertigungsnarrative und Gegennarrative einander überlappen. [...] Diese umfassenden Erzählungen bilden das unverzichtbare Reservoir für die narrative Konstruktion der Legitimation amerikanischer Politik – nicht nur in Inaugurationsreden amerikanischer Präsidenten, sondern auch in der Alltagskultur und in der ästhetischen Verarbeitung der Vergangenheit oder Gegenwart."

narratives of property outlined here must converge. For at the center of these narratives is the question of the sources of legitimate ownership.

2. Concepts: Legal and Literary Property

In her seminal collection of essays on the history, rhetoric and theory of property, *Property and Persuasion*, Carol Rose (1994) starts out with a single question, which she calls "a fundamental puzzle for anyone who thinks about property": "How do things get to be owned?" (11). In the following remarks, I would like to invest some effort into posing a slightly revised version of the same question, namely, 'How does literature get to be owned?' This is not to replace Rose's question by a different one; on the contrary, it is meant as an extension of her original question to stress the fact that literary property is indeed a form of property which challenges us to think about its legitimate origins.

To use Rose's question as an inspiration for this move has a great deal to do with her answers and especially with her shrewd and tenacious discussion of the central role of narrative and storytelling in the constitution and justification of property in its legal form, but also in its cultural practices and institutions. I will rely on Rose as one of my major guides for my own exploration of what an important early case in English law, Donaldson v. Beckett, called the 'great question of literary property.'[4]

My aim is of course much less ambitious than Rose's, but it might still appear somewhat immodest since I want to extend the inquiry beyond the confines and clarity of legal definitions and codifications into the muddled territory of literary and cultural history. Instead of following a single question about the emergence of literature, or rather literary works, as a form of property, I want to ask multiple questions, and ask them all at once. This immodesty appears to be necessary, I claim, because the question of literary ownership cannot be answered by the law alone; in fact, to give only a legal answer to the question 'How does literature get to be owned?' might result in reducing literature to a category of 'things that can be owned,' and only if they fulfil the necessary criteria. "Lawful writing" in this sense, as Martin Kayman has called it (1996, 761), may be literature defined as property in the legal sense (most likely by being tied to a specific concept of authorship and concomitant copyright regulations); but it says nothing about how this particular definition at any point in time bears on the ways in which a whole culture conceives of, claims, and practices, literary ownership.

So the foundational puzzle needs to be extended by asking more questions such as, 'How is literature owned?' and 'By whom at what time'; 'How is

[4] For a thorough discussion of this case, see Mark Rose (1988) and Ginsburg (1990).

literary ownership claimed' and 'by whom' and 'for what reason'? What are the consequences of these questions and claims? How does the legal conception of literary property react to these claims and questions? Is there a mutual interaction between the legal and the cultural understanding of what property means: what can it mean, or even what should it mean, to 'own' literature? And finally, what is owned by literature: can literature – in the act of writing as well as in the act of reading – constitute or 'create' a form of property? Is a national literary canon a form of literary 'property'?[5]

From the vantage point of history it would be easy to reject these questions as merely cultural 'epiphenomena,' and thereby to solve the question of literary property by relegating and reducing it exclusively to its legal definition. This tendency – to render the question of property as merely a legal question, property being an exclusively 'legal' category – is unfortunate, especially for literature, or more precisely, for literary history and literary theory. For, if we abide by the conventional distribution of conceptual labor between the disciplines of legal and literary studies, the question what literature is *qua literature* will be defined by literary criticism and scholarship (and probably also the readers), but how literature may be defined *as property* will be exclusively determined by the law. My point in what follows is that such a separation of attitudes and perspectives vis-a-vis the interdependence of literature as a legal form of property and literature as a cultural form of ownership (and the difference is crucial here and in the following argument) is at best counterintuitive and at worst counterproductive.

It may be helpful to explain my argument by bringing in an example of the kind of 'extended' literary ownership that I have in mind. William Faulkner's effort to graphically chart the territory of the fictional *Yoknapatawpha* county which forms the setting of almost all of his narrative works is a rather obvious and explicit instance of claiming literary ownership in a form which is sanctioned and acknowledged by the law. Faulkner had appended an original, hand-drawn version of a map to his 1936 publication of *Absalom, Absalom!* The map reproduced here (Figure 1) is a revised version produced for the 1951 edition of the novel and is based on (yet) another version of the map produced for Malcolm Cowley's edition of the *The Portable Faulkner* in 1946. Cowley's edition was meant to establish Faulkner as a reputable (and not just obscure) author for a wider American audience, but also as an international author of high reputation and value. That bid proved quite successful – Faulkner's reputation in Europe for some time had been much more favorable than at home and in 1949 he was eventually awarded the Nobel Prize of literature. The major point in Cowley's 'campaign,' however, was not Faulkner's European reputation; rather, it concerned Faulkner's aspirations towards establishing himself as

[5] For a more detailed discussion of these questions, see Schneck (2015).

a local (or territorial) author who was able to write the history of the American South by composing/inventing the parallel fictional history of *Yoknapatawpha* county. But what is most notable – and helpful for my discussion – is that for Cowley's edition Faulkner added something to his original map, quite obviously a claim for authorship and ownership. In the version reproduced here, he added the lines

> JEFFERSON, YOKNAPATAWPHA COUNTY, MISSISSIPPI
> Acres, 2400 square miles. Population: Whites 6298, Negroes 9313

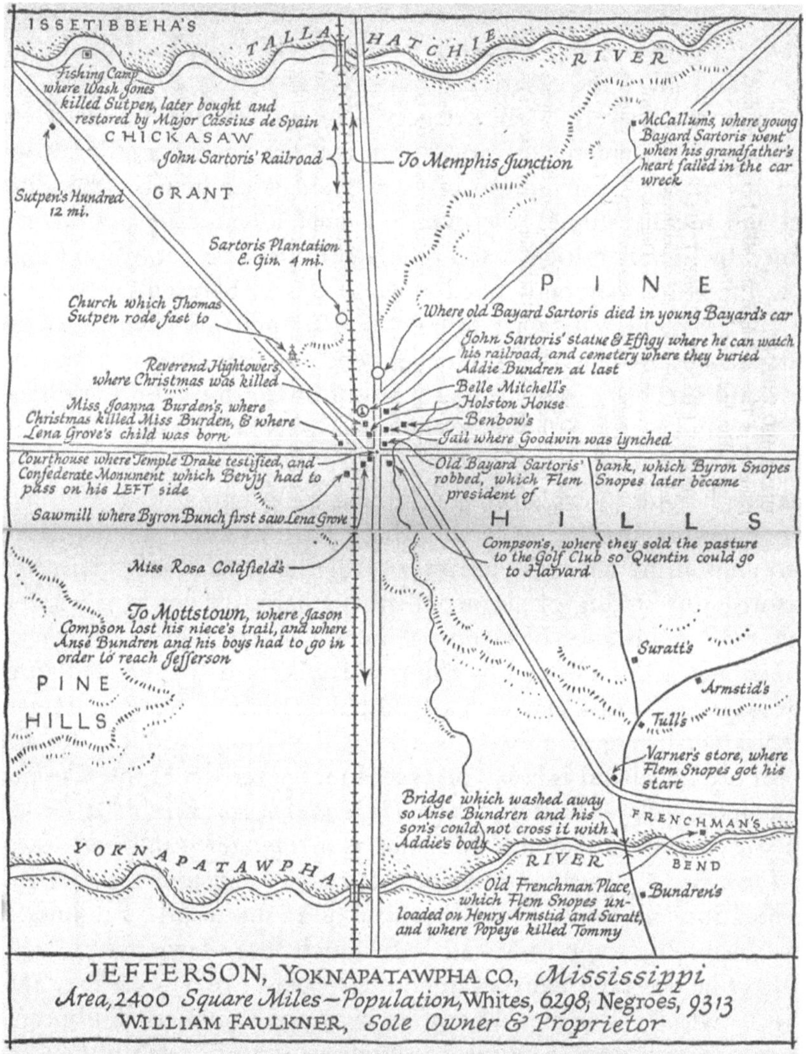

William Faulkner's map of Yoknapatawpha county,
originally drawn in 1936, amended in 1946.

and most importantly: "William Faulkner, sole owner and proprietor." Clearly then, the map represents a claim of ownership, but what kind of ownership is this? How do you claim ownership of a completely fictional territory, complete with the locations and inhabitants that only exist in your imagination? What could be the possible grounds for such a claim?

In Faulkner's case, the claim is based on his status as the author – the inventor or creator of the fictional county – and thus it somehow only represents or reinstitutes a claim which is backed by law, albeit in a slightly metaphorical and, at the same time, slightly more reifying manner:

> What is [...] remarkable about the map is that it articulates that the land is 'in fact' the possession of the author of the map. He might have wanted to retrieve the lost terrain in a symbolic way. On the other hand, the map clearly serves as Faulkner's inventory of property. Map is Territory, however, not simply because of that inscription of ownership but because of the relation between the owner/cartographer and the intrinsic faculty of a map. The map enables Faulkner to display *Yoknapatawpha* as the whole of the knowledge the author should grasp about the land. (Tokizane 2007, n.p.)

But in a much more urgent and even more absolute sense, the act of mapping a fictional imagined location as a *territory* and adding to that mapping a claim of absolute proprietorship seems 'overreaching'; it also seems besides the point in terms of legal ownership. Mark that Faulkner does not add a copyright sign to his drawing (the reproductive rights of this version rest with the publisher). So the ownership Faulkner claims is of a different order and addressed to an audience who might appreciate and understand, might in fact *acknowledge* such a claim.

Returning to Carol Rose's understanding of property originating in acts of communication about claims of possession, Faulkner's map is a clear signal of such an act, and the *form* of the act follows long-standing conventions of claiming legal title in regard to land or territory. Finally, this claim is connected or even essential to Faulkner's emphatic claim to a specific form of literary property, or more precisely a specific form of authorship or creative agency that is absolute, at least with regard to its creations. As he famously stated "I can move these people around like God, not only in space but in time too" (Meriwether & Millgate 1980, 255).

If Faulkner's (and his editor's) choices make any sense as claims of ownership it would be fair to assume that there exists an audience that would acknowledge these claims and react accordingly. In Carol Rose's words: "the original claim to property looks like a kind of speech, with the audience composed of all others who might be interested in (also) claiming the object in question" (1994, 14). But if there is indeed an audience for this kind of claim, one may ask about the specific form and response which would make such claims legitimate and effective. The question, again, must thus be considered in terms of its legal *and* its wider cultural implications.

3. Property Narratives: A Model

In order to find some structured responses to the questions I have asked in a rather disorderly manner, and which I have illustrated with a somewhat mystifying map of an imaginary territory created, governed and owned by Faulkner, I would like to propose a model for property narratives. This approach looks at the question of literary property and ownership from three different, but related angles. The model is meant as a kind of heuristic scaffolding which will allow me, in the second half of my discussion, to look at three distinct literary examples and their 'narrative claims' to literary property. The triangular perspective, it is to be hoped, will also allow me to keep the connection alive between the texts' obvious concerns with (a) specific questions of property, (b) their particular ways of representing aspects of ownership and proprietary practices and concepts in their fictional worlds, and, finally, (c) the central notions or figurations of property and ownership which in each case inform the narratives. My aim is not a detailed and individualized interpretation of the single texts, even though I will need to discuss some details more closely. The main objective is, rather, to treat the examples as representative realizations of a basic 'structure' or 'plot' that, it could be argued, dominates U.S.-American narratives of property and which explains the contrasts as well as the affinities between the examples. The 'model' narrative thus may serve as a heuristic or analytic tool to tease out the continuing resonance and correlation between narrative forms, cultural norms and authorial claims for legitimate ownership.

The three angles or aspects which, I think, essentially characterize the model narrative, could be called "Taking," "Doing" and "Making" – together these three aspects circumscribe a *processual conception* of 'original' property which came to dominate notions of property since the early modern period. Again, I am not claiming any originality on this point, certainly not in the sense that the three proposed angles alone would amount to an analytically mature model of 'property' from a philosophical perspective. The model is just meant to look at different phases of the process of 'how things get be owned.' Property has to come from somewhere, unless one would want to argue for the magical appearance of property out of the blue, and the 'taking' aspect points to that 'somewhere' as a source or a resource. At the same time, it also emphasizes the active involvement of an agent who does the taking. The agent usually is human and, in regard to the legal concept of property, a 'person' in the legal sense. This active engagement with a source or resource already connects to the 'doing' angle or aspect; it is part of the processes and practices of transformation and curation or even struggle which are culturally associated with legitimate or acknowledged forms and practices of ownership. As Neal Milner has observed, these may be expressed in the form of common "property narratives which are framed around [...] sets of social practices, myths and beliefs"; Milner calls them "rites of identity, rites of settlement, and rites of struggle" – in short, "the rites of ownership" (1993, 227).

The narratives which Milner identifies in the stories of everyday people about their property and their rights share a crucial feature with the narrative structures and plots described by Rose in the stories of common law about the origin of property and property rights. These property narratives do not simply define or constitute ownership in any positive sense, rather, what these cultural and legal narratives actually do (and are used for) is a form of claiming or 'making a case' for property rights in a contested situation in which property and the right to own are at stake. In this respect, they could and should be read as justification narratives or narratives of legitimacy in the sense of Forst's *Rechtfertigungsnarrative*.

The third aspect, the 'making' aspect, also resonates with the 'doing' aspect because it is a form of active involvement which can be described as a *practice* of ownership, and thus, can become integrated as an important element in the cultural property narratives which Milner identified. However, what distinguishes the 'making' in contrast to the 'taking' dimension of the process of 'doing property' is that 'making' results in something different from the original source or resource. Since property as a cultural and legal institution finds its most basic justification in the notion of an overall collective 'gain,' the distinction between what had been taken and what subsequently has been made, inevitably adds and actually demands an evaluative perspective to the narrative.

I am quite aware that this rough and ready description of the model despite its crudeness may start to look rather familiar because it could be understood as a basic 'type' of a larger repertoire of 'types' or 'genres' of cultural property narratives, which may also be found in legal property narratives. For instance, it might appear suspiciously close to the labor theory of property devised by John Locke. This is no accident at all. On the one hand, Locke's theory marks an important point of reference for Western concepts of property since the seventeenth century. On the other hand, there is certainly a mutual calibration at work between legal and cultural 'stories' about the origin of property, which works to align these narratives with more or less success. In fact, one might argue that the dynamic of potential difference and potential alignment between the cultural and the legal narratives is rather crucial for the mutual and self-reflexive justification of legal and cultural norms over time. So far, the 'model' simply seems to affirm the cultural predominance of a specific correlation between legal and cultural narratives of property (or claims to property rights).

Yet, even while one may understand the 'taking, doing, making' model as a basic type in the larger repertoire of property narratives in culture and in law, this acknowledgment may seem to amount to nothing more than a banality. For, if we were satisfied with pointing out similarities of legal and literary (or cultural) narrative claims, we would miss the chance of asking about and exploring the particular mutual positioning of these narratives vis-a-vis each other. It is one thing to posit that there is some sort of congruence between these narratives; it is quite another to understand and approach the cultural narratives as a sort of broader commentary and register, i.e. both as an ongoing affirmation *and* criticism of the main *forms* which enable us to justify and claim property and property rights.

My argument in what follows will focus on the relation or even congruence between the specific claims that are *narrated* in the three exemplary works of fiction that I will discuss and on the associated claims for literary property by their authors (and possibly also their readers). Both claims are made in the specific *form* of literary narrative fiction. While the fictional narratives share surprisingly many structural aspects with the basic stories and narratives discussed by Rose and Milner, the legitimacy which is claimed in each case always also refers to the specific literary form as a legitimate mode for the claim.

4. *Taking ... and Making*

My first example, **Cooper's *The Pioneers***, comes from the genre of historical 'frontier' fiction, which rose to prominence and came to dominate the critical discourse obsessed with identifying the characteristic features of a national literature in the U.S. during the first half of the nineteenth century. In fact, one could argue that James Fenimore Cooper's *The Pioneers, or, the Sources of the Susquehanna* (1823) was explicitly written in response to the criticism of Cooper's first two novels. *Precaution* (1820) was a rather crude imitation of Jane Austen's popular novels of manners, which 'flopped' rather embarrassingly. It was followed by a second slightly more successful 'historical' spy novel, set during the time of the revolutionary war (*The Spy, a Tale of the Neutral Ground*, 1821). It is important to describe the genesis of Cooper's third novel in this detailed manner, since this work, the first of the so-called *Leatherstocking Tales*, established its author as the first truly 'American' writer and novelist, nationally as well as internationally. Cooper's resonating success thus was not the result of a streak of innovative genius; rather, *The Pioneers* is the outcome of careful modulations and diligent revisions of existing forms of historical narratives, both in relation to available sources of historiography and with regard to a fairly new and successful form or model of fiction, especially in the example of Walter Scott, who quite obviously served as the major model for Cooper.

The novel has been characterized quite fittingly as a "romance of property" (Cheyfitz 1993, 125). A host of critics from different times and different theoretical backgrounds have duly noted and discussed the novel's obvious interest in and close relation to the legal discourses and debates of its time. In many ways, then, *The Pioneers* may be seen as a foundational work, whose 'key-position' for the establishment of the field of U.S.-American literature and literary criticism is acknowledged even while its specific property narrative has come to be severely criticized and, indeed, delegitimized.

The property form in question is land ownership, and the source and resource therefore is land, or more precisely, nature. As Rose has remarked, the taking and the first occupancy of land is a crucial (foundational) element of the common-law narrative of the origin of property. In terms of land ownership in the U.S., this is even more crucial since the entire system of landed property is based on the famous Supreme Court decision in *Johnson v. M'Intosh* from 1823, which is also one reason why Cooper's novel, published in the same year, has been read as a fictional affirmation of the 'discovery doctrine' which legitimized settler-colonial expansion. The Supreme Court decision argued that colonial appropriation of natives' land was legal on the grounds that the land which had been taken by the colonial powers had been 'empty' and basically in the state of nature.

Hence, the 'taking' which is being described in the novel's narrative about building a frontier settlement very obviously follows the logic of the common law's narrative of the origin of property as identified by Rose. However, for the specific narrative claim about the legitimacy of the property in question, the 'doing' is just as important. The novel takes great care to show the settlers' distinct ways of realizing and practicing their 'natural' property rights. Some practices are in conflict and lead to struggles between various factions, and some practices are harmful to the preservation of natural resources (uncontrolled mining results in wild fires just as uninhibited hunting leads to massive killing of wildlife). Obviously following a basic Lockean script, Cooper uses these occurrences within his plot to make an argument for the necessity of civic and legal order, a "system of mild laws" (Cooper 1823, vol.I, 2) as he calls it in the famous opening scene of *The Pioneers.*

And it is precisely this well-known landscape description at the beginning of the novel, which marks the convergence of the property claims *in* the novel and the property claims *of* the novel itself. This opening scene is not attached in any way to the narrative agency and the experiential sphere of the characters, and it is also not an element of the plot. In fact, one could read the novel without reading the opening paragraph, and it would still make perfect sense as narrative fiction. But that does not mean it is irrelevant. On the contrary, the opening is essential to Cooper's claim for legitimate literary ownership.[6] The opening scene in fact presents the *final* result of the process of taking, doing, and making property which the novel actually retells from the perspective of fully legitimate ownership, as the final remark of the passage indicates: "only

6 For a more detailed discussion of the scene see Schneck (2018).

forty years have passed since this whole territory was a wilderness" (I, 2). The entire landscape description thus stands as a form of retrospective priming because it frames the dominant narrative genre and the central plot – the core historical novel – from the perspective of other, earlier and more descriptive and 'taking' genres: travel narratives, exploration, and even tourist manuals. To actually place the 'making,' i.e. the *result* of taking and doing property, at the very beginning of a historical fiction about the origins of property is to insist on judging and assessing historical processes and struggles from a privileged perspective on the process of 'making' property: the privilege of authorship as ownership.

Cooper's description works like Faulkner's map, it demarcates the boundaries of legitimate proprietorship in similar ways since the fictional 'making' of property (on the level of the narrative plot) and the creative composition of the landscape (on the level of literary form) collapse into one and the same claim: authorship legitimizes ownership, and vice versa. Aesthetic form thus claims legitimacy for a form of ownership (taking, doing and making of properties) that is projected into the past and at the same time into the future. Like Faulkner's map, Cooper's landscape legitimizes a generative and reproductive form of authorial ownership, i.e. literary property which depends on (or even insists on) what could be called 'absolute dominion.'

My second example, **Charles Chesnutt's *The House Behind the Cedars*** (1900), presents a much more challenging, and indeed critical, narrative about the legitimate 'origin' of property and property rights in the U.S. Written in response to the failed efforts of reconstruction after the Civil War, the blatant legal disenfranchisement of black citizens by the Supreme Court, and the emergence of a legally fortified and culturally enhanced system of racial segregation, Chesnutt's first novel (after two successful short story collections) deconstructs the racialized fiction of free agency upon which the legitimacy of the dominant legal and cultural property narratives came to rest.

Next to the assumption of vacancy as the natural state of unpropertied nature, another major assumption of the taking, doing, and making narrative of the 'natural' origin of property rights concerns some fundamental capacities of the acting agent. Legitimate taking requires that the agent is able to act on his or her own account, both physically and mentally, i.e., s/he possesses the capacity to perform intentional physical acts in accordance with his/her motivated decision making (or planning). In the Lockean version of the basic narrative of property and property rights, free will and free mind are not just capacities that exist before or alongside property, they actually already constitute a form of property of the individual person. This notion of a normative convergence of liberty and property on the level of the individual, as Marietta Auer remarks, is a most consequential 'legitimizing trick':

> [Liberty] no longer stands alongside the concept of property, as it did with Grotius, but rather below it. Locke's concept of property encompasses not only the ownership of property and other property rights, but rather explicitly the entire individual sphere of freedom and rights of the person – 'Lives, Liberties, and Estates, which I call by the general name, Property. [...] Locke's theory of rights thus succeeds in the legitimating trick of making property, liberty, and subjective right one and the same by conceiving *liberty as a property right.* (2014, 25; my translation)[7]

This 'trick' owes a great deal to the semantic flexibility of the term 'property' (as Auer takes care to point out), with the fatal consequence that this particular convergence or collapse of personal liberty and personal property into one sphere of subjective individual rights (the "ineins [...] setzen") could serve as a foundation for the universalism of property rights reserved exclusively for those who mutually acknowledged the 'properties' they already possessed. It also made the protection of liberty contingent on the protection of property and vice versa; and it generated and reproduced universalized forms of exclusivity which in turn generated and reproduced attendant legitimizing forms of highly genderized and racialized property narratives which were meant to protect specific 'properties' (whiteness, maleness) as the only legitimate and foundational 'properties' of property.

Chesnutt's deconstruction of these foundational fictions of property relies on a fragmented form of narration which moves back and forth between different times and locations. He does not simply present one conclusive narrative, but gradually reveals and confronts different narratives of property which are mutually contingent yet also incommensurable according to the dominant cultural fiction and factual legal force of "whiteness as property" (Harris 1993, 1724).

As an author of mixed ancestry who could pass as white, but chose to identify as black, Chesnutt in obvious ways invested autobiographical as well as historical knowledge into his tragic narrative of passing. As a lawyer he also integrated legal history and even incorporated quotations from legal documents to reveal the mixed origins of property and its 'impossible' legacy, a history of property which is neither black nor white but both, and which thus must be denied and disavowed. On the one hand, by integrating legal decisions and documents in verbatim form into his fiction, and, on the other, by presenting the southern white ownership class as acting out fictional scripts taken from the historical novels of Walter Scott, Chesnutt lets his narrative hover between the factual

---

7 Original: "[Die Freiheit] steht nicht mehr wie noch bei Grotius neben, sondern vielmehr unter dem Eigentumsbegriff. Lockes Eigentumsbegriff umfasst nicht nur das Sacheigentum und sonstige Vermögensrechte, sondern vielmehr ausdrücklich die gesamte individuelle Freiheits- und Rechtssphäre der Person – 'Lives, Liberties, and Estates, which I call by the general name, Property.' [...] Lockes Rechtstheorie gelingt also das legitimatorische Kunststück, Eigentum, Freiheit und subjektives Recht ineins zu setzen, indem sie *die Freiheit als Eigentumsrecht* konzipiert." See also the similar argument in Pipes that for Locke "property necessarily entails liberty" (1999, 36). Pipes also stresses that Locke's thoughts are less original than the latter's particular phrasing.

and the fictional, showing up the complicity of racialized fictions in the construction of a racialized property regime.

The story which Chesnutt tells starts with a "stranger," "a gentleman from South Carolina," whose identity is certified by the name entry in the hotel's register by the clerk, who makes out the stranger as a man of wealth and property "probably in cotton, or turpentine" (Chesnutt 1993, 1–2). As it turns out, the stranger is a fiction because he is no stranger at all, and his name is not his real name, but his wealth and property are real. One of the structural devices Chesnutt's narrative employs is to challenge his readers' ability (and willingness) to identify with the main characters' fictional and real identities, because they inhabit and perform these identities at the same time in different spaces (in this case, North and South Carolina), which are equally both fictional and real spaces. They are fictional because they are created by the legal and cultural scripts and narratives of performing (and recognizing and identifying with) racial identity, and they are real, because these performances produce and secure real forms of wealth and power.

The same disconcerting (and for the characters dangerous and even deadly) mixing of different identities and spheres likewise happens on the level of time and temporality, since the stranger from South Carolina is visiting his own past in North Carolina in order to take his sister from the past to join him in his new fictional and real life as a white, propertied gentleman who has married into a respectable family and thus possesses all the privileges of white ownership. The 'passing' siblings thus present two property narratives, two major origins or sources of legitimate ownership; this ownership is attained but at the same time denied, because 'whiteness' is treated as property – both on the register of the real and the imaginary.

The stranger's real property and wealth are based on slave labor, but his ownership results from his fictional property of 'whiteness,' which is acknowledged and thereby legitimized by his marriage to the heiress of a plantation. (He has moved from his past history in North Carolina to the south and 'passed' as white in South Carolina.) This narrative is paralleled by his sister, who finds herself courted by another wealthy white owner soon after she has joined her brother in South Carolina. "It's a dream, only a dream," his sister announces in reaction to the courtship, as she, too, is seemingly accepted as white into society. This dream, however, gradually turns into a nightmare when her suitor learns about her past and it eventually ends with her return to the role of 'a young colored woman' and her death. Thus the novel ends with a passing 'in reverse' as it were when Rena's racial identity is confirmed and at the same time her identity as an individual character is taken from her (42; 159).

The contrasting trajectories of the conflicting narratives – which either produce whiteness as an accepted illusion of property or whiteness as a denied form of property – stand for a paradoxical and 'impossible' form of ownership.

Whiteness as a proprietory existence is both real and unreal at the same time, precisely because the two trajectories result from the *same* historical and biographical constellations: a mixing of properties occurs which produces a property that can only be claimed when its history is being disclaimed at the same time.

This impossible in-between status of the properties which Chesnutt's protagonists undeniably possess but, at the same time, are being denied by the same historical trajectory of the origin of whiteness as property, also resonates and is reflected on the level of authorship and Chesnutt's own claims for literary ownership. These claims, as Chesnutt was painfully aware, are partly complicated by the very strategy of mixing and creating dual identities within two fictional spaces which complete each other but also contradict each other or even cancel each other out. Moreover, on the level of genre and mode, Chesnutt's novel presents and employs a whole range of different forms of expression and representation that run from the comical to the tragic, from the ironic to the satirical. The novel's character descriptions include idealizations collapsing into stereotypes and racist remarks by "unreliable narrators in the third person," as critics have pointed out, which are a challenge to the reader since they be could be mistaken for the narrator's: "These [racist] sentiments rephrase [the character's] thoughts as if they are the narrator's and thus mask from many readers the truth of the tale by cryptically contradicting the logic of the text" (Hattenhauer 1993, 34).

This uneasy and challenging mixture of forms and modes establishes a variety of possible and contradictory positions (of the narrator and hence the reader) vis-a-vis the actions and characters depicted: how does one claim ironic ownership of melodrama, how can one claim to 'own' a reality that is satirized at one moment and idealized at the next? Moreover, it never really finds a proper foundation in one coherent form of experience. For one of the most poignant, and also self-reflexive, strategies of Chesnutt's formal mixing of different literary 'properties' is to emphasize how much the self-perception (the identity) of every character depends on literary forms and genres: on their literary properties, as it were. If we look at Chesnutt's narrative of property from the three angles I suggested, we might come to the conclusion that *The House Behind the Cedars* rejects and deconstructs the basic narrative plotting of the 'taking, doing, making' model. But that conclusion may be a bit too hasty because, while the novel certainly rejects and deconstructs the exclusionary fiction of 'whiteness as property,' the novel does not question the normative coherence of liberty and property, but rather critically reveals the exclusionary force of racialized fictions about the source and origin of property and property rights.

My last, and shortest, example is meant to highlight this central question of normative and narrative coherence as a major requirement and expectation of legal and cultural narratives of legitimate property and ownership. **Kaui Hart**

Hemmings's 2007 bestselling novel ***The Descendants*** connects in obvious ways to Cooper's novel (both are about landownership and inheritance laws) as well as to Chesnutt's novel, because they both share a central concern with the legitimacy of 'mixed' sources of property. What links all three novels is the essential status and central role of narratives of 'consent and descent' (Sollors 1986); more precisely, the way in which the motivated and deliberate intersection (the consent) and 'mixing' of genealogical structures (the descent) of transfer and tradition have contributed to a specific 'American' way of claiming legitimacy, in terms of both property *and* identity.

The question of property at the center of Hart Hemmings's novel concerns the possible sale of a huge piece of land (undeveloped) on the main island of Hawaii. It is owned 'in trust' by the extended descendants of the original joint owners, a Hawaiian princess, Kekipi, and an Anglo-American missionary, Edward King, who is a financial officer and estate planner working for her father. The joint ownership is the result of the princess's active resistance against the customary laws of descent (generational transfer of property by marrying in the family): she chose to marry the estate planner rather than (according to local custom) her brother. The casual manner in which the current chair of the trustees and main protagonist and narrator of the novel, Matt King, explains the complicated chain of legitimate property, already establishes the narrative's major attitude towards the property in question. This attitude is informed both by ironic detachment and cynical fatalism:

> Okay, then, what happened ... Kekipi was supposed to marry her brother, a weird Hawaiian tradition. Yikes. Just when they were ready to tie the knot, she had an affair with her estate planner, Edward, and they married soon after. [...] Anyway, they had a lot between the two of them, and when another princess died, she left three hundred thousand acres of Kauai land to Kekipi as well as her estate. Kekipi died first. Edward got it all. Then Edward set up a trust in 1920, died, and we got it all. [...] There's Edward, hollow-eyed and serious. [...] There's Kekipi, which means "rebel," her brown and flat, chubby face. Her bushy brows. Whenever I see her picture I think we would have hit it off. I can't help but smile at her. [...]
>
> My father died last year, marking the termination and dissolution of the trust. And now, land-rich and cash-poor, we, the beneficiaries, are selling off our portfolio to ... someone. I don't know.
>
> It's what I inherited. Like it or not. (Hart Hemmings 2009, 36)

What complicates the question of property and the pending sale of the estate is that King's wife has fallen into a coma after a boating accident, leaving him not only in charge of their two daughters but also with the responsibility to decide about her status in relation to the law, that is, whether she is legally alive or dead. The major family plot line in the novel turns around this question, because it marks the transfer of agency and thus of control. The paradoxical twist is that only when Matt King officially declares his wife dead, her legal will (called her 'living will') will be executable. The very idea of narrative progress thus hinges on a decision about life and death, linked to the decision about the future of property and ownership.

At the beginning of the story, Matt King is as much detached from his family and his wife, as he is from the history of his property as a family history. Thus he only gradually learns about his wife's affair with a real estate developer interested in King's property after her boating accident. The narrative thus could be read as a process of transformative ownership: letting go of his wife and accepting her duplicity and unfaithfulness, Matt at the same time regains his legitimate authority (as a father) and finally accepts the responsibility of ownership, turning from an accidental heir into a legitimate proprietor.

The property narrative which the novel unfolds is the narrative of the cynical and fatalistic acceptance of existing legal and cultural conditions of property relations (*doing* property) which have become an unreflected way of life. These conditions are only gradually reformed into meaningful and purposeful relations by the responsible acceptance of the cultural and social history of property relations. The coherence that the narrative is able to regain in the end is a coherence brought about by the re-establishment of familial relations over time, connecting the recovered past with a meaningful future.

The model of authorship and literary ownership which underlies these efforts in the novel is the scrapbook which the youngest daughter is assembling as a school project, and which she uses to create a coherent family narrative around the living absence of her mother. The scrapbook stands for an open-ended and accidental but nevertheless motivated effort to collect and bring together scraps of memory (both collective and individual) which will help to form a narrative and a literary property (as a legacy and an inheritance) which can be accepted as a collective history of consent and as a shared cultural memory of descent.

As the major re-connecting lines evolve, the Kings' family history moves backwards to the source of the property about to be alienated. That 'source' is another historical connection, the unconventional, but significantly far-reaching relation between the heiress of the royal family and her American suitor, presumably one of the missionary developers who prepared the gradual annexation of Hawaii by the U.S.A. during the nineteenth century. One of the most effective narrative twists of the novel lies in recalling to memory the complex struggle which shaped the history of Hawaiian property rights in the context of American colonization and remodeling it as a love story.[8] The origin of ownership – and its legitimacy in the novel's plot as a form of reconciliatory history – thus comes to rest on the consensual formation of intimate *and*

[8] For the complex history of native land rights and new real estate developments during the 19th-century Hawaii before annexation, see LaCroix & Roumasset (1990) and Levy (1975). For the specific legal contexts and issues the novel is situated in and refers to (e.g. the rule against perpetuities and trust law), see Roth (2013).

formal bonds, i.e. the contractual meeting of minds. No force, no violation, no asymmetry of relations, just a stubborn insistence on subjective attraction – all of these are of course at stake in the novel's strange recovery of a relation where minds did not meet, and can no longer meet, where one mind has to 'make up' another in order to find out what the wife, hovering in a comatose state between biological and legal death, actually wanted him to do with the property. While the name of the protagonist (King) is a weak reminder of a crucial concept (kingship) in relation to genealogy and inheritance, linking him to his Hawaiian progenitors, Matt King's wife clearly serves as a representative of the U.S. mainland and its economic interests. Her relation to the land as property is determined by claims of sovereignty and economic rationality 'dressed up' as an affair with a successful American mainland developer who is as much attracted to Matt's wife as he is interested in Matt's property.

The final scene of the novel, the burial of the mother's ashes at sea, while focusing on the daughters' reactions and their renewed bonding, is told from the perspective of their father, and thus successfully reestablishes a narrative legitimacy (of voice and of telling) that had almost been lost at the beginning of the novel. In fact, the two major dramatic strands which the plot follows – the restoration of the King family and the conservation of the family's property – both present a struggle for a legitimate voice (or, rather, a center of consciousness) which is able to evolve over the course of the narrative and to reconcile the claims of the family with the larger claims of the (historical) collective: the community of Hawaiian landowners, defending their land and their history against foreign 'developers' from the U.S. mainland.

Matt King's legitimate position as a responsible father and owner, preserving the family's property by refusing to sell, also restores the myth of the family as the rightful owner and conserver of the original aesthetic splendor of the landscape of Hawaii. This last point moreover highlights the claim of restored authorship which is also inscribed in the final scene and expressed through Matt's musings and observations at the end of the novel. Successfully retaining the family's property is tantamount to restoring the family, and it also means keeping a specific connection between property and authorship in place. The claim of rightful dominion is connected to the claim of narrative authority, which in turn is regained through the scrap-book as the shared work of remembrance, if only in bits and fragments. The author is still a "proprietor" (Rose 1988, 51) but this status is only secured after the ancient history of property relations has been reimagined as a story of stubborn and resilient love and desire and after Matt has accepted to speak for the dead, literally burying the silent, yet persistent claims of his wife.

5. *Conclusion: Plotting Property*

Instead of a stringent and conclusive comparison of the three individual works I have discussed, my short conclusive remarks aim to highlight their exemplary and representative character as narratives of property in the context of U.S.-American literature and culture. They thus should not be read simply as historically situated and specific narrative fictions that accidentally share an interest in questions of property and legitimate ownership. The more general motivation for bringing these works into contact across their historical time and social and cultural spaces was that their accidental interest in property was in fact a continuing and persistent historical, social and cultural trait which continually motivates and generates narrative claims, and does so in order to justify, but also to criticize, specific property regimes, their reality and their practices. Thus, in the most obvious way, because these selected fictions – and they may perhaps be argued to represent a substantial mass of fictional prose in U.S.-American literary history until today – are 'about' questions of property: they are inevitably engaged with concrete existing legal and, in a more general sense, cultural narratives about the origin and the legitimacy of property and ownership. The 'taking', 'doing', and 'making' aspects of these narratives, both in law and in literature, must be seen as the most basic form of emplotment, of 'plotting property' as it were. Legal and literary narratives of property in the U.S.-American context thus legitimize (or criticize) ownership within a larger process of historical continuity, connecting the (mythic) origin of ownership with specific forms of productive and generative use and expected specific 'yields' or realized 'gains.' Each one of the dimensions may become the basis for the justification, as well as the target of criticism, while still retaining the overall logic of the basic plot of the normative property narrative.[9]

The final point of my discussion has been to insist that the act of creating such narratives in the form of literary fictions must be seen in itself as a claim for property that is 'literary', i.e. a claim for property which is defined and realized by being literature. For Cooper, the claim of *The Pioneers* is made obvious above all through the descriptive appropriation of specific landscapes, an appropriation that is both territorial and aesthetic, merging existing literary forms of landscape description with the normative 'markers' of appropriate possession. Cooper's 'descriptive tale' (as indicated on the title page) thus lays claim to a specific legal-aesthetic form of literary fiction, indeed the 'romance of property.' For Chesnutt, in contrast, I have argued that such obvious claims for literary property are constantly frustrated by the racialized narratives of legitimate ownership and continuous dispossession, indicating the precarious position of

[9] For the specific connection between the meaning of 'plot' in the legal and the literary discourse since the early modern period, see Brückner & Poole (2003); for a discussion of property in the context of expected 'yield' as a principle, see Levy (2021).

'mixed' authorship and ownership within a legal culture of racial segregation. Finally, the reconciliatory narrative at the center of Hart Hemmings's novel restores contemporary claims of native ownership and authorship by revisiting and revising their historical formation based on trans-ethnic desire and 'mixed' genealogies – claiming the legitimacy of literary and legal property through the fragmented narrative of disruptive desire 'patched-up,' as it were, by the trust that may be invested in new responsible forms of ownership. Whether these claims are seen as legitimate depends as much on their legal and their literary assessment; the specific emplotment is never fully accidental and never fully autonomous, neither with regard to the legal nor to the literary formation and justification of property.

Works Cited

Auer, Marietta (2014) *Der privatrechtliche Diskurs der Moderne*. Tübingen: Mohr-Siebeck.

Brückner, Martin and Kristen Poole (2003) "The Plot Thickens: Surveying Manuals, Drama, and the Materiality of Narrative Form in Early Modern England." *ELH* 69.3: 617–648.

Chesnutt, Charles W. (1993) *The House Behind the Cedars* [1900]. New York: Penguin.

Clymer, Jeffory A. (2013) *Family Money. Property, Race, and Literature in the Nineteenth Century*. New York: Oxford Univ. Press.

Cooper, James Fenimore (1823) *The Pioneers or The Sources of the Susquehanna; A Descriptive Tale* [1823]. New York: Wiley.

Faulkner, William (2003) *The Portable Faulkner*. Ed. Malcolm Cowley. New York: Penguin.

Forst, Rainer (2018) *Normativität und Macht. Zur Analyse sozialer Rechtfertigungsordnungen*. Frankfurt a.M.: Suhrkamp.

Harris, Cheryl (1993) "Whiteness as Property." *Harvard Law Review* 106.8: 1707–1791.

Hart Hemmings, Kaui (2009) *The Descendants* [2007]. London: Vintage.

Johnson v. M'Intosh. (1823) 21 U.S. (7 Wheaton) 543.

Hattenhauer, Darryl (1993) "Racial and Textual Miscegenation in Chesnutt's *The House Behind the Cedars*." *Mississippi Quarterly* 47.1: 27–45.

Holloway, Karla FC (2014) *Legal Fictions. Constituting Race, Composing Literature*. Durham: Duke Univ. Press.

Kayman, Martin (1996) "Lawful Writing: Common Law, Statute and the Properties of Literature." *New Literary History* 27: 761–783.

LaCroix, Sumner and James Roumasset (1990) "The Evolution of Private Property in Nineteenth-Century Hawaii." *Journal of Economic History* 50.4: 829–850.

Levy, Neil M. (1975) "Native Hawaiian Land Rights." *California Law Review* 63.4: 848–885.

Levy, Jonathan (2021) *Ages of American Capitalism. A History of the United States.* New York: Random House.

Luck, Chad (2014) *The Body of Property. Antebellum American Fiction and the Phenomenology of Possession.* New York: Fordham.

Meriwether, James B. and Michael Millgate (1980) Ed. *Lion in the Garden.* Lincoln: Univ. of Nebraska Press.

Milner, Neal (1993) "Ownership Rights and the Rites of Ownership." *Law & Social Inquiry* 18.2: 227–253.

Pipes, Richard (1999) *Property and Freedom.* London: Harvill.

Rose, Carol (1994) *Property and Persuasion.* Boulder: Westview.

Rose, Mark (1988) "The Author as Proprietor: Donaldson v. Becket and the Genealogy of Modern Authorship." *Representations* 23: 51–85.

Roth, Randall W. (2013) "Deconstructing *The Descendants*: How George Clooney Ennobled Old Hawaiian Trusts and Made the Rule Against Perpetuities Sexy." *Real Property, Trust and Estate Law Journal* 48: 291–319.

Schneck, Peter (2015) "Who Owns Uncle Tom's Cabin? Literature as Cultural Property." *Copyrighting Creativity: Creative Values, Cultural Heritage Innstitutions and Systems of Intellectual Property.* Ed. Helle Porsdam. London: Ashgate. 129–150.

Schneck, Peter (2018) "James Fenimore Cooper, *The Pioneers, or, The Sources of the Susquehanna, a Descriptive Tale* (1823)." *Handbook of the American Novel of the Nineteenth Century.* Ed. Christine Gerhardt. Berlin/Boston: de Gruyter. 174–196.

Sollors, Werner (1986) *Beyond Ethnicity. Consent and Descent in American Culture.* New York: Oxford Univ. Press.

Stolzenberg, Nomi Maya (2000) "The Culture of Property." *Daedalus* 129.4: 169–192.

Tokizane, Sanae (2007) "Cartographical Imagination: Faulkner's Map of Yoknapatawpha." *The Faulkner Journal of Japan.* np. https://www.faulknerjapan.com /journal/no9/2007Tokizane.html. last accessed November 09, 2021.

Recht und Stimme von Oscar Wilde bis Anis Mohamed Ferchichi: Zu einem Problem der juristischen Verhandlung von fiktionaler Literatur

Hans J. Lind

Am 03. April 1895 beginnt mit *Regina v. John Douglas Marquess of Queensberry* jener Gerichtsprozess, der gemeinhin als Beginn des Endes von Oscar Wilde gesehen wird. In einem Saal des Marlborough Street Magistrates Court, dem Gericht, an dem einst Charles Dickens als Gerichtsberichterstatter tätig gewesen ist (Lock 1980, 15), befragt Edward Henry Carson unter Mandat des Marquess den Schriftsteller im Rahmen eines Kreuzverhörs. Wilde zeigt sich zunächst überheblich, und dies auch durchaus publikumswirksam. Er mokiert sich über Carsons mangelnde Vortragskunst[1] und das Publikum lacht, als Wilde die Frage: „Have you ever felt that feeling of adoring madly a beautiful male person many years younger than yourself?" wie folgt beantwortet: „I have never given adoration to anybody except myself" (Holland 2004, 91). „Have you written other [letters] in the same style?" beantwortet Wilde lapidar mit „I don't repeat myself in style" (108); Carsons Nachfrage „Is that an ordinary letter?" kann Wilde nur rhetorisch verstehen: „I think everything I write extraordinary. [...] I do not pose as being ordinary – good heavens!" (110)

Auch wenn sich die Protokolle[2] dieses veritablen Schauspiels eher als ein evasives Sprachspiel lesen, welches die gegen Wilde vorgebrachten Beweise dennoch nicht entkräften kann, so ist das Verhör aus einer anderen Perspektive interessant: Es zeigt bereits die Charakteristika einer äußerst problematischen gerichtlichen Behandlung von Literatur, die erstens in der Annahme von unmittelbarer lebensweltlicher Referenzialisierbarkeit literarischer Texte besteht (Wahrheitsfrage), zweitens in einer mangelnden Trennung von Autor und Erzähler bzw. Figur und der damit verbundenen Annahme, dass beide Stimmen und damit „Positionen" identisch sind (Carson spricht von „pose" (74) bzw. „putting forth views" (80)), und drittens in einer Verkennung intertextueller Bezüge. Hinzu kommt viertens die prozesstechnische Hilfsannahme, dass aus

[1] „Carson: That is a beautiful phrase too? Wilde: Not when you read it, Mr. Carson. When I wrote it, it was beautiful. You read it very badly" (Holland 2004, 106).

[2] Es gibt mehrere (Teil-)Abdrucke der Gerichtsprotokolle, die im Wortlaut aber teils eklatant voneinander abweichen. Merlin Hollands Edition gilt als die verlässlichste und wird in diesem Beitrag deshalb auch zugrunde gelegt.

dem Inhalt eines literarischen Werks zumindest auf den Charakter des Autors geschlossen werden könne.

Der Schwerpunkt dieses Teils von Carsons Verhör liegt dabei u.a. auf dem Versuch, Parallelen zwischen dem Autor Wilde und der Figur des Künstlers Basil Hallwood in Wildes Roman *Dorian Gray* (1890) zu etablieren. Ziel ist zu beweisen, dass Wilde, wie seine Romanfigur,[3] homosexuelle Beziehungen zu jüngeren Männern suchte – im konkreten Fall zu dem 16 Jahre jüngeren Lord Alfred Douglas. Zudem sind mehrere Briefe Wildes an Douglas Gegenstand des Verhörs, wobei es sich beim ersten Brief zumindest nach der Einlassung von Wilde um ein an Douglas gerichtetes Gedicht („prose poem", 111) handelt.

Um nachzuweisen, dass Wilde ein „posing sodomist" (100) ist, befragt Carson dann Wilde tatsächlich Satz für Satz zu Wildes Roman und zu den Briefen:

> I will suggest to you *Dorian Gray*. Is that open to the interpretation of being a sodomitical book? [...]
> Let us go over the thing phrase by phrase. [...]
> „I was jealous of every one to whom you spoke." Have you ever been jealous of a young man? [...]
> „I wanted to have you all to myself." Did you ever have that feeling? [...]
> Have you yourself ever had this feeling towards a young man? [...]
> Is it an incident in your life? [...]
> „I quite admit that I adored you madly." What do you say to that? Have you ever adored a young man, some twenty-one years younger than yourself, madly? (81–90)

Worauf Carson abzielt, ohne dies ausdrücklich zu behaupten, ist eindeutig: die lebensweltliche Referenzialisierbarkeit von Literatur, vielleicht sogar unter der Präsupposition einer naiven Erlebnispoesie. Wildes abwehrende Antwort ist hier kategorisch:

> No. It is a work of fiction I am describing [...]. You must remember that novels and life are different things. [...] You are not to ask me if I believe they really happened; they are motives in fiction. (90–103)

Carsons Insistieren auf der lebensweltlichen Referenzialisierbarkeit der Passagen beantwortet Wilde zudem in einem Fall mit dem Verweis auf die Intertextualität des infrage stehenden Textes:

> Carson: Then you have never had that feeling that you depict here?
> Wilde: No. The whole idea was borrowed from Shakespeare, I regret to say. [...] Yes, from Shakespeare's sonnets.
> Carson: [...] [Y]ou yourself have never experienced the sensation which you described there as being the sensation of this artist towards Dorian Gray?
> Wilde: No, I varied it from Shakespeare's sonnets. I took it –. (92–93)

---

[3] Wobei die homosexuellen Bezüge in der prozessgegenständlichen Fassung im Vergleich zu den früheren Versionen des Romans bereits deutlich abgeschwächt worden waren – ein Faktum, auf das auch Carson im Rahmen des Kreuzverhörs verweist (Holland 2004, 78–79, 86).

Obwohl Wildes Argument im Hinblick auf die Wahrheitsfrage zunächst insoweit aristotelisch ist, als er anstelle von Faktizität das in den Passagen Gesagte als allgemeinere (poetische) Wahrheit zu fassen sucht,[4] zielt Wildes Argumentation tatsächlich auf eine deutlich weitreichendere Autonomie der Kunst ab. Weder der Wahrheit noch der Moral soll Literatur verpflichtet sein, sondern allein der Schönheit:

> Wilde: [I]n writing a plot, a book [...] I am concerned entirely with literature, that is, with art. The aim is not to do good or evil, but to try and make a thing that will have some quality of beauty [...]. I rarely think that anything I write is true.
> Carson. Did you say „rarely"?
> Wilde: I said „rarely." I might have said „never."
> Carson: Nothing you ever write is true?
> Wilde: Not true in the sense of correspondence to fact; [...] not true in the actual sense of correspondence to actual facts of life, certainly not; I should be very sorry to think it. [...]
> Carson: „There is no such thing as a moral or an immoral book. [...] Books are well written, or badly written" [...]. That expresses your view?
> Wilde: My view of art, yes.
> Carson: Then, I take it that no matter how immoral a book was, if it was well written, it would be a good book?
> Wilde: If it were well written, it would produce a sense of beauty, which is the highest feeling that man is capable of. (74–80)

Carsons Annahme, dass Literatur dagegen apophantisch sei („A well written book putting forth sodomitical views"), weist Wilde dann auch harsch zurück: „No work of art ever puts forward views of any kind" (80).

Dass solche Literatur dann auch keinesfalls als Spiegel der Gefühle oder Erlebnisse des Autors verstanden werden darf, ist evident:

> Carson: May I take it that you [...] have never known the feeling described here?
> Wilde: I have never allowed any personality to dominate my art [...]. (90)

Wildes „Kunst" soll zudem in gewisser Weise elitär sein: Sie kann nur vom verständigen Adressatenkreis beurteilt werden[5] – und eigentlich von niemandem, außer von Wilde selbst,[6] was Wildes Verständnis von Wahrheit als irreduzibel subjektiv entspricht:

---

[4] „I think it is the most perfect description of what an artist would feel on meeting a beautiful personality that was in some way necessary to his art and life [...]. I think it is perfectly natural for any artist to admire intensely and love a young man" (Holland 2004, 90).

[5] „The views of the Philistines on art [...] are incalculably stupid." In der Passage heißt es weiter: „Carson: The majority of people would come within your definition of Philistines and illiterates? [...] Do you think that the majority of people live up to the pose you are giving us [...]? Wilde: I am afraid they are not cultivated enough. Carson: Not cultivated enough to draw the distinction [...] between a good book and a bad book? Wilde: Oh, certainly not" (Holland 2004, 81).

[6] „What concerns me in my art is my view and my feeling and why I made it; I don't care twopence what other people think about it" (Holland 2004, 81).

> Carson: „A truth ceases to be true when more than one person believes in it"?
> Wilde: [Y]es, that would be my metaphysical definition of truth – something so personal that [...] the same truth can never be appreciated by two minds [...]. (76)

Dieses Kunstverständnis wird dann auch sogleich apologetisch genutzt, wenn Wilde versucht, einen belastenden Brief an Douglas als „Gedicht"[7] einzustufen, und ihm damit eine Eignung im Rahmen eines Tatsachenbeweises abzuerkennen:[8]

> Wilde: I am afraid you are criticizing a poem [...]. I think it was a beautiful letter. If you ask me whether it is proper, you might as well ask me whether *King Lear* is proper, or a sonnet of Shakespeare is proper. It was a beautiful letter. I was not concerned with – the letter was not written – with the object of writing propriety; it was written with the object of making a beautiful thing.
> Carson: But apart from art? [...] Suppose a man, now, who was not an artist had written this letter to a handsome young man, as I believe Lord Alfred Douglas is? [...]
> Wilde: A man who was not an artist could never have written this letter. (105)

Carsons Argumentation konnte Wilde damit indes nicht entkräften. Im auf *Regina v. Douglas* folgenden, ersten strafrechtlichen Verfahren gegen Wilde[9] (*Regina v. Wilde and Taylor*, 1895) wird Sir Charles Frederick Gill als Vertreter der Anklage den Autor in ähnlicher Manier zur Bedeutung des Begriffes „shame" in einem der Gedichte von Douglas befragen (Linder 1995b).[10] Noch Sir Frank Lockwood, Vertreter der Anklage in einem zweiten Strafverfahren gegen Wilde,[11] in welchem der Autor wegen homosexueller Handlungen als „gross indecency" nunmehr zu zwei Jahren Zwangsarbeit verurteilt wurde, wird von dem „prose poem" bzw. „sonnet" Wildes als „evidence of a guilty passion" sprechen (Linder 1995a).

Man mag dem tatsächlich äußerst intelligenten und auch sprachgewandten Carson zugutehalten, dass er nicht ausdrücklich eine unmittelbare lebensweltliche Referenzialisierbarkeit von Wildes literarischem Werk behauptete,[12] diese allenfalls suggerierte. Carson bewegte sich im Hinblick auf das Ziel seiner Fragen vielmehr in einer anderen prozeduralen Praxis, die mehr als ein Jahrhundert fortdauern soll, und die darin besteht, literarische Texte zwar nicht als

---

7 „It is a poem and I have written other beautiful letters" (Holland 2004, 108).

8 Beim zweiten Brief wäre das Argument indes nicht überzeugend, weshalb wohl auch Wilde einräumt: „It isn't like the other – a prose poem. It is a letter expressive of my great devotion for Lord Alfred Douglas" (Holland 2004, 111).

9 *Regina v. Wilde and Taylor*, eröffnet am 26. April 1895.

10 In Carson'scher Manier fragt Gill weiter: „What is ‚the love that dare not speak its name'?" (Linder 1995b).

11 *Regina v. Wilde and Taylor*, eröffnet am 21. Mai 1895.

12 Carson behauptet zwar nicht, dass *Dorian Gray* ein autobiografischer Roman ist. Er suggeriert aber, dass sein Autor das Geschehen des Romans zumindest gutheißt, wenn nicht sogar selbst praktiziert. Aus dieser Stoßrichtung erklärt sich auch Carsons Insistieren auf Wildes genereller Position zur Moralität der dargestellten Handlungen, etwa im Hinblick auf *The Priest and the Acolyte*: „Do you approve of those words?" (Holland 2004, 70).

Beweis für die Tat selbst, doch aber für den Charakter eines Autors heranzuziehen: als *evidence of bad character*. Indes ist letztere Prozesspraxis eine nicht weniger problematische Praxis, die noch 1979 in *United States v. Giese* zu beobachten ist,[13] und die in gewissen Grenzen auch heute als zulässig angesehen wird – auch wenn ihr u.a. in *State v. Hanson* (1987) und *State v. Skinner* (2014) mehr als ein Jahrhundert nach dem Wilde-Prozess berechtigterweise eine (wenn auch leider nur eingeschränkte)[14] Absage erteilt wurde.

1. *Problematische Kontinuitäten I: Literatur vor Gericht im 21. Jahrhundert*

Man mag im 21. Jahrhundert leicht dazu geneigt sein, obige Prozesspraktiken als längst vergangen zu betrachten, und dies nicht ohne Grund: Anklagen wegen einer moralisch negativen Wirkung von Literatur sind zwar noch existent, aber auf wenige Fallgruppen beschränkt.[15] Jugendschutz steht als Anliegen hinter einer dieser Fallgruppen und findet sich im Vereinigten Königreich,[16] den Vereinigten Staaten[17] und in Deutschland verwirklicht.[18] Die Gefährdung des öffentlichen Friedens und des sozialen Zusammenlebens ist eine andere Fallgruppe, die neben dem Vereinigten Königreich gerade in Deutschland noch heute relevant ist, wo die Spanne von menschenverachtender Gewaltdarstellung über Volksverhetzung bis zu Holocaustleugnung reicht.[19] Im Übrigen genießt Literatur heute weite Freiheiten, die gerade auch durch eine klarstellende

13 In dem Fall ging es u.a. um die Frage, ob man den Charakter eines Angeklagten an den Büchern, die er liest, ablesen kann. Die Entscheidung war hochumstritten und enthält selbst bereits ein Sondervotum (*dissenting opinion*). *United States v. Gregory Lee McCrea* (1978) hatte die Frage beiläufig verneint.

14 Die Absage ist insoweit nur eingeschränkt, als, wie noch *State v. Skinner* zeigen wird, literarische Texte im Rahmen einer Abwägung durchaus als Beweismittel benutzt werden können. *United States v. Giese* (1979, § 60) und *State v. Hanson* (1987, 663) nehmen eine solche Abwägung tatsächlich vor, die auch von verschiedenen Prozessordnungen als Ausnahme ausdrücklich zugelassen ist, siehe etwa: *US Federal Rule of Evidence* 303–304. Für Großbritannien siehe Emson (2017, 31–32 und Kap. 15.2).

15 Im UK regeln der *Obscene Publications Act* von 1959, der *Obscene Publications Act* von 1964 und der *Theatres Act* von 1968 solche Einschränkungen der schriftstellerischen Freiheit. In den USA regelt u.a. Titel 18, §§ 1460–1466 des *United States Code* den Sachbereich. Dass *obsencity trials* durchaus noch existent sind, zeigt u.a. *Luke Records, Inc. v. Navarro* (1992).

16 U.a. der *Children and Young Persons (Harmful Publications) Act* v. 1955 (neben den beiden Obscene Publications Acts).

17 Titel 18, § 1470 *United States Code* ist einer der bundesrechtlichen Vorschriften, hinzu kommt Landesrecht (*state law*).

18 Siehe hierzu u.a. §§ 15, 18, 27 des *Jugendschutzgesetzes*.

19 §§ 130–131, 141 StGB. Im UK bietet der *Public Order Act* von 1986 ähnliche Einschränkungen.

Rechtsprechung in den USA[20] und dem UK[21] sowie durch das Postulat einer „kunstspezifischen“ Betrachtung in Deutschland[22] gesichert ist.

Tatsächlich finden sich aber Autoren deutlich häufiger wegen ihrer Werke vor Gericht, wobei es scheint, dass sich obige, äußerst problematische Prozesspraxis nicht nur in einer Vielzahl von Fällen fortgesetzt, sondern zum Wechsel ins 21. Jahrhundert quantitativ erst ihren Höhepunkt erreicht hat. Dabei lassen sich einzeln oder kumulativ die obigen drei Fehlschlüsse (Annahme der lebensweltlichen Referenzialisierbarkeit von Literatur; Gleichsetzung der Stimme von Autor und Erzähler/Figur; Verkennung der Intertextualität von Literatur) nachweisen. Hinzu kommt die fast noch häufiger in Gerichtsprozessen des anglo-amerikanischen Rechtsraums beobachtbare Annahme, dass man aus dem Inhalt literarischer Werke zumindest Rückschlüsse auf den Charakter des Autors ziehen könne.

Es ist dabei die vermutlich häufigste und einflussreichste Form von Gegenwartslyrik, die jüngst zu einem inflationären Anstieg der Fallzahlen geführt hat. Im UK den Gerichten als *drill* bekannt, und hier regelmäßig als *street realism* eingestuft, der sich unter Anlehnung an amerikanische Vorbilder im 21. Jahrhundert in London entwickelt hat, handelt es sich hier um Texte, die teils abbildend, teils verherrlichend die alltägliche Gewalt und den Drogenmissbrauch auf der Straße beschreiben. Durchgehend rhythmisiert und teils spärlich mit Musik unterlegt, zeichnen die Texte ein düsteres Bild der in der Regel minderjährigen Protagonisten. Drill ist dabei Teil einer „glokalen“[23] Jugendkultur, die sich von der Bronx aus weltweit verbreitet hat und in vielen Ländern bereits ein gewichtiger, wenn nicht der wichtigste Teil der Populärkultur geworden ist: Rap. Chicago Drill als Vorbild des London Drill teilt dabei mit dem West Coast Rap eine äußerst stereotypisierte, auf Herabsetzung, Gewalt und Drohungen reduzierte Lexis. Der aus Ladbroke Grove (West London) stammende Rhys Angelo Herbert etwa formuliert in *Play for the Pagans* (2017):

> How can his bredrin shoot up his yard and nearly murder his mum?
> That happened a few months back
> And what has he fucking done?
> He's wearing General's trackie in Trap Goes Dead
> He's a fucking bum [...]
> When I shank man up, man tear through guts
> Man, I stab for the kill

20 Siehe etwa *Miller v. California* (1973), *Pope v. Illinois* (1987), *Street v. New York* (1969) zum *expressive conduct* und *Snyder v. Phelps* (2011) zu *speech on matters of public concern.*

21 Instruktiv ist hier aus der neueren Rechtsprechung u.a. *Redmond-Bate v. Director of Public Prosecutions* (1999).

22 Siehe Bundesverfassungsgericht (1971, 1645 sowie 1984, 213).

23 Zum Rap als globales Phänomen, das sich durch Prozesse kultureller Aneignung lokal ausdifferenziert hat, siehe Klein & Friedrich (2003, 84–99) sowie Androutsopoulos (2003).

These niggas keep talking my name
This shit's about to get real. [...]
The last time I saw him, his chest got bored out
I dipped like four of them neeks
I ain't got no patience, play for the pagans
Man get smoked like trees.

Rap als Kunstform ist ein textuell sehr stark ausdifferenziertes Phänomen, das in medialer Hinsicht eine breite Spanne an Formen bietet und von stark rhythmisierten Texten mit in der Regel vier betonten Silben pro Zeile,[24] die gänzlich ohne Musikbegleitung vorgetragen werden, bis hin zu äußerst aufwendig produzierten Videoclips mit Musikbegleitung reichen, bei denen die Bildästhetik höchste kommerzielle Standards erfüllt. Bereits die rein auf Textvortrag reduzierten (Ur-)Formen, der Battle-Rap und der Acapella-Rap, weisen dabei die für eine strafrechtliche Verfolgung verantwortlichen Charakteristika auf. Während bei letzterem vorgeschriebene Texte ohne Musikbegleitung einem Publikum vorgetragen werden, ist der Battle-Rap ein in der Regel improvisierter Wettkampf, wobei die wesentliche Gemeinsamkeit beider Formen ist, dass die Texte Gewalt beschreiben, mit Gewalt drohen oder zumindest Andere beleidigen oder in sonstiger Weise verbal herabsetzen.

Auch wenn diese beiden Genres mit den in der Regel als kulturell wertvoll verstandenen *poetry slams* Überschneidungen aufweisen, welche als Form fast zeitgleich in Chicago entstanden sind[25] und sich ebenfalls weltweit verbreitet haben – wobei beide performativen Praktiken oft in einem Satz als „poetry of a new generation" (Eleveld 2003) bezeichnet werden –, unterscheiden sich Rap Battles und Poetry Slams als institutionalisierte Praktiken in drei zentralen Charakteristika: Poetry Slams wurden erstens von Beginn an als Teil einer eher ambitionierten Literatur verstanden,[26] während die beiden textzentrierten Rapformen allenfalls als Popularform qualifiziert werden. Battle- und Acapella-Rap dienten zweitens zumindest ursprünglich dem Empowerment einer äußerst prekären Bevölkerungsschicht in den Ghettos der Bronx (und später von South L.A. und Chicago), wobei die Verlagerung der Bewährungskämpfe von der Straße auf die Bühne als vertretende Konfliktbewältigung auch ein Charakteristikum des in Brixton geborenen UK Drill sowie des oft faktisch als „Migrantenrap" verstandenen Gangsta-Rap in Deutschland ist (Klein & Friedrich 2003, 80). Drittens finden sich Poetry Slammer in der Regel nicht für ihre Literaturproduktion vor Gericht gestellt, Rapper indes schon.

---

[24] Die „Grundwährung" im Rap ist *16 bars*: Eine Strophe besteht regelmäßig aus 16 Zeilen, wobei jede Zeile wiederum aus 16 Silben (4 Hauptbetonungen) besteht (RTC 2020).

[25] Wobei auch insoweit teils personelle Übereinstimmungen bestehen, als relevante Battle-Rapper tatsächlich der Poetry Slam Szene angehörten.

[26] Wobei nicht verschwiegen werden soll, dass auch Poetry Slams in den USA früh als Mittel eines Empowerments ethnischer Minderheiten genutzt wurden, siehe Algarin (1994) und Holman (1994).

Es gibt aber, wenn es sich auch um eine Populärform handelt, insoweit gewichtige Argumente, Rap Lyrics als literarisches Genre anzuerkennen und in diesem Sinne auch mit den anderen Literaturformen rechtlich gleich zu behandeln, als sie, wie ich an anderer Stelle darlege (Lind 2022a), wesentliche Charakteristika von Literatur im Allgemeinen bzw. von Lyrik im Besonderen aufweisen. Tatsächlich ist die Literarizität von Rap nicht nur in den Vereinigten Staaten als Geburtsort des Genres anerkannt, wo Rap sogar als „the new vanguard of American poetry" (Gates 2011, S. xxvi)[27] gefeiert wurde. Vielmehr mehren sich auch im Vereinigten Königreich[28] und in Deutschland[29] entsprechende Stimmen, was gerade auch aufgrund der extremen Bedeutung des Genres als Jugendkultur bedingt ist. Rap wird hier als „Straßenpoesie"[30] verstanden, welche den marginalisierten Bevölkerungsschichten eine Stimme gibt.

In allen drei Ländern ist indes leider auch die Verurteilung von Autoren des Genres wegen ihrer Texte an der Tagesordnung, wobei in Deutschland möglicherweise auch aufgrund der verzögerten Etablierung der Populärform die Fallzahlen noch niedrig sind und sich eine einheitliche Prozesspraxis bisher nicht abschätzen lässt. Was das glokale Genre indes eint, ist, dass sich vor Gericht in der Regel Minderheiten für ihre Texte verantworten müssen. In den USA sind es fast ausschließlich Afro-Amerikaner, deren lyrische Texte als Beweismittel ausgewertet werden, im UK und in Deutschland in der Regel People of Color sowie Personen mit Migrationshintergrund.

In den USA sind die Verfahren kaum noch zählbar – ein Bericht einer Kollaboration der University of Richmond, Virginia, mit der University of Georgia hat mehr als 500 Gerichtsverfahren erfasst (Nielson 2020; Nielson & Dennis 2019).[31] Für das UK wird von der University of Manchester in einem Forschungsprojekt[32] momentan ebenfalls eine entsprechende Liste erstellt, deren Ergebnisse noch ausstehen. Gleiches gilt für ein Projekt an der London School

---

27 Zitiert in „MOTION" (2019, 13).

28 Zum UK Rap siehe u.a. Wacker (2019) und Bramwell (2015). Quinn (2005) folgt in den Kapiteln 5 und 6 ihrer Monografie dem Ansatz Henry Louis Gates' (1988), dass Rap einer langen Tradition des „vernacular storytelling" entspringt.

29 Wolbring (2015, 133–139); Gruber (2017). Zu „Lyrics" als Lyrik siehe von Ammon & von Petersdorff (2019, 7–14).

30 Schon früh wurde in den USA Rap als „street poetry" eingeordnet. Curtis Lyle berichtet bereits 1982 in einem Gespräch mit Amiri Baraka von Rap als „poetry […] of the street" (Reilly 1994, 228). Steven Dougherty spricht 1986 im *People Weekly Magazine* anlässlich L.L. Cool J. von Rap als „raw street poetry […] set to a booming beat" (Peters 1990, 48). Im UK lässt sich der Begriff ebenfalls nachweisen, siehe etwa Linden (1997, 50). In Deutschland wurde der Begriff zur veritablen Selbstbezeichnung der Rapper: Alpa Gun, *Die Stimme der Strasse* (2010); Alpa Gun, *Keine Angst* (2020); Asche, *Straßenpoesie* (2021); Bushido & Animus, *Lichter der Stadt* (2019); Carzza, *Straßenpoesie* (2020).

31 Nielsons Arbeit ist in Rechtskreisen indes bereits deutlich länger bekannt. Er war u.a. Mitverfasser der *amici curiae briefs* in *Elonis v. United States* (2014), in *Bell v. Itawamba Country School Board* (2015) sowie in *Knox v. Commonwealth* (2019).

32 AHRC AH/T000058/1 „Prosecuting Rap: Criminal Justice and UK Black Youth Expressive Culture". Das Projekt wird von Prof. Eithne Quinn geleitet.

of Economics.[33] Gemein ist beiden Ländern dabei, dass die Gerichtspraxis hier tatsächlich immer noch äußerst problematisch ist: In Rap Lyrics Geschildertes wird als in der Lebenswelt tatsächlich geschehen angesehen, womit literarische Texte im Rahmen des Tatsachenbeweises Verwendung finden können. Da die Angeklagten in der Regel selbst Autoren der Texte sind, werden diese Texte in alter Manier faktisch als Geständnis für eine begangene Straftat gelesen. Subsidiär werden Rap-Texte als *evidence of bad character* erfasst.

Besagte Literatursorte scheint eine derart ergiebige Quelle von Beweisen zu sein, dass Staatsanwälte die Ermittler tatsächlich vor Hausdurchsuchungen auf die Relevanz von Rap Lyrics als Beweismittel aufmerksam machen. In einem Handbuch für Strafverfolgungsbehörden wird den Ermittlern die Suche nach Rap-Texten sogar nachdrücklich empfohlen (Jackson 2004). Das *Attorney's Bulletin* geht sogar so weit, Rap kurzerhand als tatsachenbasierte Erlebnislyrik zu behandeln, wobei lyrisches Ich und Autor kurzgeschlossen werden:

> In today's society many gang members compose and put their true-life experiences into lyrical form [...]. Law enforcement officials must remain mindful of [...] the opportunities to obtain inculpatory evidence. (Lyddane 2006, 1)[34]

In Deutschland wurde unter derselben Präsupposition jüngst die Wohnung von Rapper Fler (bürgerlich: Patrick Losenský) von einem Sondereinsatzkommando vergeblich nach Sprühfarbe durchsucht. Hintergrund war eine Textzeile von *Dieser Boy* (2019), die lautete: „Komm' im Bentley, doch male nachts die U-Bahn. / Ein Millionär, der nie schläft, muss was zu tun haben. [...] Bin ich schuldig? Natürlich. Selbstverständlich / [...] Bin dieser boy."

In den USA wurde in jüngerer Zeit Alex Medina angeklagt und verurteilt, wobei Rap-Texte als Geständnis interpretiert wurden, die u.a. den Passus enthielten: „Never did it for the fame / cuz that ain't right, / Did it cuz I had love for my homies and the life" (New York Times 2014). Antwain Stewards *Rap Bad Newz* wurde ebenfalls als Beweismittel in einem Mordprozess herangezogen. Der Text lautete: „Listen, walked to your boy and I approached him / 12 midnight on his traphouse porch and / Everybody saw when I motherfuckin' choked him / But nobody saw when I motherfuckin' smoked him / Roped him, sharpened up the shank then I poked him" (Daily Press 2013; Daily Mail 2013). Ronell Wilson (aka Rated R) wurde wegen Mordes zum Tode verurteilt, wobei Beweismittel u.a. Lyrics waren, die lauteten: „Come teast Rated U better have dat vest and Dat Golock / leave a 45 slogs in da back of ya head / cause u cause I'm getin dat Bread / I ain't goin stop to ‚m dead" (*United States v. Wilson*, 2010). Jonair Tyreece Moore (aka Spade / High C) wurde wegen Drogenhandels verurteilt, wobei Lyrics Verwendung fanden, um zu beweisen, dass Moore ein

[33] Geleitet wird das Projekt von Abenaa Owusu-Bempah.
[34] Zitiert nach Dennis (2007).

Drogendealer war. Der Text lautete u.a.: „The police all know me and I have narcotics" (*United States v. Moore*, 2011).

In einer nicht unbeachtlichen Anzahl von Fällen im Vereinigten Königreich wurden Rap-Texte ebenfalls als Beweismittel dafür eingeführt, dass die Angeklagten Mitglieder kriminelle Banden oder Drogendealer waren.[35] Ein Bericht der britischen Bürgerrechtsorganisation *Justice* führt hierzu aus: „The CJS [d.h. Criminal Justice System, HJL] has come to misconstrue drill as a form of realism, depicting what the artists have directly seen, heard and done. As a consequence, lyrics are often adduced as biographical, and therefore admissible evidence" (Justice 2021, 40). In *Regina v. Simpson & Anor* (2019) wurden Rap Lyrics vom Englischen Court of Appeal zwar nicht als Geständnis gewertet, aber doch als „evidence of the appellant's bad character" (§ 13).[36] Gleiches gilt für eine Vielzahl weiterer Fälle, wie z.B. *Regina v. Zafran Akhtar Saleem* (2007) und *Regina v. Mucktar Khan* (2018).

Letzteres entspricht jener bereits angesprochenen, äußerst problematischen Prozesspraxis, literarische Texte wenn nicht als direkte Beweismittel für eine Straftat, so doch zumindest subsidiär im Carson'schen Sinne als Beweis für den kriminellen Charakter des Autors zu lesen. Viele Fälle ähneln dabei auch insoweit dem Wilde-Verfahren, als, wie bei Wilde,[37] unter anderem Texte als *character evidence* beigezogen wurden, die nachweislich vor der prozessgegenständlichen Tat geschrieben wurden und damit zumindest nicht als Geständnis gewertet werden konnten – ein Problem, mit dem sich höchstrichterlich u.a. *State v. Skinner* (2014) beschäftigen musste.

2. *Wer spricht? Über Rollen und Realität(en) im Rap*

Es gibt im Rap zwar tatsächlich Texte, die sich für eine referenzielle Lektüre anbieten, und hierbei handelt es sich nicht nur um Ausnahmen, sondern um ein veritables Subgenre von Ausdruckspoesie im Rap. Tupacs *So many tears* (1995), verfasst in Erwartung der Todesstrafe, ist hier im Genre sicherlich ein Paradigma. Rapper von Notorious B.I.G. über Eminem bis Jay-Z haben das Genre ebenfalls als Medium genutzt, um ihre Drogensucht und andere persönliche Rückschläge zu beschreiben (Grove 2021).

---

35 Z.B. [2021] EWCA Crim 673; [2016] EWCA Crim 668; [2014] EWCA Crim 48; [2014] EWCA Crim 54.

36 Zudem wurden die Texte als Beweis für Bandenmitgliedschaft herangezogen: „At trial the prosecution were allowed to adduce particular evidence [...]. This included [...] rap lyrics written by the appellant said to illustrate conflict and violence between the CR0 and CR7 gangs" (*Regina v. Simpson & Anor*, 2019).

37 Wildes *Dorian Gray* wurde nachweislich vor dem Beginn seiner Beziehung mit Lord Alfred Douglas geschrieben und konnte insoweit nicht als unmittelbares Beweismittel für dieses konkrete Verhältnis dienen.

In London erweist sich das gefühlsbasierte Subgenre als durchaus bedeutsamer Gegenpart zum UK Drill, wobei sich autobiografische Darstellungen mit Gefühlsschilderungen vermischen. Der Rapper Michael Ebenezer Kwadjo Omari Owuo Jr. (aka Stormzy) schreibt in *Do Better* (2019):

Have you ever had to sacrifice your health?
Ever had to sacrifice yourself? [...]
God, hold me down ,til I drown
It's like I nearly fell into the ground.[38]

Autobiografisch führt Owuo dann auch fort:

Was a troublesome youth, had desire for war [...]
Spend time in my sneaks or spend a night in my thoughts
You walk a mile in these, I walk a mile in yours
Ah, man, all the things I been battling through the year
Wonder if my bro woulda made it if I was there
Number twenty-five on my little list of fears.

Der in Streatham aufgewachsene David Orobosa Omoregie (aka Dave) sinniert in *Screwface Capital* (2019):

I ain't got a memory of when dad was around
Still a child when I turned man of the house
Tell me what you know about a bag full of bills
And your mom crying out
Saying, „Son, I can't take it"
And then staring in the mirror for an hour
With a tear in your eye like
„I gotta go make it."

Berwyn (bürgerlich Berwyn Du Bois) reflektiert in *Glory* (2020) ebenfalls seine eigene prekäre Situation:

Lately, I been drinkin' a lot
And maybe it's in my DNA
Maybe it's the way things have been goin' for me
Lately, I been thinkin' a lot
Maybe I'll always be a slave
Maybe I'll never break these chains
Maybe I need a twist of faith
One of them nothin' was the same like Drizzy Drake's
And this is transparency and God forbid that I fail
,Cause I'd hate to see my mother end up back in that jail
And immigration sent a letter, said they're grantin' me bail.

[38] Soweit nicht anders angegeben, sind nachfolgend die Transkriptionen der in der Regel nicht gesondert veröffentlichten Texte dem Internetdienst lyricfind.com entnommen.

In Deutschland haben u.a. Capital Bra & Samra mit *Tilidin* (2019) und KC Rebell & RAF Camora mit *Neptun* (2019) jüngst ähnliche Beispiele autobiografischer Ausdruckslyrik geliefert.

Es sind diese eindeutigen Verbindungen mancher Rapformen zur Ausdruckspoesie, die sicher auch dazu geführt haben, dass von den Gerichten die Genregrenzen innerhalb des Rap ignoriert und gerade auch Lyrics aus dem hoch intertextuellen Genre des Gangsta-Rap fälschlicherweise als realitätsabbildend behandelt wurden. Dies wird dadurch gefördert, dass es auch im Gangsta-Rap (inklusive des Drills) tatsächlich Fälle von lebensweltlich referenzialisierbaren Texten gibt. Gonzales Reese Wardlaw (aka Snoop) wurde so wegen eines Mordes auf dem Parkplatz eines Restaurants der Olive Garden Kette verurteilt. Beweismittel waren u.a. ein Rap, in dem es heißt: „[H]it ‚em in his chest […] caught ‚em dead at da Olive Garden" (Bleier 2014). In *Greene v. Commonwealth* (2006) ließ das Berufungsgericht einen Rap-Text als Beweismittel zu, in dem der Angeklagte nach der Tat die Ermordung seiner Ehefrau beschreibt: „Bitch made me mad, and I had to take her life. / My name is Dennis Greene and I ain't got no fucking' wife" (83). Das Gericht führte aus, der Text „establishes premeditation and motive and in the Appellant's own words" (87). In *People v. Lee* (2011) rappte der Angeklagte im direkten Anschluss an die Tat: „I didn't want to shoot you, didn't want to kill you, bitch, but you wouldn't give me any" (627). Berechtigt waren die Verurteilungen sicher auch in *United States v. Wilson* (2010) und *United States v. Belfast* (2010).

Diese Einzelfälle lassen aber leicht übersehen, dass der Gangsta-Rap des 21. Jahrhunderts als dasjenige Subgenre des Rap, das als Beweismittel am ergiebigsten ist, gleichzeitig am höchsten ästhetisiert ist, wobei intertextuelle Bezüge einen in der Frühzeit des Genres noch vorhandenen Realitätsbezug oft größtenteils, wenn nicht sogar vollständig ersetzt haben.

Hinzu kommt, dass die Sprechersituation gerade im Gangsta-Rap äußerst problematisch ist, eine Dissoziation der Stimmen von Autor und lyrischem Ich zumindest mittlerweile nicht die Ausnahme, sondern vielmehr die Regel ist.[39] Bei den literarischen Personae des Gangsta-Rap handelt es sich nämlich um Standardfiguren, deren Charaktereigenschaften und Taten vom Genre vorgegeben sind. Gleiches gilt für die Narrative des Genres. Auch wenn Gangsta-Rap sich immer wieder als naturalistisches Genre geriert, bei dem das Leben selbst die Texte schreibt,[40] weisen diese Narrative nämlich eine äußerst geringe Spannbreite auf.

Zudem sind selbst die Erzähltechniken des Rap kulturell determiniert. Henry Gates Jr. (1988, 2011) hat nachgewiesen, dass Rap in einer langen Tradition afro-amerikanischen Erzählens steht, zu der auch die Praktiken von *boast*

[39] Wenn auch versteckt durch die genretypische „pretence of no pretence" (Rose 2008).

[40] „Meine Texte schreibt das Leben / Ich brauch nicht mehr zu tun, als'n Stift zur Hand zu nehmen" (Sido, *Interview* 2004).

(Übertreibung) und *diss* (Herabsetzung) gehören. Wie der *amicus brief* in *State v. Skinner* ausführt, gilt dies tatsächlich auch für Lyrics im Gangsta-Rap:

> The intention of the narrator of the [rap, HJL] yarn is to tell outrageous stories that stretch and shatter credibility, overblown accounts about characters expressed in superlatives […]. [B]y definition the traditional yarn is always […] one outrageous lie after another. („Brief" 2013, 9)

Für Gates (2011) machen die spezifischen Praktiken des Zitats und des Sampling[41] Rap Lyrics zudem zum Paradigma postmoderner Lyrik: „Rap is the postmodern version of an African American vernacular tradition" (xxv); „rap is signifying in a postmodern way" (xxii).[42]

Aufgrund der starken intertextuellen Ausrichtung an amerikanischen Vorbildern ist die „Stimme der Straße" im Rap als glokales Phänomen eine im doppelten Sinne geliehene Stimme: Sie ist erstens die Stimme einer stereotypen Rollenfigur. Zweitens ist die Stimme des glokalen Rap, der sich anders als der amerikanische Gangsta-Rap nicht auf ein „eigenes Ursprungsnarrativ" beziehen kann, eine Stimme, die im Rahmen einer kulturellen Appropriation erst geliehen und „zur Sprache gebracht" werden muss (Dietrich & Seeliger 2013, 113). Ich weise an anderer Stelle zudem nach, dass der glokale Gansta-Rap des 21. Jahrhunderts in einem tendenziell sogar postfaktischen Zeitalter verwurzelt ist, aber gleichzeitig als hochgradig intertextuelle Rollenlyrik verstanden werden muss, die dieselben Narrative in stets neuer Form abarbeitet, womit das Genre als Formkunst mehr mit mittelalterlicher Lyrik gemein hat, als mit der Ausdruckspoesie der Neuzeit (Lind 2022a).

Das Verständnis von Gangsta-Rap als Rollenlyrik wurde tatsächlich bereits früh von Rappern vorgebracht. Die erste Detroiter Crew von Marshall Bruce Mathers III (aka Eminem) nannte sich „D12" (Dirty Dozen), weil jedes Mitglied der sechsköpfigen Gruppe jeweils noch eine literarische Persona mitbrachte. Der deutsche Rapper Lukas Strobel (aka Alligatoah) bezieht sich ebenfalls auf diese Tradition, wenn er ausführt: „Alligatoah ist ja eine fiktive Band, die aus zwei Terroristen besteht, die in mir wohnen und die habe ich auch verkörpert. […] Jetzt spiele ich andere Rollen" (Splash!Mag 2012). Der deutsche Rapper Anis Mohamed Youssef Ferchichi (aka Bushido) versuchte, sich vor dem Bundesverwaltungsgericht sogar mittels eines Gutachtens von seiner literarischen Persona „Sonny Black" zu distanzieren. In dem Gutachten heißt es, Ferchichi „habe in den Texten mit verschiedenen Stilmitteln eine Kunstwelt […] geschaffen, die keinen Bezug zu seiner Person aufweise" (BVerwG 2019, Rn. 5).

Wie wenig im Gangsta-Rap als hochkommerzielles Genre Autor und Rollenfigur heute noch miteinander zu tun haben, zeigt allein schon ein Blick auf

41 „Rap's signature characteristics is the parody and pastiche of its lyrics, including ‚sampling,' which is just another word for intertextuality" (Gates 2011, xxiv).

42 Wobei „signifying" als „the language games of black language games" bezeichnet wird (Gates 2011, xxiii).

die Biografien der bekanntesten Gangsta-Rapper des 21. Jahrhunderts (Seeliger 2019; Lind 2022a). Nicht nur in den USA und dem UK prahlen Straßenrapper gerne mit ihren Vorstrafen und Konflikten mit der Polizei, sondern auch in Deutschland. Straffällige Gangsta-Rapper wie Haftbefehl und Gzuz sind hier aber allenfalls kleine Fische – und machen daraus durchaus kein Geheimnis. Der Rapper Aykut Anhan (aka Haftbefehl), der laut seiner Texte 82 Morde begangen haben will (*Musikexpress* 2016), gibt offen zu, „nie jemanden ernstlich verletzt zu haben" (Spiegel 2014, 131). Auf die Diskrepanz angesprochen, die zwischen seinem Privatleben und seinen Texten besteht, spricht Anhan von einer „bewusst gewählten Ästhetik". Er erklärt weiter: „Das ist HipHop, eine Kultur mit eigenen Codes" (133). Kristoffer Jonas Klauß (aka Gzuz) von *187 Straßenbande* formuliert ebenfalls auffallend ehrlich: „Wenn ich darüber rappe, wenn ich meine Tochter ins Bett bringe, verkauft sich das eben nicht so gut" (ProSieben 2018). Auch in den USA ist Gangsta-Rap längst ein höchstkommerzialisiertes Feld, wobei hier von den Plattenlabeln tatsächlich auch Druck dahingehend ausgeübt wird, Rapper zum Wechsel in dieses gewinnträchtige Genre zu bewegen (Cubrin 2014, 190). Auch dort sind sich die Künstler darüber im Klaren, dass Gangsta-Rap ein kommerzielles Konsumprodukt darstellt, welches eine entsprechende „pretence" erfordert. Der aufgrund seiner Texte wegen Mordes angeklagte und erstinstanzlich auch verurteilte Antwain Steward (aka Twain Gotti) erklärte so in einem Interview: „I just found something that I'm talented at and found a way to make money off of it. [...] [L]ike it or not, gangsta rap is what sells" (PBS Newshour 2014).

Der fiktionale Charakter des Rap, der spätestens im 21. Jahrhundert mit der Kommerzialisierung des Gangsta-Rap zur Regel geworden ist, bestand aber schon bei der Urform des Rap, dem in der Bronx geborenen East Coast Rap. Denn hier hatte diese performative Sozialform gerade auch die Funktion, die Gewalt von der Realwelt auf die Bühne zu heben: Anstelle mittels echter Gewalt konnten sich die Protagonisten in verbalen Rap-Battles stellvertretend auf der Bühne bewähren,[43] womit das so oft unter dem Verdacht, kriminelle Einstellungen zu verbreiten und zu fördern stehende Genre in Wirklichkeit Menschleben rettete. Ferchichi reflektiert für den Deutschrap jüngst Ähnliches in autobiografischen, an seine Kinder gerichteten Lyrics:

> Der Papa ist ein ganz guter Rapper, der heißt Bushido [...]
> Doch weil Papa in sein'n Liedern böse Sachen sagt
> Denkt die ganze Nachbarschaft, dass er auch böse Sachen macht
> Aber Papa sagt die Sachen, die er sagt
> Nur damit er nicht mehr tun muss, was Papa früher tat. (Bushido, *Papa* 2017)

[43] In der Forschung oft als individuelles Empowerment verstanden, siehe dazu Lind (2022a).

Nichtsdestotrotz ist es ein globales Phänomen, dass von Ämtern, Strafverfolgungsbehörden und Gerichten immer wieder Autor und literarische Person kurzgeschlossen oder Rap-Texte als lebensweltlich unmittelbar referenzialisierbare Erlebnislyrik verstanden werden – auch wenn diese Praxis bereits höchstinstanzlich ausdrücklich kritisiert wurde:

> [W]e are not persuaded by the opinions of courts in other jurisdictions that view rap music lyrics ‚not as art but as ordinary speech' and have allowed their admission in evidence as literal statements of fact. (*Commonwealth v. Gray*, 2012)[44]

United States v. Foster (1991) zeigt bereits eine frühe Variante einer problematischen Praxis, die in *State v. Hanson* etablierten Prinzipien einer Trennung von Autor und Figur zu umgehen, indem fiktionale Texte zumindest als Beweis für Fachwissen hinsichtlich krimineller Praktiken herangezogen wurden, welches wiederum als „evidence for knowledge and intention" hinsichtlich einer konkreten Straftat dienen kann (§ 46). In *United States v. Foster* (1993) wurden die Lyrics „Key for Key, Pound for pound / I'm the biggest Dope Dealer and I serve all over town / Rock 4 Rock Self 4 Self" dann auch als Beweismittel zugelassen. Das Berufungsgericht führt hierzu aus:

> [State v.] Hanson underscores the need to recall that the rap verse was not admitted to show that Foster was, in fact, „the biggest dope dealer"; it was not admitted to establish that Foster was the character portrayed in the lyrics. But in writing about this „fictional" character, Foster exhibited knowledge of an activity that is far from fictional. He exhibited some knowledge of narcotics trafficking, and in particular drug code words. It was for this limited purpose that the verse was admitted, and it is for this limited purpose that its relevance is clear. (§ 55)

Auch wenn die Verurteilung in Sachen Foster im Hinblick auf die erdrückende Beweislage sicherlich gerechtfertigt war, ist zumindest diese Passage des Urteils höchst problematisch. Was Foster hier zum Vorwurf gemacht wird, ist allein, dass er, wie vermutlich alle Jugendlichen aus prekären Vierteln und wie mittlerweile sicherlich sogar der Großteil von Jugendlichen gutbürgerlicher Herkunft, die regelmäßig Rap Texte produzieren oder rezipieren, die „Sprache der Straße" sprach und verstand. Folgt man der Argumentation von *United States v. Foster*, reicht es, kurz gesagt, aus, sich im intertextuellen literarischen Spiel des Gangsta-Rap kompetent zu betätigen, wobei bereits literarisches Wissen kriminalisiert wird. Wie begehrt solche prozessualen Kunstgriffe heute noch sind, zeigt die äußerst ähnliche Argumentation in *United States v. Moore* (2011).

---

44 Der *Court of Appeal* nimmt diese Argumentation auf, wenn er ausführt: „Absent some meaningful method to determine which lyrics represent real versus made up events, or some persuasive basis to construe specific lyrics literally, the probative value of lyrics as evidence of their literal truth is minimal" (*People v. Coneal*, 2019).

3. *Bedrohliche oder bedrohende Texte?*

Problematisch ist zudem ebenfalls eine Gerichtspraxis, die von den USA ihren Ausgang genommen und nunmehr auch Europa erreicht hat. Gemeint ist das Verständnis von Rap-Texten und damit von Literaturproduktion als eigene Straftat. Einst die Domäne der *obscenity trials*, stehen heute bei diesen eine veritable Kriminalisierung von Literaturproduktion bedeutenden Verfahren die Bedrohung, Beleidigung oder Verleumdung realer Personen im Zentrum. Rap Lyrics werden hier aufgrund ihrer genretypischen Eigenheit (Dominanz von Gewaltnarrativen, Herabsetzung und Bedrohung als performative Praktiken des Diss) öfter missverstanden als andere Literaturformen. Das eigentliche Problem dieser Gerichtsverfahren ist dabei ebenfalls eine Verkennung der Natur dieses literarischen Genres, wobei hier nunmehr zwei Varianten der Fehlbeurteilung zu unterscheiden sind. Die erste Variante betrifft die vermeintliche Bedrohung oder Herabsetzung eines unbestimmten Personenkreises, die zweite die Herabsetzung oder Bedrohung namentlich konkretisierter Personen.

Zur ersten Variante gehören die Fälle *People v. Oduwole* (2013), *Jones v. State* (2002) und, in Teilen, AG Tiergarten 2013 (*NWA*). Im Fall Olutosin Oduwoles wurde ein im Auto gefundener Sechszeiler eines Studenten, der laut *expert witness testimony* lediglich „formative stages of a rap song" darstellte, vom erstinstanzlichen Gericht als „terrorist threat" gewertet.[45] Im Falle Blake Jones wurde einer von mehreren Rap Lyrics, die der Angeklagte regelmäßig mit einer Schulfreundin austauschte und die einen namentlich unbestimmten Sprecher („I") sowie einen namentlich unbestimmten Adressaten hatten („you"), als Bedrohung („true threat") verstanden.

Narratologisch gesehen liegt der Fehler in solchen Fällen darin, reale und fiktive Kommunikationssituation zu verwechseln: Statt ein Kommunikationsverhältnis zwischen Rollenfigur und fiktiver Person bzw. einem fiktiven Personenkreis anzunehmen, wurden die Texte als direkte Kommunikation zwischen Autor und einem realen Personenkreis gelesen. Der Fehler lässt sich nicht nur mit einem narratologischen Fiktionalitätskriterium[46] beschreiben, sondern auch sprachhandlungstheoretisch: Ein fiktionaler Sprechakt wurde in diesen Fällen von den Strafverfolgungsbehörden fälschlicherweise als faktual verstanden. Ob man dabei fiktionale Sprechakte in der Tradition John Searles nur als „pretence" begreift (Searle 1975, 325; Beardsley 1978, 169–170), oder aber bei fiktionalen Sprechakten von Sprechakten sui generis ausgeht (Wolterstorff

[45] Die Verurteilung wurde vom Berufungsgericht aufgehoben. Das Gericht sah aber in der Behandlung der Lyrics als faktual keinen Fehler. Grund für den Freispruch war vielmehr, dass laut Berufungsgericht die Schwelle von der straflosen Vorbereitungshandlung zum strafbaren Versuch noch nicht überschritten worden war.

[46] Fiktionalität verstanden als Dissoziation von Autor und Erzähler/Sprecher: Hamburger (1957); Kayser (1958); Genette (1993); Cohn (1990; 1999).

1981, 332; Currie 1985, 385–387), ist dabei unbeachtlich: In jedem Fall hätte das Gericht eine tatsächliche Bedrohung („true threat") verneinen können.[47]

Komplexer sind die Fälle der zweiten Variante, da diese sich eher schlecht mit einem narratologischen Kriterium fassen lassen. So hatte das Landgericht Köln die Verurteilung eines Teilnehmers einer Battle-Rap-Veranstaltung bestätigt, weil dieser seine Kontrahentin verbal herabgesetzt hatte (LG Köln 2010). Eine Analyse der Sprecherpositionen allein hilft in dieser Fallgruppe tatsächlich nicht weiter: Der verurteilte Teilnehmer nahm keineswegs eine andere Rolle ein und Adressat der verbalen Herabsetzungen war unstrittig besagte Kontrahentin.[48] Eine sprachhandlungstheoretische Betrachtung hätte hier indes eine Lösung geboten: Wie die im Battle-Rap üblichen Gewaltdrohungen sind in diesem Genre Beleidigungen nicht nur genretypisch, die entsprechenden Sprechakte sind vielmehr fiktional. Ob man dabei die vorliegenden Sprechakte nur als „pretended" begreift, oder aber bei fiktionalen Sprechakten von Sprechakten sui generis ausgeht, führt wie schon bei der ersten Variante zu ein und demselben Ergebnis: In jedem Fall hätte das Gericht bereits das Vorliegen einer Beleidigung (qua Rechtsgutsverletzung) verneinen können. Zumindest das Amtsgericht Tiergarten verneinte drei Jahre später eine strafbare Bedrohung im Rahmen eines Disstracks in Searle'scher Manier mit der durchaus zutreffenden Begründung, dass solche Äußerungen in der Regel nicht „ernsthaft" seien (AG 2013, 906).

Gemein ist beiden Varianten dabei, dass der neuralgische Punkt die Frage ist, aus welchem Horizont der illokutionäre Status der Aussage zu bewerten ist. Auch hier ist die mögliche Spanne weit und reicht von subjektiven Äußerungs- oder aber Empfängerhorizonten bis hin zu objektiven Bestimmungsversuchen.[49] Damit wird auch in den gerichtlichen Entscheidungen eine Spanne geboten, die jener Debatte in der Fiktionalitätstheorie ähnelt, ob Fiktionalität eine objektivierbare Frage des Textes, der Intention des Textproduzenten oder lediglich eine Rezeptionsweise und damit eine Rezipientenhaltung ist.[50] Es scheint dabei in Rechtskreisen zumindest dahingehend Einigkeit zu bestehen, dass eine rein textsemantische Analyse nicht ausreicht, sondern vielmehr der

[47] Im Falle Oduwole wurde die Verurteilung ebenfalls vom Berufungsgericht aufgehoben. Auch hier wurde nicht auf die Fiktionalität der Lyrics abgestellt, vielmehr auf die fehlende Konkretisierung eines tatsächlichen Empfängers: „Finally, there is no evidence from which to find or infer that the defendant had identified a particular audience for his communications" (*People v. Oduwole* 2013, § 49).

[48] Man hätte einzig den Einwand erheben können, dass tatsächlich „für" das Publikum gesprochen wurde – was aber eher den perlokutionären Zweck der Äußerung betrifft. Und es mag auch Battle-Rap geben, in dem die Teilnehmer als Rollenfigur agieren (siehe dazu auch den nachfolgenden Abschnitt 4. „Problematische Kontinuitäten II").

[49] Siehe *United States v. Elonis* (2016), III A.; BGH (2009, 253); BVerfG (1971, 1648); BVerfG (2007, 41); BVerwG (2019, Rn. 34).

[50] Siehe Lind (2020a, 32, 53 Fn. 300).

pragmatische Kontext mit zu berücksichtigen ist.[51] Gerichte nehmen dabei regelmäßig eine „verständige Durchschnittsperson" als Maßstab, wobei bei Beleidigung hinzukommen soll, dass eine solche vom tatsächlichen Empfänger zudem als Herabsetzung „empfunden" wird (Fischer 2020, § 185 StGB, Rn. 14). Bei Zivilverfahren wegen Verletzung des Persönlichkeitsrechts ist die Lage indes komplexer. Hier wird, wie ich an anderem Ort ausführe (Lind 2022b), teils ein Sonderkreis an Rezipienten als Maßstab genommen,[52] der sogar in Analogie zu Carsons Evokation eines unverständigen Leserkreises[53] ein vielleicht gar nicht intendierter oder zumindest nicht allgemeiner Persönlichkeitskreis ist – was sogar ausdrücklich Fehllektüren wie die faktuale Lektüre von textintern oder paratextuell als fiktional markierten Texten mit einschließen kann (VG Köln 2006, Rn. 26; BVerfG 2007, 43–44). Ähnliches kann aus Gründen des Jugendschutzes gelten.[54]

Die Komplexität des Problems und die Schwierigkeiten der Gerichte, Rap als literarische Praxis dogmatisch richtig zu fassen, zeigt auch ein Fall, der tatsächlich unter beide Varianten subsumierbar ist. In dem verfahrensgegenständlichen Text holten die Angeklagten Michael Schindler (aka Shindy) und Anis Mohamed Ferchichi (aka Bushido) gleich zu einem Rundumschlag aus:

> Halt die Fresse, fick die Presse, Kay, du Bastard bist jetzt vogelfrei
> Du wirst in Berlin in deinen Arsch gefickt wie Wowereit
> Fick die Polizei, LKA, BKA
> Meine Jungs verticken Elektronik so wie Media Markt
> Jeden Tag im Fadenkreuz, ich zeig dir, wie der Hase läuft
> Arabisch-deutsche Sippe und ich jage euch, ihr Partyboys
> Du versteckst dich, doch ich finde dich wie Google Maps
> Ich verkloppe blonde Opfer so wie Oli Pocher [...]
> Und ich will, dass Serkan Tören jetzt ins Gras beißt,
> Was für Vollmacht, du Schwuchtel wirst gefoltert
> Ich schieß' auf Claudia Roth und sie kriegt Löcher wie ein Golfplatz.

Während die Medien sogleich von einer Straftat ausgingen („Aufruf zu Gewalt" (Stern 2013), „Aufruf zum Mord" (Rottmann 2013)) und unter anderem Klaus

---

[51] „[...] [S]o darf nicht verkannt werden, dass dieses sich vornehmlich an Jugendliche und junge Erwachsene richtende Lied sich einer Sprache bedient und bedienen muss, die vom Empfängerhorizont verstanden wird und den dementsprechenden Sprachcode verwendet" LG Berlin (2014), 904. Vgl. auch Fischer (2020), StGB § 185, Rn. 17.

[52] „[E]ngere Bekanntenkreis" (BGH 2009, 253); „nicht unbedeutender Leserkreis" (BVerfG 1971, 1648; BVerfG 2007, 41).

[53] „Carson: An illiterate person reading *Dorian Gray* might consider it a sodomitical book?" (Holland 2004, 80).

[54] Die Figur des „gefährdungsgeneigten", d.h. eines ‚labilen' Lesers, (BVerwG 2019, Rn. 34), vom dem eine mögliche Fiktionalität bzw. eine eventuell vorliegende „ironische ‚Brechung' des Geschilderten [...] nicht verstanden" wird (VG Köln 2006, Rn. 22), geht explizit von der Möglichkeit von konventionswidrigen (Fehl-)Lektüren aus. Gleiches gilt für die Ausführungen des BGH (1968, 1777) zu Lesern, die Gattungsbezeichnung oder distanzierendes Vorwort ignorieren.

Wowereit Anzeige wegen Beleidigung erstattete, die Behörden zudem wegen Volksverhetzung ermittelten, zeigten das Amtsgericht Tiergarten und das Landgericht Berlin als mit dem Vorgang befasste Gerichte ein klares Bewusstsein, dass der Text zwar geschmacklos, aber durchaus genretypisch ist und deshalb vermutlich keine Verurteilung rechtfertigt. Die Begründung der Entscheidung erweist sich indes als ein Potpourri verschiedenster Theorieansätze, die teils durchaus reflektiert, teils aber auch etwas unbeholfen angewandt werden. Eine Beleidigung von Wowereit und Serkan Tören verneint bereits das Amtsgericht mit dem Argument, dass Wowereit nicht Adressat der Äußerungen gewesen sei (AG Tiergarten 2013, 906). Die Realperson Kenneth Glöckler (aka Kay One) sieht das Gericht indes eindeutig als Adressat der Lyrics (906). Besonders problematisch erscheinen für das Gericht dabei die an den Letzteren gerichteten und zudem homophoben Lanzen des Textes. Anstelle die Frage des Vorliegens eines fiktionalen Sprechaktes zu stellen, behilft sich das Gericht hier damit, eine Beleidigung durch einen Kunstgriff zu verneinen: Der Passus „Du wirst in den Arsch gefickt wie Wowereit / […] Du Schwuchtel wirst gefoltert" sowie die Referenzen auf die im Rap als durchgehend herabwürdigend verstandene Homosexualität („Männer lutschen keine Schwänze") sucht das Gericht mit dem fragwürdigen Argument zu banalisieren, dass Homosexualität an sich kein Makel sei, womit die „Reduzierung" eines Menschen auf seine Homosexualität und deren Praktiken nicht „den Tatbestand der Beleidigung" erfülle (906). Dies widerspricht aber bereits der einleitenden Bemerkung des Gerichts, dass zur Ermittlung des „Sinns" einer Aussage „der gesamte Kontext, in dem sie gefallen ist", zu beachten ist (904) und nach dem „Sprachcode" des Rap der Vorwurf von Homosexualität und deren Praktiken unzweifelhaft als herabsetzend verstanden wird. Gerettet hat hier das Gericht in Teilen, dass zumindest für die Verfolgung einer Beleidigung[55] des heterosexuellen Glöcklers („Du Schwuchtel", etc.) ein Strafantrag fehlte (904). Die auch ohne Strafantrag verfolgbaren tätlichen Bedrohungen mehrerer Beteiligter wurden dann aber durchaus zutreffend mit dem mangelnden „Eindruck der Ernstlichkeit" der Äußerungen verneint (906), wobei leider illokutionärer Status und perlokutionärer Zweck des Sprechaktes nicht ausreichend klar voneinander getrennt werden. Denn diese Feststellung soll laut Gericht gerade auch für die Bedrohung des Kenneth Glöckler gelten, da es sich bei solchen Herabsetzungen lediglich „um eine genretypische Erscheinung handelt, bei der wechselnde Allianzen und Feindschaften durchaus auch als Instrument der Bekanntheitssteigerung und Vermarktung der eigenen Produkte eingesetzt und genutzt werden" (906). An anderer Stelle wird dann zudem die Überzeugung geäußert, dass im Rap das

[55] „Angesichts dessen ist auszuschließen, dass sich die Textpassage ‚[…] Du Schwuchtel wirst gefoltert' auf den früheren Bundestagsabgeordneten Tören bezieht. Vielmehr wird an dieser Stelle die Beleidigung und Bedrohung des durchgehend angesprochenen „X" [d.h. Kenneth Glöckler, HJL] fortgesetzt" (AG Tiergarten 2013, 906).

„Beleidigen, Diffamieren und auch Bedrohen anderer Rapper" tatsächlich ein „Stilmittel"[56] sei (905) – was in der technisch ebenfalls unklaren Formulierung einer neueren Entscheidung des Landgerichts München nachhallt, dass solche Beleidigungen im Rap „Teil der Kunstform" seien (LG 2019).

Das Landgericht Berlin als nächsthöhere Instanz erkennt zwar ebenfalls, dass ein Disstrack bei „Jugendlichen und jungen Erwachenden" als „Empfängerhorizont" aufgrund eines abweichenden „Sprachcodes" möglicherweise einen anderen Sinn hat (LG Berlin 2014, 904) – was es dem Gericht ermöglicht hätte, die Frage zu stellen, ob hier nicht die Angriffe lediglich fingiert wurden. Das Gericht fügt dann aber stattdessen das wenig differenzierende Argument hinzu, dass bei der Passage „Kay, du Bastard bist jetzt vogelfrei, / du wirst in den Arsch gefickt wie Wowereit" für den „Empfänger" die „Bedeutung" nicht „zwingend auf dem Vergleich", sondern möglicherweise stattdessen „auf dem Reimwort" läge (904) – womit eine hermeneutische Betrachtungsweise des Gerichts den Schritt zu einer narrativen oder gar sprachhandlungstheoretischen Lösung verhindert.

Das Amtsgericht hatte sich hier ebenfalls bereits mit einem hermeneutischen Argument beholfen: Dass nämlich nur dann eine Strafbarkeit gegeben sei, wenn keine Lesart möglich ist, die eine Rechtsgutsverletzung ausschließt (AG Tiergarten 2013, 904–905)[57] – womit zumindest der Polysemie von Literatur in angemessener Weise Rechnung getragen wurde. Das Gericht fügt als Argument zudem hinzu, dass die „Intention" offensichtlich die „Provokation" des Kenneth Glöckler sei, und nicht „Volksverhetzung, Beleidigung oder ähnliches" (LG Berlin 2014, 904), womit, wenn auch nicht der illokutionäre Status der Äußerung, so doch zumindest einer der perlokutionären Zwecke richtig erkannt wurde.[58]

Die Entscheidungen der beiden Gerichte stehen zudem im Widerspruch zu einer Fülle von Verurteilungen von Rappern wegen herabsetzender Inhalte im Deutschrap. Die Verurteilung wegen antisemitischen Inhalten im Rap ist etwa bereits weit fortgeschritten, wobei neben Volksverhetzung oft auch der Tatbestand einer Kollektivbeleidigung erfüllt ist,[59] und die Zahl an Verurteilungen von Rechtsrappern wegen ihrer Texte in dieser Fallgruppe ist bereits durchaus beachtlich (Lind 2021). Zudem wurden bereits 2008 mehrere Rapper aus dem Genre des Horror-Rap wegen Lyrics, in denen die namentlich

[56] Zum Begriff des „Stilmittels" siehe BVerwG (2019, Rn. 38) mit weiteren Nachweisen auf die Rechtsprechung u.a. des Bundesverfassungsgerichts (*Mutzenbacher*, etc.).

[57] Was der ständigen Rechtsprechung des Bundesverfassungsgerichtes entspricht.

[58] Dass Feindschaften im Rap oft lediglich medienwirksam inszeniert und damit vielleicht sogar nur fingiert werden (unter dem perlokutionären Zweck der Bekanntheitssteigerung und Gewinnerzielungsabsicht), spricht das Gericht aber nicht an.

[59] Holocaustleugnung etwa wird nämlich nach der ständigen Rechtsprechung gleichzeitig als Kollektivbeleidigung begriffen: als „Beleidigung aller Juden" (Fischer 2020, Vorb. § 185–200 StGB, Rn. 10).

genannte Politikerin Monika Griefahn (vermeintlich) bedroht wurde, tatsächlich auch verurteilt. Die Medien sprachen hier, wie im Falle Schindlers und Ferchichis, von „Anstiftung zum Mord" (Tagesspiegel 2008). Auch die Rapper Felix Blume (aka Kollegah) und Nuhsan Coskun (aka Jigzah) wurden noch 2019 wegen eines Rap Tracks,[60] in welchem die Töchter von Unternehmer und Reality-TV-Darsteller Robert Geiss lyrisch bedroht wurden, erfolgreich gerichtlich zur Rechenschaft gezogen (Heitmeier 2021). Auch das Landgericht München bejahte jüngst eine Rechtsgutsverletzung bei verbalen Herabsetzungen im Rahmen eines Disstracks (LG München I 2019). Das Bundesverwaltungsgericht hat schließlich jüngst entschieden, dass Ferchichi in seinem Album „Sonny Black" keineswegs „beabsichtigt hat, die Demütigung und Herabwürdigung von Frauen und Homosexuellen als Stilmittel in ein Konzept ‚Inszenierung des Gangsterbosses B[ushido]' einzubetten" (BVerwG 2019, Rn. 65) – eine Argumentation, die sich durchaus auf den im Jahr 2013 vor dem Amtsgericht Tiergarten streitgegenständlichen Text von Ferchichi und Schindler übertragen ließe.

Das Landgericht München I scheint[61] in oben bereits zitierter Entscheidung (LG München I 2019) das Problem von Beleidigungen innerhalb eines Disstracks zudem überhaupt nicht über die Frage des illokutionären Status der Äußerung zu lösen, sondern über die Rechtswidrigkeit der Verletzung.[62] Damit entspricht es einer vertretbaren Position, die mit Rap als Genre institutionalisierte Praxis des Diss (wie den Battle-Rap insgesamt) eher als Boxkampf zu begreifen, bei dem es zu einem tatsächlich Rechtsgüter verletzenden verbalen „Schlagabtausch" kommt (VG Köln, Rn. 22)[63] und nicht als *Wrestling* (Catchen), d.h. als einen bloßen Schaukampf, in dem Rechtsgutsverletzungen nur vorgetäuscht werden. Aber auch diese, erstmals im Rahmen des Verfahrens vor dem Kölner Verwaltungsgericht von der Bundesprüfstelle zur Sprache gebrachten Position scheint insoweit Probleme mit der dogmatischen Einordnung zu haben, als das Problem des illokutionären Status des Sprechaktes (bzw. das narratologische Pendant einer möglicherweise doppelten Kommunikationssituation) zwar durchaus erkannt wurde, die Entscheidung der Frage der Fiktionalität

---

60 Kollegah & Jigzah, *Medusablick* (2018).

61 Das Urteil ist (bisher) nicht veröffentlicht, es stehen mir daher nur Pressemitteilungen zur Verfügung (z.B. LTO (2019)), die zwar ausgewertet werden können, eine genaue Beurteilung gerade der dogmatischen Begründung der Entscheidung aber nur bedingt zulassen.

62 So wäre dann auch erklärbar, dass eine Beleidigung der Kinder Ferchichis durch den Disstrack bejaht werden konnte, gleichzeitig aber hinsichtlich der Eltern mit der Begründung verneint, dass diese selbst verbal ausgeteilt hatten. Das zivilrechtliche Verfahren (wegen Persönlichkeitsrechtsverletzung) unterscheidet sich vom Strafverfahren dabei primär im Hinblick auf den Vorsatz (Intention), wie der BGH (2009) äußerst anschaulich darlegt. Es gibt aber Besonderheiten bei der Bestimmung des Schutzbereichs.

63 Was zudem erlaubt, Rappern selbst in der Lebenswelt ein verbales „Recht auf Gegenschlag" (Fischer 2020, § 193 StGB, Rn. 21) zuzuerkennen.

aber in einer etwas unbeholfenen Parataxe offengelassen wird. Man liest dort nämlich, dass es im Battle-Rap um „das Niedermachen eines realen oder imaginären Gegners/Konkurrenten" gehe (Rn. 22).

4. Problematische Kontinuitäten II: Rolle als Realität

Die gerichtliche Behandlung von Battle-Rap und Disstracks zeigt nicht nur das prozessrechtliche Scheitern eines narrativen Fiktionalitätskriteriums, vielmehr werden hier auch die Probleme eines sprachhandlungstheoretischen Verständnisses offenbar. Der neuralgische Punkt ist hier das Authentizitätspostulat des Rap. Gerade im Gangsta-Rap des 21. Jahrhunderts fallen Rolle und Realität immer auffälliger auseinander, wobei diese Diskrepanz von der Fangemeinde keineswegs als Widerspruch wahrgenommen wird: Auch wenn die gerade im Gangsta-Rap behaupteten Straftaten (allen voran Morde) kaum ernst genommen werden, scheint ein Konsens darüber zu bestehen, dass die Rapper dennoch „real" bzw. „echt" sind. Authentizität wird dabei nicht nur in den Texten selbst behauptet. Vielmehr gehört es mit zum genretypischen Diss, anderen Rappern *realness* abzusprechen.

Der Grund einer Vereinbarkeit solcher Widersprüche liegt darin, dass Rap zumindest im 21. Jahrhundert als besondere Ausformung einer performativen Kultur begriffen werden muss. Realness ist in der glokalen Kultur des Rap nämlich lediglich eine „Inszenierungsstrategie"; als „Herstellungspraxis" besteht sie in einer lediglich performativen Bestätigung des tradierten Normenkodex (Klein & Friedrich 2003, 9). Authentisch bzw. real ist im Rap folglich nicht, was wahr ist, sondern vielmehr, was „glaubhaft in Szene gesetzt wird" (9). Dieses Problem eines abweichenden, genrespezifischen Authentizitätsbegriffs gesellt sich zu der ohnehin schon bestehenden theoretischen Frage, ob Lyrik als solche überhaupt fiktional sein kann (Kablitz 2008).

Für Gerichte ist dabei besonders problematisch, dass die Performance in der Rapkultur am Bühnenrand nicht aufhört und sich damit die Probleme des Authentizitätsanspruchs weiter in der Lebenswelt fortsetzen. In den USA wurde dies schon früh bemerkt. Der *amicus curiae brief* in *United States v. Elonis* (2015) vergleicht Rapper äußerst zutreffend mit Catchern, „that stay in character even after they have left the stage" („Amicus Brief" 2014, 14) – und bezieht sich damit auf ein Charakteristikum der Rapkultur, welches Tricia Rose (2008) als „[r]ap's pretence of no pretence" bezeichnet hat: „[T]hey act *as if* they live the life they rap about". In der Forschung wird die Persona im Rap deshalb auch als „soziale Rolle im Sinne Goffmans" begriffen (Wolbring 2015, 172). Hinsichtlich Disstracks wird dabei von einem „Dreiklang" gesprochen: „Diss-Rap, zugehöriges Musikvideo – und eine Fortsetzung des Streits auf Instagram und Co." In Wirklichkeit handele es sich nämlich „um die Auseinandersetzung zweier Kunstfiguren in einem Song, durch die dritte Social-Media-Ebene aber findet dieser künstliche und künstlerische Streit dann den Weg in die Realität" (Kleiner 2019).

Dieses Charakteristikum einer steten Vermischung beider Ebenen ist auch dafür verantwortlich, dass in ein und demselben Text Realname und Pseudonym abwechseln können, das Sprecher-Ich sich, wie in den verfahrensgegenständlichen Texten Ferchichis, textintern gleichzeitig als Musiker bzw. Produzent im Rap-Business inszeniert, wie als Gangster.[64] Für Rap als hochkommerzialisiertes Genre ist zudem bedeutsam, dass der Ambivalenz hinsichtlich des Verhältnisses von Autor und Persona im Gangsta-Rap eine besondere wirkungsästhetische Funktion zukommt. Denn „die Inkarnation des Transgressiven kann ihre volle Wirkungsmacht nur entfalten, wenn Rolle und Person nicht klar abgrenzbar sind". Erforderlich soll hierzu eine Darstellung sein, bei der „Rollenmuster, Drohgesten und dem ideologischen Konsens zuwiderlaufende Elemente nicht auf eine ‚uneigentliche', d.h. metaphorische Lesart reduziert werden können und ein rein referenziell-realistisches Verständnis sich gleichwohl ebenfalls ausschließt, ohne dass das Ganze als reine Stilübung erscheint" (Sokol 2007, zitiert nach Wolbring 2015, 173).

Dieses bewusst ambivalent gehaltene Authentizitätspostulat des Rap stellt aus rechtlicher Perspektive nicht nur ein Problem dar, wenn es darum geht, Texte als referenziell zu behandeln und damit als Beweismittel zuzulassen, oder aber die Texte selbst als strafbewehrte Äußerungen zu verstehen (*true treat*, etc.). Wie konfliktträchtig solche Vermischungen von Rolle und Realität vielmehr sind, zeigt sich gerade im Hinblick auf Anklagen von Rappern wegen ihres Verhaltens in sozialen Netzwerken sowie in der alltäglichen Lebenswelt. Auch wenn bei den Gerichten ein Bewusstsein dafür zu bestehen scheint, dass Rapper auch in der Realwelt Feindschaften lediglich medienwirksam inszenieren („Selbstinszenierung", OVG NRW 2015) wurden diese wiederholt wegen Beleidigung und Bedrohung verurteilt (u.a. LG Berlin 2011). Der jüngste Fall ist hier die Verurteilung des Rappers Patrick Losenský (aka Fler). Im März 2021 wegen Bedrohung und Beleidigung von Polizisten und Journalisten zu zehn Monaten Haft auf Bewährung sowie einer Geldstrafe von 10.000 Euro verurteilt, rechtfertigte der Rapper vor Gericht seine Taten wie folgt: „Für mich ist es künstlerische Freiheit, dass ich mich verhalte, wie sich ein Rapper verhält". Seinen Verteidiger ließ er ausführen: „Er ist auch eine Kunstfigur, das ist seine Rolle" (Idowa 2021). Bereits 2019 war Losenský wegen einer Beleidigung in Rap Lyrics verurteilt worden.

Die für den Rap typische Vermischung von Rolle und Realität, die Gerichten eine Beurteilung erschwert, ist dabei nicht nur ein Problem der Rapkultur im Besonderen, die als Kultur der aktiven Aneignung sogar zu einer Vermischung

---

[64] Siehe etwa zu Ferchichi: *Stress ohne Grund* (2013), *Fotzen* (2014), *Leben und Tod des Kenneth Glöckler* (2017).

von Rolle und Realität zwingt (Gruber 2017, 67 m.w.N.), sondern vielmehr von performativen Szenekulturen im Allgemeinen – und eine Konsequenz der allgemeinen Tatsache, dass Identitäten kommunikativ bzw. medial hergestellt werden (Reckwitz 2008, 135–148; Kron & Horacek 2009). Gerade marginalisierte Gesellschaftsschichten und -szenen sind im Rahmen individuellen wie kollektiven Empowerments auf solche Praktiken besonders angewiesen; Rolle und Realität werden hier oft ununterscheidbar (Lind 2022a).

Wie viele Verurteilungen im UK und den USA zeigen, machen letztere Fälle tatsächlich sogar die Mehrzahl der Verurteilungen aus. Gerade der Nachweis von Bandenmitgliedschaft von gänzlich unbekannten Rappern mittels Lyrics hat sich in den Vereinigten Staaten und dem Vereinigten Königreich zu einer veritablen Prozesspraxis entwickelt und wurde von Verbänden durchaus berechtigt kritisiert (Justice 2021, 40). Denn die Inszenierung vieler Jugendlicher in Rap-Texten, sozialen Netzwerken und sogar der Realwelt als Rapper, Gangsta und Bandenmitglied ist oft nicht mehr als „pretence“ und „puffery“ im Rahmen alltäglicher Prozesse jugendlicher Identitätsbildung. Was von den Gerichten als kriminelle „Gang“ begriffen wurde, würden wir außerhalb der Rapkultur eher als Clique bezeichnen (Justice 2021, 10, 32). Dass von Jugendlichen gerade die Rollenmuster der Rapkultur übernommen werden, lässt sich mit der Einsicht der Subjektstheorie erklären, dass die Ausbildung des Selbst nur in sozialen Umgebungen möglich ist, als „Reflexion in sozialen Kontexten“ (Kron & Horacek 2009, 22–23). Rap bietet als performative Kultur dabei sowohl im Rahmen verbalen als auch im Rahmen nonverbalen kommunikativen Handelns (Sprachcode, Kleidung, Verhaltensweisen) äußerst attraktive „szenespezifische Ausdrucksmöglichkeiten für die Inszenierung der eigenen Identität“ (Gruber 2017, 67). Hinzu kommt, dass der Gangsta mit seinen „Attributen von Hypermaskulinität, Authentizität, Wettbewerbsorientierung und Ghettobezug“ gerade auch als Medium des Empowerments eine attraktive Identitätsfigur ist, weil er „wie kaum eine andere Rolle Souveränität verkörpert“ (Wolbring 2018, 4).

Damit soll nicht behauptet sein, dass die performativen Praktiken des Rap in der Lebenswelt nicht auch dazu führen können, dass Jugendliche dazu gezwungen werden, dem von ihnen inszenierten Bild zu entsprechen – und in Konsequenz auch tatsächlich straffällig werden.[65] Die Teilnahme an den sozialperformativen Praktiken des Rap rechtfertigt für sich allein aber den besagten, in Gerichtsprozessen oft zu beobachtenden Kurzschluss eindeutig nicht, weshalb selbst die gängige Prozesspraxis, Texte, die vor einer tatsächlich gesche-

[65] Es lassen sich vielmehr tatsächlich Fälle nachweisen, in denen den Worten Taten folgten, siehe Wolbring (2015, 495) sowie Lind (2020b, 129). Siehe auch BPJM (2015, 20).

henen Tat verfasst wurden, beweisrechtlich als „proof of knowledge, motive or intent“[66] zu nutzen, äußerst kritisch beurteilt werden sollte.

5. *Alter Wein in neuen Schläuchen? Zwei „Grundsatzurteile“*

Es ist nicht überraschend, dass in Anbetracht der problematischen Natur solcher Verurteilungen gerade auch von Bürgerrechtsverbänden eine höchstrichterliche Klärung der gerichtlichen Verhandlung von Literatur im 21. Jahrhundert sehnsüchtig erwartet wurde. Mit *State v. Skinner* und dem *Esra*-Beschluss des Bundesverfassungsgerichts liegen nunmehr zwei höchstrichterliche Entscheidungen vor, die sich dezidiert mit der Frage der Justiziabilität von fiktionaler Literatur befassen, wobei es sich in beiden Fällen um literarische Werke handelte, die die Grenze von Realität und Fiktion bewusst verflüssigten. Beide Entscheidungen enttäuschen indes insoweit in ein und derselben Hinsicht, als in beiden Entscheidungen der Grad der Ähnlichkeit von lebensweltlichem Geschehen und fiktionaler Darstellung de facto zum Entscheidungskriterium wurde.

State v. Skinner liest sich zwar zunächst insoweit als äußerst vielversprechend, als die Entscheidung mit einer Vielfalt von Vorurteilen hinsichtlich des Verhältnisses von Literatur und Lebenswelt aufräumt. Zum zu vermeidenden Fehler einer lebensweltlich referentialisierenden Lektüre von fiktionalen Texten führt das Gericht etwa äußerst zutreffend aus:

> One would not presume that Bob Marley, who wrote the well-known song „I Shot the Sheriff," actually shot a sheriff, or that Edgar Allan Poe buried a man beneath his floorboards, as depicted in his short story „The Tell-Tale Heart.“ (*State v. Skinner* 2014, 251)

Das Gericht formuliert zudem als Ergebnis:

> Fictional forms of inflammatory self-expression such as poems, musical compositions, and other writings about bad acts, wrongful acts, or crimes, are not properly evidential. (239)

Schließlich bezieht sich das Gericht zudem auf das in *State v. Hanson* etablierte Prinzip, dass man aus dem Inhalt eines literarischen Werkes nicht auf den Charakter des Autors schließen sollte.[67]

Für obige Prozesspraxis, Rap-Texte als Beweismittel für den Charakter des Verfassers zuzulassen, ist die Entscheidung aber in einer Hinsicht äußerst problematisch: Das Gericht bestätigt ausdrücklich die geltende Rechtsprechung,

---

66 State v. Skinner (2014, 246, 252). Vgl. auch US v. Foster (1991); State v. Evans (2001); Joynes v. State (2002); State v. Villados (2011); Holmes v. State (2013); People v. Minnifield (2014); State v. Lewis (2016); State v. Garlington (2020).

67 „[...] [T]he proposition that an author's character can be determined by the type of book that he writes“ (State v. Skinner 2014, 253).

dass literarische Texte als Beweis für den *bad character* des Angeklagten statthaft sein können, nunmehr aber mit der maßgeblichen Einschränkung, dass das Kriterium eines „starken Nexus“ zwischen Text und Tat erfüllt sein muss (239, 252). Da die Entscheidung nahelegt, dass ein solcher Nexus bereits vorliegt, wenn „substantial similarity with the alleged crime“ gegeben ist,[68] hat damit über die Hintertür der Referenzgedanke de facto wieder Eingang in das Beweisverfahren gefunden: Eine unmittelbar lebensweltlich referenzialisierende Lektüre ist für fiktionale Texte im Beweisverfahren zwar weiterhin ausgeschlossen, literarische Texte wirken sich aber als *character evidence* dann negativ für das Verfahren aus, wenn eine beträchtliche Ähnlichkeit zwischen Tat und literarischer Darstellung besteht. Was zu der paradoxen Situation führt, dass die Referenzfrage zwar ausdrücklich verabschiedet wurde, um dann aber sofort wieder in neuem Kleid zu erscheinen. *United States v. SB 12 13* (2015), eine Entscheidung, die sich auf *State v. Skinner* bezieht und die Entscheidung ausdrücklich bestätigt, hat Rap Lyrics dann im konkreten Fall auch als Beweismittel zugelassen.

State v. Skinner ähnelt in dieser Hinsicht der viel diskutierten Entscheidung des Bundesverfassungsgerichts zu Maxim Billers autofiktionalem Roman *Esra*, der Gegenstand des wohl pressewirksamsten Romanverbotsverfahren im 21. Jahrhundert war. In der *Esra*-Entscheidung musste der erkennende Senat darüber entscheiden, ob ein autofiktionaler Roman Persönlichkeitsrechte Dritter verletzen kann, und hat dies auch bejaht. Zwar ist der Beschluss insoweit richtig, als das Gericht eine im Ergebnis angemessene Abwägung zwischen dem allgemeinen Persönlichkeitsrecht von in dem Roman potentiell dargestellten realen Personen auf der einen Seite und der Kunstfreiheit des Autors auf der anderen getroffen hat. Zudem ist die Entscheidung insoweit auch richtungsweisend, als erstmalig in Deutschland eine höchstrichterliche Vermutung für die Fiktionalität von Romanen als literarische Werke eingeführt wurde – womit, wie bei *State v. Skinner*, berechtigt Hoffnung auf eine maßgebliche Änderung der Gerichtspraxis im Hinblick auf die Verhandlung literarischer Werke bestand. Wie ich an anderer Stelle ausführe (Lind 2022b; Lind 2023), ist die *Esra*-Entscheidung indes in einem unscheinbaren, äußerst unglücklich formulierten Passus höchst problematisch: Sie erhebt die Ähnlichkeit von Lebenswelt und fiktionaler Darstellung nicht nur durchaus zutreffend zu einem der rechtlich zu berücksichtigenden Faktoren im Rahmen der Interessenabwägung zwischen Persönlichkeitsrecht und Kunstfreiheit, sondern macht diese möglicherweise sogleich zum Kriterium eines graduell verstandenen Fiktionalitätsbegriffs[69] –

[68] Abschnitt III A. der Entscheidung sowie die im Abschnitt III B. genannten Beispiele (einschließlich der Verweise auf *Greene v. Commonwealth* und *Bryant v. State*, der das Kriterium des „strong nexus“ entnommen ist) zeigen, dass eine „substantial similarity with the alleged crime“ (State v. Skinner 2014, 252) als ausreichend anzusehen ist.

[69] „Je stärker der Autor eine Romanfigur von ihrem Urbild löst und zu einer Kunstfigur verselbständigt (‚verfremdet‘ […]), umso mehr wird ihm eine kunstspezifische Betrach-

womit weder sprachhandlungstheoretische noch narratologische Kriterien bei der gerichtlichen Bestimmung der Fiktionalität eines Werkes zum eigentlichen Kriterium werden. Im Ergebnis folgt der *Esra*-Beschluss des Bundesverfassungsgerichts im Hinblick auf das Fiktionalitätskriterium damit der Einschätzung des *Esra*-Urteils des Bundesgerichtshofs (BGH 2005), nach dem eine erhebliche Ähnlichkeit zwischen „Urbild" und „Abbild" zur „Aufkündigung" des Fiktionsvertrages führen soll.[70] Damit hat aber auch im *Esra*-Beschluss des Bundesverfassungsgerichts der Referenzgedanke zumindest über die Hintertür erneut Eingang gefunden. Hinzu kommt, dass im Esra-Beschluss an einer Stelle vorschnell Autor und Erzähler kurzgeschlossen werden,[71] es zudem als Faktualitätssignal gewertet wird, wenn „aus der Perspektive des Romans eigenes Erleben des Ich-Erzählers geschildert wird" (BVerfG 2007, 43).

Während sich die *Esra*-Entscheidung im Hinblick auf die Fiktionalitätsvermutung bereits klar in den Entscheidungen der Judikative fortschreibt,[72] ist bisher nur schwer ablesbar, ob und wie sich das eher beiläufig formulierte Fiktionalitätskriterium auf die Entscheidungen der Strafgerichte in den für diesen Beitrag skizzierten Falltypen auswirken wird. Ich hoffe aber, dass es sich bei der missglückten Fiktionalitätsdefinition eher um einen folgenlosen Lapsus handelt – denn es ging, wie ich an anderer Stelle darlege (Lind 2023), bei der viel gerügten „je-desto"-Formel der Entscheidung tatsächlich gar nicht um die Formulierung eines Fiktionalitätskriteriums. Sollte dies indes geschehen, dann wäre die Lage im Ergebnis nicht anders als in *State v. Skinner*: Bereits eine quantitativ erhebliche Ähnlichkeit von Realität und literarischem Text würde dann ausreichen, um Autoren literarischer Texte in alter Manier zu belangen.

Die Bundesprüfstelle argumentierte jüngst in dieser Manier, wenn sie ausführt, die literarische Persona „‚B[ushido]' sei keine fiktive Figur, weil die geschilderten Erlebnisse zum Teil deutliche Bezüge zum Leben des Klägers aufwiesen".[73] Das Bundesverwaltungsgericht hat diese Feststellungen im Rah-

tung zugutekommen. Dabei geht es bei solcher Fiktionalisierung [sic!] nicht notwendig um die völlige Beseitigung der Erkennbarkeit, sondern darum, dass dem Leser deutlich gemacht wird, dass er nicht von der Faktizität des Erzählten ausgehen soll. […] Je stärker Abbild und Urbild übereinstimmen, desto schwerer wiegt die Beeinträchtigung des Persönlichkeitsrechts" (BVerfG 2007, 42).

70 „Wer wie im Streitfall als Schriftsteller Personen in einer Weise erkennbar macht, daß sich Romanfiguren einer real existierenden Person eindeutig zuordnen lassen, kündigt die Übereinstimmung zwischen Autor und Leser auf, daß es sich beim literarischen Werk um Fiktion handelt" (BGH 2005, 2847-2848).

71 „[….] Figur der Lale […], weil der Autor [nicht Erzähler, sic!] sie anders als Esra ganz überwiegend nicht aus eigenem Erleben schildert" (BVerfG 2007, 43).

72 Zu den Nachwirkungen der Entscheidung siehe auch Raue (2009) sowie Bülow (2013).

73 Die Entscheidung ist nur in Auszügen veröffentlicht. Obiges Zitat ist in dem mir vorliegenden Bescheid interessanterweise nicht enthalten, wird aber vom Bundesverwaltungsgericht in indirekter Rede wiedergegeben (BVerwG 2019, Rn. 3).

men seiner Entscheidung übernommen (BVerwG 2019, Rn. 1, 64–66),[74] wobei das Gericht analog der Carson'schen Prämissen autorenschaftlicher *pose* bzw. einem *putting forward views* argumentiert, wenn es die Frage, welche „Botschaft" die Texte „vermitteln" (BVerwG 2019, Rn. 67), dahingehend entscheidet, dass durch das Werk „eine bejahende Tendenz gegenüber Straftaten zum Ausdruck gebracht wird" (BVerwG 2019, Rn. 31). Zu eigen gemacht hat sich das Gericht zudem die Ansicht, dass die literarische Figur „B..." in diesen Texten „erkennbar als alter ego des Klägers [d.h. Ferchichi, HJL] auftritt" (BVerwG 2019, Rn. 68).

Zitierte Literatur

Algarín, Miguel (1994) „The Sidewalk of High Art." *Aloud: Voices from the Nuyorican Poets Café.* Hg. ders. und Bob Holman. New York: Henry Holt.

„Amicus Curiae Brief of the American Civil Liberties Union in Support of Petitioner. (2014) The Supreme Court of the United States. Anthony Douglas Elonis v. United States" – No. 13-983 –.

Androutsopoulos, Jannis, Hg. (2003) *HipHop: globale Kultur – lokale Praktiken.* Bielefeld: transcript.

Beardsley, Monroe (1978) „Aesthetic Intentions and Fictive Illocutions." *What is Literature?* Hg. Paul Hernadi. Bloomington: Indiana Univ. Press. 161–177.

Bleier, Evan (2014) „Rap Lyrics Used to Convict South Carolina Man of Murder at Olive Garden." *United Press International.* 20. Februar 2014. Web. 09. November 2021.

Bramwell, Richard (2015) *UK Hip-Hop, Grime and the City. The Aesthetics and Ethics of London's Rap Scenes.* London/New York: Routledge.

„Brief of Amicus Curiae of the American Civil Liberties Union of New Jersey in Support of Defendant-Respondent (2013) Criminal Action State of New Jersey, Plaintiff-Appellant v. Vonte L. Skinner, Defendant-Respondent. The Supreme Court of New Jersey." A-57/58-12 (071764).

Bülow, Karoline (2013) *Persönlichkeitsrechtsverletzungen durch künstlerische Werke.* Berlin: Duncker & Humblot.

Cohn, Dorrit (1990) „Signposts of Fictionality. A Narratological Perspective." *Poetics* 11.4: 775–804.

Cohn, Dorrit (1999) *The Distinction of Fiction.* Baltimore and London: Johns Hopkins Univ. Press.

Cubrin, Charis (2014) „Rap on Trial." *Race and Justice* 4: 185–211.

[74] Beurteilungen des Zwölfergremiums der Bundesprüfstelle werden als Sachverständigengutachten behandelt, siehe BVerwG (1992).

Currie, Gregory (1985) „What is Fiction?" *Journal of Aesthetics and Art Criticism* 43.4: 385–392.

Daily Mail (2013) „Rapper Charged with Homicide after allegedly Bragging about unsolved Double Murder in his Song." 31. Juli 2013. Web. 09. November 2021.

Daily Press (2013) „Newport News Rapper Charged in Killings." 10. Oktober 2013. Web. 09. November 2021.

Dennis, Andrea (2007) „Poetic (In)Justice? Rap Music Lyrics as Art, Life, and Criminal Evidence." *Columbia Journal of Law and the Arts* 31: 1–42.

Dietrich, Mark und Martin Seeliger (2013) „Rap als ambivalente Subjektskultur." *Psychologie und Gesellschaft* 37: 113–135.

Eleveld, Mark (2003) (Hg.) *Slam, Hip Hop & The Poetry of a New Generation.* Chicago: Sourcebooks MediaFusion.

Emson, Raymond (2017) *Evidence*. 5. Aufl. London: Macmillan Education UK.

Fischer, Thomas (2020) *Strafgesetzbuch und Nebengesetze*. München: C.H. Beck.

Gates, Henry Louis jr. (1988) *The Signifying Monkey. A Theory of African-American Literary Criticism*. Oxford: Oxford Univ. Press.

Gates, Henry Louis jr. (2011) „Foreword." *The Anthology of Rap.* Hg. Adam Bradley und Andrew DuBois. New Haven: Yale Univ. Press. xxii–xxvii.

Genette, Gerard (1993) *Fiction and Diction*. Übers. Catherine Porter. Ithaca: Cornell Univ. Press.

Grove, Rashad (2021) „24 Rap Songs That Address Mental Health & Depression." Web. 09. November 2021. Https://www.okayplayer.com/music/rap-songs-that-address-mental-health-depression.html.

Gruber, Johannes (2017) *Performative Lyrik und lyrische Performance: Profilbildung im deutschen Rap.* Bielefeld: transcript.

Hamburger, Käte (1957) *Die Logik der Dichtung*. Stuttgart: Klett.

Heitmeier, Kevin (2021) „Verfahren gegen Kollegah nach Zahlung von 100.000 € Schmerzensgeld erledigt." *Lhr-Law Magazin*. 07. Juni 2021. Web. 09. November 2021. Https://www.lhr-law.de/magazin/medienrecht-und-persoenlichkeitsrecht/verfahren-gegen-kollegah-nach-zahlung-von-schmerzensgeld-erledigt/.

Holland, Merlin (2004) (Hg.) *The Real Trial of Oscar Wilde*. New York: Harper Collins.

Holman, Bob (1994) „Congratulations. You have found the Hidden Book. An Invocation." *Aloud: Voices from the Nuyorican Poets Café.* Hg. Miguel Algarín und ders. New York: Henry Holt.

Hyde, H. Montgomery (1987) (Hg.) *The Trials of Oscar Wilde. Regina (Wilde) v. Queensberry. Regina v. Wilde and Taylor*. Aldershot: Gregg Publishing.

Idowa (2021) „Urteil: Rapper Fler bekommt Bewährungsstrafe.“ *Idowa online*. 03. März 2021. Web. 09. November 2021. Https://www.idowa.de/inhalt.urteil-rapper-fler-bekommt-bewaehrungsstrafe.34d49221-420a-4223-8ca4-d9285cac24cd.html.

Jackson, Alan (2004) *Prosecuting Gang Cases. What Local Prosecutors Need to Know*. Alexandria: American Prosecutors Research Institute. Web. 09. November 2021. Https://www.nationalpublicsafetypartnership.org/clearinghouse/Resource/467.

Justice (2021) *Tackling Racial Injustice: Children and the Youth Justice System. A Report.* Web. 09. November 2021. Https://justice.org.uk/wp-content/uploads/flipbook/46/book.html.

Kablitz, Andreas (2008) „Literatur, Fiktion und Erzähler nebst einem Nachruf auf den Erzähler.“ *Im Zeichen der Fiktion. Aspekte fiktionaler Rede aus historischer und systematischer Sicht. Festschrift für Klaus W. Hempfer zum 65. Geburtstag*. Hg. Irina Rajewski und Ulrike Schneider. Stuttgart: Franz Steiner Verlag. 13–44.

Kayser, Wolfgang (1958) „Wer erzählt den Roman?“ *Die Vortragsreise. Studien zur Literatur*. Hg. Wolfgang Kayser. Bern: Francke. 82–101.

Klein, Gabriele und Malte Friedrich (2003) (Hg.) *Is this real? Die Kultur des HipHop*. Frankfurt a. M.: Suhrkamp.

Kleiner, Marcus (2019) „Gericht zum Rapper-Streit Bushido/Fler: Kinder sind tabu. Marcus S. Kleiner im Gespräch mit Hannes Stepputat und Britta Schultejans.“ Auszüge aus: *Die Welt Online*. 11. Dezember 2019. Web. 09. November 2021. Https://medienkulturanalyse.de/wp/2019/12/11/die-welt-gericht-zum-rapper-streit-bushido-fler-kinder-sind-tabu/.

Kron, Thomas und Martin Horacek (2009) *Individualisierung*. Bielefeld: transcript.

Lind, Hans (2020a) „Theorizing fictional discourse: Toward a Reassessment of the Fact–Fiction Dichotomy in Legal Theory and Practice.“ *Fictional Discourse and the Law*. Hg. ders. Abingdon/New York: Routledge. 1–64.

Lind, Hans (2020b) „Rap on Trial.“ *Fictional Discourse and the Law*. Hg. ders. Abingdon/New York: Routledge. 124–137.

Lind, Hans (2021) „Keeping it real: Zu den rechtlichen Problemen literarisch inszenierter Authentizität.“ *Rap: Politisch. Rechts? Ästhetische Konservatismen im Deutschrap*. Hg. Nicolai Busch und Heidi Süß. Weinheim: Beltz Juventa. 163–190.

Lind, Hans (2022a) ",Ich bin die Stimme von der Straße‘: Zum didaktischen Potential von Rap-Texten als Form der Gegenwartslyrik.“ *Literatur im Unterricht. Texte der Gegenwartsliteratur für die Schule*. Hg. Jan Standke. Trier: Wissenschaftlicher Verlag (im Erscheinen).

Lind, Hans (2022b) ",Quod licet Iovi, non licet bovi?‘ Zu den Gesetzen der Fiktion in Literatur und Recht.“ *Lizensur fiktionaler Literatur.* Hg. Eric Achermann, Daniel Arjomand und Nursan Celik. Stuttgart: Metzler (im Erscheinen).

Lind, Hans (2023) „Zensur und Fiktion [Arbeitstitel].“ *Zensur. Handbuch für Wissenschaft und Studium.* Hg. Nicola Roßbach. Baden-Baden: Nomos. Preprint über ssrn.com erhältlich.

Linden, Amy (1997) „Rap Screen Savers.“ *Billboard.* 22. November 1997. 46–50.

Linder, Douglas (1995a) (Hg.) „Closing Speech for the Prosecution by Solicitor-General Frank Lockwood.“ *The Criminal Trials of Oscar Wilde.* Web. 09. November 2021. Http://law2.umkc.edu/faculty/projects/ftrials/wilde/prosecclose.html.

Linder, Douglas (1995b) (Hg.) „Testimony of Oscar Wilde.“ *The Criminal Trials of Oscar Wilde.* Web. 09. November 2021.

Lock, Joan (1980) *Marlborough Street. The Story of a London Court.* London: Robert Hale Ltd.

LTO (2019) „Bei Kindern hört das Dissen auf.“ *Legal Tribune Online.* 11. Dezember 2019. Web. 09. November 2021.

Lyddane, Donald (2006) „Understanding Gangs and Gang Mentality: Acquiring Evidence of Gang Conspiracy.“ *United States Attorney's Bulletin* 54.3: 1–64.

„MOTION FOR LEAVE TO FILE BRIEF AS AMICI CURIAE AND BRIEF OF AMICI CURIAE MICHAEL RENDER („KILLER MIKE“), ERIK NIELSON, AND OTHER ARTISTS AND SCHOLARS IN SUPPORT OF PETITIONER No. 18–949 IN THE Supreme Court of the United States JAMAL KNOX, Petitioner, v. COMMONWEALTH OF PENNSYLVANIA, Respondent“ (2019).

Musikexpress (2016). November 2016. Web. 09. November 2021. https://www.musikexpress.de/wp-content/uploads/zeitung/musikexpress/ATvzN7mxpcBgb/index.html#/1.

New York Times (2014) „Prosecutors Hear Evidence in Songs.“ 26. März 2014. Web. 09. November 2021.

Nielson, Erik (2020) „Prosecutors are increasingly – and misleadingly – using Rap Lyrics as Evidence in Court.“ *The Conversation.* 17. März 2020. Web. 09. November 2021. Https://theconversation.com/prosecutors-are-increasingly-and-misleadingly-using-rap-lyrics-as-evidence-in-court-131440.

Nielson, Erik and Andrea Dennis (2019) *Rap on Trial: Race, Lyrics, and Guilt in America.* New York: The New Press.

PBS Newshour (2014) 29. Juni 2014. Web. 09. November 2021. Https://www.pbs.org/newshour/show/rap-lyrics-used-evidence-court.

Peters, Erskine (1990) *Fundamentals of Essay Writing.* Oakland: Regent Press.

ProSieben (2018) „Gzuz: Emotionales Interview! 187-Rapper enthüllt private Details." 16. Mai 2018. Web. 09. November 2021. Https://www.prosieben.de/stars/video/gzuz-emotionales-interview-187-rapper-enthuellt-private-details-clip.

Quinn, Eithne (2005) *Nuthin' but a „G" Thang: The Culture and Commerce of Gangsta Rap.* New York: Columbia Univ. Press.

Raue, Peter (2009) „Kunstfreiheit, Persönlichkeitsrecht und das Gebot der praktischen Konkordanz. Gedanken zum Esra-Urteil des Bundesverfassungsgerichts und dem Contergan-Fall." *AfP* 40.1: 1–6.

Reckwitz, Andreas (2008) *Subjekt*. Bielefeld: transcript.

Reilly, Charlie (1994) (Hg.) *Conversations with Amiri Baraka*. Jackson: Mississippi Univ. Press.

Rose, Tricia (2008) *The Hip Hop Wars: What We Talk About When We Talk About Hip Hop – And Why It Matters*. New York: Basic Civitas.

Rottmann, Kerstin (2013) „Aufruf zum Mord: Staatsanwalt prüft Hass-Song von Shindy & Bushido." *Die Welt Online*. 13. Juli 2013. Web. 09. November 2021.

RTC (2020) „16 Bars: Die Währung im Rap. https://rap-text.com/16-bars. Web. 09. November 2021.

Searle, John (1975) „The Logical Status of Fictional Discourse." *New Literary History* 6.2: 319–332.

Seeliger, Martin (2019) „Autobiografien deutscher Gangstarapper im Vergleich." *Verhandelte Globalisierung*. Hg. ders. Cham: Springer. 129–152.

Spiegel, der (2014) „‚Es geht um nichts. Um Scheiß.' Der Gangsta-Rapper Haftbefehl erzählt vom Leben in Deutschlands Problemvierteln." *Der Spiegel* 50: 130–133.

Splash!Mag (2012). Web. 09. November 2021. Www.youtube.com/watch?v=eMIpwVW4FhM&list=HL1349963052&feature=mh_lolz.

Stern, der (2013) „Bushido bestreitet Aufruf zur Gewalt." *Stern Online.* 15. Juli 2013. Web. 09. November 2021.

Sturm, Jan Felix (2018) „Gesetzeskraft und Bindungswirkung von Entscheidungen des Bundesverfassungsgerichts." *JA* 7: 682–694.

Tagesspiegel (2008) „Anstiftung zum Mord." *Tagesspiegel online*. 11. Juni 2008. Web. 09. November 2021.

Von Ammon, Frieder und Dirk von Petersdorff (2019) „Einleitung." *Lyrik/Lyrics. Songtexte als Gegenstand der Literaturwissenschaft.* Hg. dies. Göttingen: Wallstein.

Wacker, Julian (2019) „Grime Poetry: Black British Rap Lyric(s) in the Twenty-First Century.“ *Poem Unlimited: New Perspectives on Poetry and Genre*. Hg. David Kerler und Timo Müller. Berlin/Boston: De Gruyter.

Wilde, Oscar (1890) *Dorian Gray*. London: Ward, Lock and Co.

Wolbring, Fabian (2015) *Die Poetik des deutschsprachigen Rap*. Göttingen: V&R unipress.

Wolbring, Fabian (2018) ",Ich bin mehr Gangster als mein Gangster-Image.‘ Zum Verhältnis von Gangsta-Rap und Kriminalität.“ *BPB*. 23. Februar 2018. Web. 09. November 2021. Https://www.bpb.de/apuz/265106/gangsta-rap-und-kriminalitaet.

Wolterstorff, Nicholas (1981) „Response to Beardsley on ‚Fiction as Representation.‘" *Synthese* 46.3: 174–189.

Urteilsverzeichnis

AG Tiergarten (2013) Beschluss des Amtsgerichts. 19. November 2013 – (279 Ds) 222 Js 1201/13 (101/13) = ZUM 2015, 904.

Bell v. Itawamba Country School Board (2015) 799 F.3d 379 (5th Cir.).

BGH (1968) Urteil des Bundesgerichtshofs. 20. März 1968 – I ZR 44/66 = NJW 1968, 1773BGH (2005) Urteil des Bundesgerichtshofs. 21. Juni 2005 – VI ZR 122/04 = NJW 2005, 2844.

BGH (2009) Urteil des Bundesgerichtshofs. 24. November 2009 – VI ZR 219/08 = ZUM 2010, 251BPJM (2015) Entscheidung der Bundesprüfstelle für jugendgefährdende Medien Nr. 6055. 09. April 2015. *Bundesanzeiger* AT: 30. April 2015.

BVerfG (1971) Beschluss des Ersten Senats des Bundesverfassungsgerichts. 24. Februar 1971 („Mephisto“) – 1 BvR 435/68 = NJW 1971, 1645.BVerfG (1984) Beschluss des Ersten Senats des Bundesverfassungsgerichts. 17. Juli 1984 („Anachronistischer Zug“) – 1 BvR 816/82 = BVerfGE 67, 213.

BVerfG (2007) Beschluss des Ersten Senats des Bundesverfassungsgerichts. 13. Juni 2007 („Esra“) – 1 BvR 1783/05 = NJW 2008, 39.

BVerwG (1992) Urteil des Bundesverwaltungsgerichts. 26. November 1992 – 7 C 20/92 = NVwZ 1993, 675.

BVerwG (2019) Beschluss des Bundesverwaltungsgerichts. 04. November 2019 – 6 C 18.18 = BVerwGE 167, 33.

Commonwealth v. Lamory Gray (2012) 978 N.E. 2d 543 (463 Mass. 731).

Greene v. Commonwealth (2006) No. 2004-SC-00046-MR (197 S.W.3d 76).

Jones v. State (2002) 347 Ark. 409 (64 S.W.3d 728).

Joynes v. State (2002) 797 A.2d 673, 677 (Del.).

Holmes v. State (2013) 129 Nev. Adv. Op. 59 (Nev.).

Knox v. Commenwealth (2019) 139 S. Ct. 1547.

LG Berlin (2011) Urteil des Landgerichts. 15. November 2011 – 27 O 393/11 = ZUM-RD 2012, 94.

LG Berlin (2014) Beschluss des Landgerichts. 04. März 2014 – 512 Qs 69/13 = ZUM 2015, 903.

LG Köln (2010) Urteil des Landgerichts. 14. Juli 2010 – 28 O 857/09 = BeckRS 2010, 19920.

LG München I (2019) Urteil des Landgerichts. 11. Dezember 2019 – 25 O 16530/19.

Luke Records, Inc. v. Navarro (1992) 960 F.2d 134.

Miller v. California (1973) 413 U.S. 15.

OVG NRW (2015) Beschluss des Oberverwaltungsgerichts. 03. Juni 2015 – 19 B 463/14 = ZUM 2015, 913.

People v. Coneal (2019) A152529 (Cal. Ct. App.).

People v. Minnifield (2014) Ill. App. 113778 (Ill. App. Ct.).

People v. Oduwole (2013) Ill. App. 5th 120039 (985 N.E.2d 316).

People v. Lee (2011) 51 Cal. 4th 620 (Cal.).

Pope v. Illinois (1987) 481.U.S. 497.

Redmond-Bate v. Director of Public Prosecutions (1999) EWHC Admin 733.

Regina v. Junior Simpson & Anor (2019) EWCA Crim 1144.

Regina v. Mucktar Khan (2018) EWCA Crim 2893.

Regina v. Zafran Akhtar Saleem (2007) EWCA Crim 1923.

Snyder v. Phelps (2011) 562 U.S. 443 (131 S. Ct. 1207), 179 L.Ed.2d 172.

State v. Garlington (2020) No. P1-2017-0542 A&B (R.I. Super.).

State v. Hanson (1987) 731 P.2d 1140 (46 Wash. App. 656).

State v. Evans (2001) 01AP-594 (Ohio Ct. App.).

State v. Lewis (2016) 195 So. 3d 1206 (La.).

State v. Villados (2011) NO. 30442 (Haw. Ct. App.).

Street v. New York (1969) 394 U.S. 576 (89 S.Ct. 1354), 22 L.Ed.2d 572.

State v. Skinner (2014) 218 N.J. 496 (N.J.).

United States v. Belfast (2010) 611 F.3d 783 (11th Cir.).

United States v. Elonis (2016) 12-3798 (3d Cir.).

United States v. Foster (1991) 939 F.2d 445 (7th Cir.).

United States v. Foster (1993) 986 F.2d 541 (D.C. Cir.).

United States v. Giese (1979) 597 F.2d 1170 (9th Cir.).

United States v. McCrea (1978) 583 F.2d 1083 (9th Cir.).

United States v. Moore (2011) 639 F.3d 443 (8th Cir.).

United States v. SB 12 13 (2015) 785 F.3d 832 (2d Cir.).

United States v. Wilson (2010) 07-1320 (2d Cir.).

VG Köln (2006) Urteil des Verwaltungsgerichts. 17. Februar 2006 – 27 K 6557/05 = NJOZ 2006, 3565.

Abkürzungsverzeichnis

AG	Amtsgericht
AHRC	Arts and Humanities Research Council
BeckRS	Beck'sche Rechtsprechungssammlung
BGBl	Bundesgesetzblatt
BGH	Bundesgerichtshof
BGHZ	Entscheidungen des Bundesgerichtshofs in Zivilsachen
BPJM	Bundesprüfstelle für jugendgefährdende Medien
BVerfG	Bundesverfassungsgericht
BVerfGE	Entscheidungen des Bundesverfassungsgerichts
BVerwG	Bundesverwaltungsgericht
BVerwGE	Entscheidungen des Bundesverwaltungsgerichts
BvR	Aktenzeichen einer Verfassungsbeschwerde zum Bundesverfassungsgericht
Cal. Ct. App.	California Courts of Appeal
EWCA Crim	England and Wales Court of Appeal (Criminal Division)
EWHC Admin	England and Wales High Court (Administrative Court)
F.2d	Second series of the Federal Reporter
F.3d	Third series of the Federal Reporter
GRUR	Gewerblicher Rechtsschutz und Urheberrecht
L.Ed.2d	United States Supreme Court Reports, Lawyers' Edition
LTO	Legal Tribune Online
N.E. 2d	North Eastern Reporter Second
NJOZ	Neue Juristische Online-Zeitschrift
NJW	Neue Juristische Wochenschrift
StGB	Strafgesetzbuch (deutsches) in der Fassung der Bekanntmachung vom 13. November 1998 (BGBl. I, 3322), das zuletzt durch Artikel 3 des Gesetzes vom 8. Oktober 2021 (BGBl. I, 4650) geändert worden ist
S.W.3d	South Western Reporter Third
U.S.	United States Supreme Court

ZUM	Zeitschrift für Urheber- und Medienrecht
ZUM-RD	Zeitschrift für Urheber- und Medienrecht – Rechtsprechungsdienst

The Criminal Charge: A Narratological Bow Tie?

Jeanne Gaakeer

No practice of law takes place in the absence of stories.
(Elkins 2019, 5)

1. *Telling a Better Story*

The rise of narrative jurisprudence and, before it, the "turn to interpretation" in law have traditionally been contrasted with the idea of objectivity in law cherished in legal positivism (Elkins 1985,134–135). In the second half of the twentieth century, legal and literary scholarship refuted the kindred notion that language is a neutral vehicle and argued that the articulation of reality by linguistic means presupposes a process of contextual, selective interpretation. This contextual approach to interpretation is not without its pitfalls. From an epistemological point of view, there are some narratological issues to consider.

Firstly, the judge in her function as a reader-narrator describes not only the world as she finds it, in the file and the narratives of those involved, and/but this is also the world on which she will pronounce judgment. Secondly, law, and especially criminal law, constitutes its own referential world in that the criminal charge offers a legal translation of a pre-legal reality of events and actions. Interdisciplinary, narratological research is thus faced with the question whether or not these issues imply a return to the long obsolete descriptive approach to language. This pivotal problem was pointed out already in the 1980s by the criminal law professor 't Hart (1983).

The first issue highlights why law and legal studies belong to the humanities. The second issue urges us to consider the problem of referentiality from the perspective of legal narratology, and to do so more carefully than has been done to date. It is along these lines that I develop my argument in what follows – to offer yet another interdisciplinary intersection between law and the humanities and not to provide an avenue of escape from legal theory and doctrine.

The written criminal charge provides guidelines for the various narratives that make up a criminal case. The defendant's story as well as the narratives produced by the legal professionals involved are thus framed: "trials always function through a framework of storytelling" (Ferguson 1996, 84–85). The metaphor in the title of this article, the 'narratological bow tie', suggests that procedures of the law are subject to a process of knotting and tying in a to-and-fro movement. Firstly, legal storytelling is a progress from diversity to unity. The stories in the pre-trial stage, namely those by the defendant, the victim, the witness, and the police on 'what happened', come to form a unity on account of the criminal charge with its normative, textual specification of what constitutes a criminal offence. There is therefore a movement from the left side of the bow tie to the 'knot' in the middle. Then, secondly, at the trial stage, there is a reverse shift from the unity of the 'knot' (which corresponds to the charge) to diversity. Based on the criminal charge, a multiplicity of narratives and arguments is brought forward in court, and these constitute the right side of the (first) bow tie. Finally, in the judicial decision, there is once again a return to unity, if only for the moment, figured in the 'knot' of yet another, the second, bow tie. This process, although not an infinite regress (the proceedings must come to an end in the foreseeable future: *lites finiri oportet* 'legal disputes must come to an end') is repeated in appeal and cassation and, in some cases, before a supranational court. Because the plot thickens in the hierarchy of courts, legal narratology matters (Chestek 2008).

Depending on the legal system and the jurisdiction, the wording of the criminal charge may or may not undergo changes during the pre-trial and the trial stages, in the lower court as much as in the appeal. In the Netherlands, for example, the public prosecutor is *dominus litis*, i.e. the 'master of the dispute' who decides to bring a charge and who decides on the text of the charge and on any amendment deemed necessary during the trial stage. If such an amendment is brought forward, the first question that the judge asks herself is: does this affect the scope and content of 'the fact' as delineated in the original charge? If a charge of murder is amended with the subsidiary charge of manslaughter, this is certainly not the case because manslaughter is the lesser charge. Yet if a charge of 'fencing,' i.e. of intentionally handling illegally obtained goods, is amended to a theft, the judge might very well answer in the affirmative. Why? Because the human act behind the two charges is different, and so are the actual punitive consequences. Even if the statutory norm provides a comparable punishment, the protected societal interests encapsulated in the statutory norm differ. As a result, the punishment meted out for theft will usually be higher, at least in the Netherlands. Such an amendment will of course meet with resistance from the defense. Contrariwise, if there is something wrong with the final wording of the charge (e.g. when the name of the city in which the crime presumedly took place is incorrect) nothing can be done by the judge if the prosecutor fails to amend the charge during trial, and she must acquit. The same applies when the public prosecutor makes a mistake as far as the choice of the offence or the form of participation are concerned (e.g. introducing the role of joint author where there is evidence only for the role of accomplice).

In other European countries, the judge is allowed more freedom. Evidently, if more changes can be made to the text of the charge during the proceedings, then this poses more problems for the defense. If the defendant has told her story to the police in her own words, truthfully from her perspective, then this poses the question whether or not it fulfills its function, i.e. does it work to her advantage when viewed against the charge? Can she still change her story when faced with a more differentiated charge? The situations of storytelling differ at various stages of the proceedings as does perhaps the way in which the chronology of events is given its narrative form. At the end of the day, the judge must distinguish between events and human acts that can and such that cannot be regarded as legally relevant facts. For narratologists, these choices present a great challenge due to the concept of *mens rea*, the mental element of the defendant's intention to commit a crime, which is theorized differently in common law and civil law jurisdictions. The judge must also differentiate between narratives that are plausible in a legal context and those that are not, and between narratives to which a legal value may or may not be attributed.

Thus, the story of the judge as reader-narrator relies on her interpretation and evaluation of what others have told her. Certainly, her decisions in this respect have penal consequences. Success in this evaluative and interpretive process depends on *phronèsis*, judicial practical wisdom (Gaakeer 2019). Such wisdom includes a certain narrative knowledge or narrative sensitivity that enables the judge to conduct an assessment of competing narrative truths (which may also be historical truths), the result of which is conviction in both senses of the word.

In what follows, I address issues concerning narrative and norm in the pre-trial stage (section two). In section three, I take into consideration that the criminal charge is structured differently in various European legal systems. I do so in order to ask what consequences these differences may have for the plethora of narratives in the discursive practice of the criminal case. Ultimately, the aim of this essay is to acknowledge these narratives' relevance for legal narratology.[1] I am not trying to out-argue the expert narratologists in the field, but I will at least try, from the perspective of legal practice, to out-narrate them to some extent (Caputo 2018, 177).

[1] Two caveats are in order here. I am aware of the differences between common law and civil law jurisdictions. The groundwork that I aim to offer here is also important for criminal law systems in which, for example, plea bargaining is an option; any narrative mistake in the defendant's initial story can have grave negative consequences later on. Secondly, I am also aware of the (ideological distinctions with respect to the) terminological differences in the field of narratology and its main concepts, such as narrativity, story and plot. Compare Gaakeer (2015).

2. *Beginning*

2.1. 'Know your Bloody Facts First'

How can anyone "know their bloody facts first" (Heilbron 2019, 2)? Allow me to start with an example. § 261[2] of the Dutch *Code of Criminal Procedure* refers to the concept of 'fact' as the statement of the underlying substantive offense contained in the accusation, i.e. the charge. The charge should also contain the circumstances, i.e. the secondary facts by means of which the offense may be inferred, such as time, place and manner of execution (*modus operandi*). Together they serve to delineate what the defense needs to prepare against. In court, facts are only *assumed* to have happened, at least for the moment, due to the requirement of judicial impartiality and suspension of judgment. Paraphrasing Aristotle, we could say that the charge is the mimesis of the action, the (referential) construction of events and the reenactment of 'what happened.' But Aristotle (1999 [335 BC], 8, 1451a 16–18 (57)) also offers an important warning, namely: "Any entity has innumerable features, not all of which cohere into a unity; likewise, an individual performs many actions which yield no unitary action."

What, then, are actual facts when viewed against the abstract legal norm? How does the profile of a crime, i.e. the legislator's criminalization of specific human behavior and the legislator's' underlying reasons for doing so, impact on the distinction of what is and what is not a fact? This issue is especially acute given the risk of over-criminalization as a result of contemporary technological developments in artificial intelligence. Furthermore, what are actual facts when viewed from the perspective of the prosecutor's understanding of substantive criminal law and her reasons for charging a citizen with a specific, alleged act or activity? It is one thing to criminalize specific human behavior, but quite another to claim that criminal responsibility should be attributed to this specific individual. Any statement of facts is always already guided by the normative background of existing legal rules concepts and by case law. Both have a formative influence on the narratives of all parties involved in legal cases. There is no unmediated application of objective legal norms to the facts. It is the case itself that matters. As Esser (1964) put it, "Erst die Kasuistik teilt uns mit, was Rechtens ist" (288), i.e. it is the facts of the case that tell us what is legally the case. The movement between fact and norm is always dialectic. Speaking with Engisch (1963, 15), it is like the gaze which wanders to and fro ("Hin- und Herwandern des Blickes"). The written rule may well be the starting point for a debate or the basis for further argument and reasoning, but it is not the sole determinant of the outcome. As von Arnauld (2017, 320) points out, the

[2] In Dutch, these sections are called "articles."

justification of "the reconstruction of the process of norm application through narratological means" is found in the case. However, jurists should bear in mind the influence of their own interpretive frameworks on both fact and norm. Both professionally and personally, we cannot escape our hermeneutic situation of being culturally and situationally determined.

Jurists are in need of guidance as far as the production and the reception of narratives is concerned. Firstly, they have to be made aware of the distinction between narrative in the sense of a story told (what narratologists call the *histoire*) and narrative as the manner in which a story is being transmitted so as to have a specific impact on its audience (*narration* and *discours*). In legal practice, this distinction is crucial. To employ Cardozo's image, legal professionals have to develop a linguistic antenna sensitive to peculiarities beyond the level of the signifier, because the form and content, the 'how' and the 'what' of a text, are interconnected (Cardozo 1925). In other words, and from a narratological perspective, jurists will benefit from learning to differentiate – consciously and conscientiously – between *story* or *what* is told, and *discourse* or *how* the story is told.

Secondly, legal professionals need to realize that 'story' comprises *both* events (either actions or happenings) *and* characters that themselves initiate actions or get involved in happenings, all in specific temporal and spatial settings. These distinctions are crucial in criminal law. For example, as noted above, for the presumption of innocence and that of *mens rea* one needs to ask: is an act committed in the knowledge that a specific result will or is almost certain to occur, i.e. is the actor aware of the foreseeable consequences of particular actions or circumstances? Or is the act the result of negligence, namely when someone knows about its possible consequences but does not sufficiently take account of them; or else is the action an act of deliberate recklessness? For the sake of illustration, let us examine a case of alleged reckless driving in Dutch law. The case concerned a collision between a Porsche and another car, resulting in the death of its five passengers. The conductor of the Porsche had been driving at double the maximum speed. The Dutch Supreme Court judged the behavior of the Porsche driver to be 'extremely negligent' in accordance with Dutch law but not 'intentional,' i.e. consciously; it was argued that he had not consciously accepted the possible consequence of being killed himself.[3] The concept of recklessness is the subject of ongoing debate, not least because societal views on this issue strongly differ from judicial decisions. When is an occurrence an act (i.e. a deliberate action) and when is it merely an event? The answers co-depend on the valuation of the facts, the circumstances and our

[3] Dutch Supreme Court 15 October 1996, ECLI:NL:HR:1996: ZD0139. For European decisions that have a European Case Law Identifier (ECLI), see the European e-justice portal <e-justice.europa.eu>. For a German example, see the Bundesgerichtshof, 18 June 2020, BGH-4StR 482/19.

professional perceptions which are influenced by our judicial training, culture, and background.

Thirdly, jurists should be aware of the manifold ways in which narratives are transmitted and pay careful attention to chronology, narrative voice, narratorial presence as well as point of view. The 'how' matters also in the sense that it can render a narrative credible. Especially in jury trials, where the persuasiveness of the story is often prioritized to the detriment of an empirical verification of evidence, poetic effect may win the case. The role of a defense lawyer in common law is to refute the prosecution's claims to narrativity, or rather to puncture their narrative:

> [...] a jury will only convict if the prosecution case exhibits some Aristotelian coherence and, rather than offer a counternarrative, the defense lawyer must convince the jury that the crime may be the result of random or inexplicable action or circumstance – that the true facts are either confusing or aesthetically disappointing. (Weisberg 1996, 69)

Again, narrative matters.

2.2. Voice and Text: Determining or Being Determined by the Narrative?

When it comes to ascertaining the facts, the pre-trial stage needs to be differentiated from the trial stage of the proceedings. In the pre-trial stage of police interrogations, narratological research could focus on the defendant's narrative voice, on the way in which the narrative construction or constitution of the facts takes place, temporally and spatially, and on the narrative coherence of the world thus constructed, all viewed in the light of the (preliminary) charge. A word of caution is here in order. Perceptions of the facts may deceive. If a suspect is caught red-handed, what we think we perceive may not be what actually happened. Well-known scenarios and scripts regarding suspicious demeanor may lead to errors in interpreting the suspect's initial story, and subsequently to a specific charge that may be unwarranted. When that happens, how can the suspect now turned defendant be successful when offering a different but equally plausible explanation of events later in the proceedings? Our natural tendency to structure reality by means of narratives may prove to be a trap, since we tend to apply set stories as set rules.

Furthermore, initial perceptions can guide the rest of the investigation, e.g. the interrogation of witnesses and forensic investigations at the crime scene. When, on the other hand, information about the suspect is the result of prolonged investigation (e.g. in drug-trafficking cases), it is tempting to confront the defendant with only those facts and/or allegations that confirm the prosecutor's reason to start investigating the case in the first place. Because of the bond between facticity and normativity, this issue is of crucial importance.

The following example will help to clarify these points. Recent research on false allegations of rape suggests that the prototypical story of women filing a false complaint does not include elements such as kissing – kissing being an aspect connected to consensual sex – nor does it mention that the (fabricated) rapist apologized or was friendly afterwards. By contrast, in presumably true stories of rape victims, kissing often occurs and the rapist does indeed often apologize and is frequently friendly after the act. Yet juries tend to believe that an allegation of rape is false when the alleged rape was preceded by a kiss (Zutter et al. 2017, 3–4, 7). This example goes to show that we need to become aware of our prejudices concerning typical behavior that co-occurs with a specific crime and must avoid them. A crime may imply a narrative that is totally different from what we typically expect. In other words, our "poetic needs" may deceive us, as may our "cognitive baggage" and the coded cultural meanings aligned with it (Berns 2018, 201).

As Alber points out, "[w]hen recipients narrativize texts (including performances), they deal with the question of 'who did what to and with whom, when, where, why, and in what fashion' in the represented world" (2017, 363). This question, which originates with Quintilian, is pivotal also in the field of legal narratology (Quintilian 2001, L, V, 10, § 20). Many interrogations do not follow the format of these rather open questions but instead ask the defendant to confirm the events that the investigation process has produced as the most likely story. Even more frequently, the records do not provide the exact questions asked by the police. If the record is presented as a continuous first-person narrative, or if it consists only of selected legally relevant passages, although the narrative is presented as a unified whole, then the judge-qua-reader cannot recognize any irregularities. For instance, she will not be able to determine whether the story suggests a chronology or linearity of events where in fact there was none, or whether parts of the defendant's account were accidentally or deliberately left out and, if so, for what reasons. If there is no audio(-visual) recording, the judge cannot ascertain these omissions.

Human narratives often deviate from a chronological ordering of events, in legal surroundings as much as anywhere else. Moreover, narratorial presence is an issue to consider. There can be (unmarked) shifts in narratorial voice, the narrator's presence as an actor in the story may be more or less recognizable, and extradiegetic narrators may suddenly take over. This is the case, for example, when a narrative closely associates hearsay evidence with the narrator's own knowledge. Jurists should therefore pay careful attention to two aspects that narratologists call narrative level and narrative person. On the one hand, they should consider the level at which the narrating occurs, i.e. whether the narrator is situated outside or inside the story world (extradiegetic vs. intradiegetic narration). On the other hand, the relationship between the narrator and the story must be taken into account, i.e. whether the narrator is also a character in the story or not. Narratologically, this corresponds to the distinction between homodiegetic narration (the 'I' or narrating self relates his/her own story) and heterodiegetic narration (the narrator relates what others have said and done) (Kearns 1999, 101).

I suggest that, in criminal law, the (extradiegetic-heterodiegetic) omniscient third-person narrator of a criminal record is especially problematic when it comes to fact-finding: how are we to verify the sources of information presented in the narrative? What action or intention is attributed to whom? What role did the narrated person have – accomplice? witness-bystander? victim? expert witness? Equally problematic is the situation in which the suspect is the homodiegetic narrator and the reader cannot scrutinize the question-and-answer structure behind the interrogation, a structure that is decided by the interrogating police officer who, given her training and experience, may act under the influence of a similarity between the suspect's story and the prototypical story that is the codified legal norm.

The seminal work of Komter (2019) on Dutch criminal law suggests that the long-dominant method of interrogation which produced a linear narrative in the style of a monologue is now more and more being replaced by a more balanced criminal record in a question-and-answer style or in the form of a "recontextualised monologue," in which the interrogating police officer's statements concerning her knowledge of the case are recorded alongside the suspect's comments (Komter 2019). However, this does not mean that the criminal record is an actual transcript of what has been said during the interrogation. Indeed, there may be huge discrepancies between story time and discourse time. Komter points out several examples in which utterances recorded in the transcript are much more formal or complex than could be expected from the suspect in question (and which do not agree with what the suspect actually said, as the audio-recording proves). Furthermore, there are also examples of narratives in which details are related in such a manner that they indicate a problem of referentiality, i.e. when they move into the direction of the constitutive elements of the criminal charge. Komter's work has been corroborated by further research which shows that only 19 to 21 percent of what the suspect says during an interrogation is recorded in the form of a transcription. This includes the suspect's answers to questions as well as the narrative that results from "investigative interviewing," a form of interrogation that allows her to tell her story in her own words (Malsch et al. 2015, 11).

Judges need to assess to what extent the written reports adequately 're'-present the characters' alleged actions and the events as they actually occurred. To do so, the quality of the police work is important because it influences how we read for the plot in the written files. Judges also need to realize that it is a fiction to think that one can visually perceive whether the suspect/defendant is lying. Prudence is required when interpreting body language and/or perceived unease and nervousness. Such non-verbal behavior is not necessarily a sign of lying. The only objective indications of lying are evasive answers to direct questions (Malsch et al. 2018). In other words, what I want to point out is that the requirements of the statutory rule prove problematic. The more specific the statutory norm is, i.e. when it requires qualificative elements such as "constitutive events" that "are necessary for the story to be the story it is" (Abbott 2021, 22), the greater the risk of referentiality.

Another complication that narratological research on suspects' or defendants' statements has not yet taken into consideration is the following: in the Netherlands more than 250.000 people have an IQ lower than 70 and 2.5 million people have an IQ between 70 and 85. These people are cognitively impaired to the extent that their linguistic ability as well as their understanding of space and time are often severely reduced. It seems reasonable to assume that the numbers are comparable in other countries. Since it is precisely this group of people that is proportionally overrepresented among suspects/defendants, this factor likewise impacts the narratives produced in interrogation. Moreover, we have not even taken into consideration the effect of false sympathy, trickery, or pressure, either real or perceived, during interrogation. Every police interrogation is a stressful situation and not every suspect is a repeat player (Malsch & de Boer 2019). Finally, the use of visual material such as photos taken of the victim or camera footage of the crime scene may also affect the narrative (Verhoeven et al. 2020).

3. *Middle: The Knotty Relationship between Norms and Narratives*

3.1. Seeing the One as the Other

The preliminary stage with its narratological diversity comes to an end when the writ of summons is issued against the defendant. It contains the charge that guides the genesis of narratives and decisions in the trial stage. Its defining unity, the first 'knot' of the (first) bow tie, brings the alleged crime into focus. At the preliminary stage, the prosecutor could still opt for dismissal of the case. Once the trial is under way, this is no longer possible; should the prosecutor have second thoughts about the evidence, she can only ask for acquittal. Thus, the prosecutor carries a double burden. As far as the wording of the definitive charge is concerned, she must make the correct legal choice. At the same time, prosecution is an ethical decision because the presumption of innocence requires that no citizen be dragged into criminal proceedings without good reason.

During the trial stage, the pivotal question is the following: what does the allegation (considered as a text) mean when viewed from the perspective of criminal law? This leads to several follow-up questions. Thus: does this perspective increase the risk of a semantic collapse between accusation and guilt, as is the case in Kafka's "In the Penal Colony," where facts and norms literally fuse on the convict's back? In other words, is there the risk that the German concept of "Sachverhalte," i.e. the facts and circumstances, will all too easily be qualified as "Fälle von Tatbeständen," i.e. elements of the (codified) offence (Hassemer 1968, 11–12)? The trained practitioner is faced with two tasks. Firstly, she must recognize what is literally the case from a legal point of view and, secondly, when she then uncovers the decisive element(s) of the case, she must continue to be attentive to her potential professional bias. As Aristotle pointed out, when people contemplate resemblance, "they understand and infer what each element means, for instance 'this person is so and so'" (Aristotle 1999 [335 BC], 4, 1448b5 (39)). Put differently, when making sense of facts and circumstances, we are all influenced by organizing frameworks such as schemas and scripts (Sherwin 1994, 50). Thus, we should consider our frameworks carefully and acknowledge that they influence our notions of credibility and persuasiveness in actual legal decision-making. Another way of characterizing this conundrum is to point out that our bias which depends on schemas and scripts is somewhat similar to syllogistic reasoning. A script can prompt us to rearrange the facts in such a way as to make them fit into its framework; similarly, syllogistic reasoning may bend the truth by bringing the facts into conformity with the major premise. One might think of the Procrustean bed as an analogue. In short, this corresponds to the fallacy of referentiality at its worst.

Furthermore, there is the risk that stock story, deep frame and script on the one hand, and confirmation bias or belief perseverance, on the other, are mutually getting reinforced. After all, negative information is "weighted more heavily than positive information in forming impressions of others" (Chestek 2015, 50). Theoretically, the reciprocal relation of facts and norms is not deductive and syllogistic, but that does not mean, that in our practical legal lives, the tensions between fact and norm are easily resolved, textually or 'factually.' What is more, most of our European criminal codes were drawn up in the nineteenth century, yet we attribute meaning to their norms in the twenty-first century. That the interpretation of the laws and norms can only be performed contextually can be seen as both the beauty and the burden of legal decision-making, and this applies especially when the norm of criminal law contains terms that are not geared towards facticity.

Allow me to illuminate this problem by means of an example. § 310 of the Dutch *Criminal Code* runs as follows: "A person who removes any property belonging in whole or in part to another, with the object of unlawfully appropriating it, is guilty of theft and liable to a term of imprisonment of not more than four years or a fine of the fourth category."[4] The word "property" in the statutory norm needs factual specification in the criminal charge because the defendant needs to be informed what exactly it is that the prosecutor claims she has stolen; otherwise, she cannot defend herself. Did she break into a house and steal one plastic watch or five gold watches and three silver bracelets? The Dutch Supreme Court decided that the term "property" was factual enough if the written charge was unambiguous as to the nature of the stolen property. However, the term "an image of a sexual act" in § 240b of the Dutch *Criminal Code* on child pornography was not considered to be unambigious.[5] In analogy with societal views on the concepts of recklessness and negligence, other norms may likewise suffer from what Schroth (1971, 109) calls stereotypical terminology. An example of this is the obsolescent German term *Unzucht* for illicit sexual acts; this lexeme does not only have a negative connotation, but for many people commonly evokes a strong evaluative affect of censure and repugnance that may influence the decision-making process.

From a narratological perspective, it should be noted that in Germany, other than in the Netherlands, the writ of summons consists of the "abstrakte Anklage," the criminal offence in terms of the codified norm, and the "konkrete Anklagesatz," the narrative description of 'what happened' [6] When it comes to the qualification of the committed offence, the German judge is thus less constrained by the codified norm than her Dutch colleague. If the discussion in court of 'what happened' permits it, she can requalify behavior that is termed theft in the charge differently, for example as "handling illegally obtained goods." However, if such new qualification were to entail the inclusion of aggravating circumstances and hence an increase in the penalty should the defendant be found guilty, then the judge must give the defense the opportunity to respond (Stevens et al. 2017, 104–105). This can lead to a deferment of the trial. In Belgium, too, the judge can modify the constitutive elements of the crime with which a defendant has been charged. When this is done, the same complex of facts and circumstances will lead to the application of a different paragraph in the *Criminal Code*. The Belgian criminal charge is called *saisine*; it refers to the scope of the case before the court as delineated by the prosecutor. This means that *autosaisine*, the extension of the charge by the judge, is prohibited. However, so long as the complex of facts remains the same, the Belgian

[4] I quote from the English translation of the Dutch *Criminal Code* by Rayar (1997), and the European Judicial Training Network's (unofficial) translation available at http://www.ejtn.eu/PageFiles/6533/2014/20seminars/Omsenie/WetboekvanStrafrecht_ENG_PV.pdf. Where modification was required due to recent changes to specific paragraphs, the translation is mine.

[5] Dutch Supreme Court 20 March 2018, ECLI:NL:HR2018:394; Dutch Supreme Court 24 June 2014, ECLI:NL:HR:2014:1497.

[6] For the comparative legal aspect, as far as the criminal charge is concerned, I draw on Stevens et al. (2017).

judge can re-qualify the facts and convict the defendant following another paragraph of the *Criminal Code*. What is more, when this 'rabbit' emerges from the narratological 'top hat,' the judge can convict "sous sa plus haute expression pénale," i.e. impose the highest possible penalty (Stevens et al. 2017, 55–56).

Allow me to elaborate on this point by means of a comparison between the Dutch and German codified norms applied to aggravated forms of theft and their translations into the criminal charge. This comparison is worthwhile for a number of reasons. First, the juxtaposition of legal systems requires us to be specific in our narrative analyses of legal cases. Note that the European Court of Human Rights accepts a variety of legal systems in Europe without regarding it as their duty to harmonize these systems. Secondly, and even more importantly, a comparative perspective is necessary if legal narratology is to have any impact on legal practice.

§ 312 of the Dutch *Criminal Code* on aggravated theft could be translated into a concrete charge that may run like this:

> The above-mentioned person summoned to appear in court is charged with the crime that on or about 12 June 2019, in Rotterdam, he has taken away, with a view to misappropriation, a smartphone, in any case a good, belonging, wholly or partly, to X, in any case to another person or other persons, which act was preceded, accompanied or followed by an act of violence against X, consisting of multiple kicks to the body and head of said X, in order to procure said smartphone.

Compare how the §§ 242 and 252 of the German *Criminal Code* translate into the following concrete charge:

> 'X und Y werden angeklagt, in Hamburg am 31.10.2006 gemeinschaftlich handelnd bei einem Diebstahl auf frischer Tat betroffen, gegen eine Person Gewalt verübt zu haben, um sich im Besitz des gestohlenen Gutes zu erhalten, indem sie:
> gegen 05:50 Uhr in der Gaststätte A in der a-Straße 2 in [Postleitzahl] Hamburg im bewusst und gewollten Zusammenwirken arbeitsteilig handelnd unter erheblichen Alkoholeinfluss stehend (der Beschuldigte X ein Atemalkoholgehalt von 1,55 ‰ und der Beschuldigte Y von 1,56 ‰) der Beschuldigte X eine Flasche Whisky "Jim Beam" vom Tresen entnahm und in seinen Hosenbund verstaute, sodann beide Beschuldigte zum Ausgang der Gaststätte gingen, dabei von der Zeugin A aufgehalten wurden, der Beschuldigte Y daraufhin die Zeugin zurückzog, schüttelte, schubste und daran hinderte, den Beschuldigten X am Verlassen und damit an der Mitnahme der Flasche Whisky zu hindern, um zumindest auch den gemeinsamen Besitz der zuvor entwendeten Flasche "Jim Beam" zu erhalten. Verbrechen, strafbar nach §§ 242 Abs. 1, 252, 25 Abs. 2 StGB.' (Stevens et al. 2017, 183)[7]

> X and Y are being charged that, having been caught in the act of theft perpetrated on 31 October 2006 in Hamburg, to have committed violence against a person in order to retain the stolen good in the following manner: that at around 05.50 hrs in restaurant A [name] in the a-Street [name of Street] in [postal code] Hamburg, X and Y while they were under the influence of a considerable amount of alcohol [X a breath alcohol

[7] For the German *Criminal Code* (*Strafgesetzbuch*), see https://dejure.org/gesetze/StGB/ and https://germanlawarchive.iuscomp.org/.

> level of 1,5‰ and Y a breath alcohol level of 1,56‰] knowingly and intentionally as joint authors, X took a bottle of Whiskey Jim Beam from the shelf and put it in his waistband, after which act both accused went to the door of the restaurant, where they were being prevented from leaving by witness A, [and that] defendant Y then pulled her back, shook her up and punched her in order to keep her from obstructing their exit and preventing their taking away the bottle of whiskey, in order to retain the joint possession of said bottle of Jim Beam. Offence punishable according to §§ 242(1), 252, 25(2) of the German *Criminal Code*. (Stevens et al. 2017, 183; translation Monika Fludernik)

The German concrete charge provides a much more detailed narrative than the Dutch one. Thus, German defendants who, together with the charge, receive documents containing the evidence that the prosecutor bases her case on, can try to get their story right and avert the looming danger that their behavior will be identified as belonging to the category of the abstract norm. A complication in the German format of the criminal charge, at least in comparison with other jurisdictions, is its complexity. The individual defendant's concrete charge frequently contains (the acts of) all participants or accomplices to the crime that she is being charged with, including information as to whether juvenile court jurisdiction applies. This renders entangling the charge (what she herself is charged with) and, subsequently, finding the most effective story more difficult.

Put differently, if the defendant manages to clearly differentiate *her* story from the story encapsulated in the charge, she may be acquitted. The judicial qualification of the offense is based on the specific act which alone establishes the offense or fails to do so. For all participants, it is a matter of offering the most convincing of the (available) "perspectival narratives" (Brooks 2006, 10). Especially in legal systems in which court proceedings are based on the principle of orality, one needs to pay attention to the fact whether from a narrative perspective everything relevant is brought to the fore. This is crucial, for instance, in France, where a trial before the *Court d'Assises* with a jury has an oral character. In Germany, too, the so-called "Mündlichkeitsprinzip" requires that any written document contained in the case file is read aloud in court. Likewise, in Norway, the "bevisumiddelbarhetsprinsipet"[8] requires that all the evidence is orally presented in court. As an example, let us take the case of a French judge who instructs the jury incorrectly about the charge of murder because she fails to mention that, if premeditation cannot be proved, a conviction for manslaughter will be possible; an acquittal will be the likely outcome due to procedural error. Neither the prosecutor nor the surviving relatives of the murder victim will be happy with this conclusion of the proceedings, to say the least. Appeal will undoubtedly be the result. The stories told in the court of appeal will once more diverge, though probably in different ways than

[8] Thanks is due to Frode Helmich Pedersen (Bergen University) for providing me with this Norwegian term.

during the trial of the first instance. And with these stories, the narratological conundrums typical of trials re-emerge with a vengeance.

The impact of narrative also affects the victim impact statement. What is their narrative scope and relevance in jury trials and elsewhere? Is a victim impact statement literally just that, a narrative about the impact of the crime on a victim's life, or is the victim allowed to discuss the evidence and ask for a conviction? If the victim details her suffering and trauma, how is one to deal with emotions running high? If the victim is a party to the legal process, how will the victim's permission to address the evidence and sentencing influence the judge's decision? The victim's story may be in conflict with the presumption of innocence of the defendant.

The criminal trial relies on the narrative competence of all parties involved. However, the defendant has the right to remain silent and sometimes her defense lawyer will advise her to follow this strategy. Should the defendant try to tell her story in her own words, i.e. without attention to the legal terminology applicable in her case, this may have negative consequences. At the trial stage, the specific truth conditions and procedural constraints of criminal law, including the rules of evidence, influence the stories that are being told. The defendant needs a lawyer to translate her view of the facts into legal terms. Her story must stay clear of the charge yet cohere with the charge's semantic framework, especially with the legal qualification of her act. In summary, the more extensive the description of the human actions under consideration in the criminal charge, the greater is the risk that a referential view on language will prevail. That is to say, the greater the detail in the charge as far as the description of the human activity that is deemed criminal it contains, the greater the risk that in the fact-finding process the prosecutor and the judge may seek for evidence to cover all the details, taking everything literally. Thus, narrative strategies employed by the defense lawyer may backfire.

3.2. Resisting (Pre-)Figuration

The hermeneutic circularity of the relation between facts and norms is further complicated by aspects of temporality.[9] This trajectory is inescapably a vicious circle. If any human act is regarded as "*an activity and a desire in search of a narrative*," then every human experience is always "already mediated by all kinds of stories we have heard," as Ricoeur (1986, 129; original emphasis) noted. For Ricoeur, the temporality of the world of action – what jurists or lawyers call 'the brute facts' – is always already influenced by our pre-understanding. For example, we have a certain preunderstanding in criminal law about how a robbery is usually planned and how it takes place. Speaking with Ricoeur (1984,

[9] I have discussed this in greater detail elsewhere, see Gaaker (2019, 145–152).

55), "[e]very narrative presupposes a familiarity with terms such as agent, goal, means, circumstance, help, hostility, cooperation, conflict, success, failure, etc., on the part of its narrator and any listener". This knowledge influences the way in which the brute facts translate into legal facts in legal contexts. Therefore, we should not unconditionally accept our pre-understandings, at least at this early stage of narrative prefiguration. The circularity between facts and norms or scripts involved here should alert us to the necessity of acknowledging our faulty tendency to hold on to a type of story we have identified in relation to the case at hand irrespective of contrary information. Ricoeur correctly points out that "to understand a story is to understand both the language of 'doing something' and the cultural tradition from which proceeds the typology of plots" (57). Any profession has specific plots on which it relies. This means that

> [...] an event must be more than just a singular occurrence. It gets its definition from its contribution to the development of a plot. A story, too, must be more than just an enumeration of events in a serial order; it must organize them into an intelligible whole, of a sort that we can always ask what is the 'thought' of this story. In short, emplotment is the operation that draws a configuration out of a simple succession. (65)

This is what Ricoeur called the stage of *mimēsis*$_2$. Such a translation of 'what happened' into a manageable form to be used in the trial stage includes propositions that adumbrate the realm of metaphor. The 'as-if' (Vaihinger 1924 [1911], 92), the seeing of the one thing in the other, entails the suggestion of a 'what if.' At the same time, it must steer clear of the risk that the 'if plot' of statutory rules (Sternberg 2008) becomes an 'as-if plot' in the negative sense. This is the case if one adds facts and circumstances to the charge that a defendant is charged with and that are suggestive of the criminal act as charged. This may fuel bias and lead to a conviction for which there is no sufficient evidence. Hence, plot analysis is clearly crucial.

All participants in the criminal trial offer their suggestions for what they claim is the most plausible emplotment. They either try to connect the case to the legal norm or disconnect the case from it. With storytelling comes the need to woo the audience, to seduce, making legal storytelling "duplicitous" (Douzinas et al. 1991, 110). For judges, rule application in criminal trials "consists both in adapting the rule to the case by way of qualifying the act as a crime, and in connecting the case to the rule, through a narrative description taken to be truthful" (Ricoeur 2007, 55–56). This narrative description, then, is also guided by one's theory of the case, i.e. the combination of facts and legal theories supporting one's case. And the theory of the case, in its turn builds on a narrative theory: one must be prepared to offer another story should the opponent's narrative so require. For example, when the prosecutor in her argument focuses on the proof of the primary charge, the defense may need to offer a story on the basis of the subsidiary charge in order to effect damage control in cases where the evidence is so overwhelming that no judge will acquit. These processes are even more pronounced in common law settings with adversarial proceedings, where the control that parties have is greater than in inquisitorial settings. The sum-total, then, of the centripetal and centrifugal forces of stories and counter stories, in the movement from diversity to unity at the trial stage, what I have called the knot of the bow tie, depends both on substantive and procedural law.

4. *Conclusion: Tying the Bow, Connecting Facts and Norms*

4.1. Conclusion I: The Decision

Since narratives in court are always in competition with one another, a decision is called for. The judge's decision is based on the material facts (*facta probanda* – 'facts here to be proved') expressed in the charge and the weighing of the evidence, both in the written file and as presented in the participants' narratives. The judge as narratee must appropriate the various texts into her own judicial world and emplot them to arrive at her decision. This is the stage of refiguration or, in Ricoeur's terms, *mimēsis*$_3$, in which the judge explains her view of the 'new world' that is the result of the interaction of *mimēsis*$_1$ and *mimēsis*$_2$. *Mimēsis*$_3$ is the stage of application: our pre-understanding is informed and transformed by *our* act of configuration, when figuration executes its power of redescription and so becomes effective. When *mimēsis*$_1$ and *mimēsis*$_2$ interact, our earlier pre-understandings also become subject to change. Narration is a form of explanation. In bringing together heterogeneous facts and circumstances woven into competing narratives of opposing parties, the judge draws on the written and unwritten sources of law that are themselves part of the stage of *mimēsis*$_1$ as much as they are the result of an earlier application: namely, an earlier *mimēsis*$_3$, when one considers the dynamic process of law's development of precedents and refined interpretations of existing norms as a story. The judge must decide because her decision helps to create law.

Any such emplotment and application requires insight into narratology. Narratology is necessary because the decision-making process is guided by one's interpretive framework. Secondly, both narrative and legal interpretation involve a judgment about probability, verisimilitude and truth, based on the whole of one's knowledge of the world. As Floris Bex notes, "one of the main dangers of stories is that a coherent story is judged as more believable than an incoherent story, regardless of the actual truth of the story" (2011, 79). Furthermore, from a judicial practical perspective, the lower courts' narratives are always composed in such a way as to withstand scrutiny by a higher court in appeal, and the same is true for the higher courts with a view towards scrutiny by courts of cassation. Put differently, these narratives are composed with an eye on the legal and factual feasibility of the evidence that has been chosen to legitimize the decision. The politics of judging matters. For example, the Dutch Supreme Court in the cassation procedure can deliver a 'factual' judgment on the Court of Appeal's decision, a juridical judgment, or a mixed, i.e. a factual and juridical judgment. While the 'factual' judgment is a marginal test that only considers whether the Court of Appeal's view on the facts is 'not incomprehensible,' the juridical judgment considers whether the Court's decision does or does not contain an incorrect view of the (application of the) law, and so does the mixed judgment. Thus, judges may in practice follow Aristotle's advice to leave out anything unnecessary, that is, anything that distracts from the main storyline of the (juridical) judgment, because in the legal context, such unnecessary detail could give any higher court a reason to reverse or quash the judgement. Obviously, such brevity may compromise the judicial narrative, especially when 'events' in the file become 'legal facts' and are translated into a causal chain of events that produces legal consequences, or when condensation prevails where detail was required. This is yet another reason why the form and content of judicial narratives, the 'how' and the 'what,' are of huge significance.

4.2. Conclusion II: Reality and Fiction

In the end, literally and figuratively, the judge-narrator who determines the outcome of the trial cannot escape what White (1984) wrote about narratorial character:

> [...] a writer always gives himself a character in what he writes; it shows in the tone of voice he adopts, in the signals he gives the reader as to how to take that tone of voice, in the attitude he invites his reader to have toward the world or toward people or ideas within it, in the straightforwardness or trickiness with which he addresses his reader – his honesty or falseness – and in the way he treats the materials of his language and culture. (15)

If the judge as a narrative addressee is misled by narratives, either by deliberate policy or on account of her own prejudices, her own narrative voice and text may end up misjudging both as far as its form and content are concerned. The judge's narrative can be a response to all kinds of triggers that evoke subconscious or unconscious reactions. Both the constitution of the facts and the interpretation of the statutory norms depend on judicial habitus (Bourdieu 1991, 12) as well as professional and private background. For instance, the judge may ask biased questions such as "Surely you could have run away when you saw him grab that knife?" or "Surely you could have dressed differently when you went out late at night?". Thus, a training in philosophical-legal hermeneutics and narratology is important, precisely because of the dangers of referentiality or factuality as (a) legal fiction. To return to the problem of referentiality once more, it is important that judges

> […] should never forget that language, by virtue of the infinitive generative but also *originative* capacity – in the Kantian sense – which derives from its power to produce existence by producing the collectively recognized, and thus realized, representation of existence, is no doubt the principal support of the dream of absolute power. (159; original emphasis)

Equally important is the judicial reflection on the violence of law's outcomes (Cover 1986). Ultimately, the judge must learn to resist hasty closure. Legal-narratological research should therefore strive for two things: a multilateral re-contextualization of topics, both theoretical and practical, and the recognition of the experiences of the main actors in the criminal trial and procedure.

Works Cited

Abbott, H. Porter (2021) *The Cambridge Introduction to Narrative*. Cambridge: Cambridge Univ. Press.

Alber, Jan (2017) "Narratology and Performativity. On Processes of Narrativization in Live Performances." *Narrative* 25.3: 359–373.

Aristotle (1999) *Poetics* [335 BC]. Ed. and Trans. Stephen Halliwell. Cambridge, London: Harvard Univ. Press.

Arnauld, Andreas von (2017) "Norms and Narrative." *German Law Journal* 18.2: 309–329.

Berns, Sandra (2018) *To Speak as a Judge. Difference, Voice, and Power* [1999]. Milton Park: Routledge.

Bourdieu, Pierre (1991) *Language and Symbolic Power*. Ed. John B. Thompson. Trans. Gino Raymond and Matthew Adamson. London: Polity Press.

Brooks, Peter (2006) "Narrative Transactions – Does the Law Need a Narratology?" *Yale Journal of Law & Humanities* 18.1: 1–38.

Caputo, John D. (2018) *Hermeneutics, Facts, and Interpretation in the Age of Information*. London: Pelican.

Cardozo, Benjamin N. (1925) "Law and Literature." *Yale Review* 14: 699–718.

Chestek, Kenneth D. (2008) "The Plot Thickens: The Appellate Brief as Story." *Journal of the Legal Writing Institute* 14: 127–169.

Chestek, Kenneth D. (2015) "Of Reptiles and Velcro: The Brain's Negativity Bias and Persuasion." *Nevada Law Journal* 15: 605–631.

Cover, Robert (1986) "Violence and the Word." *Yale Law Journal* 95: 1601–1629.

Criminal Code, Germany, DOI: https://dejure.org/gesetze/StGB/ and DOI: https://germanlawarchive.iuscomp.org/.

Criminal Code, the Netherlands, DOI: http://www.ejtn.eu/PageFiles/6533/2014%20seminars/Omsenie/WetboekvanStrafrecht_ENG_PV.pdf.

Douzinas, Costas, Ronnie Warrington and Shaun McVeigh (1991) *Postmodern Jurisprudence. The Law of Text in the Texts of Law*. London, New York: Routledge.

Elkins, James R. (1985) "On the Emergence of Narrative Jurisprudence. The Humanistic Perspective Finds a New Path." *Legal Studies Forum* 9: 123–156.

Elkins, James R. (2019) "Preface to 'Narrative Jurisprudence. A Law, Lawyers, and Stories Bibliography'." *Legal Studies Forum* 43.1–2: 3–7.

Engisch, Karl (1963) *Logische Studien zur Gesetzesanwendung*. 3rd expanded edition. Heidelberg: Winter.

Esser, Josef (1964) *Grundsatz und Norm in der richterlichen Fortbildung des Privatrechts*. 2nd edition. Tübingen: Mohr.

Ferguson, Robert A. (1996) "Untold Stories in the Law." *Law's Stories. Narrative and Rhetoric in the Law*. Ed. Peter Brooks and Paul Gewirtz. New Haven: Yale Univ. Press. 84–98.

Gaakeer, Jeanne (2015) "Futures of Law and Literature: A Jurist's Perspective." *Recht und Literatur im Zwischenraum. Aktuelle inter- und transdisziplinäre Zugänge/Law and Literature In-Between. Contemporary Inter- and Transdisciplinary Approaches*. Ed. Christian Hiebaum, Susanne Knaller and Doris Pichler. Bielefeld: transcript. 71–103.

Gaakeer, Jeanne (2019) *Judging from Experience. Law, Praxis, Humanities*. Edinburgh: Edinburgh Univ. Press.

Hart, August C. 't (1983) *Strafrecht en Beleid. Essays*. Leuven: Acco.

Hassemer, Winfried (1968) *Tatbestand und Typus. Untersuchungen zur strafrechtlichen Hermeneutik*. Köln: Heymann.

Heilbron, Hilary (2019) *Rose QC. The Remarkable Story of Rose Heilbron. Trailblazer and Legal Icon*. Oxford: Hart Publishing.

Kafka, Franz (1971), "In the Penal Colony" [1919]. *Franz Kafka, The Complete Stories*. Ed. Nahum N. Glatzer. Trans. Willa and Edwin Muir. New York: Schocken Books.

Kearns, Michael (1999) *Rhetorical Narratology*. Lincoln: Univ. of Nebraska Press.

Komter, Martha (2019) *The Suspect's Statement. Talk and Text in the Criminal Process*. Cambridge: Cambridge Univ. Press.

Malsch, Marijke, R. Kranendonk, J. de Keijser, H. Elffers, M. Komter and M. de Boer (2015) *Kijken, luisteren, lezen. De invloed van beeld, geluid en schrift op het oordeel over verdachtenverhoren*. Apeldoorn: Politie & Wetenschap, Nederlands Studiecentrum Criminaliteit en Rechtshandhaving.

Malsch, Marijke, J. van Zanten and H. Elffers (2018) "Pinokkio's neus: leugens en het gedrag van de verdachte in een verhoorsituatie." *Delikt en Delinkwent* 35: 1–16.

Malsch, Marijke, and Meike M. de Boer (2019) "Interviews of Suspects of Crime: Law and Practice in European Countries." *The Oxford Handbook of Criminal Process*. Ed. Darryl K. Brown, Jenia I. Turner and Bettina Weißer. Oxford: Oxford Univ. Press. 317–340.

Quintilian, Marcus Fabius (2001) *The Orator's Education*. Books 1–12 [1521]. Ed. and Trans. Donald A. Russell. Cambridge: Harvard Univ. Press.

Rayar, Louise (1997) (Trans.) *The Dutch Penal Code*. Littleton: Rothman.

Ricoeur, Paul (1984) *Time and Narrative* (vol. 1). Trans. Kathleen McLaughlin and David Pellauer. Chicago: Univ. of Chicago Press.

Ricoeur, Paul (1986) "Life: A Story in Search of a Narrator." *Facts and Values. Philosophical Reflections from Western and Non-Western Perspectives.* Ed. Marinus C. Doeser and J. N. Kraay. The Hague: Martinus Nijhoff. 121–132.

Ricoeur, Paul (2007) *Reflections on the Just*. Trans. David Pellauer. Chicago: Univ. of Chicago Press.

Schroth, Ulrich (1971) "Zum Problem der Wertneutralität richterlicher Tatbestandsfestlegung im Strafrecht." *Rechtstheorie. Ansätze zu einem kritischen Rechtsverständnis*. Ed. Arthur Kaufmann. Karlsruhe: Müller. 103–110.

Sherwin, Richard K. (1994) "Law Frames: Historical Truth and Narrative Necessity in a Criminal Case." *Stanford Law Review* 47.1: 39–83.

Sternberg, Meir (2008) "If-Plots: Narrativity and the Law-Code." *Theorizing Narrativity*. Ed. John Pier and José Ángel García Landa. 29–107.

Stevens, Lonneke, Marjolein Cupido, Bas de Wilde, Elinor Fry and Sonja Meijer (2017) *De tenlastelegging als grondslag voor de rechterlijke beslissing. Een rechtsvergelijkend onderzoek naar de inrichting van de tenlastelegging en de gebondenheid eraan bij het bewijs, de kwalificatie en de straftoemeting in Nederland, België, Frankrijk, Italië en Duitsland*. Ed. WODC and Ministerie van Veiligheid en Justitie. Den Haag: Boom uitgevers.

Vaihinger, Hans (1924) *The Philosophy of 'As If'. A System of the Theoretical, Practical and Religious Fictions of Mankind* [1911]. Trans. Charles K. Ogden. London: Routledge and Kegan Paul.

Verhoeven, Willem Jan, G. Vanderveen, L. van Dillen, S. Kruit and M. Hysaj (2020) "Verbeelding in de verhoorkamer. De invloed van het gebruik van beeldmateriaal in het verhoor op verhoortechnieken en proceshouding." *Politiewetenschap* 117. Web. 10 September 2020 https://www.politieenwetenschap.nl/cache/files/61b9fa5087f49PW117.pdf.

Weisberg, Robert (1996) "Proclaiming Trials as Narratives: Premises and Pretenses." *Law's Stories. Narrative and Rhetoric in the Law.* Ed. Peter Brooks and Paul Gewirtz. New Haven: Yale Univ. Press. 61–83.

White, James Boyd (1984) *When Words Lose Their Meaning. Constitutions and Reconstitutions of Language, Character, and Community*. Chicago: Univ. of Chicago Press.

Zutter, André W.E.A. de, Robert Horselenberg and Peter J. van Koppen (2017) "Filing False Vice Reports: Distinguishing True from False Allegations of Rape." *The European Journal of Psychology Applied to a Legal Context* 9.1: 1–14.

The Rhetorical Use of Plot-Construction in Judgments

Frode Helmich Pedersen

1. Introduction

Plot has been described as one of the most elusive of all narratological concepts (Dannenberg 2005, 435). In this contribution I would like to formulate some of the central problems about plot and discuss a few examples of how plot-construction can be used rhetorically in the court's story of facts as it is presented in the judgement. These stories are (in the Norwegian legal system) generally accepted as the "material truth" of what happened in the case but can also be read as a way for the court to justify its own decision. One could say, therefore, that the stories presented in the judgement serve two masters, who may not always agree with each other. On the one hand, the court's story should adhere to the principle of truthfulness and give a balanced and evidence-based rendering of the relevant events; on the other, it must present these events in a way that makes the court's decision appear just, sound, and reasonable. While these two dimensions of the court's narrative are often in line with each other, there may also be instances where they come into conflict. This may occur, for instance, when there has been put forward credible testimony or evidence before the court that does not quite fit with the story that most convincingly supports the court's conclusion. In such cases the rhetoric of persuasion may demand adjustments to the story that would not have been necessary if the sole purpose of the story had been to present a balanced and truthful account of what happened. Such adjustments may be effected in a number of ways. In a well-documented study of Norwegian criminal trials from 2008, the folklorist Audun Kjus claims that what he calls "tightly paring down of the narrative" is a common way to do this in judgements. According to Kjus, "tightly paring down" a narrative means creating a narrow time frame for the plot so that inconvenient facts can be left out of the narrative simply because they occur at points in time which the narrative – as it is presented in the judgment – does not cover (Kjus 2010, 70). The phenomenon can be viewed as an aspect of plot-construction, which always includes a decision about where a particular story begins and where it ends. In this contribution I will discuss a concrete example of the rhetorical use of plot-construction which differs somewhat from the phenomenon discussed by Kjus, but where the basic problem is similar, i.e., how to conceal, cover up or make inconspicuous, inconvenient aspects of the case through storytelling or, more specifically, plot-construction. The main example is taken from the judgments in the much-discussed Orderud-case (2001/2002), where four people were convicted of "aiding and abetting" a shocking triple murder of an elderly couple and their grown-up daughter at a farmhouse in eastern Norway.[1] My analysis concerns both judgements in the case, issued by two different judicial instances, i.e. two courts of different instances, as well as the story put forward by the Norwegian prosecuting authority.

2. *Theoretical Points about Plot and the Rhetoric of Storytelling*

Before we turn to the concrete example, it is necessary to clarify some theoretical points about plot and the rhetoric of storytelling. How should we define 'plot'? As the reader will be aware, plot is often defined as a kind of configuration of the story.[2] In order to understand what that means, we must first agree what a 'story' is.[3] As I understand it, the story is a thing of the mind, a mental construction, where events are chronologically ordered and arranged within a general framework of causality. If we imagine, for instance, a sequence of events where Mr. Smith got a letter and then Mrs. Johnson crashed her car, we do not have a story. If we imagine instead that Mr. Smith got a letter, which caused him to call his sister, Mrs. Johnson, who then crashed her car, we do have a story. When we are dealing with factual narratives, it is important not to confuse the story level with the level of reality itself, which I prefer to call the *happenings*, following a suggestion by Karlheinz Stierle (1973, 531). This distinction corresponds to the difference between what really exists and *claims* about what really exists. When we are dealing with the story-level of a factual narrative, we are dealing with *claims* about reality, that is: of what happened,

---

1 https://en.wikipedia.org/wiki/Orderud_case.

2 In theoretical discussions of the term plot, Seymour Chatman's formulation of plot as "story-as-discoursed" (1978, 43) and Peter Brooks's definition of plot as "the dynamic shaping force of the narrative discourse" (Brooks 1992, 13) are frequently mentioned.

3 In what follows I will use the narratological terms in a way that differs somewhat from the standard model of Genette, Chatman, Rimmon-Kenan and others. I use *story* to designate the chronologically ordered sequence of events, which is, in factual stories, selected from the raw material of experience. The level underneath the story (for factual stories) is the level of reality, which I refer to as *happenings*. *Discourse* is used to refer to the verbal presentation of the story, in which events may be referred to independently from their chronological order. *Plot* is used in this article to mean a modelling or configuration of the story – the way the story is shaped. In factual stories, the "story" (understood as the 'content' of the narrative) can always be extended further back in time on the basis of new information. This does not hold for the plot, which is tied to the concrete presentation. Plot differs from discourse both because the discourse includes verbal phenomena that do not properly belong to the "plot" and because it may refer to points in time that lie outside the scope of both story and plot. If a legal narrative about a brawl in a bar opens with brief discussion of changing attitudes to violence from the 1950s until today, one cannot say that the plot therefore begins in the 1950s. It does, however, make sense to say that the discourse begins with a glance at events in the 1950s.

who did what to whom, when, where, and why. These claims can be true or false and they may be more or less plausible. Such categories do not apply to the level of reality.[4]

The story is, according to narrative theory, always presented to us in the form of a *discourse*. This is the same as saying that we extrapolate the story from what is presented to us by the discourse. What we get through this operation is – at least ideally – a chronologically ordered sequence where the most important events are causally linked. When this story is a factual narrative of the kind we are presented with in criminal cases, we may view the entire story as *one* claim about what happened in the case.

I would like to turn now to the question of rhetoric, understood as a means of persuasion. It is generally accepted that the discourse – any discourse – has a rhetorical aspect to it. If the narrator, for instance, describes a person as "crafty" rather than using a possible alternative such as "goal-oriented," the choice of words can be regarded as part of the overall rhetoric of the discourse, which seeks to nudge the reception of the story in a particular direction. A similar use of rhetoric can be found at the level of the story. Consider the following example: In the judgement of a Norwegian murder case (often referred to as the Tengs-case), the court-as-narrator includes, through an external analepsis, an earlier incident where the young male defendant had allegedly complained very intensely to his teacher about some test-results at school. By including this event in the story about the murder, the defendant is characterized in an unfavorable manner (i.e., as a person who may react violently when his sense of self-worth is questioned), which fitted well with the court's view of what happened at the scene of the crime. The event could just as well have been left out – no essential information would thereby have been lost – but was included for rhetorical reasons.[5]

So far, we have briefly looked at how rhetoric may be at work at the level of the discourse as well as that of the story. We turn now to the rhetoric of plot-construction. As a narratological term, plot is perhaps best viewed as the presentation of the story; not its verbal presentation, but its arrangement, how the story is laid out. Plot does not so much concern *what* is included in the narrative as *when* or *where* it is included; at what point in the discourse the events are told and, further, what events are highlighted and what events are placed in the background. From this brief description it should already be evident that plot-construction can be used for rhetorical purposes, for instance by directing the reader's attention toward certain events or facts rather than others. In legal storytelling, the highlighted events will typically be the ones which can be used to support the story's main conclusion, whereas the events that are placed in

4 Compare Pedersen (2021, 69–70).

5 The defendant was acquitted in the court of appeal. The case is currently being investigated by a cold case unit and a different man has been charged with the murder.

the background may contain information that is less convenient to the overall drift of the story.

In general, I think it important that the analysis of narratives in judgements pays close attention to these three aspects of narrative construction: the composition of the story, the wording of the discourse (i.e., the stylistic level of the discourse), the design of the plot (the presentation of the story-elements). The analysis should, in short, be able to expound the rhetorical effects produced on each of these levels. In the following analysis of the Orderud-case, I will focus on the question of how plot-construction can be used rhetorically by the court in order to persuade the reader of the soundness and plausibility of its conclusions and, more generally, to create an impression of the court's authoritative command of the facts of the case. But before I do that, it is necessary first to give a brief overview of the case.

3. *About the Orderud Case*

The Orderud murder-case is one of the most commented-on criminal trials in recent Norwegian history. The murders were committed over twenty years ago, but the case is still very much present in the Norwegian press, not least because two of the convicted defendants (who have since been released from jail) are currently fighting to get their case reopened in order to prove their innocence. The case was unusual in many ways, which is one of the reasons why the various stories about it have captured the imagination of the general public and why it has been the subject of several books and film documentaries.

The case concerns a triple murder, carried out with firearms at the Orderud farm on May 22, 1999. The shooting took place during the night when the victims were at home in their beds. The victims were an elderly couple, who were the formal owners of the large farm on which they lived, and their grown-up daughter, who had a successful career at the Norwegian Ministry of Defense. The daughter was staying with her parents for the weekend. Four people were investigated as suspects: The couple's son Per, who had run the farm for many years, and his wife Veronica, who lived together in the farm's main building, near the scene of the crime. Among the defendants were also Veronica's sister, Kristin, and her boyfriend Lars. They were both connected to the criminal underworld in Oslo. A crucial point about the case from a legal point of view is that the four defendants all ended up being charged with, and later convicted of, *aiding and abetting* the murders and not with carrying out the actual killings. The reason for this was that the police could not find enough evidence at the scene of the crime to conclude with any degree of certainty who had been present there at the time of the killings. They did, however, claim to be able to prove a motive for the murder as well as producing evidence that Per had obtained several firearms with the help of his sister-in-law and her boyfriend.[6] One of the defendants, Kristin, who was a drug addict at the time, claimed that Per and Veronica had indeed planned the murder of Per's parents. The motive, according to her, had to do with the ownership of the farm. Per's father had, after an initial oral agreement that the entire property would be transferred to Per, postponed the deal, and was now moving to secure part of the farm's property for his daughter, who was among the victims. The prosecution was able to prove that the son, Per, had falsified his father's signature in order to secure the farm for himself – a fact which Per eventually admitted. All four defendants were convicted of aiding and abetting the murder, and with respect to Per and Veronica it mattered little that they were not charged with having committed the actual murders, since they got the maximum sentence under Norwegian law, 21 years. Kristin was sentenced to 16 years of imprisonment and her boyfriend Lars got 18 years.

4. *One Story, Three Beginnings*

An initial point of interest in the story about the Orderud case is the significant hole at its very center: neither the police nor the court, nor anyone else who was willing to talk, could give an account of what happened on the night of the killings. The question is, then, how one can go about constructing a narrative about these murders convincing enough to convict the four defendants, given that one cannot relate the event of the actual killings nor identify who perpetrated them.

The Norwegian justice system produced three different written narratives about the crime in the course of the criminal process. The first is found in the indictment, which is issued by the public prosecuting authority, and which is always quoted in full in the judgement. The second is formulated in the judgment of the first instance of court, Nes Herredsrett, from 2001, and the third is presented in the judgment issued by the court of appeal, Eidsivating lagmannsrett, from 2002. These three narratives are very different from one another, both with respect to how they begin and with respect to how they deal with the hole at the center of the story.

I should like to start with a general comment on the beginning of a narrative. The beginning of a narrative is to my mind an aspect of plot-construction. The beginning is often used to establish the main theme of the story or the

[6] Two of the pistols that had been obtained by Per had not been used in the murders. A third gun, a revolver, had according to ballistic analysis been used at the scene of the crime but Per denied ever having had access to this gun, which belonged to Lars and was accessible to Kristin.

narrator's attitude to the main events.[7] In this case, there was not a great deal of disagreement with respect to the story level: that is, all the main events were more or less viewed in the same way in all three narratives. Nevertheless, they differ greatly in the way the story is told, including where the plot begins.

Starting with the narrative found in the indictment, we will first take a closer look at the significance of the beginning. How does this narrative begin? Interestingly, the narrative formulated by the prosecuting authority begins at the moment where Per and Veronica's presumed intention of killing Per's parents is first concretely acted upon: "In the fall of 1998 Veronica and Per Orderud approached Kristin Kirkemo and Lars Grønnerød and asked them whether they could provide them with a firearm."[8] From this point on, the events are seamlessly knitted together up until the events at the scene of the crime. Rhetorically speaking, this is a *logos*-oriented plot-construction, which, through its strong focus on causality, is designed to appeal to the readers' reason. The central function of this plot-construction is to show how the narrative's ending is anticipated already at its very beginning. At the moment of the plot's opening, the string of events that end with the killings are set in motion in such a way that the murders are seen as an all but direct consequence of the act of requesting the firearms. The events of this narrative are arranged almost as if they were subject to a domino effect or a chain reaction.

Moving on to the narrative of the first instance of court, we notice already in the first sentence that this is an entirely different way of telling the story: "Per Orderud has lived his entire life at the Orderud farmstead. His father Kristian Orderud, born in 1918, started running the farm in his teens. He was a relatively dominating person who had strong opinions about how the farm should be run."[9] The beginning is here placed at a much earlier point in the story, with the father's take-over of the farm in the early 1930s. Through this opening, the court signals that this is a narrative about a generational conflict and, more concretely, a conflict about the farm. Through its wide and far-reaching perspective, this is an *ethos*-oriented plot-construction in the sense that it signals a thorough and truth-seeking human seriousness, which is mainly concerned with the question that was on everyone's mind during the trial: How could it be possible that a presumably decent man and able farmer like Per Orderud, whose tender relationship with his mother was well-known in the area, could decide to brutally kill both of his parents over a such trivial conflict – which was all the less significant to Per, one would assume, seeing as his allod (*allodium* or 'right to inherited estate') to the farm had never been questioned. In order to explain this conundrum, the narrative of the court of

---

7 In his classical work *Metahistory*, Hayden White talks about the "inaugurating event," which is necessary in order to transform a chronicle into a story (2014, 7).

8 Quoted from the judgement of Nes Herredsrett, TNESS-2001-51. The translation is mine.

9 TNESS-2001-51. The translation is mine.

the first instance carefully examines the lives of those involved in the story in a way that resembles a Bildungsroman or a biography. In addition, the narrative goes into a thorough review of several other murder cases where the motive was less than rational and hard to understand. The court is then able to conclude that it is indeed possible that Per planned the murders.

Turning now to the court of appeals, whose judgement is still legally valid, we observe that this narrative begins at the opposite end compared to the narrative presented by the first instance of court, i.e., with the discovery of the bodies:

> At about 11 pm on May 23, 1999 [Kristian's brother] drove up to the Orderud farmstead in Sørumsand. Earlier this Sunday, he had tried several times to get in touch with his brother, Kristian Orderud, over the phone. Kristian Orderud lived in a house at Orderud farm with his wife, Marie Orderud. This Pentecost weekend their daughter, Anne Orderud Paust, was visiting her parents. When [Kristian's brother] arrived at the house he found the front door locked. He had keys to it and let himself in but did not manage to get past the entry. He went round the house and up to the terrace and saw the murdered bodies of Kristian Orderud, Marie Orderud and Anne Orderud Paust inside the house.[10]

This opening, where we follow the witness from his premonitions that something is amiss to the horrifying discovery of the dead bodies, resembles the openings of the plots we often find in crime fiction. This way of telling the story is suspense-arousing and designed to draw the reader into the action. Through its plot-construction, the court-as-narrator here invites the reader to imagine what it would be like to discover your family murdered in this manner. This is therefore, rhetorically speaking, a pathos-oriented plot, which places the central emphasis on the shocking nature of the murders. Whereas the narrative in the first instance of court emphasized *the need to understand* how these murders could happen, the narrative of the court of appeal is more concerned with demonstrating that the murders are something that should and must be *strongly condemned*.

As we can see, what we have here are three plot-constructions that make use of each of the main means of persuasion in rhetoric: logos, ethos, pathos. We have also seen how the court, by choosing one opening rather than another, is able to direct the readers' attention in ways that highlight certain aspects of the case.

5. The Gap in the Story and How It Is Dealt With

We turn now to the major gap in the story, which resulted from the fact that the police investigation did not succeed in uncovering who was present at the

[10] LE-2001-666. Obtainable at www.lovdata.no. The translation is mine.

scene of the crime. The first thing to notice is that the gap is not properly described as a plot-hole but should rather be seen as a hole in the story itself and as such a *premise* for the plot-construction. The hole concerns the question of what we know about the reality of the crimes and is not an effect of any particular way of constructing the story. The second thing we should note is that the hole *is a problem* for a story about the Orderud murders intended as a factual basis for the conviction of the four defendants. The main reason for this is the lack of any clear, evidence-based connection between the alleged planning of the murders, which all four defendants are said to have been involved in, and the movement and actions of the murderers on the night of the crime. The question that will concern us in what follows is how this gap between planning and execution was dealt with in the three official stories produced by the criminal justice system in this case.

As we have seen, the three stories in question differ significantly from one another and the same is true for their handling of the gap in the story. We found three distinct rhetorical strategies at work with respect to the beginning of the plot in the three narratives. Similarly, we find three different strategies in the way that they deal with the gap. In the story of the indictment, the narrator hides or covers up the hole; in the story formulated in the first judgement, the hole is left open; and, finally, in the story formulated by the court of appeal, the narrator tries to *fill in* the hole. The task of the following analysis is to examine the specific problems connected with each way of dealing with the gap.

The narrative in the indictment is short and has a strong focus on causality. The narrative movement from the phase of planning to the carrying out of the killings looks seamless at the first glance:

> On the night of April 3, 1999 at Orderud farm Per Orderud received a revolver cal. 38 with ammunition from Lars Grønnerød in exchange for one of the pistols that Kristin Kirkemo had acquired. The exchange of weapons took place as a result of Per Orderud's request. After prior consideration the murders were committed in the following manner: [here follows a technical description of the shots fired and their impact on the bodies of the victims].[11]

In this narrative the plot is constructed in such a way as to make the hole inconspicuous. This is done by going directly from Per's obtaining the firearm to the technical description of the murders. One thereby gets the impression that at least Per must have been present at the scene of the crime, since he has, in the previous sentence, received one of the weapons that were used at the scene of the crime. But in fact, no such claim is made in this story. While Per is the subject in the sentence about the gun, the following sentence makes no reference to any particular subject. It is simply stated that the murders were committed in the manner which is deductible from the investigation of the

[11] TNESS-2001-51.

crime-scene. The rhetorical trick consists in constructing a causally oriented story where the causal link is heavily implied throughout the sequence, including the causal connection between Per's receiving the gun and the execution of the killings. Close reading is required in order to notice that the subject is in fact lacking in the sentence which follows immediately after the sequence about the gun. In this way a causal connection is implied without being stated outright, and this is what I am referring to when I claim that the hole is concealed. This is partly an effect of the story's discourse (leaving out the subject), and partly a result of plot-construction (strong focus on presenting the reader with a causally arranged string of events).

In the narrative presented by the first instance of court, the gap is handled very differently compared with the story of the indictment. Instead of concealing the hole, the hole is openly discussed at various stages of the court's presentation of the case. For example, the court clearly states that it is unclear whether there were "one or several perpetrators" present at the scene of the crime, adding that the findings at the crime-scene "are much too uncertain to claim with any reasonable degree of certainty that any of the three defendants can be tied to the execution of the murders."[12] In other words, the court is here quite outspoken about the fact that what happened on the night of the murders is largely unknown, focusing instead on establishing a motive for each of the defendants and on proving that planning had occurred, and that Lars had instructed Per and Veronica in how to use a firearm. This way of handling the gap is in line with the ethos-oriented nature of this narrative in the sense that the court-as-narrator is honest about what it does not know. The problem with this narrative is that the hole weakens the plausibility and overall soundness of the story. It does so not only because it is possible that there was more than one plan to kill the same people, but also because it is possible that one or more of the defendants were unaware that any serious attempt on the life of Per's parents was being suggested. The court, in its narrative, is trying to overcome this problem by focusing on establishing a clear motive for all of the defendants.

Turning now to our third narrative, formulated in the judgment issued by the court of appeal. We can observe here a third strategy with respect to how the gap in the story is dealt with. The connection between the planning and the carrying out of the murders is presented in a similar way compared to the narrative in the court of first instance, but with a significant addition. After having established Per's acquisition of the firearms, the court-as-narrator tells us that "after deliberation, Per left the completion [of the plan] to others."[13] This is an attempt to *fill in* the hole in the story in the sense that the missing link between the planning and execution of the murders is partially brought forward:

---

[12] TNESS-2001-51. The reason why the court only mentions three of the defendants is that it concluded that Lars had an alibi for the night of the crime.

[13] LE-2001-666.

Per has planned everything, with the help of his wife and the other defendants, and then left it to others to carry out the plan. Read in isolation, this addition makes the story more complete and would therefore seem to lessen the gap that troubled the other narratives. But on closer look, the opposite is true: the addition creates far more problems for the story than it solves.

First, it should be noted that the whole operation is illegitimate. The gap belongs to the narrative's story-level, and one cannot fill in such a gap through plot-construction alone. Any attempt to fill in such a gap must involve introducing new elements at the level of the story, which requires the introduction of new evidence or source material. However, this is not done in this case: the new plot element is introduced without any new information to support it. To my mind, this strategy is fatal to the plausibility of the entire narrative. By attempting to bridge the two separate parts of the story, and thus partly getting rid of the hole, several *other* holes immediately open up: Who were these other people? What did they receive as compensation? Why has there been no mention of such a compensation in the rest of the story? What could be the reason why no evidence for such a compensation has been discovered? How did Per come into contact with these people? How did they arrive at the scene of the crime? And if Per did indeed leave the killings to others, who were presumably professionals, why did he and his wife stay at the farm's main building on the night of the killings instead of securing an alibi for themselves by going away? In fact, they left early the next day before the bodies were discovered.

Instead of filling in the hole, the addition to the plot made by the court of appeal has the effect of creating a plethora of new holes in the narrative. This illustrates a central characteristic of stories in general: that they cannot simply be viewed as linear sequences but must be regarded as organic wholes, in the sense that each point in the story is not only connected to what comes immediately before it and after it but also to a host of other story-elements. A change made at one point in the narrative may therefore have unforeseen consequences for other parts of the narrative and may, as in this case, have a negative effect on the narrative's overall coherence. And when a factual narrative loses coherence, it also becomes less plausible. Plausibility is of course crucial to any instance of legal storytelling and of particular importance when the story is used by a court as a basis to convict people of murder. In Norway, as in many other legal jurisdictions, the standard of proof in criminal cases is that the guilt of the defendant must be established beyond reasonable doubt in cases of conviction. The standard of proof may be reformulated in terms of narrative plausibility. According to the Norwegian legal scholar Eivind Kolflaath, this can be done by stating that a conviction is admissible only when the court is unable to construct an evidence-based story to support an acquittal after having examined all the evidence in the case (2013, 156). I will leave the question open as to whether this criterion has been met in the Orderud case, but would like to suggest that the possibility that it is *not* met increases when the story that serves as a basis for conviction is incoherent or implausible.

6. Conclusion

We have seen in this contribution that rhetoric is at work at all levels of legal storytelling, including the stories which are presented in judgements. In order to analyze the story's rhetoric, it is useful to pay attention to the particular rhetorical maneuvers that takes place both at the story-level and discourse-level of the narrative as well as that of the plot. The example of the Orderud case shows us that establishing *the beginning* is a crucial part of plot-construction, not least because the beginning tends to set the tone and establish the theme of the entire narrative. The example also shows that different possibilities exist with respect to handling problems at the narrative's story-level through plot construction, while at the same time pointing towards an important *restriction* on plot-construction in factual narratives: One cannot, in the effort to construct as plausible a plot as possible, introduce elements to the plot that are without basis on the narrative's story-level. Any introduction of new narrative elements at a factual narrative's story level requires the support of new evidence or source material. The narrative in the legally binding judgment in the Orderud case illustrates the kinds of problems that can result from the violation of this restriction. The fact that this judgment is still actively contested, almost twenty years after it was issued, suggests that problems in narrative construction may point to serious flaws in the evidentiary foundation of the case.

Works Cited

Brooks, Peter (1992) *Reading for the Plot*. Revised edition. Cambridge, MA: Harvard Univ. Press.

Chatman, Seymour (1980) *Story and Discourse*. Ithaka, NY: Cornell Univ. Press.

Dannenberg, Hilary P. (2005) "Plot." *Routledge Encyclopedia of Narrative Theory*. Ed. David Herman, Manfred Jahn and Marie-Laure Ryan. London/New York: Routledge. 435–439.

Kjus, Audun (2010) *Stories at Trial*. Liverpool: Deborah Charles Publications.

Kolflaath, Eivind (2013) *Bevisbedømmelse i praksis* [The Evaluation of Evidence in Practice]. Bergen: Fagbokforlaget.

Pedersen, Frode Helmich (2021) "The Court's Story of Facts." *Narratives in the Criminal Process*. Ed. Frode Helmich Pedersen, Espen Ingebrigtsen, Werner Gephard. Frankfurt a. M.: Klostermann.

Stierle, Karlheinz (1973) "Geschehen, Geschichte, Text der Geschichte." *Geschichte, Ereignis und Erzählung*. Ed. Reinhart Koselleck and Wolf-Dieter Stempel. München: Fink.

White, Hayden (2014) *Metahistory* [1973]. Baltimore: Johns Hopkins Univ. Press.

Erfahrungs- oder Tatsachenbericht? Das Zeugnis der Überlebenden Maryla Rosenthal im 1. Frankfurter Auschwitz-Prozess

Dominique Hipp

1. Zeugen in Prekärer Lage

Strafprozesse dienen dazu, die (Un-)Schuld der Angeklagten zweifelsfrei zu beweisen. In der Folge sind sie es, die im Mittelpunkt der Hauptverhandlungen stehen, und die verschiedenen hinzugezogenen Beweismittel – Gutachten, Indizien, Zeugenaussagen – dienen somit der Klärung der Handlungen des Angeklagten (Henne 2007, 81–83). Das gleiche Phänomen – die Angeklagten als zentrale Figur im Strafgerichtsverfahren – gilt für die Verfahren zu nationalsozialistischen Gewaltverbrechen (NSG) der Nachkriegszeit in der Bundesrepublik Deutschland (BRD). Jenseits der erzählerischen Besonderheiten war auffällig, welch geringen Einfluss dagegen das Erzählen der Überlebenden auf die Prozessdynamik hatte. Auch wenn bereits die Anklageschrift implizit eine Anerkennung des verbrecherischen Handelns war, das Geschehen hatte stets einen klaren Fokus auf die Angeklagten, weshalb die (west)deutschen Prozesse nur der Beginn einer Auseinandersetzung mit NS-Verbrechen sein konnten. Die Möglichkeiten, die die juristischen Verfahren bieten, sind also eine beginnende Auseinandersetzung mit den vergangenen Verbrechen, finden aber klare Grenzen ihrer Möglichkeiten in der Wahrnehmung des Erlebten und Erzählten der ZeugInnen jenseits der Funktion eines Beweismittels (Hipp 2020, 212–213).

Gleichzeitig ist die Beschäftigung mit den Zeugnissen, konkret mit den Aussagen der Überlebenden vor Gericht, ebenso erkenntnisfördernd wie die mit dem Erzählen der Angeklagten. Der Grund findet sich einerseits in den juristischen Gegebenheiten bzw. dem Fortgang des Gerichtsverfahrens. Darin stellt der Zeugenaufritt einen theatralen Höhepunkt dar (Weitin 2016, 47). Zweifel und Unstimmigkeiten sollen durch das unvermittelte Erzählen der vergangenen Ereignisse aus der Sicht eines ehemaligen Beobachtenden „vereindeutigt werden“ (58). Diese fast schon heroische Zuschreibung, die den ZeugInnen im Strafprozess zugedacht wird, steht im Widerspruch zur Unsicherheit und zum Zweifel, die jeder Zeugenaussagen entgegengebracht werden bzw. werden müssen und worin sich die prekäre Lage der Überlebenszeugen begründet (53). Das Dilemma der Überlebenszeugen findet sich also nicht nur in der Tatsache, dass die Shoah ein Ereignis ohne Zeugen war und immer noch ist, sondern auch in der Tatsache, dass ihre Aussagen in den juristischen Kategorien von wahr oder falsch bzw. glaubhaft und nicht-glaubhaft kategorisiert wurden. Die Verfahren reduzierten also die Zeugnisse auf ihren faktischen Gehalt und ihre Funktion vor Gericht, denn im Strafprozess ist das Zeugnis ein „im formellen rechtlichen Sinne [...] mündliche oder schriftliche Aussage eines Zeugen über selbst wahrgenommene, rechterhebliche Tatsachen zum Zwecke des rechtlichen Beweises" (Scholz 2011, 25). Diese juristische Wertung kann die Besonderheit der Aussagen in ihrer konkreten Verfasstheit als Zeugnis nicht greifen. Der vorliegende Aufsatz befasst sich daher mit der Frage, wie ein quellenkritischer Umgang mit den in den juristischen Verfahren entstandenen Zeugenaussagen aussehen kann, der die Besonderheiten eines erinnernden Erzählens, aber auch das Erleben der Shoah greifen kann, also das Ausgesagte als Erfahrungs- und nicht als Tatsachenbericht berücksichtigt. Aus diesen Gründen basieren die folgenden Gedanken und die daraus resultierende Argumentation unter anderem auf philosophischen Überlegungen zum Themenkomplex Zeugenschaft und dem prekären Status von Überlebenszeugen vor Gericht.[1] Diese entscheidenden philosophischen Überlegungen werden dann verknüpft mit den Aussagen der Zeugin Maryla Rosenthal im Ersten Frankfurter Auschwitz-Prozess.

2. *Die Besonderheit von Zeugen in NSG-Verfahren*

Gerichtsverfahren sind stets ein Aushandeln zwischen Recht und Gerechtigkeit – bei Verfahren der *transitional justice*[2] gilt dies umso mehr. Agamben (2003) trifft für diesen Aspekt eine wichtige begriffliche Unterscheidung zwischen Augenzeugen und Überlebenszeugen. Ist Ersterer glaubhaft in seinen Aussagen, weil er als Außenstehender nur eine beobachtende und somit distanzierte Rolle eingenommen hat, so vertritt der Überlebenszeuge das gegenteilige Prinzip. Weil ÜberlebenszeugInnen keine außenstehenden BeobachterInnen, sondern Teil des vergangenen Ereignisses waren, verleiht ihnen dieses Beteiligtsein eine ethisch-moralische Position, die ihnen Glaubwürdigkeit wie auch Glaubhaftigkeit verleiht. Richtigerweise sieht Agamben darin eine Erweiterung ihrer juristischen Position, allerdings stellt dies wiederum im Juristischen eben ein

---

[1] Gerichte begegnen den ZeugInnen mit einem „methodische[n] Zweifel" (Schmidt 2009, 8). Die Unzuverlässigkeit von Erinnerung ist im juristischen Rahmen bei dem Umgang mit ZeugInnen von Beginn an mitgedacht. Der vorliegende Aufsatz will deshalb die Frage nach der besonderen Evidenz durch (Überlebens-)ZeugInnen stellen und sieht sich deshalb nicht in den Zusammenhang der verschiedenen gedächtnistheoretischen Überlegungen eingebunden.

[2] *Transitional justice* meint eine Übergangsjustiz von einer Diktatur zu einer Demokratie. Sie macht es sich zur Aufgabe, die im vorherigen politischen System begangenen Verbrechen rechtlich zu ahnden. Gesellschaftliche, politische und rechtstaatliche Strukturen befinden sich ebenfalls im Umbruch (Hipp 2020, 211–212).

Problem dar, da es den Zweifel an den Aussagen bestärkt, weil ÜberlebenszeugInnen eben nicht (nur) objektive BeobachterInnen waren, sondern auf Grund der besonderen Lagerstrukturen ein unmittelbarer Teil des Geschehens waren (14–15).[3]

Die Aufgabe der NSG-Verfahren war neben der strafrechtlichen Ahndung auch an eine emanzipatorische Idee angelehnt, denn durch die Anerkennung der ZeugInnen als Geschädigte findet ebenso eine Würdigung des Erlebten statt. So setzen sich die NSG-Verfahren der BRD zum Ziel, die Verbrechen der NS-Zeit zu verurteilen und Recht im Sinne der Opfer zu sprechen. Die Verfahren werden als ein Weg gesehen, das Leiden der Überlebenden von nationalsozialistischen Verbrechen anzuerkennen. Dieses Vorhaben gelingt jedoch kaum, weil die juristischen Verfahren den Aussagen und deren Zeugnischarakter nicht gerecht werden können. Warum dies scheitern muss, eröffnet Lacans Überlegung. So trennt Lacan nicht zwischen dem Gesagten und dem Sprechenden. Er sieht das ‚Was' des Erzählens an zweiter Stelle, wenn es um die Konstitution einer Subjektidentität geht. Entscheidend ist in seinen Augen vielmehr das Gegenüber, das durch die Zuhörerschaft überhaupt erst die Möglichkeit einer Trennung vom Gesagten und Sagendem zu überwinden schafft. Diese potentielle Überwindung einer Zweiteilung ist für Lacan entscheidend, um ein Zeugnis abgeben zu können, und gleichzeitig für die AdressatInnen, um das Gesagte als Zeugnis zu fassen (Haas 1975, 44).

Der vorliegende Aufsatz zeigt deshalb die quellenkritischen Möglichkeiten, aber auch Grenzen im Umgang mit den Aussagen der Überlebenden in juristischen Verfahren zu Verbrechen in den nationalsozialistischen Konzentrations- und Vernichtungslagern auf. Ein erstes Problem stellt die fehlende oder nur fragmentarische Dokumentation des Prozessgeschehens von westdeutschen NSG-Verfahren dar. Die deutsche, aber auch die österreichische Strafprozessordnung sieht bis heute keine umfassende Protokollierung der Hauptverhandlung vor. Zeugenaussagen im Prozessgeschehen selbst und die gesamte Dynamik der Hauptverhandlung lassen sich also nicht mehr rekonstruieren. Die Situation des historiografischen Umgangs mit den Aussagen von Überlebenden in juristischen Verfahren ist somit auf der Basis zahlreicher vergangener Prozesse schlicht nicht möglich, weil die im Prozess gemachten Aussagen nicht dokumentiert wurden. Die konventionalisierte Fokussierung auf die Person des Angeklagten zeigt sich ebenfalls in der unvollständigen Dokumentation der Aussagen, unter anderem in den Protokollen der österreichischen Volksgerichtsprozesse der Jahre 1945 bis 1955. Selbiges gilt genauso für die bundesrepublikanischen Verfahren. Sind im Falle der österreichischen Volksgerichtsprozesse die Hauptverhandlungen protokolliert worden, so ist doch die Überliefe-

[3] Die perfide Struktur der Häftlingsgesellschaft – nicht zu verstehen als soziale Struktur – schloss das Unbeteiligtsein für die Inhaftierten aus, vielmehr war die unfreiwillige, aktive Teilhabe notwendig, um ein Überleben möglich zu machen (Kranebitter 2014, 28–32).

rung der Zeugenaussagen nur unzureichender Art – biografische Daten und Gründe für die Inhaftierung der Häftlinge in einem der nationalsozialistischen Konzentrationslager lassen sich nur lückenhaft klären, und die Fragen der anderen Prozessbeteiligten an die Zeugen sind nicht niedergeschrieben.

Eine Ausnahme – hinsichtlich der Dokumentation – bilden aber die Frankfurter Auschwitz-Prozesse. Bei den von Juni 1959 bis Oktober 1962 andauernden Ermittlungen fanden die Aussagen von fast 1.500 ZeugInnen und von mehreren hundert Beschuldigten Eingang in die Untersuchungen. Auf Grund der Fülle an Akten und Materialien hatte der Bundesgerichtshof Tonbandaufnahmen als Gedächtnisstütze unter der Voraussetzung einer Einwilligung der aussagenden ZeugInnen erlaubt. Die nach Prozessende geplante Löschung der insgesamt ca. 430 Stunden Tonbandaufnahmen konnte durch Hermann Langbein, dem Generalsekretär des *International Auschwitz Commitee* verhindert werden (Wojak 2009, 328–329). Für nachfolgende Analysen birgt dies den großen Vorteil, dass der textbasierten, schriftlichen Überlieferung die Tonbandaufnahmen als Korrektiv gegenübergestellt werden können. So soll auch im Folgenden die Aussage der Zeugin Maryla Rosenthal aus dem Ersten Auschwitz-Prozess analysiert und den philosophischen Überlegungen zur Zeugenschaft produktiv entgegengestellt werden.

Die Frage war oder ist nun, mit welchem anderen quellenkritischen Blick die Aussage von ZeugInnen wahrgenommen werden kann, um die juristische Fokussierung auf die Angeklagten zu durchbrechen und somit den Besonderheiten der Überlebenszeugen Rechnung zu tragen. Es geht also um nicht weniger als den Versuch, eine Lücke im Werkzeug der Quellenanalyse zu schließen und gleichzeitig über eine mögliche Lösung eines Dilemmas nachzudenken. Der entscheidende Punkt ist, die Aussagen der Reduktion auf ihre Funktion im juristischen Kontext, der Funktion als Beweismittel, zu entheben und durch die Einordnung in die Kategorie als Zeugnis für Erkenntnismöglichkeiten jenseits der bloßen Information zu erweitern.

3. Zeugnis vs. Zeugenaussage

Was aber genau unterscheidet die Wahrnehmung von Erzähltem als Zeugnis von der Wahrnehmung von Erzähltem als Zeugenaussage? Und welche Folgen hat die unterschiedliche Wahrnehmung des Gesagten für die AdressatInnen? Bevor der vorliegende Text aber auf das Zeugnis von Überlebenszeugen eingeht, soll hier ein kurzer Exkurs zur *testimony*-Debatte skizziert werden, um das philosophische Grundproblem zur Vermittlung von Wissen durch einen Zeugen aufzugreifen.

Zeugen stellen die Mittelbarkeit dar, durch die das Wissen an den Einzelnen oder die Einzelne gelangt. Gemäß dem Ideal der Aufklärung soll aber das eigene Wissen und die daraus ableitbare Erkenntnis aus dem eigenen Verstehen entstehen und eben nicht durch Dritte vermittelt werden. Dies liegt zum einen an der Skepsis gegenüber jeglichem Vermittelten, aber auch am aufklärerischen Impetus des ‚Ich'. Der Zeuge als Medium stellt in dieser Sicht also insofern ein Problem dar, als er sich zwischen das eigene Erkennen und das Erkennen des Ichs stellt. Der Reduktionismus lehnt Zeugnisse als Wissensquelle aus genau diesem Grund ab (Krämer et al. 2017, 13). Eine Kritik an dieser verkürzten Sicht auf Zeugenschaft ist die mangelnde Berücksichtigung der Überlebenszeugen. Die Überlebenden treten nicht nur in der Funktion von bloßer Wissensvermittlung auf, sondern sie treten vielmehr als „politisch-moralische Autorität [auf], die ihnen zuwächst kraft der solitären Erfahrung eines Ereignisses, das nicht nur erlebt, sondern überlebt wurde" (16). Eine reduktionistische Sicht berücksichtigt diesen Umstand nicht. Überlebenszeugen sind diese politisch-moralische Autorität nicht aufgrund ihrer Aussage, sondern aufgrund ihres erlebten Leids. Sie umgibt deshalb eine „Aura eines Außerordentlichen" (17), der epistemische Faktor ist in der Folge für die Bewertung des Erzählten nicht entscheidend.

Grundlegend für den Zeugnischarakter ist darüber hinaus die Beglaubigung durch das Publikum (Schmidt 2016a, 121). Für den Zeugen ist somit die kommunikative Situation, also eine Zuhörerschaft entscheidend, die ihn durch ihre Anwesenheit zum Zeugen macht. Durch die sprachliche Handlung des Zeugen wird ein „wechselseitiges soziales Verhältnis geschaffen" (Krämer et al. 2017, 18), das in dieser dialogischen Form Vertrauen schafft, weshalb die anti-reduktionistische Sicht das Zeugnis durchaus als Wissensquelle anerkennt. Ebenso setzen sich die ZeugInnen durch das Publikum ebenso dessen Erwartungen aus. Diese Erwartungen unterscheiden sich ebenso wie das Erzählen der Zeugen in Form, Anspruch und auch in den Inhalten von den Kontexten, in denen sie über das Vergangene erzählen. Der Komplex der Zeugenschaft erfordert also sowohl die Berücksichtigung des ‚institutionellen' Rahmens als auch die einer möglichen Kritik am Publikum, denn erwartungsgemäß orientieren sich die Sender zumeist an den Ansprüchen der AdressatInnen (Krämer 2011, 123). Authentizität ist deshalb an dieser Stelle ein entscheidendes Stichwort und kann die problematische Seite dieser kommunikativen Situation markieren. Denn „[a]uthentisch nennt ein Beobachter die Übereinstimmung einer Beobachtung [...] mit seiner Erwartung (bezüglich einer Person oder eines Objekts)" (Schilling 2020, 41). Zeugen und auch Überlebenszeugen sind somit stets mit den Erwartungen ihres Publikums konfrontiert. Vor Gericht ist die Erwartung vom Ziel der Urteilsfindung geprägt.[4] Gilt vor Gericht durch die Reduktion auf die Funktion als Beweismittel und dem Zeugen als eben solches Mittel, nicht mehr

[4] Agamben (2003) formuliert so auch die Grenzen der Terminologien wie (Un-)Schuld und Verantwortung. Beide sind dem Theologischen und Juristischen entlehnt. Das Juristische gibt vor, durch das richterliche Urteil sowohl Wahrheit als auch Gerechtigkeit herstellen

und nicht weniger, so kommt diese Objektivierung einer Re-Traumatisierung gleich, und ihr ist gleichzeitig durch die asymmetrische Gesprächssituation eine Machtdemonstration des Gerichts gegenüber dem Zeugen eingeschrieben[5] (Steyerl 2015, 21).

3.1. Zeugenaussagen und ihre Funktion in Gerichtsverfahren

Aufgabe des Publikums ist es aber auch nicht nur, dem Gesagten, sondern auch dem Sprechenden zu glauben, wenn eine Zeugenaussage ‚gelingen' soll. Glaubwürdigkeit und Glaubhaftigkeit sind also fundamental für ein Zeugnis und müssen durch die AdressatInnen quittiert werden. Diese Korrelation von Person und Erzählung, die für das faktuale Erzählen per se typisch ist, ist für den Zeugnischarakter nicht nur pragmatisch, sondern auch moralisch entscheidend. Bereits an dieser Stelle zeigt sich ein erster Konflikt mit dem juristischen Kontext und den Aussagen der Überlebenden, die als Zeugnisse zu charakterisieren sind. Sind doch gerade die Individualität und Einmaligkeit nicht für die Qualität des Beweismittels der Zeugenaussage entscheidend. Vielmehr ist im Prozess die reine Funktionalität des Ausgesagten von Belang, weshalb u.a. der Richter im Frankfurter Auschwitz-Prozess Maryla Rosenthal wiederholt auch als ‚Frau Zeugin' anspricht. Es ist also nicht die einzelne Person, ihr Erleben und ihr Erzählen, sondern die Funktionalität und die personifizierte Beispielhaftigkeit, die für das Gerichtsverfahren entscheidend sind. Wären die Aussagen einzigartig, wäre – im juristischen Sinne gedacht – die Stärke ihrer Beweiskraft deutlich geringer.

Zeugenaussagen werden wie alle anderen Beweismittel als argumentativ und für die Wahrheitsfindung nützlich oder unbrauchbar kategorisiert. Das individuelle Erleben kann im juristischen Verfahren keine Rolle spielen. Um im juristischen wie auch geschichtswissenschaftlichen Diskurs ein möglichst genaues Gesamtbild über die Vergangenheit zu erlangen, sind unter anderem die Gegensätze von ‚wahr' und ‚falsch' entscheidend. Denn „während das Zeugnis [...] in jeder Hinsicht singulär ist, unterliegt die Zeugenschaft einer Logik des Beweises, aus der sich Kriterien von Überprüfbarkeit, Übereinstimmung und Bestätigung ableiten" (Weigel 2000, 127). Es ist also genau das entscheidende Charakteristikum des Zeugnisses, das im Widerspruch zur Rolle des Zeugen vor Gericht als Beweismittel steht. In der Folge kann das Gericht in der aus-

zu können. „Dem Recht geht es [aber] ausschließlich um das Urteil, unabhängig von Wahrheit oder Gerechtigkeit" (16).

5 Steyerl (2003, 21) thematisiert die Ambivalenz, mit denen die Umgebung auf Zeugnisse reagiert. Einerseits stehen sie unter Verdacht, andererseits stellen sie eine der entscheidenden Zugänge zur Vergangenheit dar. Gleichzeitig können nicht alle gleichermaßen von ihren Erlebnissen erzählen bzw. Gehör finden.

schließlichen Wahrnehmung des Zeugnisses als Beweismittel keinen Beitrag zum emanzipatorischen Akt des Erzählens beitragen, denn

> [d]amit ist das Zeugnis [eine] Erinnerungsrede, die sich auf eine singuläre Erfahrung bezieht – aber jenseits des Gegensatzes von Fiktion und Faktizität situiert [ist], da sich das Zeugnis allein auf die vergangene, dem allgemeinen Bewusstsein und kollektiven Gedächtnis unzugängliche Erfahrung bezieht, die dem Individuum zugestoßen ist. (Weigel 2000, 116)

Wegen dieses Erlebens, das die Autorität eines Überlebenszeugen ausmacht und sich in dessen Zeugnis wiederfindet, spricht Sibylle Schmidt von einer „internen Wahrheit“ (Schmidt 2016b, 205), die sich im Erzählen des Überlebenden finden.

3.2. Folgen der Funktionalisierung der Zeugenaussagen

Die Einzigartigkeit steht somit im Widerspruch zur Funktion des Zeugen im Gerichtsverfahren, wo er stets einem „methodische[n] Zweifel“ (Schmidt 2009, 8) unterliegt und vor allem durch eine Plausibilität wie auch Kohärenz gemessen an den anderen Aussagen und Beweismitteln an Gültigkeit gewinnt bzw. verliert. Dieses systemisch bedingte Misstrauen gegenüber den Aussagen der Überlebenden stellt den ethisch-moralischen Konflikt von NSG-Verfahren in Bezug auf den Umgang mit den darin erbrachten Zeugnissen dar (Schmidt 2009, 25). Ist es doch gerade das Ziel der nationalsozialistischen Vernichtung gewesen, ein Ereignis zu schaffen, dessen Wesen ein nicht Belegbares ist. In der Folge ist gleichzeitig „[d]as Spezifikum des Zeugnisses vom Holocaust, [...] dass es sich um singuläre, auch isolierende Erfahrungen handelt, mit denen jeder Zeuge radikal allein steht“ (49). Diese frappierende Zeugnislosigkeit der Shoah schlägt sich auch nieder in dem Gerücht als wichtige Informationsquelle im Lageralltag. Die Häftlinge mussten sich auf das Hörensagen verlassen, weil die reale tödliche Gefahr die einzig verbriefte Realität war. Diese Unbestimmtheit war ein strukturelles Merkmal der umfassenden und allgegenwärtigen Willkür der nationalsozialistischen Konzentrations- und Vernichtungslager. Dies zeigt sich auch bei der Zeugin Maryla Rosenthal im Ersten Frankfurter Auschwitz-Prozess. Das Gericht will eine eindeutige und zweifelsfreie Aufklärung des Sachverhalts. Weil es aber ein Trugschluss ist, die Shoah detailliert aufklären zu können, muss dieses Vorhaben scheitern. ZeugInnen wie Maryla Rosenthal sahen sich oftmals den Erwartungen eines Gerichts ausgesetzt, dass sie die/eine „richterliche Suche nach materieller Wahrheit im Gerichtsverfahren“ (Barton 2017, 94) maßgeblich unterstützen sollten. Die Aussagen der ÜberlebenszeugInnen konnten dies aber oftmals aufgrund emotionaler bzw. traumatischer Überforderung nicht leisten.

Gleichzeitig findet sich in der Zeugenlosigkeit der Shoah auch der Grund für ihre Singularität; durch die Einmaligkeit bzw. den außerordentlichen Charakter ist weder Vergleichbarkeit noch Referentialität für das Ereignis gegeben. Das Wissen um den Holocaust ist also durch die Erstmaligkeit des Ereignisses in kein vorher generiertes wie auch verbreitetes Erfahrungswissen einzuordnen. Diese fehlenden ‚Ähnlichkeiten' zu vorherigen Ereignissen bringt die Zeugnisse hinsichtlich eines Vertrauens durch das Publikum in eine prekäre Situation. Hier findet sich somit ein weiteres entscheidendes Dilemma für die Zeugnisse der Überlebenden.

Ein weiterer wichtiger Aspekt neben der faktischen Unmöglichkeit des Bezeugens eines stattgefundenen Ereignisses findet sich im Involviertsein der Überlebenden in den Abläufen der Vernichtung, was bedeutet, dass „Häftlinge […] beständig im Bewußtsein, auf Kosten und an Stelle eines anderen Lagerinsassen überlebt zu haben" (Schmidt 2009, 52), weiterlebten. Gehen wir also davon aus, dass „[e]in Zeuge ein Beobachter [ist], der über das, was er gesehen oder gehört hat, möglichst wahrheitsgemäße Aussagen machen soll" (Weitin 2016, 47), werden die Schwierigkeiten wie auch Unmöglichkeiten eines Zeugnisses über die Shoah deutlich. Anders als herkömmliche Zeugen sind die Zeugen der Shoah Teil der vergangenen Vorkommnisse gewesen, deshalb emotional unmittelbar betroffen und traumatisiert. Die gerichtlich geforderte neutrale und objektive Position eines außenstehenden Beobachtenden ist ihnen unmöglich. In der Folge ist für das Zeugnis über die Shoah nicht nur das Was, sondern das Wie des Erzählens und somit die „Performanz des Zeugnisses" (Schmidt 2009, 53) entscheidend. Weigel (2000, 128) bezeichnet das Zeugnis deshalb auch als eine Form der Klage. So ist das zuhörende Publikum, das ja durch sein Vertrauen nicht nur die Glaubwürdigkeit des Zeugen, sondern auch die Glaubhaftigkeit des Ausgesagten ermöglicht, auch für die erwähnte Performanz notwendig. Es kommt also auf die Wahrnehmung der „Schwierigkeit, ja [der] Unmöglichkeit des Bezeugens" (Schmidt 2009, 91) an. Ein Gerichtsprozess kann dieser Unmöglichkeit aber keinen Raum geben. Ist die Anerkennung der Zeugenschaft mit einem Vorhandensein eines Publikums verbunden, taucht ein weiteres Problem für die Zeugen der Shoah auf – das Gerichtsverfahren drängt sie so unter Umständen erneut in einen wortwörtlichen ohnmächtigen Zustand, da das Publikum über die Entscheidungsmöglichkeit verfügt, ob dem geäußerten Zeugnis Gültigkeit zugesprochen wird oder nicht. Es ist deshalb letztlich ein Irrtum, von einer Dokumentation in Bezug auf die Aussagen der Überlebenden der Shoah zu sprechen. Es sind vor allem die Leerstellen, die die Zeugnisse festhalten.[6]

---

[6] Stengel (2019, 577) wählt den Begriff der ‚Dokumentation' in Bezug auf die Überlebenszeugen. Diese Begrifflichkeit aus dem Faktischen vermag es nicht, die Subjektivität des Zeugnisses zu berücksichtigen.

Schmidt (2009) fasst das Wesen des Zeugnisses folgerichtig zusammen:

> Es [d.h. das Zeugnis, DH] umfasst den Bericht eines Dritten, der ein unbeteiligter Beobachter ist, aber auch den eines Überlebenden, der von einer erschütternden Erfahrung gezeichnet ist. Mannigfaltiger noch sind die verschiedenen Formen von Wissen, für die ein Zeugnis je nach Kontext fruchtbar gemacht wird. Wie vor allem hinsichtlich des Überlebenszeugnisses deutlich wird, geht jedoch das Zeugnis nie ganz in den Funktionalisierungen als Beweis, Quelle oder Exempel auf – wenngleich es auch nur in dieser Form zu einem positiven Wissen werden kann. Der nicht archivierbare Rest des Zeugnisses – der zugleich seine Singularität ausmacht – besteht in seiner Performativität. (93)

Letztlich weist erst die philosophische – und auch die erinnerungspolitische Debatte – dem Zeugnis für unterschiedliche Bereiche eine entscheidende Rolle als Erkenntnisquelle zu. Denn Wissen generiert das Individuum durch ein Netz von Zeugnissen, denen es Vertrauen schenkt. In der Folge erhält das Nachdenken über Zeugnis und Zeugenschaft eine moralische wie auch soziale Wende, die im Falle der Überlebenden der Shoah um eine ethische Seite erweitert wurde.

Die Postmoderne macht es sich deshalb zur Aufgabe, „die Beschränktheit des rein epistemischen Zugangs aufzuzeigen" (Schmidt 2011, 60). Begrifflich lässt sich dieser Zusammenhang noch einmal deutlicher machen mit Blick auf eine „diskursive Wahrheit" (Krämer 2017, 149). Diese Form der Wahrheit meint ein argumentatives Aushandeln ihrer selbst, wobei der Diskurs dort beginnt, wo die AdressatInnen Zweifel an den Äußerungen der Zeugen formulieren. Ein Gerichtsverfahren dient dazu, Sachverhalte zu klären und entsprechend ihrer Befunde Recht zu sprechen bzw. ein Urteil zu verkünden. Diese Urteilsfindung verläuft auf argumentativem Wege, wird also ausgehandelt zwischen verschiedenen Prozessbeteiligten. Argumentation wird also auch im Strafprozess verstanden „als das Geben und Nehmen von Gründen in Bezug auf einen strittigen Punkt" (Hannken-Illjes 2019, 31). Da aber die Aussagen von Überlebenszeugen durch ihre Subjektivität nicht nur Wahrheit, sondern vor allem Wahrhaftigkeit vermitteln, ist es nicht die Glaubhaftigkeit der Aussagen, sondern vielmehr die Glaubwürdigkeit der Person, die entscheidend für NSG-Verfahren und noch entscheidender für die Zeitzeugenschaft der Shoah ist.[7] Ihre Aussagen werden vom Gericht in ihrer Funktion als Argumente für die eigene Beweisführung bzw. für die Urteilsfindung als argumentative Schritte genutzt. Der erzählerische Wert gerät dabei aber außer Acht. Ist die Argumentation in ihrer Funktion somit vor allem situativ zu verorten, so muss aber das Zeugnis der Überlebenden in der Aufgabe einer Erzählung verstanden werden, das ex-

---

7 „Wahrhaftigkeit [...] verstanden als Anspruch, der nicht auf die Wahrheit einer Aussage, sondern einer Person in ihrem Verhältnis zu dem, was sie sagt, bezogen ist [...]." (Krämer 2017, 150).

plizit oder auch implizit „gebunden [ist] an die Ausbildung und Versicherung von Identität" (36).

Ob es dem Gericht in NSG-Verfahren wie dem Frankfurter Auschwitz-Prozess gelingt, durch das Zuhören die Seite der Performativität zu erfüllen und so den Aussagenden den Weg zu Subjektivität wie auch aus der Lagerhaft zu ermöglichen, soll die zugrunde liegende Frage der folgenden Analyse der Aussage von Maryla Rosenthal darstellen. Gleichzeitig gilt es aber ebenso, quellenkritische Möglichkeiten aufzuzeigen, die es vermögen, den Zeugnissen in ihrer Ambivalenz zwischen Einmaligkeit und gleichzeitig repräsentativem Charakter gerecht zu werden und so das Dilemma ein Stück weit aufzulösen.

4. Maryla Rosenthal als Zeugin beim 1. Frankfurter Auschwitz-Prozess

Maryla Rosenthal[8] sagte am 26. Verhandlungstag, den 13. März 1964, in dem insgesamt zwanzig Monate andauernden Prozess vor Gericht aus. Rosenthal wurde 1908 in Krakau geboren, im April 1942 von der Gestapo verhaftet und drei Monate später nach Auschwitz deportiert. Dort war sie nach einer kurzen Zeit in einem Arbeitskommando als Dolmetscherin und Schreiberin in der Politischen Abteilung des Stammlagers und ab 1944 in der Politischen Abteilung im sog. ‚Zigeunerlager' tätig. Im Januar 1945 wurde sie weiter in das Frauenkonzentrationslager Ravensbrück deportiert. Zum Zeitpunkt ihrer Aussage vor Gericht im Jahr 1964 war Maryla Rosenthal 55 Jahre alt.[9]

Ein vor Gericht geladener Zeuge unterliegt, im Gegensatz zur angeklagten Person, sowohl einer Aussage- als auch einer Wahrheitspflicht. So klärt Hans Hofmayer, der vorsitzende Richter am 26. Verhandlungstag, vor Beginn ihrer Vernehmung die Zeugin Maryla Rosenthal im Rahmen der Hauptverhandlung über ihre Rechte, aber vor allem über ihre Pflichten als Zeugin auf:

> Frau Rosenthal, Sie sollen hier als Zeugin vernommen werden. [Pause] Es ist menschlich erklärlich, daß Sie sehr ungern an diese Zeit zurückdenken, die hier wiederum in diesem Prozeß auftaucht. Aber wir müssen Sie trotzdem bitten, Ihr Gedächtnis anzustrengen und uns alles zu sagen, was Sie von dieser Zeit noch wissen. Sie müssen nach gesetzlicher Vorschrift auf Ihre Aussage hin beeidigt werden. Und Ihr Eid bezieht sich auch darauf, daß Sie nichts verschwiegen haben. Ich muß Sie deshalb noch mal bitten,

[8] Das Fritz Bauer Institut hat auf der Homepage https://www.auschwitz-prozess.de die Tonbandmitschnitte sowie deren Deskriptionen als pdf-Datei des Auschwitz-Prozesses 1963–1965 zugänglich gemacht. Die wörtlichen Zitate meiner Analyse beziehen sich auf die 25-seitige pdf-Datei der Aussage Rosenthals. Ebenso habe ich die Tonbandaufnahmen berücksichtigt. Im Folgenden werde ich Zitationen aus diesem Dokument mit ‚Rosenthal' und der jeweiligen Seitenzahl der entsprechenden pdf-Datei versehen. Siehe https://www.auschwitz-prozess.de/zeugenaussagen/Rosenthal-Maryla/, zuletzt abgerufen am 06. November 2021.

[9] Siehe Fritz Bauer Institut: Der Auschwitz-Prozess, http://www.auschwitz-prozess-frankfurt.de/index.php?id=55, zuletzt abgerufen am 07. November 2021.

> uns alles zu sagen, selbst dann, wenn Ihnen die Aussage schwerfallen sollte, selbst dann, wenn Sie lieber über diese Dinge schweigen würden. Ich muß es Ihnen aber sagen im Interesse der Wahrheitserforschung und möchte Sie bitten, Ihre Pflichten hier ganz besonders ernst zu nehmen. Es ist meine Pflicht, Sie hinzuweisen auf die Bedeutung des Eides und Sie hinzuweisen auf die Strafen, die auf Meineid angedroht sind. (Rosenthal 1964, 1)

Die Zeugenaussage vor Gericht ist also dieser Belehrung entsprechend ein Beweismittel, das dazu beitragen soll, dem inquisitorischen Paradigma des deutschen Strafrechts – dem Ziel der Wahrheitsfindung – dienlich zu sein. Sie, die Zeugenaussage, soll zur Rekonstruktion des Tathergangs dienen und korrespondierend mit den anderen Zeugenaussagen als Korrektiv gegenüber den Aussagen der Angeklagten zur Klärung der Schuldfrage beitragen. Der Richter macht deutlich, dass die Aussage der Zeugen eine Beweisfunktion zu erfüllen hat. Dieser „Sprechakt [der] Beweisführung“ (Weigel 2000, 120) trägt die Kontrolle seiner Inhalte in sich, weswegen die berichteten Tatsachen überprüft werden, um zu klären, ob die Aussage glaubhaft ist oder nicht. Gleichzeitig setzen das rechtstaatliche Verfahren und die Strafprozessordnung voraus, dass der Zeugenaussage neutral begegnet wird. So auch der vorsitzende Richter Hofmayer, wenn er zwar Verständnis für die Schwierigkeiten einer Aussage über das Erlebte der Zeugin Rosenthal formuliert, aber auch verdeutlicht, dass das Ziel der Wahrheitsfindung dem überzuordnen ist. Umgekehrt ist aber auch implizit Ziel und Motivation der ZeugInnen, dass ihnen geglaubt wird. Letztlich verfolgen also die Zeugin Rosenthal und das Gericht als Zuhörerschaft das gleiche Ziel – beide wollen einen Beitrag zur Aufklärung der Tat leisten.

Nachdem der rechtliche Rahmen, mit dem auch der Referenzrahmen der folgenden Aussagen – das formale wie auch institutionalisierte Setting eines Gerichts – zu Beginn der Vernehmung durch den Richter klar verbalisiert worden ist, folgt die Klärung der biografischen Formalien wie Alter, Beruf, Wohnsitz und Familienstand. Dies geschieht in einem Wechsel aus kurzen Fragen und ebenso kurzen, informierenden Antworten. Dem schließt sich, initiiert durch die Aufforderung des Richters, eine längere Schilderung Rosenthals ihrer Zeit in Auschwitz an. Da die Tonbandaufnahme bei dieser längeren Passage – Maryla Rosenthal spricht über sechs Minuten – keine signifikanten Pausen oder keinerlei Verwendung von Füllwörtern hören lässt, ist davon auszugehen, dass Rosenthal hier eine frühere Schilderung wiederholt oder sie diese eigens für den Gerichtsprozess memoriert hat. So schildert sie ihren Einsatz bei einem Arbeitskommando und den dortigen körperlichen Anstrengungen, denen sie auf Dauer nicht gewachsen gewesen wäre sowie die körperlichen Erniedrigungen, mit denen sie und die anderen Häftlinge täglich konfrontiert wurden (Rosenthal 1964, 3). Rosenthal benennt das Grundproblem der Zeugenschaft, indem sie zwei Mithäftlinge mit einer Warnung an sie zitiert: „[W]as Sie hier sehen und hören, das haben sie nicht gesehen und nicht gehört, sonst bezahlen Sie das mit ihrem Leben“ (3). Die Idee, die Vernichtung der Juden als Ereignis ohne ZeugInnen zu planen, belegt Rosenthal so mit dieser Äußerung und führt ihr Dilemma wie auch das der anderen ZeugInnen deutlich vor Augen, denn die tatsächlichen Zeugen der Vernichtung haben die Shoah nicht überlebt. So schildert und kommentiert sie ihren Aufenthalt im Lager auch als einen des dauerhaften Ausnahmezustands, wenn sie sagt: „Also ich war ganz benommen. Ich konnte das gar nicht verarbeiten, wo ich mich befinde und was das überhaupt ist" (3).

Rosenthal untermauert bei emotionalen Teilen ihrer Aussage diese wiederholt mit direkten Zitaten, so auch bei dem SS-Angehörigen Wilhelm Boger und seiner Androhung von Folter gegenüber den Häftlingen. Im Falle des Tatnachweises von Boger – da sie als Schreibkraft für Boger arbeitete, sollte ihre Aussage vor allem zur Klärung seiner Straftaten beitragen – verdeutlicht sich die Ambivalenz zwischen einer neutralen Zeugenschaft und ihrem damaligen Involviertsein, aber auch die Anforderungen des Publikums, denen sich Rosenthal ausgesetzt sieht, weil sie nicht nur stille Beobachterin der Vorkommnisse in Auschwitz, sondern als Häftling Teil des Systems des Vernichtungslagers Auschwitz war. Der Anspruch des Gerichts ist es, von ihr eine detaillierte und exakte Aussage zu erhalten. Ihre Charakterisierung Bogers als ihr gegenüber „sehr menschlich und sehr anständig" (3) ist der Subjektivität ihres Erlebens geschuldet, und die Rolle des Gerüchts als vage, aber für das Lager typische Informationsquelle benennt sie ebenfalls: „Gesehen habe ich nichts, denn ich war im Büro. Aber da hat sich vieles herumgesprochen" (4). Auch wenn es um die Aufklärung des Schicksals des Häftlings Lilli Tofler[10] geht, waren es das Gerücht und die bisherigen Erfahrungen im Lager, die die Mithäftlinge das Schicksal der inhaftierten Frau erahnen ließen, „[u]nd dann habe ich gehört, sie wurde in den Bunker gebracht, in den berüchtigten Bunker 11. Und dann haben wir gehört, sie wurde erschossen" (8). Doch Maryla Rosenthal kann oftmals keine eindeutigen Informationen über ihr Erlebtes in Auschwitz wiedergeben. So entgegnet sie auf die Frage, ob es sich bei den Verhören durch Boger um polnische Häftlinge gehandelt habe: „Ich glaube, das waren fast immer polnische Häftlinge, politische Häftlinge." Der Richter daraufhin: „Sie glauben, es waren fast immer", was die Zeugin mit „Ja" beantwortet (9).

Vieles, was die Zeugin weiß, hat sie nicht selbst gesehen, vieles, woran sie sich erinnern kann, ist ihr also nicht selbst widerfahren, und gleichzeitig prägten die Gerüchte im Lager ihr dortiges Erleben immens und somit auch das Zeugnis, das sie darüber abgibt. So antwortet Rosenthal auf die Frage, was sie von den Erschießungen im Männerlager wusste, in vollkommen selbstverständlicher Weise: „Man hat davon gesprochen" (17). Der Richter benennt dies aber unter anderem als ein Defizit ihrer Aussage: „Sie wissen es auch nur vom Hörensagen, daß sie [d.h. Lilli Tofler, DH] erschossen worden sein soll" (8).

10 Lilli Tofler war ein Häftling in Auschwitz, die von der SS erschossen wurde. Die Aufklärung des Mordes war ein Vorhaben des Gerichts.

Gemessen an den juristischen Erwartungen, stellt Maryla Rosenthals Aussage so keinen Beweis für die Ermordung Lilli Toflers dar.

Mit dem weiteren Verlauf ihrer Aussage wird aber auch deutlich, dass die Zeugin durch ihr Erzählen zunehmend in die Logik des Lageralltags von Auschwitz (zurück)gelangt, weshalb sie Bogers Folterungen nicht nur neutral schildert, sondern sein Handeln als dessen Aufgabe rechtfertigt.[11] Da sie aber sein Verhalten als ‚schlimm' kategorisiert und sein Pflichtbewusstsein durch ein direktes Zitat Bogers darstellt – „Auf welche Art und Weise ich das mache, geht Sie nichts an. Ich muss zu meinem Ziel kommen" (11) – zeigt ihren retrospektiven Blick auf das Vergangene, das zu beurteilten sie damals und auch im Gerichtsverfahren durchaus in der Lage war. Es zeigt aber noch viel deutlicher – was eingangs bereits vorweggenommen wurde –, dass der Wert eines Zeugnisses sich nicht in der Wiedergabe von Fakten erschöpft, sondern in erster Linie in der Vermittlung einer subjektiven Lebenswirklichkeit.

Deutlich wird ihre Zeugenaussage in der Rolle eines Beweismittels noch einmal gegen Ende der Ausführungen. Der Staatsanwalt thematisiert Rosenthals Abweichungen zwischen ihren Aussagen bei der polizeilichen Vernehmung und insistiert nachdrücklich, um eine möglichst genaue und glaubhafte Aussage zu erhalten (19). Und auch der Nebenklagevertreter will vor allem die Richtigkeit und Zuverlässigkeit ihrer Aussage eruieren, wenn er fragt, „Frau Zeugin, haben Sie vorher schon ein sehr schlechtes Gedächtnis gehabt, oder haben Sie im Lager nervliche oder Gedächtnisschäden erlitten?" (21) Das Bewusstsein des Nebenklagevertreters über die psychischen und physischen Folgen einer Lagerhaft in Auschwitz ist weniger einem Mitgefühl geschuldet als der juristisch notwendigen Einordung und Bewertung der Aussagen von Maryla Rosenthal für eine argumentative Verwendung im Verfahren und für das spätere Urteil.

5. *Erfahrungsbericht vor Gericht – Ein Fazit*

Durch die Reduktion auf die Funktion im juristischen Prozess geht der erzählerische Überhang – also der Anteil, der sich in den Aussagen jenseits von richtig oder falsch findet und die Aussagen zu Zeugnissen macht – verloren. Warum gab es diese Informationen nur in Form von Gerüchten? Was steckt hinter dieser damaligen Form des gerüchteweisen Erzählens unter den Häftlingen? Welche Folgen hat das für das Leben im Lager, aber auch für die Erinnerung an das damalige Erleben? Diese Fragen vermag das Gericht nicht zu stellen, weshalb an diesem Punkt das quellenkritische Moment meiner Überlegungen

11 „Wenn ein Häftling nicht aussagen wollte […] oder wenn er nach dem Begriff von Herrn Boger was sehr Schlimmes getan hat und er mußte von ihm rausbekommen, was das war, dann war er auch schlimm" (Rosenthal 1964, 11).

ansetzt. Und auch die Zeugin Rosenthal selbst markiert im Laufe der Vernehmung deutlich ihr Wissen um die Geschehnisse im Lager auf der Grundlage von Gerüchten, thematisiert die emotionale Überforderung und beschreibt ihre Wahrnehmung nach ihrer Ankunft in der Politischen Abteilung (3).

Schmidts oben zitierte Definition von Zeugnis berücksichtigt die Subjektivität des Erlebten und sieht das Erzählen der Überlebenden vor Gericht zuvorderst als Erfahrungsgeschichte und weniger als Tatsachenbericht. Die besondere Subjektivität entsteht durch die ungeteilte Erfahrung der Handlungsgegenwart von Zuhörerschaft und den Erzählenden. Die Zuhörenden waren im Gegensatz zu den Erzählenden nicht Teil der vergangenen Ereignisse. Das Zeugnis soll deswegen die Erfahrung des Geschehenen bezeugen und vermittelt im Zuge dessen Erfahrungstatsachen.

Durch die Ungleichzeitigkeit von Handlungsgegenwart und dem Zeitpunkt der Aussage, durch die Referenzrahmen der Handlungsgegenwart – also das Leben als Häftling in einem Konzentrations- bzw. Vernichtungslager, die dortige tagtägliche Entwürdigung und dem Ausgesetztsein der Lager-SS –, aber ebenso durch den Referenzrahmen des Gerichts – also der Herausforderung, seinen ehemaligen Peinigern erneut gegenübertreten zu müssen und die erlebten Qualen in einem für das Gericht verwertbaren Bericht wiederzugeben – verdeutlicht sich noch einmal die Dringlichkeit einer anderen Perspektive, die das Erzählte der Überlebenden als Zeugnis greift. Die Zeugin Rosenthal wirkte beispielsweise während ihrer Aussage zum Angeklagten Boger so stark verunsichert, dass einer der Nebenklagevertreter fragte, ob sie sich in Anwesenheit des besagten Angeklagten nicht zu sprechen traue. Die Gefahr einer sekundären Traumatisierung durch das Gerichtssetting beeinflusst das Erzählte ebenfalls in einem erheblichen Maße, und auch die Tatsache, dass viele der Überlebenden über ihre Erfahrungen erstmals vor Gericht sprachen, führte zu einer erheblichen Verunsicherung der Aussagenden.

Im Falle der Überlebenden Rosenthal wird besonders deutlich, wie beharrlich das Gericht auf die Klärung der Faktenlage pocht. Wenn auch nicht unfreundlich, dann doch in so nachdrücklicher Art, dass es gemessen am Erlebten der Zeugin mehr als nur befremdlich erscheint. Das Beweismittel der Zeugenaussage dient also in erster Linie dem Ziel eines juristischen Verfahrens zur Klärung des Sachverhalts und einer sachgemäßen Beurteilung der begangenen Straftaten.

Die Aussagen der Geschädigten – um den juristischen Terminus an dieser Stelle zu verwenden – sind ohne Zweifel als Beweismittel genau für diese Zielsetzungen unerlässlich. Die Möglichkeit einer Nebenklage, die im Falle der Frankfurter Auschwitz-Prozesse wahrgenommen wurde, stützt die Überlebenden in der offiziellen Anerkennung als Geschädigte. Diese Möglichkeit, sich am Prozess zu beteiligen, garantiert aber noch lange nicht, dass das Urteil einen adäquaten Gerechtigkeitsdiskurs initiieren konnte.

Eine wichtige Besonderheit für alle Strafprozesse ist der Angeklagte als Anlass und Zentrum des gerichtlichen Geschehens. Die Aussagen der Zeugen sollten eine Beweisfunktion erfüllen, die im Rahmen der Institution Gericht einen Beitrag zur Tätergeschichte leisteten. Das eigene, subjektive Erleben sollte aber im Hintergrund bleiben. Die Verfahren konnten die „Geste des Bezeugens“ (Weigel 2000, 123) nicht wahrnehmen. Es waren aber die eigenen Erfahrungen des Lagerlebens und die Erfahrungen mit den Angeklagten, die sie schilderten, um dem Ziel eines Beweismittels und dem Erzählen vor Gericht gerecht werden zu können. Verharrt die Einordnung und Verwendung der Aussagen von ÜberlebenszeugInnen auf der juristischen bzw. gerichtlichen Funktion, verkennt dies den Wert solcher Quellen über die Shoah. Eine Einordnung der Aussagen als Zeugnisse und narrative zeithistorische Quellen kann dies hingegen verhindern. Vielmehr erzählen die Überlebenden in ihren Zeugnissen ein persönliches und individuelles Erleben – auch ihre verfahrensrechtliche Position als Geschädigte ändert daran nur wenig. Das bedeutet, dass die vergangenen NSG-Verfahren dem Zeugnischarakter der Überlebenden nicht umfassend Rechnung tragen können. Vielmehr führte das Wieder-Erleben im Erzählen oftmals zu einer Re-Traumatisierung. Der heutige Blick auf diese Aussagen sollte deshalb losgelöst von einer Beurteilung mit juristischen Kategorien von wahr und falsch bzw. glaubhaft und nicht-glaubhaft sein. Eine narratologische Perspektive auf die Aussagen der Zeugen als historische und erzählende Dokumente, also die Wahrnehmung als narrative Quelle mit einer entsprechenden Analyse macht es unter anderem möglich, sowohl deren subjektiven als auch repräsentativen Charakter zu würdigen. Auf diese Weise kann die Erfahrung der ZeugInnen als genuin subjektives Erleben wahrgenommen werden.

Wirft man noch einmal einen Blick auf die Überlegungen von Krämer zum Zeugen als Medium, wird ein weiteres Problem in Bezug auf die Zeugenschaft und der Gleichzeitigkeit von Medium und Person in Verfahren zu Verbrechen in Konzentrationslagern deutlich. Als Häftlinge der Konzentrations- und Vernichtungslager waren sie nicht nur bloße Opfer der Gewalt, sondern sie wurden ihrer Identität und Menschlichkeit beraubt. Krämer sieht aber die Integrität des Personseins als Bedingung einer Zeugenschaft, da ein signifikantes Merkmal von Zeugenschaft die Gleichheit von Medium und Person ist. Mit der Wahrnehmung der Zeugenerzählungen als Zeugnis – also der Wahrnehmung des Erzählten als Erinnerungsrede über ein singuläres Erlebnis – kann diesem Umstand Rechnung getragen werden (Krämer 2008, 248).

Mit der erinnerungspolitischen Wende der ausgehenden 1970er und 1980er Jahre verändert sich die Wahrnehmung von Zeugenschaft in der Bundesrepublik über die Shoah grundlegend. Nicht der Zeuge als Beweismittel vor Gericht, sondern der Zeitzeuge, der sein subjektives Erleben in verschiedenen Kontexten – pädagogisch, didaktisch, historiografisch, museal, etc. – erzählt, steht zentral als moralische Instanz. Der Fall Wilkomirski[12] bringt diese Position erneut ins Wanken, greift aber das Zeugnis in seinem einzelnen und besonderen Wert nicht an. Vielmehr wird Wilkomirskis Buch *Bruchstücke* (1995) als Angriff auf die Einzigartigkeit der Zeugnisse verstanden und deshalb diskursumfassend abgelehnt (Jureit & Schneider 2010, 23–25; Stengel 2019, 578). Ähnlich aber wie im Falle der Gerichtsverfahren sehen sich die ZeitzeugInnen ebenfalls nicht einem Publikum ohne Erwartungen gegenüber. Vielmehr trägt diese Form der Zeugenschaft Anforderungen in einem erinnerungspolitischen Diskurs an die Überlebenden heran. Diese Funktionalisierung schafft sowohl für die Erzählenden als auch für die Erinnerungspolitik Probleme. Weder das Dilemma noch die prekäre Situation der Überlebenszeugen der Shoah kann letztlich aufgelöst werden, allerdings kann das Verständnis der Aussagen als Äußerungen über ein subjektives Erleben eine erneute Objektivierung der Überlebenden verhindern.

Zitierte Literatur

Agamben, Giorgio (2003) *Was von Auschwitz bleibt: Das Archiv und der Zeuge*. Frankfurt a.M.: Suhrkamp.

Barton, Stephan (2017) „Über-Zeugen im Strafverfahren." *Über Zeugen: Szenarien von Zeugenschaft und ihre Akteure (Trajekte)*. Hg. Matthias Däumer, Aurélia Kalisky und Heike Schlie. Paderborn: Wilhelm Fink. 93–110.

Haas, Norbert (1975 (Hg.) *Jacques Lacan. Schriften II.* Olten/Freiburg: Walter.

Hannken-Illjes, Kati (2019) ",Siehe da, es gab Ermessensspielräume': Argumentatives Erzählen – erzählendes Argumentieren." *LiLi* 49.1: 29–49.

Henne, Thomas (2007) „Zeugenschaft vor Gericht." *Zeugenschaft des Holocausts. Zwischen Trauma, Tradierung und Ermittlung*. Hg. Michael Elm, Gottfried Kößler. Frankfurt a.M.: Campus. 79–91.

Hipp, Dominique (2020) *Von NS-Konzentrationslagern erzählen: Angeklagte vor Gericht über Dachau, Mauthausen, Ravensbrück und Neuengamme*. Bielefeld: transcript.

Jureit, Ulrike und Christian Schneider (2010) *Gefühlte Opfer: Illusionen der Vergangenheitsbewältigung*. Stuttgart: Klett-Cotta.

Krämer, Sybille (2008) *Medium, Bote, Übertragung: Kleine Metaphysik der Medialität*. Frankfurt a.M.: Suhrkamp.

[12] 1995 erschien das Buch *Bruchstücke* von Binjamin Wilkomirski, der sich als Überlebender der Shoah ausgab und den Inhalt des Buches als sein Erleben. Drei Jahre später stellte sich heraus, dass Wilkomirski kein Überlebender der Shoah war. Binjamin Wilkomirski ist das Pseudonym von Bruno Dössekker, der 1941 in der Schweiz geboren wurde.

Krämer, Sybille (2011) „Vertrauen schenken: Über Ambivalenzen der Zeugenschaft.“ *Politik der Zeugenschaft. Zur Kritik einer Wissenspraxis*. Hg. Sibylle Schmidt, Sybille Krämer und Ramon Voges. Bielefeld: transcript. 117–139.

Krämer, Sybille (2017) „Spur, Zeuge, Wahrheit: Zeugenschaft im Spannungsfeld zwischen diskursiver und existentialer Wahrheit?“ *Über Zeugen: Szenarien von Zeugenschaft und ihre Akteure (Trajekte)*. Hg. Matthias Däumer, Aurélia Kalisky und Heike Schlie. Paderborn: Wilhelm Fink. 147–165.

Krämer, Sybille, Sibylle Schmidt und Johannes-Georg Schülein (2017) „Zeugenschaft als philosophisches Problem: Zur Einleitung in den Band.“ *Philosophie der Zeugenschaft: Eine Anthologie*. Hg. dies. Münster: mentis. 7–23.

Kranebitter, Andreas (2014) *Zahlen als Zeugen. Soziologische Analysen zur Häftlingsgesellschaft des KZ Mauthausen*. Mauthausen-Studien, Bd. 9. Wien: New Academic Press.

Rosenthal, Maryla (1964) Deskription ihrer Zeugenaussage, DOI: https://www.auschwitz-prozess.de/zeugenaussagen/Rosenthal-Maryla/.

Schilling, Erik (2020) *Authentizität: Karriere einer Sehnsucht*. München: C.H. Beck.

Schmidt, Sibylle (2009) *Zeugenschaft. Ethische und politische Dimensionen*. Frankfurt a.M.: Peter Lang.

Schmidt, Sibylle (2011) „Wissensquelle oder ethisch-politische Figur? Zur Synthese zweier Forschungsdiskurse über Zeugenschaft.“ *Politik der Zeugenschaft. Zur Kritik einer Wissenspraxis*. Hg. dies., Sybille Krämer und Ramon Voges. Bielefeld: transcript. 47–66.

Schmidt, Sibylle (2016a) „Spuren der Authentizität: Zur körperlichen Dimension von Zeugenschaft.“ *Der Spur auf der Spur*. Hg. Sandi Attia, Ingrid Streble, Nathalie Le Boudece und Alice Volkwein. Heidelberg: Universitätsverlag Winter. 119–127.

Schmidt, Sibylle (2016b) „Können Täter Zeugnis ablegen?“ *Zeugen in der Kunst*. Hg. Sybille Krämer und dies. Paderborn: Wilhelm Fink. 195–209.

Scholz, Oliver R. (2011) „Das Zeugnis anderer – sozialer Akt und Erkenntnisquelle.“ *Politik der Zeugenschaft. Zur Kritik einer Wissenspraxis*. Hg. Sibylle Schmidt, Sybille Krämer und Ramon Voges. Bielefeld: transcript. 24–45.

Stengel, Katharina (2019) „Opferzeugen in NS-Prozessen: Juristische Zeugenschaft zwischen Beweis, Quelle, Trauma und Aporie.“ *Jahrbuch des Dubnow-Instituts* XVIII: 577–610.

Steyerl, Hito (2015) *Die Farbe der Wahrheit: Dokumentarismen im Kunstfeld*. Wien/Berlin: Turia + Kant.

Weigel, Sigrid (2000) „Zeugnis und Zeugenschaft, Klage und Anklage: Die Geste des Bezeugens in der Differenz von ‚identity politics', juristischem und historiographischem Diskurs." *Zeugnis und Zeugenschaft*. Hg. Rüdiger Zill. Berlin: Akademie Verlag. 111–135.

Weitin, Thomas (2016) „Den Auftritt des Zeugen beobachten." *Zeugen in der Kunst*. Hg. Sybille Krämer und Sibylle Schmidt. Paderborn: Wilhelm Fink. 47–59.

Wojak, Irmtrud (2009) *Fritz Bauer 1903–1968: Eine Biographie*. 2. Auflage. München: C.H. Beck.

Onlineressourcen

Https://www.auschwitz-prozess.de.

Http://www.auschwitz-prozess-frankfurt.de/index.php?id=55.

Legal Narratives as Imaginary Constructions: Siegfried Kracauer, Historiography and Law's Stories

Arild Linneberg

1. *On the Construction of Legal Narratives*

At the University of Bergen, "The Bergen School of Literature- and Law-studies", our research group have had two research projects funded from RCN (Research Council of Norway), the first one called "The Dramaturgy of Miscarriages of Justice: On the Construction of False or Fictitious Stories in Court" (2009–2013), the second had the title "A Narratology of Criminal Cases" (2016–2021).[1] Both were international interdisciplinary projects within the fields of Law and the Humanities. Moreover, the University of Bergen financed our "Center for Humanistic Legal Studies" (2013–2019).

Our main focus has been on *the construction of legal narratives*, not only from a narratological point of view, but in the context of new and classical rhetoric, semiotics, hermeneutics and critical theory (Linneberg 2021). In this paper I will point at Siegfried Kracauer's relevance for the understanding of law's stories, especially the importance of his philosophy of history, or rather his theory of historiography.

2. *Discontinuity in Space and Time*

"The room that Kracauer has been allocated in the Frankfurt School is sparse," Gertrud Koch wrote in *Siegfried Kracauer zur Einführung* (Koch 1996, viii).[2] Since then, there have been significant attempts to bring Kracauer out from behind the shadows cast by his friends of the Frankfurt School. Anyway, I will start with a short introduction to Kracauer, before discussing the parts of his œuvre that I find most interesting concerning legal discourse.

Siegfried Kracauer (1889–1966) was born in a German-Jewish family in Frankfurt. He held a doctoral degree in architecture and for some years he even worked as an architect. Furthermore, he studied sociology (Georg Simmel

---

[1] The first led by Arild Linneberg with the fulltime researchers Johan Dragvoll and Bjørn Chr. Ekeland, the second led by Frode Helmich Pedersen, both projects with parttime researchers from Nordic and European countries and the US. For some of the results, see Dragvoll et al. (2014), Helmich Pedersen et.al. (2021), Linneberg (2021, 2022).

[2] Quoted from the English edition, *Siegfried Kracauer. An Introduction* (Koch 2000).

was his teacher) and philosophy, and he was a prominent writer in Germany under the Weimar Republic. From 1922–1933 he was the feuilleton-editor in *Frankfurter Zeitung*, where he wrote more than fifteen hundred articles, essays and reviews of literature and film. He and his wife Lili[3] lived in Berlin from 1931 to 1933. After the Reichstag Fire in February 1933, they moved to Paris. From 1933 to 1941 they were refugees in Paris and Marseille. In April 1941 they managed to flee to the US with the last ship with refugees from Lisbon to New York. After the second world war Kracauer became a leading film theorist, and in cooperation with the research group "*Poetik und Hermeneutik*" in Giessen he contributed to a shift of the paradigm in the philosophy of history.[4] From 1941 until his death in November 1966, the Kracauers lived in New York.[5]

The exile years highly influenced Kracauer's thoughts about his own biography and more generally his concept of history. He began to think of history and life not in terms of continuity, but in terms of discontinuity in space and time. His own lifeline was disrupted, and he began to consider disruption as a main characteristic feature of history as such. Walter Benjamin once wrote that "history is a constellation of dangers" (Benjamin 2002, 470). Due to his own experience in exile Kracauer began to regard history as a constellation of danger, fear, suffering and hope (Bratu Hansen 2012, 281–283).

To perceive history as a coherent development did not correspond with reality: real history was characterized by contingency, chance and open-endedness. Naturally, the traditions of general history became highly problematic, traditional history-writing did not grasp what it was meant to do according to the well-known expression "*wie es eigentlich gewesen*".

3. *"The horrible last-minute run of the transcendental subject"*[6]

In 1921 Kracauer wrote a review of Georg Lukács's *Die Theorie des Romans. Ein geschichtsphilosophischer Versuch über die Formen der großen Epik* (Kracauer 1921). Lukács discussed the historical development of the western canon of epic literature on the basis of and as a parallel to Hegel's philosophy of history. Kracauer then got the idea to write about the most popular literature at the time, the detective novel, on the basis of and as a parallel to some main concepts in Sören Kierkegaard's philosophy and Kant's *Zur Kritik der Urteilskraft*. It was a brilliant idea, but as it seems it was too original for its time, because after all Kracauer wrote his treatise on the detective novel in the years from 1922–1925, but

---

3 Lili Kracauer (born Ehrenreich) (1893–1971), at the time Lili and Siegfried Kracauer met (in 1926), she was librarian at *Institut für Sozialforschung* in Frankfurt.

4 The group was constituted in 1963, its most prominent members were Hans Robert Jauß, Clemens Heselhaus, Hans Blumenberg and Wolfgang Iser.

5 For a more detailed account, Später (2016).

6 See Linneberg (2022).

it was first published in 1971: *Der Detektiv-Roman. Ein philosophischer Traktat* (Kracauer 1979).

To a Norwegian it is interesting that one of Kracauer's main examples is taken from Sven Elvestad (1884–1934) alias Stein Riverton, the most famous writer of detective novels in Norway. Elvestad wrote 98 detective novels, 89 of them were translated into German in the author's lifetime, and many of them are still being published anew, above all in Germany. His novel *Døden tar inn på hotellet* (Elvestad 1921) – "Death checks in at the Hotel", was printed in Germany in 1923, *Der Tod kehrt im Hotel ein*.

Kracauer's *Der Detektiv-Roman* was published in English in 2007 as *The Detective Novel: A Philosophical Treatise*. A central quotation in a central chapter in the book, "The Hotel Lobby", is taken from Elvestad's novel. The storyteller tells us: "Once again it is confirmed that a large hotel is a world unto itself and that this world is like the rest of the large world" (Elvestad 1921, 37, Kracauer 1995a, 184). The novel's story about what is taking place in the hotel is so to speak a story about what is taking place in the large world. The detective novel mirrors society: "Just as the detective discovers the secret that people have concealed, the detective novel discloses in the aesthetic medium the secret of a society bereft of reality, as well as the secret of its insubstantial marionettes" (Kracauer 1995a, 175).

The detective as a figure is almost pure reason. The detective represents a higher reason, the principle of rationality. Because of their intelligence, their *ratio*, the detectives stand above other humans, they are almost divine.

The detectives are "rationally constructed complexes" and as such "comparable to the transcendental subject" (Kracauer 1995a, 177). As an individual the detective is "detached from the existential stream of the total person" and "reduced to an unreal, purely formal relation" (Kracauer 1995a, 177). Kant himself "still believed there was a seamless transition from the transcendental to the preformed subject-object-world" and was therefore "able to overlook this horrible last-minute sprint of the transcendental subject". The transcendental subject's last-minute sprint can be observed in the hotel lobbies in these novels: In "tasteful lounge chairs [...] a civilization intent on rationalization comes to an end" (Kracauer 1995a, 190–191).

The detective novel is a rational construction of reality which discloses the rationality underlying this reality. Kracauer compares this rationally constructed complex with the abstract idealistic philosophical systems since the Enlightenment. These systems intend to circumscribe and define the totality, but because they are too abstract, they do not catch the empirical reality, they do not embrace human existence and everyday life. They are not capable of grasping reality in its totality.

Kracauer considers the detective novel as a further development of the abstract philosophical systems, or rather as a new version of the abstract system of rationality. In the last chapter of the book, Kracauer argues that the solving of the mysteries, the solution of the problem, in the detective novel is not a real one, but an aesthetic construction. It is *Kitsch* (Kracauer 1979, 131–134). The image of reality in the detective novel is not a true picture, it presents an illusion, the illusion that we can grasp reality through rational abstractions.

Kracauer's remarkable conclusion is that the abstract philosophical systems are *Kitsch* as well, and for the same reason. The detective novel and the philosophical systems both create apparently coherent stories meant to explain the hidden meaning of the world we live in. But both types of stories are insufficient constructions of reality, not reality itself.

4. *"Reality is a construction"*

In the first chapter of *Die Angestellten* (1929–1930)[7], Kracauer states that "*Wirklichkeit ist eine Konstruktion*" – "reality is a construction" (Kracauer 2016, 16). At the time this was an extraordinary statement. Kracauer discusses the new journalistic genre "reportage" and he concludes that "the reportage photographs life"[8] (Kracauer 2016, 16, my translation). He draws a connection between photography and writing.

The first time Kracauer highlights this connection is in his essay "Photography" (Kracauer 2014a). An important subject in this essay is the problem of referentiality. What do we see when we look at a picture of someone, for instance a photography of our grandmother? "Did the *grandmother* look like this?" Kracauer asks (Kracauer 2014a, 28). We know we see the grandmother in the picture, because someone has told us who the photographed person is:

> The viewer of old photographs feels a shiver. For they make present not the knowledge of the original sitter but the spatial configuration of a moment; it is not the human being that emerges from the photograph but rather the sum of everything that can be subtracted from that being. (Kracauer 2014a, 37)

Already in the opening sequence of the essay, Kracauer points at the distance between what we see in the photography and the photographed person. The photography is a technological reproduction of reality: "If one looked through a magnifying glass, one could recognize the grid, the millions of tiny dots that form the [film] star […]. But the subject of the picture is not the network of points; it is the living star" (Kracauer 2014a, 27).

A photograph is a construction of reality, a reportage is photographed reality, and so is history-writing. Taking the "principle of Goethe philology" as a point of departure, Kracauer draws a remarkable line from photography to historiog-

---

7 First published in Frankfurter Zeitung 1929, then as the book in 1930.
8 Kracauer (2016, 16): "*Die Reportage photographiert das Leben.*"

raphy. In the Goethe Society's *Jahrbücher* he found a series of photos, and his comment to this finding is amazing:

> The principle of Goethe philology is that of the *historicist* thinking that has become dominant at approximately the same time as modern photographic technology. Its representatives assume, overall, that one can explain any phenomenon purely by tracing its origins. [...] Photography provides a space-continuum; historicism would like to fulfil the time continuum. The entire mirroring of the intra-temporal course of a period contains, according to historicism (*Historismus*) the meaning of everything that has happened in that time. [...] For historicism, it is a matter of the photography of time. What could correspond to its photography of time is a huge film which would depict the processes linked together in it from all sides. (Kracauer 2014a, 30)

It is exactly this correspondence between historiography and film that is Kracauer's main concern in his writings on film and history.

5. Photography, Film and History

Kracauer's first interventions in the interconnections linking photography, film and history we find in his film-reviews and essays on film in the twenties. In the essay "Calico World" he analyzed "the illusionist studio wizardry in various UFA films" (Levin 1995, 24). Kracauer showed "how stupid and unreal film fantasies are the daydreams of society, in which its actual reality comes to the fore. [...] The more incorrectly they present the surface of things, the more correct they become and the more clearly they mirror the secret mechanism of society" (Kracauer 1995b, 333). "Everything guaranteed nature," Kracauer here wrote about these film illusions, the only problem being that these constructions of reality actually repress access to the real. All we have is constructions of reality, not reality itself.

His brilliant book *From Caligari to Hitler* (1947) deals with the cinematic history of the Weimar Republic, "the psychological history of German film". The horror movies paved the way for the horror of Hitler's Nazi regime, and teach us about the sociopsychological climate leading up to the Third Reich.

Theory of Film. The Redemption of Physical Reality (1960) is more optimistic when it comes to the contributions of filmic constructions of reality. According to Kracauer, films could help us to see the beauty of our physical environment and thus contribute to save our habitat on earth.

In history writing it is almost the other way around. History writing is not only constructions of historical reality, but false constructions of real life.

5.1 A Realistic and a Formative Tendency

When Kracauer died in November 1966 he had not finished his final work, *History. The Last Things Before the Last.* Completed by Paul Oskar Kristeller it was published in 1969. Like Aristotle Kracauer meant that it was very much truth in fiction. According to Kracauer authors like Laurence Sterne, Lev Tolstoj, Marcel Proust and Franz Kafka not only gave more insight into the real life of a historical epoch than did the works of historians, but these authors also reflected more profound on the philosophical problems of history-writing.

In his foreword Kristeller wrote that Kracauer tended "to criticize the general theories of history formulated by Hegel and Nietzsche, Spengler and Toynbee, Croce and Collingwood, and to disregard the theories of Heidegger and the analytical philosophers" (Kristeller 1969, xiii).

The problem was not fictitious stories about history in literary fiction; the problem was that it is very much fiction in the factitious stories told in the general history-writing. In his last work Kracauer focused on this problem when he analyzed the construction of stories in historiography.

In the "Introduction" to *History* Kracauer recalls his earlier studies of photography:

> I realized in a flash the many existing parallels between history and the photographic media, historical reality and camera reality. Lately I came across my piece on "Photography" and was completely amazed at noticing that I had compared historicism with photography already in this article of the twenties. (Kracauer 2014b, 4)[9]

Kracauer always recognized film as a photographic medium and discussed the referential problem in film and history in accordance with his discussion of photography. Based on his *Theory of Film* he stated that film and history share two main characteristic features; they both have a realistic and a formative tendency (Kracauer 1960).

A film refers to elements of reality, that is the realistic tendency. However, the filmic reproduction of these elements of reality regroup the elements into a new order in new sequences of events. This regrouping of elements is the formative tendency. The overall problem is not that film and history do not refer to reality, but how they do it, in what way, i.e. the relation between the realistic and the formative tendencies.

5.2 The historian as a detective

In his treatise on the detective novel Kracauer for the first time analyzed the construction of stories in philosophy and fiction. And in his work on historiog-

[9] In October 1950 Kracauer received some of his old manuscripts from Germany and in a letter to Adorno October 1, 1950, he wrote this comment (Adorno 2008, 449).

raphy Kracauer actually discusses the historian as a detective. The historian is a detective, but of what sort? "Collingwood should have read more detective novels," Kracauer writes, because the historian Collingwood acts like a Sherlock Holmes, finding facts, clues, traces and solves the problem by putting these traces, clues and facts into a storyline. The historian, however, should act more like the detective Arnold Pike in Philip MacDonald's *Murder gone mad* (1931), because Arnold Pike not only finds the facts and makes a story out of them; the most important characteristic of Arnold Pike as a detective, is his interpretations and thus the understanding of the facts (Kracauer 2014b, 77–78).

The problem with historiography in general is not the realistic tendency, but the formative one. The storytelling in historiography is a distortion of the real because of the stylistic devices and rhetorical tricks that the history-writer uses to establish a false coherence (*Schein*), fill in gaps, and create a continuity where there is none. Instead of keeping in mind the incongruences of reality, historiography fabricates what Kracauer calls *the fata morgana of unity* (Kracauer 2014b, 164–191).

6. *Historiography as Imaginary Constructions*

Historiography creates "pseudo-scientific" imaginary constructions of reality (Kracauer 2014b, 191–221). A main reason is that traditional storytelling in history-writing is based on outdated novel-structures from the psychological, realistic novels with outdated plot structures and their principles of coherence and continuity. A more updated way of telling stories should be based on structures taken from modern novels, from the works of authors like Virgina Woolf or Marcel Proust. Or even from old writers like Laurence Sterne. Kracauer's main example and his favorite among story tellers is Laurence Sterne and *The Life and Opinion of Tristram Shandy, Gentleman* (1759–1767).

At the end of the last chapter before the last of *History. The Last Things Before The Last*, Kracauer asks: "The general historian's problems; is there a solution to them?" (Kracauer 2014b, 189). He continues: "Tristram Shandy's answer to the question of how to penetrate chaos is so memorable that I cannot resist the temptation of reproducing it".

Since, after all, this lengthy quotation from Sterne's novel is so important to Kracauer and so enlightening, I will also quote his quotation here:

> Could a historiographer drive on his history, as a muleteer drives on his mule – straight forward; – for instance from Rome all the way to *Loretto*, without ever once turning his head aside, either to the right hand or to the left, – he might venture to foretell you to an hour when he should get to his journey's end; – but the thing is, morally speaking, impossible. For, if he is a man of the least spirit, he will have fifty deviations from a straight line to make with this or that party as he goes along, which he can no ways avoid. He will have views and prospects to himself perpetually

> soliciting his eye, which he can no more help standing still to look at than he can fly; he will, moreover, have various
> - Accounts to reconcile;
> - Anecdotes to pick up;
> - Inscriptions to make out;
> - Stories to weave in;
> - Traditions to sift;
> - Personages to call upon;
> - Panegyrics to paste up on this door;
> - Pasquinades at that; – All which both the man and his mule are quite exempt from. To sum up all; there are archives at every stage to be look'd into, and rolls, records, documents, and endless genealogies, which justice ever and anon calls him back to stay the reading of: – In short, there is no end of it … (Kracauer 2014b, 189)[10]

"General history, then, is a hybrid," Kracauer concludes after the quotation; what "to us appears as an 'imaginary construction,' has been the *raison d'être* of general history most of the time." Our preoccupation with the course of history "is grounded in religious prophecy, theological computations, and metaphysical ideal about mankind's lot". These "old questions, goals, and mirages" linger on, join forces "with the needs and interests which arise from the historian's involvement in the affairs of his day". Together both the contemporary and traditional concerns invite the historian "to account for temporal sequence, the past as a whole". Therefore, the historian "cannot help driving his mule straight to Loretto" (all Kracauer 2014b, 190).

7. *Non-Narrative Elements in Non-Linear Processes*

What is at stake in Kracauer's recount and discussion of this passage from Sterne's novel? In my opinion he focuses on an antinomy of narrative and non-narrative elements that is indicated in Sterne's comment on historiography. To drive the mule straight to Loretto is to tell a continuous story without breaks caused by reality's incongruent flow of events, people, things, what we could call non-narrative elements that do not fit in in a seamless storyline. The subtitle of *Theory of Film* was *The Redemption of Physical Reality*. In the foreword, Kracauer mentions the first film he remembers to have seen as a young boy and what intoxicating impression it made upon him:

> What thrilled me so deeply was an ordinary suburban street, filled with lights and shadows which transfigured it. Several trees stood about, and there was in the foreground a puddle reflecting invisible house façades and a piece of the sky. Then a breeze moved the shadows, and the façades with the sky below began to waver. The trembling upper world in the dirty puddle – this image has never left me. (Kracauer 1960, xi)

[10] Kracauer's quotation is from the paperback edition of the novel (Sterne 1940, 36–37).

Film could show us such marvels of everyday life, help save the beauty of the physical world and "do justice to the human condition in our time. Perhaps our condition is such that we cannot gain access to the elusive essentials of life unless we assimilate the seemingly non-essential?" (Kracauer 1960, xi).

For the historian, to save reality would mean to work out the dichotomy between the realistic and the formative tendency, I think that implies to clear up the antinomy of narrative and non-narrative elements.

To Kracauer the language of what Walter Benjamin called "the optical unconscious" was similar to the language of the unconscious; a dream-like flow of pictures (Benjamin 2015 [1931]). The surface-structure of reality as we experience it is actually similar to this dream-like flow of pictures, Kracauer argues; such is the real structure of historical reality with all its contingency and incongruences. The surface-structure of reality is similar to the structure of the unconscious. In accordance with this view, Kracauer argued for another concept of reality, based on sense perception, based on cinema (Bratu Hansen 2012). This implied a fundamental critique of both the abstract, idealistic and of the positivistic philosophies and world views, a critique grounded in an alternative view of reality with a weight on non-linear processes and thus a different concept of temporality.

The task of the historian is to try to live up to such expectations.

8. *The Construction of Reality in Law's Stories*

The construction of reality in legal narratives could be considered as inherent historiography. Imaginary constructions have been the *raison d'être* not only in historiography, but in law's stories, from the police reports via the prosecutors to the judges' judicial opinions in the verdicts. The use of stylistic devices and rhetorical tricks to establish a false coherence in a fata morgana of unity instead of keeping reality's incongruences in mind, characterizes most of the criminal cases I have investigated and analyzed through the years.

I could have demonstrated my conclusion so far with examples from many of the cases we in our research group have looked into and written about during a period of more than twenty years. But my main concern today was only a try to sketch the relevance of some prominent aspects of Siegfried Kracauer's impressing work on historiography for the study of legal narratives. He showed us how to proceed.[11]

[11] See Linneberg (2021).

Works Cited

Adorno, Theodor W. (2008) *Theodor W. Adorno – Siegfried Kracauer. Briefwechsel 1923–1966.* Ed. Wolfgang Schopf. Frankfurt a. M.: Suhrkamp.

Benjamin, Walter (2015) "Small History of Photography" [1931]. *On Photography. Walter Benjamin*. Ed. and trans. Esther Leslie. London: Reaktion Books.

Benjamin, Walter (2002) "On the Theory of Knowledge, Theory of Progress." *The Arcades Project*. Ed. and trans. Howard Eiland and Kevin McLaughlin. Cambridge/London: Harvard Univ. Press. 456–488.

Bratu Hansen, Miriam (2012). *Cinema and Experience. Siegfried Kracauer, Walter Benjamin and Theodor Adorno*. Berkeley/Los Angeles: Univ. California Press.

Dragvoll, Johan et al. (2014). *The Rhetoric of Miscarriages of Justice* (in Norwegian). Oslo: Vidarforlaget.

Elvestad, Sven (1921) *Døden tar inn på hotellet*. Christiania: Helge Erichsen & co.

Helmich Pedersen, Frode et al. (Ed.) (2021) *Narratives in the Criminal Process.* Series of the Käte Hamburger Center for Advanced Study in the Humanities, Law as Culture, vol. 26. Frankfurt a. M.: Vittorio Klostermann.

Koch, Gertrude (1996) *Siegfried Kracauer zur Einführung*. Hamburg: Junius Verlag. English edition: (2000) *Siegfried Kracauer. An Introduction*. Trans. Jeremy Gaines. Princeton: Princeton Univ. Press.

Kracauer, Siegfried (1921/22) "Georg von Lukács' Romantheorie." *Neue Blätter für Kunst und Literatur,* 4.1: 1–5. in Siegfried Kracauer *Schriften 5.1. Aufsätze (1915–1926)*, Frankfurt a. M.: Suhrkamp. 117–123.

Kracauer, Siegfried (1947) *From Caligari to Hitler: A Psychological History of the German Film*. Princeton: Princeton Univ. Press.

Kracauer, Siegfried (1960) *A Theory of Film. The Redemption of Physical Reality*. New York: Oxford Univ. Press.

Kracauer, Siegfried (1979) *Der Detektiv-Roman. Ein philosophischer Traktat* [1971]. Frankfurt a. M.: Suhrkamp.

Kracauer, Siegfried (1995a) "The Hotel Lobby" [1928]. *The Mass Ornament. Weimar Essays*. Ed. and trans. Thomas Y. Levin. Cambrigde/London: Harvard Univ. Press. 173–189.

Kracauer, Siegfried (1995b) "Calico World" [1928]. *The Mass Ornament. Weimar Essays*. Ed. and trans. Thomas Y. Levin. Cambrigde/London: Harvard Univ. Press. 281–290.

Kracauer, Siegfried (2007). *The Detective Novel. A Philosophical Treatise.* Cambridge: Polity Press.

Kracauer, Siegfried (2014a) "Die Photographie" [1927]. *The Past's Threshold. Essays on Photography*, Ed. Philippe Despoix and Maria Zinfert, trans. Conor Joyce. Zürich: diaphanes.

Kracauer, Siegfried (2014b) *History. The Last Things Before the Last* [1969]. Completed by Paul Oskar Kristeller. New York: Oxford Univ. Press.

Kracauer, Siegfried (2014c) *Das Ornament der Masse. Essays* [1963]. Mit einem Nachwort von Karsten Witte. Frankfurt a. M.: Suhrkamp.

Kracauer, Siegfried (2016) *Die Angestellten. Aus dem neuesten Deutschland* [1930]. Frankfurt a. M.: Suhrkamp.

Leslie, Esther (Ed.) (2015) *On Photography. Walter Benjamin*. London: Reaktion Books.

Levin, Thomas Y. (1995) "Introduction." *The Mass Ornament. Weimar Essays*. Ed. and trans. Thomas Y. Levin. Cambrigde/London: Harvard Univ. Press.

Linneberg, Arild (2021) "Stories, Law, and Justice – on the Place of Narratives in the Field of Law and Humanities." *Narratives in the Criminal Process*. Ed. Frode Helmich Pedersen et. al. Frankfurt a. M.: Vittorio Klostermann. 253–275.

Linneberg, Arild (2022) "The Last-Minute Sprint of the Transcendental Subject: Siegfried Kracauer, Sven Elvestad and the Detective Novel." *Studies in Crime Writing*, Newberry College: South Carolina, forthcoming 2022.

Lukács, Georg (1965) *Die Theorie des Romans. Ein geschichtsphilosophischer Versuch über die Formen der großen Epik* [1920]. München: Luchterhand.

Später, Jörg (2016) *Siegfried Kracauer. Eine Biographie.* Frankfurt a. M.: Suhrkamp.

Sterne, Laurence (1940) *The Life and Opinions of Tristram Shandy, Gentleman* [1759–1767]. New York: Odyssey Press.

Literatur- und Rechtsgeschichte, geschult am Roman

Claudia Lieb

Im neunzehnten Jahrhundert bildete sich an deutschsprachigen Universitäten eine Hochphase interdisziplinärer Zusammenarbeit von Philologen und Juristen aus (Lieb & Strosetzki 2013; Lieb 2021). Parallel zu den literarischen Innovationen, die rund um die Epochenschwelle von Spätaufklärung und Frühromantik entstanden, orientierten sich führende Wissenschaftler aus Philologie und Jurisprudenz theoretisch und methodisch neu, als sie die Geschichte von Literatur und Recht erforschten. Die daraus resultierenden Arbeiten zur Geschichte des Rechts und der Nationalliteratur trugen maßgeblich zur Formung der deutschen Identität im langen neunzehnten Jahrhundert bei, als die nationale Selbstfindung im Mittelpunkt des Interesses stand.

Zu den methodischen Innovationen der Literatur- und Rechtsgeschichtsschreibung gehört der Abschied vom alten Wissensmodell der *Historia Literaria* – einer umfassenden Gelehrtengeschichte, die das Wissen der vier Fakultäten Philosophie, Theologie, Jurisprudenz und Medizin zusammenfasste. Zwar gibt es noch bis weit ins neunzehnte Jahrhundert hinein Darstellungen, die sich daran orientieren, z. B. Jacob Grimms Vorlesung *Die Geschichte der deutschen Literatur von der ältesten bis zur neuesten Zeit* (1834–1837). Diese Art historiografischen Arbeitens wird jedoch im Lauf des Jahrhunderts aufgegeben: Man erkennt, dass die alte Fakultätsordnung kein adäquates Schema mehr bildet, um akademisches Wissen zu organisieren. Dies liegt zum einen daran, dass die Universität selbst in weit mehr Fächer und Arbeitsgebiete ausdifferenziert ist als in Philosophie, Theologie, Jurisprudenz und Medizin. Zum anderen erscheint es seit etwa 1850 aufgrund des kontinuierlich wachsenden Textmaterials in den Wissenschaften nicht mehr angemessen oder auch nur möglich, die immer länger werdende Reihe der Autor- und Quellennamen mehr oder minder willkürlich aufzuschreiben, historisch perspektiviert nur durch das Schema der Chronologie und einige wenige Sätze des Kommentars.

Unterdessen entwickelt sich eine neue Form der Geschichtsschreibung, die sich strukturell in Philologie und Jurisprudenz durchsetzen wird und bis heute nachwirkt. In etlichen Spielarten und Varianten entwickeln die Autoren der neueren Literatur- und Rechtsgeschichte ein einflussreiches Vorgängermodell weiter: diejenige Vorstellung von Biografie, die Christoph Martin Wieland und etliche andere Romanautoren als Kern ihrer Romane betrachten.

Innerhalb der Literatur ist das Modell der Romanbiografie flexibel und dynamisch, weil es für den Roman keine verpflichtende Poetik gibt. Außerdem ist die Romanbiografie noch jung, sie etabliert sich erst um 1750. In den folgenden Jahrzehnten bricht sie im deutschsprachigen Raum als dominante Schreibart von Romanen durch. Wohl aufgrund seiner Beliebtheit und seiner Flexibilität erscheint das biografische Modell gut geeignet, denjenigen Fächern als Ideenfundus zu dienen, die nach modernen Formen wissenschaftlicher Geschichtsschreibung suchen. Vergleicht man die Anlage und Reflexion biografisch ausgerichteter Romanerzählungen mit der Historiografie der Literatur und des Rechts, so lässt sich ein gemeinsamer Pool von Arbeitsweisen und Systematisierungen ausmachen. Dieser Zusammenhang ist in der Forschung bislang nur angedeutet worden (Harth 1996).

Übergreifend hat Reinhart Koselleck (1985) auf eine Wechselbeziehung zwischen „Historik" und „Poetik" aufmerksam gemacht. Sie hängt damit zusammen, dass sich im späten achtzehnten Jahrhundert ein neues Geschichtsverständnis abzeichnet, so Koselleck. Dass dieses Geschichtsverständnis nicht mehr viele additive Geschichten wahrnimmt, sondern die eine singuläre,

> gleichsam herausgehobene Geschichte, die alle wiederholbare Exemplarität hinter sich ließ, war nun nicht zuletzt das Ergebnis einer verschobenen Grenzbestimmung zwischen Historik und Poetik. Die epische Einheit, die von Anfang und Ende her bestimmt ist, wurde zunehmend auch der Geschichtserzählung zugemutet. (51)

Zwischen dem Erzählen von Geschichte und dem Erzählen selbst besteht notwendig eine Parallele. Koselleck zitiert in diesem Kontext Justus Möser, der dem „Geschichtschreiber" ein poetisches Erzählen abverlangte, als er 1780 den Plan einer deutschen Reichsgeschichte seit dem Ewigen Landfrieden des Jahres 1495 entwarf: Sie müsse „in eine einzige Handlung, in eine einzige Darstellung verwandelt werden" und habe „mit dem Helden" der Geschichte anzufangen – eine Methode, die schon seit langem von dem „Epopoeen-Dichter" verwendet werde (Möser 1842, 149–152; vgl. Koselleck 1985, 51). Dichtung und Geschichtsschreibung beeinflussen sich gegenseitig:

> Im Maß, als der Historie eine größere Darstellungskunst abgefordert wurde, wie sie – statt chronologischer Reihen – die geheimen Motive eruieren, ein pragmatisches Gefüge erstellen sollte, um dem zufälligen Geschehen eine innere Ordnung abzugewinnen, im gleichen Maße wirkten Forderungen der Historie in die Poetik hinein. [...] So verschränkten sich die Ansprüche von Poetik und Historik, das eine wirkte in das andere hinein, um den immanenten Sinn der 'Geschichte' ans Licht zu bringen. (Koselleck 1985, 52–53)

Was Koselleck allgemein ‚Poetik' nennt, lässt sich hervorragend auf die Poetik des Romans beziehen – und nicht zuletzt auf die vorgelagerte Praxis des Romans, die mit der Fiktion des authentischen Nacherzählens wirklicher Begebenheiten spielt. Dies soll zunächst am Beispiel von Wielands *Geschichte des Agathon* (1766/67) betrachtet werden, einem der bekanntesten Romane der damaligen gelehrten Welt.

1. *Wielands* Geschichte des Agathon

Wielands zweiter großer Roman erscheint 1766/67 in zwei Bänden, 1773 erweitert und 1794 nochmals ergänzt in der Fassung letzter Hand. Er spielt im Griechenland zur Zeit Platons. Der Protagonist Agathon schwärmt für Platon und betrachtet ihn als Lehrer eines absoluten Tugendideals. Weil dieses Tugendideal aber der Natur des Menschen widerspricht, zeigt Wielands Roman, dass und wie Agathon dagegen verstößt – je drastischer, desto besser. Überdies hat Wieland seinem Helden einen Erzieher an die Seite gesetzt, den Sophisten Hippias. Dieser versucht vergeblich, Agathon „von seinem liebenswürdigen und tugendhaften Enthusiasmus zu heilen" und ihn zu einer pragmatischeren „Denkungsart zu bringen" (Wieland 1986 [1766/67], 14). Am Ende der letzten Fassung ist und bleibt Agathon, was er von Anfang an war: ein unverbesserlicher Platon-Verehrer. Wieland hält seinen Protagonisten blind für die Einsicht, dass er weder zur Wahrheit noch zur Weisheit gelangt ist, damit das Lesepublikum umso klarer sehe.

Was die Gesamtanlage des Romans betrifft, so operiert Wieland mit einer wichtigen Herausgeberfiktion. Der Autor tritt im Vorbericht der Erstausgabe nicht als Romanautor, sondern als „Herausgeber" einer *Geschichte* auf, derjenigen *des Agathon*. Sie könnte „in der Tat aus einem alten Griechischen Manuskript gezogen" worden sein, sagt er, ja, womöglich könnte es „gerichtlich erwiesen" werden, „daß sie in den Archiven des alten Athens gefunden worden sei" (11). Die Metapher des Gerichts unterstreicht die vermeintliche Wahrheit der Geschichte; Wieland lässt seinen Roman im Gewand der Edition erscheinen und suggeriert, dass die Geschichte des Romans auf authentischen Quellen beruht. Er baut diese Fiktion weiter aus, indem er einen klaren Bezug zur Geschichte des antiken Griechenlands herstellt:

> Gesetzt, daß wirklich einmal ein Agathon gewesen, (wie dann in der Tat, um die Zeit, in welche die gegenwärtige Geschichte gesetzt worden ist, ein komischer Dichter dieses Namens den Freunden der Schriften Platons bekannt sein muß) [...]. (11)

Ist diese Prämisse wahr, dann ist dem Herausgeber zufolge der Schluss zulässig, „daß Agathon und die meisten übrigen Personen, welche in seine Geschichte eingeflochten sind, wirkliche Personen sind" (12). Außerdem betont er, dass „alles, was das Wesentliche dieser Geschichte ausmacht, ebenso historisch, und vielleicht noch um manchen Grad gewisser sei, als irgend ein Stück der glaubwürdigsten politischen Geschichtschreiber, welche wir aufzuweisen haben": Das, was der Roman erzählt, ist also ebenso echt wie historisch wahr, wie der Herausgeber „ganz zuverlässig versichern" kann (12). Um diese These zu erhärten, bezeichnet er sich selbst als „Geschichtschreiber" (637).

Wieland inszeniert ein Vexierspiel mit der Fiktionalität des Romans und der Faktualität des erzählten Stoffs. Beide treffen sich im Punkt der ‚Geschichte' – ein doppelbödiges Wort, das hier zweierlei bedeuten kann: *fabula* und *historia*.

Der Vorbericht trachtet danach, den Unterschied von *fabula* und *historia* zu betonen und ihn gleichzeitig durchzustreichen. Diesem Paradox entspricht die sprachliche Gestaltung. Der häufig benutzte Konjunktiv weist das Gesagte zwar als Möglichkeit und damit als *fabula* aus. Trotzdem steckt Wieland hier den Rahmen einer historischen Mimesis ab: die Nacherzählung wirklicher Begebenheiten. Genau das heißt Erzählen im Modus des Romans, darauf läuft die Deduktion hinaus. Dieses Erzählen beruht angeblich auf einer quellenbezogenen Aufbereitung von Tatsachenmaterial, und es soll glaubwürdiger und gewisser sein als die eigentliche Geschichtsschreibung. Es geht um die emphatische Erhöhung des Romans, darum, den Roman auf Kosten der Geschichtsschreibung zu adeln.

Behauptet Wieland einerseits die Identität von Romanautor und Historiker, von Roman und authentischer Geschichte, so grenzt er andererseits das Romanschreiben von der Geschichtsschreibung ab. Denn einen Roman schreiben heißt, die Geschichtsschreibung zu übertreffen. Als der Herausgeber erklärt, was den besonderen Reiz seiner *Geschichte* ausmacht, da zeigt sich, dass sie in einem wesentlichen Punkt von jener der politischen Geschichtsschreiber abweicht. Wo letztere lediglich die Eckdaten der Biografie erfassen könnten – wann Agathon „geboren worden, [...] sich verheiratet, wie viel Kinder er gezeugt, und [...] an was für einer Krankheit er gestorben sei“ (11) –, da hat Wielands Geschichte noch mehr zu bieten: die *„Seelengeschichte Agathons“* (591 [Originalhervorhebung]). Folglich liegt das poetische Wesen des Romans in diesem nach innen gerichteten, „psychologischen Gange der Geschichte“ (589). Der äußere historische Gang ist aber unauflöslich mit ihm verwoben und daher ebenso wichtig. Die Verbindung von Außen- und Innenwelt bildet die Antwort auf die Frage: „[W]as würde uns bewegen können, seine [d.h. Agathons, CL] Geschichte zu lesen“? (11) Die bloße Biografik kann jedenfalls niemanden dazu bewegen, teilt der Herausgeber mit: Der Dichter ist der bessere Historiker.

Mit der Dichotomie von äußerer und innerer Geschichte transformiert Wieland den Dualismus von Körper und Geist, der im Zentrum der Philosophie der Aufklärung steht (Kondylis 2002). Die Fiktion der authentischen inneren und äußeren Geschichte hält Wieland in seinen Vorreden sowie im Roman selbst durch. So dreht sich etwa das neunte Buch des zwölften Kapitels um den „Gemütszustand unsers Helden“, als er des Hochverrats angeklagt im Gefängnis sitzt. Es handelt sich um die „merkwürdigste Epoke seines Lebens“ (Wieland 1986 [1766/67], 593). Dabei beteuert der Erzähler, dass

> Wir uns zum Gesetz gemacht haben, die Leser dieser Geschichte nicht bloß mit den Begebenheiten und Taten unsers Helden zu unterhalten, sondern ihnen auch von dem, was bei den wichtigen Abschnitten seines Lebens in seinem *Innern* vorging, alles mitzuteilen, was die Quellen, woraus wir schöpfen, uns davon an die Hand geben. (593 [Originalhervorhebung])

Schließlich ist Agathon ein „Mann, der von seinen frühesten Jahren an mehr in seiner eigenen *Ideenwelt*, als *außer sich* zu leben gewohnt war" (594 [Originalhervorhebung]).

Wie sich hier abzeichnet, konzentriert sich die Darstellung auf eine zentrale Figur, den „Helden" oder auch „Charakter". Dazu heißt es programmatisch in der Vorrede, dass der Herausgeber die „Hauptabsicht" hat, den Leser mit einem besonderen „Charakter [...] bekannt zu machen", und zwar „von allen seinen Seiten" (12) – mit seinem inneren und äußeren Leben. Das Modell des Romans ist die poetisierte Biografie.

Die antike Rhetorik kennt einige feste Formen biografischen Schreibens, so Laudatio (Lobrede), Nekrolog (Totenrede) und Panegyrikus, der als Loblied oder Lobrede, in Versen oder in Prosa gestaltet sein kann. Von dieser Folie weicht Wieland ab, indem er Agathon als ganz und gar nicht lobenswerten Helden präsentiert. Er gibt allerdings vor, der rhetorischen Tradition zu folgen, wenn er etwa Agathons liebenswerten Enthusiasmus betont. Dabei ist zu beachten, dass sich Wieland begrifflich und sachlich einer weiteren antiken Form literarischen Schreibens bedient, nämlich derjenigen, die seit Theophrast „Charakter" heißt. Sie ist für die Literatur- und Rechtsgeschichte des neunzehnten und noch des zwanzigsten Jahrhunderts zentral.

Das antike Modell „Charakter" sieht vor, die Eigenart von meist fiktiven oder typisierten Personen am Beispiel eines Hauptmerkmals (z. B. Geiz) zu beschreiben. In der englischen Literatur findet es schon zu Beginn des siebzehnten Jahrhunderts Anwendung, so in Joseph Halls *Characters of vertues [sic!] and vices* (1608). Am Ende des Jahrhunderts publiziert Jean de La Bruyère sein berühmtes Werk *Les charactères de Théophraste, traduits du grec, avec les charactères ou les mœurs de ce siècle* (1688) [Die Charaktere Theophrasts, übersetzt aus dem Griechischen, zusammen mit den Charakteren und Sitten dieses Jahrhunderts]. La Bruyère charakterisiert seine Landsleute anhand von heterogenen Merkmalen: der Hof, die Stadt, die Konversation, das menschliche Herz usw. Wie der Titel seines Buchs ankündigt, tendieren *Les charactères* in Richtung Geschichtsschreibung (Asmuth 2007). Johann Jakob Bodmer und Johann Jakob Breitinger führen Theophrast und La Bruyère in den 1720er Jahren zusammen und definieren das Genre im Sinn einer nationalen Historiografie als die „subtilen und ordentliche Beschreibungen aller derjenigen Qualitäten, durch welche sich eine gantze Nation oder Person underscheidet" (Bodmer & Breitinger 1891 [1721–1722], 26). Um 1800 ist es schließlich so beliebt, dass es einen neuen, modernisierten Namen erhält, der beide Bedeutungsvarianten einschließt: „Charakteristik".

Wielands *Agathon* dürfte daran beteiligt gewesen sein, die Charakteristik im deutschsprachigen Raum zu popularisieren. Nicht nur der Held, auch etliche Nebenfiguren und Völker werden hier fleißig charakterisiert, das zeigt schon ein flüchtiger Blick auf die Erstfassung. Deren Kapitel heißen „Charakter der

Syracusaner, des Dionysius und seines Hofes", „Charakter des Dion. Anmerkungen über denselben [...] Eine Probe" (Wieland 1986 [1766/67], 567).

Je weiter der Roman in seinen erweiterten Fassungen voranschreitet, desto dominanter wird die Charakteristik. Dem Vorbild des englischen Romans folgend, stellt Wieland fiktionale Lebensläufe dar. Einige Beispiele aus der letzten Fassung mögen dies belegen: Unter dem Titel „Archytas und die Tarentiner. Charakter eines seltnen Staatsmanns" (570) erzählt der Roman kursorisch die Biografie von Archytas, einem Mentor von Agathon. Dieser wiederum tut seine eigene Biografie kund: „Agathon erzählt die Geschichte seiner Jugend, bis zu dem Zeitpunkte, da er seinen Vater fand" (564). Es folgt die „Fortsetzung der Erzählung Agathons, von seiner Versetzung nach Athen bis zur Bekanntschaft mit Danae" usw., bis Wieland seinen Helden im letzten Buch endlich zum Biografen und das heißt: zum Romanschreiber kürt. „Agathon faßt den Entschluß, sich dem Archytas noch genauer zu entdecken, und zu diesem Ende sein eigener Biograph zu werden" (565–572). Was bis hierher als mündliche Erzählung des Agathon firmiert hat, muss nun verschriftlicht werden. Denn

> die Besorgnis, daß ihm bei einer mündlichen Erzählung, im Feuer der unvermerkt sich erhitzenden Einbildungskraft, mancher erhebliche Umstand entfallen, oder ohne seinen Willen manches in ein verschönerndes Licht, manches in einen zu dunklen Schatten gestellt werden könnte, brachte ihn auf den Gedanken, seine Beichte schriftlich abzulegen, und *die Geschichte seiner Seele* in den verschiedenen Epoken seines Lebens so getreu und lebendig, als er sie in der Stille einsamer Stunden in sein Gedächtnis zurück rufen könnte, zu Papier zu bringen. (737–738 [Originalhervorhebung])

Religiös überhöht durch die Metapher der Beichte steht das Medium Schrift dafür ein, dass Agathons Lebensgeschichte authentisch ist. Das behauptet zumindest der Erzähler. Er täuscht so über das fiktionale Moment einer jeden autobiografischen Erzählung hinweg. Diese autofiktionale Eigenschaft biografischer Texte leitet sich von dem Bewusstsein ab, „dass jede Autobiographie unter Einsatz der Fiktion arbeitet" (Wagner-Egelhaaf 2013, 8). Durch das Arrangement von Fakten und deren sprachliche Bearbeitung lasse „die (Auto)Fiktion [...] den Autor als denjenigen, der fingiert und sich selbst fingiert, in Erscheinung treten" (9–10). Dies geschieht etwa dadurch, dass das erzählende Ich die eigene Lebensgeschichte retrospektiv durch konzeptualisierende Muster deutet.

Auf Agathon bezogen sind dies die Muster der inneren Geschichte und der Epochengliederung („verschiedene Epoken"). Damit verbunden ist ein drittes Muster: die Topografie, erzählt Agathon doch, wie er von Delphi erst nach Athen, dann nach Syrakus gekommen ist und von hier aus nach Tarent. Als konzeptualisierte Lebensgeschichte ist die Erzählung fiktional, so wie auch ihr Erzähler ein fiktionaler ist. Wieland gibt seine Fiktion zu erkennen, indem die Romanbiografie namens „Geschichte" oder Erzählung selbst zum Gegenstand der Erzählung wird. Indem er Agathon seine eigene Geschichte erzählen und sogar schreiben lässt, verdoppelt Wieland das Modell des Romans als poetische Biografie. Es handelt sich um einen Roman im Roman – Wieland wandelt das seit dem englischen Renaissancetheater beliebte Spiel im Spiel ab, indem er es auf den Roman überträgt.

Das Spiel mit biografischen und autobiografischen Elementen durchzieht seinen Text bis zu der Konsequenz, dass Agathon zugleich Gegenstand des Romans und Urheber seiner eigenen Biografie ist. Diese wiederum wird als mysteriöser Ursprung der *Geschichte des Agathon* eingesetzt:

> Auf diese Weise entstand nun die von Agathon selbst aufgesetzte geheime Geschichte seines Geistes und Herzens, welche, aller Wahrscheinlichkeit nach, die erste und reinste Quelle ist, woraus die in diesem Werk enthaltenen Nachrichten geschöpft sind. (Wieland 1986 [1766/67], 738)

Die ominösen fingierten Quellenangaben sind Bestandteil eines ästhetischen Spiels, in dem historisch Distanziertes und generisch weit Versprengtes in einem einheitlichen Fokus gespiegelt und als eigenständiges Kunstwerk etabliert werden: die Biografik und die Philosophie der Antike, das elisabethanische Drama, der zeitgenössische englische Roman und nicht zuletzt der platonische Dialog: „Eine Unterredung zwischen Agathon und Archytas" (572) bietet die Fassung letzter Hand.

Da Agathon sich als unbelehrbarer Platoniker erweist, ist es nur folgerichtig, dass er am Ende auch im Stile Platons spricht, während er ansonsten modernere autobiografische Erzählformen wie den Gedankenbericht bevorzugt. Der Clou besteht darin, dass Agathon seinen platonischen Dialog selber „zu Papier brachte", und zwar als „Anhang" zu seiner Autobiografie, die er gerade zu schreiben begonnen hat (740). Er wird also unter der Hand zu einem Doppelgänger Platons, dessen Werk aus Dialogen besteht, jedoch nur zu einem dilettantischen. Denn Agathon hat „von allen diesen Gesprächen nur ein einziges" aufgeschrieben (740).

Dabei sticht zweierlei ins Auge. Wielands Roman entzieht sich der traditionellen Gattungstrias von Gedicht, Epos und Drama, weil er andere Gattungen bedient und mischt. Sie sind von einer übergeordneten Instanz her gedacht, und diese Instanz ist nicht die Dichtkunst, die Gedicht, Epos und Drama kennt. Es ist die „Gattung" des „Menschen" (595): Der Mensch führt mit einem anderen ein Gespräch, er wird eines Verbrechens angeklagt und erzählt davon, der Mensch schildert sein Leben als Ganzes, und von all dem berichtet der Roman. Durch die anthropologische Grundierung kann Wieland den narrativen Diskurs namens „Geschichte" sowohl historisch als auch überzeitlich markieren: In seinem Roman trifft die antike philosophische Gattung des Dialogs auf die moderne erzählende Autobiografie, die selbst wieder auf das antike Vorbild der Charakteristik zurückgeht.

Die Mimesis bestimmter Quellen mündet in eine Metamorphose dieser Quellen im Roman: Dieses Prinzip macht die Abhandlung „Über das Historische im Agathon" durchsichtig. Es handelt sich um eine Ergänzung, die den ersten Teil des Romans in den Fassungen von 1773 und 1794 einleitet. Darin reflektiert Wieland das historische Erzählen selbst nebst den Ordnungsmustern, die ein solches Erzählen aufweisen kann. Wieland geht davon aus, dass „der Ort und die Zeit der Begebenheiten sowohl als verschiedene in dieselbe verflochtene Personen wirklich historisch sind" (574). ‚Historisch' meint hier zunächst nichts anderes als „nach den Begriffen gesprochen, welche die Alten davon gaben" (576). Dahinter verbirgt sich eine quellenbezogene Echtheitsvorstellung, wie sie von „Gelehrten" erwartet werden darf:

> Die Gelehrten werden beim ersten Anblick in dem *Tempel von Delphi*, wo Agathon erzogen wurde, eben denselben Delphischen Tempel erkennen, den uns *Euripides* in seinem *Ion*, und *Pausanias* in seiner Beschreibung von Grächen schildert. (576 [Originalhervorhebung])

Das Geschäft des Romanschreibers besteht also in der Übersetzung bzw. im authentischen Nacherzählen, das des Lesers im Wiedererkennen des Alten; die enge intertextuelle Beziehung zwischen Romanerzählung und antiker Belegstelle beglaubigt die historische Wahrheit des Erzählten. Dabei sei angemerkt, dass der Gelehrte Wieland seine Belege hier philologisch versiert in Fußnoten angibt. Nach demselben Muster schreitet er „Zeitrechnung", „Chronologie" und Figureninventar ab, räumt allerdings ein, dass sein Roman „einige merkliche Abweichungen von der historischen" Quellenlage aufweist (575–576). Dies führt zu der Frage: Was leistet die Dichtkunst hier? Sie dient der Präzisierung und Ausschmückung der Ursprungstexte: Wieland habe „der Erdichtung nicht mehr verstattet, als die historischen Begebenheiten näher zu *bestimmen* und völliger *auszumalen*" (583–584 [Originalhervorhebung]).

In seinem Vorbericht zur letzten Fassung reflektiert Wieland rückschauend die rund dreißig Jahre währende Entstehung seines Romans. Dabei erscheint der Roman selbst als Gebilde mit einem Ursprung und einer Entwicklungsgeschichte. Die Abhandlung „Über das Historische im Agathon" wird nun durch Erläuterungen über das Historische *des* Agathon ergänzt. Anders gesagt: Die *Geschichte des Agathon* wird als die Geschichte der Geschichte des Agathon aufgerollt. Deren Ursprung wurzelt in der Lebensgeschichte des Verfassers, nämlich „in der Denkart, worin die *Idee* des Werkes in seiner Seele empfangen wurde" (590 [Originalhervorhebung]) – ein emphatisches Bekenntnis zur inneren Geschichte. Auch die äußere Geschichte kommt nicht zu kurz, da Wieland von persönlichen Umständen berichtet, „durch welche der gute Agathon beinahe in der Geburt verunglückt wäre" (590). Zudem thematisiert er die verschiedenen Ausgaben des Romans, so die „*Zürcher Ausgabe* von 1767" (589 [Originalhervorhebung]). Zur äußeren Geschichte eines Textes gehören dessen Fassungen, während die innere Geschichte dem entspricht, was der Autor „in seinem Kopf entworfen hatte" (589).

In diesem letzten Vorbericht wendet Wieland die autobiografische Fiktion der retrospektiven Wahrheit, der authentischen Nachschrift und Nacherzählung wirklicher Begebenheiten auf sich selbst an. Er stilisiert sich zur historischen Figur, an der vor allem die Idee interessiert. Diese aber ist nicht wandelbar, sondern überzeitlich. Damit schließt Wieland präzise an denjenigen Kern an, den er im ersten Vorbericht ausgeflaggt hatte.

1766 ging es ihm um „das Wesentliche" der *Geschichte des Agathon*. Dabei kommt die aristotelische Unterscheidung von Wesen und Zufall, Substanz und Akzidenz zur Anwendung. Als Aristoteles das Wissen vom Seienden über dessen akzidentelle Eigenschaften hinaus auf das Wesentliche hin perspektivierte, verpflichtete er die Philosophie auf die Substanzvorstellung. Analog dazu vermeldet die erste Vorrede zur *Geschichte des Agathon*, „alles, was das Wesentliche dieser Geschichte ausmacht", sei historisch, wohingegen die „Neben-Umstände, die Folge und besondere Bestimmung der zufälligen Begebenheiten, und was sonsten zur Auszierung, welche willkürlich ist, gehört", erdichtet seien (12). Die Substanz liegt im Historischen.

‚Historisch' meint hier allerdings nicht das Vergangene, sondern das Überzeitliche. Es meint die aus der Geschichte abstrahierte Idee, genauer „ein System von Ideen" (766), nämlich diejenigen allgemeinen Grundsätze, die sich aus der Geschichte des Menschen ableiten lassen. Wieland fasst sie unter das Schlagwort der *„menschlichen Natur"* (594 [Originalhervorhebung]). Sie wird dadurch exemplifiziert und begreifbar, dass der Roman mehrere Ideensysteme vorführt, so das „System des Hippias" (599), des Archytas, des Agathon und selbstverständlich dasjenige des Herausgebers. Die daraus entstehende Polyperspektivität prägt den Text.

Um die menschliche Natur zu ergründen, muss ihr vermuteter Ursprung, die griechische Antike aufgesucht werden, und diese gilt es zu charakterisieren – „der eigene Charakter des Landes, des Orts, der Zeit, in welche die Geschichte gesetzt wird", werde niemals außer Acht gelassen, desgleichen die menschlichen Charaktere: vor allem Agathon, aber auch Psyche, Pythia, Dionysius und wen die griechische Antike sonst aufzubieten hat (11–12). Daraus folgt: Die „Wahrheit", die von der Geschichte erwartet werden darf, „bestehet darin, daß alles mit dem Lauf der Welt übereinstimme, daß die Charakter nicht willkürlich, und bloß nach der Phantasie, oder den Absichten des Verfassers gebildet, sondern aus dem unerschöpflichen Vorrat der Natur selbst hergenommen" seien (11). Weder die Ereignisfolge noch die Figurenzeichnung sind wesentlich für die Geschichte, vielmehr ist es die anthropologische Einsicht in die Natur des Menschen. Und diese allgemeingültige Erkenntnis kann aus dem Besonderen, dem Einzelfall abstrahiert werden: aus der Natur des Agathon.

Wielands Romanprojekt ist so komplex, dass die gelehrten Zeitgenossen und Nachgeborenen es kontrovers diskutieren. Das sichert ihm eine Bekanntheit, die kaum zu unterschätzen ist. Gotthold Ephraim Lessing feiert den Roman bereits in den 1760er Jahren in seiner *Hamburgischen Dramaturgie*: Es sei „der erste und einzige Roman für den denkenden Kopf von klassischem Geschmack. Roman? Wir wollen ihm diesen Titel nur geben, daß er einige Leser mehr dadurch bekommt“ (Lessing 1973, 555). Lessing betont die Neuheit und die Radikalität, die Wielands Roman von der zeitgenössischen Romanproduktion trennt.

Wielands *Geschichte des Agathon* birgt sämtliche Ordnungsmuster, die für die Literatur- und Rechtsgeschichtsschreibung des neunzehnten Jahrhunderts entscheidend sein werden: innere und äußere Geschichte, Biografik als Charakteristik, damit verbunden Topografie, Epochengliederung, Konstruktion neuer Gattungen und ein Systemgedanke, der die Identität der Figuren bestimmt. Nicht zuletzt macht auch der Gedanke Schule, dass zur äußeren Geschichte eines Textes dessen Fassungen und Ausgaben zählen, während die innere Geschichte der Autorpsyche entspricht. Da Wieland all das im Blick auf die Antike ausexerziert, ist sein Modell zunächst für Spezialisten der Antike interessant. Den philologischen und juristischen Germanisten obliegt es, das Modell zu nationalisieren und es auf die ‚deutsche Antike‘ zuzuschneiden. Dieser Entwicklung schreitet die Romantheorie voran, die vor allem die innere Geschichte betont.

2. *Blanckenburgs* Versuch über den Roman

Wielands kühnes, verschachteltes Romangebäude wird in der zeitgenössischen Romantheorie nicht als irgendein, sondern als *das* Modell des Romans gewertet. Das hängt damit zusammen, dass Friedrich von Blanckenburg früh und an prominenter Stelle die Vorlage dafür liefert. Er sucht die noch junge Gattung des Romans zu kodifizieren und veröffentlicht 1774 die erste deutschsprachige Monografie, die dem Roman gewidmet ist: *Versuch über den Roman*. Er strotzt nur so vor direkten und indirekten Zitaten aus der *Geschichte des Agathon*.

Im Vorbericht heißt es, Romane würden nicht nur für müßige Frauenzimmer geschrieben, „sondern auch für den denkenden Kopf. *Solcher* Romane aber haben wir vielleicht nicht mehr, als zwey oder drey; – vielleicht gar nur *einen*“: den „Agathon“ (Blanckenburg 1965 [1774], VII [Originalhervorhebung]). Ihn hat Blanckenburg vor langer Zeit gelesen, wie er schreibt, daneben auch Fieldings *Tom Jones*, und er „sah bey jedem Schritt, der darinn geschieht, zurück auf die menschliche Natur“ (VII). Später habe er viele andere Werke dieser Gattung und „gewiß die wichtigsten“ gelesen; und auch bei dieser Lektüre hat Blanckenburg Wielands Methode verwendet „und also aus der menschlichen Natur, gelernt und abstrahiert“ (VIII).

In diesem Stile geht es weiter, zunächst mit der Unterscheidung von Substanz und Akzidens, die Blanckenburg auf seine eigene Theorie anwendet. Nicht über „die zufällige Form“ des Romans will er schreiben, auch nicht „über die Menge und Auswahl der spielenden Personen“, sondern über das, was „in Beziehung auf wichtigere Dinge, davon gesagt werden muß“ (XII). In der Folge steckt er mit Wieland gesprochen das System der Ideen ab. Hierzu zählt die wirkmächtige Beobachtung: „Die Romane entstanden nicht aus dem Genie der Autoren allein; die *Sitten* der Zeit gaben ihm das Daseyn" (XIII [Originalhervorhebung]). Dieser Gedanke eines deterministischen Prinzips liegt jeder Epochenkonstruktion zugrunde.

Anschließend bestimmt Blanckenburg die inhaltliche Substanz des Romans: den Menschen. Der Romandichter

> soll uns den *Menschen* zeigen, *wie* er ihn, nach der eigenthümlichen Einrichtung seines Werks, zu zeigen vermag. Das übrige alles ist Verzierung und Nebenwerk. Die verschiedenen Formen, die der Roman haben kann, müssen alle von einer Materie seyn. Von dieser ist hier nun, als dem Wesentlichsten, die Rede; nicht von der Gestalt, von dem Modell des Dinges. (XV [Originalhervorhebung])

Was nun das „*Allerwesentlichste*" (8 [Originalhervorhebung]) des Romans betrifft, so hebt Blanckenburg etliche Punkte hervor, die Wielands laufend zitierter Roman ihm vorgibt: etwa die Gliederung der Geschichte in Epochen, Gattungsmischung, „die Personen [sind] selbst die Erzehler" (517) und immer wieder der „Charakter" mit seiner inneren und äußeren Geschichte, wobei der Schwerpunkt auf der inneren liegt: Im Roman ist „das *Seyn* des Menschen, sein innrer *Zustand* das Hauptwerk" (18 [Originalhervorhebung]). Genauso wie im wirklichen Leben sollen das „*Innre* und das *Aeußere* des Menschen" eng zusammenhängen (263 [Originalhervorhebung]); der Dichter muss „uns also nur *innre* Geschichte" geben, „das andre hängt von seiner Willkühr ab!" (383–384 [Originalhervorhebung]) Nur und erst dadurch wird der Autor zum Dichter:

> Wir sehen, bey dieser Behandlung, die Personen anschauend mit all' ihren Eigenthümlichkeiten vor uns. Sie treten gleichsam aus dem Gemälde hervor; wir können sie von allen andern genau unterscheiden. Mit einem Wort, nur durch diese Behandlung allein kann der Dichter […] seine Personen *individualisiren*; durch diese Behandlung allein kann er das werden, was er seyn will – *Dichter*. (309–310 [Originalhervorhebung])

Trotz zahlreicher Querverweise auf die antike Poetik und Rhetorik sowie auf andere Romane bildet der *Versuch über den Roman* eine Reformulierung derjenigen Romantheorie und -praxis, wie sie in Wielands *Geschichte des Agathon* erscheint. Dementsprechend versteht Blanckenburg sein Werk zwar als moderne, von den Alten unterschiedene Poetik, mit der er dem „jungen Romanendichter" (241) ein Regelwerk zum Verfassen von Romanen an die Hand gibt. Vor allem jedoch hat er die „Geschichte oder Charakteristik der Romane überhaupt" (7) verfasst. Er adaptiert also die Terminologie und das Verfahren, die bei Wieland zentral sind. Was kaum ein Jahrzehnt dem Roman vorbehalten war, wandert nun in die Romantheorie.

Besonders wichtig erscheint in Blanckenburgs Charakteristik das Verhältnis des Ganzen und seiner Teile: Die erste Hälfte seines *Versuchs über den Roman* fasst das Ganze ins Auge („Von dem Anziehenden einiger Gegenstände", 3), die zweite Hälfte trägt die Überschrift „Von der Anordnung und Ausbildung der Theile und dem Ganzen eines Romans“ (245). Da es bislang keine Regeln dafür gibt, wie dieses Verhältnis für den Roman zu denken ist, entsteht ein Freiraum: Was zwischen dem Teil und dem Ganzen, dem Besonderen und dem Allgemeinen vermittelt, kann Blanckenburg neu bestimmen. Er setzt als Vermittlungsfigur die Psyche ein und bezeichnet sie als innere Geschichte des menschlichen Individuums. Sie steht im Mittelpunkt sowohl des Schreibens als auch des Lesens von Romanen.

Zur inneren Geschichte zählen für Blanckenburg alle *„Eigenthümlichkeiten der Sitten einer Person“* (230 [Originalhervorhebung]). In diesem Kontext verlässt er jedoch das Paradigma der menschlichen Natur und notiert, der Dichter möge doch „die Sitten, die Personen aus seinem Volke“ nehmen, so dass sie „viel Nationelles“ verkörpern (233). Blanckenburg fordert nicht mehr und nicht weniger als den deutschen Roman, der die innere Beschaffenheit der Nation illustriert.

Dieser lässt nicht lange auf sich warten. 1774, im Erscheinungsjahr des *Versuchs über den Roman*, publiziert Johann Wolfgang Goethe die erste Fassung von *Die Leiden des jungen Werthers*. Blanckenburg wird den Roman 1775 rezensieren (Blanckenburg 1775). Es folgen, um nur die Spitze des Eisbergs anzudeuten, Johann Carl Wezels *Herrmann und Ulrike. Ein komischer Roman* (1780), Karl Philipp Moritz' *Anton Reiser. Ein psychologischer Roman* (1785–1790) und Goethes *Wilhelm Meisters Lehrjahre. Ein Roman* (1795/96). Parallel dazu kommen weiterhin antikisierende Romane auf den Markt, etwa von dem Bestsellerautor August Gottlieb Meißner: *Alcibiades* (1781–1788), *Spartakus* (1793), *Epaminondas* (1798) und *Julius Caesar* (1799). Wie sich schon an den Titeln ablesen lässt, sind sie alle am Modell der Romanbiografie orientiert. Dies wirkt wiederum auf die Romantheorie zurück: „Seit Goethes Wilhelm Meister waren sich die meisten Ästhetiker und Kritiker darin einig, daß der Roman den Menschen als Individuum schildern solle, sein privates Leben, insbesondere die Entwicklung und Bildung seiner Persönlichkeit“ (Steinecke 1976, 26) – der Roman soll den Menschen anhand seiner inneren Geschichte charakterisieren.

Bis in die 1830er Jahre bleibt der Individualroman das vorherrschende Modell in der Romantheorie. Um 1840 tritt ihm ein weiteres Modell an die Seite: der „historische Roman“ (146). In diesem Zusammenhang verlagert sich der Schwerpunkt vom Wesen des Individuums zum Wesen der Geschichte selbst. Parallel dazu lassen sich in der Literatur- und Rechtsgeschichtsschreibung analoge narrative Schwerpunktsetzungen beobachten.

3. *Äußere Geschichte und innere Geschichte in Philologie und Jurisprudenz*

Nachdem Wieland und Blanckenburg im Blick auf den Roman zwischen äußerer und innerer Geschichte unterschieden haben, führt Gustav Hugo eine analoge Unterscheidung in die Rechtswissenschaft ein. In seinem *Lehrbuch der Rechtsgeschichte bis auf unsre Zeiten* (1790) sondert er die herkömmliche Gelehrtengeschichte von diesem neuen Geschichtsmodell ab:

> Es sind vorzüglich drey Punkte, die in der Rechtsgeschichte verbunden werden können: 1. Geschichte der Quellen des Rechts, – vom wem und wie Veränderungen bewirkt worden sind, wohin natürlich auch die Geschichte des Staats selbst gehört, soweit sie auf das Recht Einfluß hat; gleichsam als das Aeusserliche der Rechtsgeschichte; 2. Geschichte des Rechtssystems, – Inhalt der Quellen systematisch geordnet. 3. Geschichte des Studiums, der Bearbeitung durch Rechtsgelehrte. (Hugo 1790, 2–3)

In der zweiten Auflage von 1799 führt Hugo seine Vorstellung von der „äußern und innern Geschichte des Römischen Rechts" weiter aus (Hugo 1799, VII), und es dauert nicht lange, bis Hugos Konzept in der juristischen Germanistik ankommt: Im ersten, 1808 erschienenen Band seiner *Deutschen Staats- und Rechtsgeschichte* zitiert Carl Friedrich Eichhorn die entsprechenden Passagen aus Hugos Lehrbuch, bevor er das Verfahren selbst anwendet. Es gilt zunächst, so Eichhorn mit Hugo, „die *äußere Rechtsgeschichte*" darzustellen,

> welche die Quellen des geschriebenen Rechts aufzählt, die Zeit ihrer Entstehung bestimmt, sie nach ihren Veranlassungen, Verfassern, Quellen, ihrem Geiste und ihrer Gültigkeit charakterisiert, und ihre nachherigen Schicksale, unter welche auch ihre Bearbeitung gehört, erzählet. (Eichhorn 1808, 2–3 [Originalhervorhebung])

Äußere Rechtsgeschichte soll nun mehr sein als politische Geschichte: Sie erweist sich als eminent philologisches Vorhaben mit textkritischem Schwerpunkt, und sie soll im Modus des Erzählens gestaltet werden. In einem erzählerischen Zusammenhang steht auch „die *innere Rechtsgeschichte*, welche sich mit den Begriffen und Sätzen des positiven Rechts selbst, ihrem meist sehr rohen Anfange, ihrer allmäligen [sic!] Verfeinerung und auch wohl ihrer nachherigen Verunstaltung, beschäftigt." Diese sieht „bey den Quellen [...] auf den Inhalt", jene auf die Form und Geschichte der textuellen Überlieferung (3 [Originalhervorhebung]).

Das Schema innerer und äußerer Rechtsgeschichte wird im neunzehnten Jahrhundert eigentlich überall verwendet, von Eichhorn über Friedrich Carl von Savigny bis hin zu Karl von Amiras *Grundriss des Germanischen Rechts* aus dem Jahr 1897. So verwundert es nicht, dass es auch in die Philologie einzieht. Bereits 1807 importiert es der Altphilologe Friedrich August Wolf, augenscheinlich im Rückgriff auf Hugo: Die „*äussere Geschichte der Litteratur*" handelt von „den schriftlichen Werken der Griechen und Römer, von deren

Verfassern, ihrem Leben und den Umständen, unter denen sie schrieben", notiert er in seiner *Darstellung der Altertumswissenschaft*, und er fährt fort:

> Hier betrachten wir die Werke fürerst als *Continentia*, als Denkmäler ihrer Zeitalter und Urheber; weshalb uns hier die Biographik der Schriftsteller am meisten beschäftigt, mit beständigem Bezug auf die Staats-Geschichte und die Fortgänge der höhern Cultur. Die zweite Abtheilung muss auf die *Contenta* der Werke gerichtet seyn, und sie ergibt die *innere Geschichte* [...] oder die Geschichte des Ursprungs, Wachsthums, blühenden Zustandes und Verfalls der Litteratur. (Wolf 1986 [1807], 60–61 [Originalhervorhebung])

Die Trennung von innerer und äußerer Geschichte hängt mit der doppelten Funktion zusammen, die Literatur und Recht im Horizont einer Literatur- bzw. Rechtsgeschichte einnehmen: Die „literarischen Texte sind sowohl Quellen für die Erkenntnis dieser Geschichte als auch Ereignisse [...] in ihr" (Weimar 2003, 278). Diese Doppelfunktion trifft ebenso auf rechtliche Texte zu. Es ergibt sich also für Literatur- und Rechtshistoriker das „Dilemma, zwischen der Beschreibung der gegenwärtigen Werke und der Beschreibung der aus ihnen zu erkennenden und bestehenden vergangenen Geschichte wählen zu müssen und doch auf keine von beiden verzichten zu dürfen" (279). Der methodische Ausweg liegt in der analytischen Trennung beider Ebenen, um den Preis jedoch, dass sich die Quellen vor die Geschichte schieben, die aus ihnen erkannt wird. So heißt es z. B. in Wilhelm Eduard Wildas *Das Strafrecht der Germanen* (1842) über das salische Recht:

> Dadurch, dass es in verschiedenen Bearbeitungen von ungleichem Alter uns erhalten ist, giebt es manche beachtenswerte Fingerzeige für das Fortschreiten der Rechtsentwickelung, wie keine der verwandten Rechtsquellen sie darbietet. Doch hat man dem freilich noch weniger die Aufmerksamkeit zugewendet, als man sich bemüht hat, die Räthsel der verderbten Malbergs-Glossen zu deuten. Dass der Wolfenbüttler und Münchner Text uns die älteste Form, in welcher die *lex Salica* erhalten ist, darbieten, darüber dürfte wohl kaum eine Meinungsverschiedenheit entstehen können. Allein auch diese ältesten Texte enthalten das Recht in einer von seiner ursprünglichen Form sehr abweichenden Gestalt. Dass man dasjenige, was auf heidnischem Glauben darin beruhte, sorgfältig daraus zu vertilgen gesucht hat, sagen die Vorreden selbst. (82–83)

In dieser Art beschreibt Wilda auf nicht weniger als 115 Seiten etliche Texte, bevor er im zweiten Teil den Inhalt dieser Texte in eine fast 900-seitige Narration integriert. Analog dazu notiert Amira noch ein halbes Jahrhundert später in dem erwähnten *Grundriss des Germanischen Rechts*:

> Die älteste Lex [...] ist das Gesetzbuch des west- oder salfränkischen Stammes, die Lex Salica. Ein Prolog derselben erzählt in der Hauptsache glaubwürdig, noch in der Zeit der Kleinkönige seien von diesen vier Männer ernannt worden, welche in drei Gerichtsversammlungen nach sorgfältigem Durchsprechen aller Streitfälle das Rechts so ‚gesagt' hätten, wie es in der L. Sal. stehe. Diese Weisthümer sind in der ursprünglichen Gestalt nicht erhalten [...]. Dagegen ist die Lex des Chlodowech (*Pactus* oder *Tractatus legis Salicae*) nicht in unveränderter Fassung bewahrt, sondern nur

der Grundtext von fünf Hauptredaktionen [...]. Der Grundtext ist wahrscheinlich erst nach 507 abgefasst und hat das westgot. Edikt des Eurich benutzt. (Amira 1897, 15)

Auch in der philologischen Germanistik wird die *„äußere* Geschichte der Literatur [...] das Feld topographisch-antiquarischer Bemühungen", wie Jürgen Fohrmann (1989, 36–37) nachgewiesen hat. Er nennt z. B. August Kobersteins *Grundriß der Geschichte der deutschen National-Litteratur* (1827), wo die ‚äußere Geschichte' in die langen Fußnoten des Anmerkungsteils geschoben wurde. Seit den 1830er Jahren lässt sich jedoch ein Übergang zur inneren Geschichtsschreibung ohne Berücksichtigung der äußeren Geschichte beobachten. Dies wirkt modellbildend und wird im Ansatz noch heute praktiziert. Den Anfang dieser Entwicklung bildet Karl Rosenkranz' Literaturgeschichte, die sich nurmehr als „innere" annonciert: Die *Geschichte der Deutschen Poesie im Mittelalter* (1830) sei das Ergebnis „innerer Geschichtschreibung" – zwar sei die äußere als eine Art Hilfswissenschaft die Voraussetzung der inneren, doch rühmt sich Rosenkranz, „nie von Handschriften" und „Ausgaben" zu sprechen (Rosenkranz 1830, IV). Stattdessen geht es ihm um die „Geschichte" als „der sich selbst erzeugende Geist". Denkmäler dieses Geistes seien *„die Nibelungen, der Titurel, Tristan, Morolf, der Krieg auf Wartburg, und Reinicke Fuchs* [...]. Die innere Geschichtsschreibung hat das Wesen und den Gehalt solcher hervorragenden Gebilde zu enthüllen und so sie selbst zu begreifen" (3–4).

Das enthüllende Begreifen gelingt dadurch, so die Theorie, dass der in den Quellen lebende Geist der Geschichte durch den Geist des Interpreten verdoppelt bzw. aktualisiert wird: Die „Fremdheit" bzw. „Dunkelheit" eines mittelalterlichen Textes „soll verschwinden und soll erkannt werden, daß der Geist, welcher jene Produkte erzeugte, derselbe ist mit dem, welcher nun ihrer sich erinnert" (4). Ähnlich wie bei vielen anderen zeitgenössischen Literarhistorikern mutiert auch bei Rosenkranz der Geist zur Maske des Autors bzw. Volks, dessen Beschaffenheit mittels der Texte erkannt werden soll. Sinnigerweise bezieht er sich auf Texte, deren Verfasser nicht bekannt sind (etwa das *Nibelungenlied*), aber auch auf solche, deren Autor man kennt. In der Praxis heißt das allerdings, dass Rosenkranz' Literaturgeschichte mehrheitlich aus Inhaltsangaben besteht, die durch interpretative Passagen eingeleitet werden. Eingespannt ist das Ganze in eine historisch-systematische Konstruktion, die sich grob an Gattungen, vor allem aber an literarischen Stoffen und Motiven orientiert (Weimar 2003, 304–311; Goßens 2011, 379–388). Die Schnittmenge von erkennendem und erkanntem Geist ist der Inhalt.

Nachdem Rosenkranz die Literaturgeschichtsschreibung programmatisch auf den Inhalt verpflichtet und die Textkritik daraus entlassen hat, können sich Literaturgeschichte und Editionsphilologie zu eigenständigen philologischen Disziplinen ausbilden. Auch die Rechtsgeschichtsschreibung verselbständigt sich im neunzehnten Jahrhundert zu einer Disziplin innerhalb der Jurisprudenz. Dies bleibt der Textkritik hier versagt, und so verharren die Angaben zu Textgestalt, Überlieferung usw. in der Rechtsgeschichte selbst. Obwohl Juristen diese ‚äußere Geschichte' im ganzen neunzehnten Jahrhundert nicht verabschieden werden, wird die ‚innere Geschichte' in der Regel stärker gewichtet und ausgearbeitet. ‚Innere Geschichte' wiederum entpuppt sich meist als Charakteristik: von individuellen Autoren einerseits, von „Völkerindividuen" (Savingy 1840, 19) andererseits (Lieb 2021).

4. Schlussbemerkungen

Der biografische Roman und seine Poetik der authentischen Narration historischer Ereignisse ist nicht das einzige Paradigma, auf das sich die neuere Literatur- und Rechtsgeschichtsschreibung des neunzehnten Jahrhunderts stützt. Trotzdem bleibt festzuhalten, dass die Unterscheidung von innerer und äußerer Geschichte, die in Roman und Romantheorie der Epochenwende von der Spätaufklärung zur Romantik populär wird, sich als Impulsgeber für den akademischen Diskurs erweist und um 1800 in literatur- und rechtsgeschichtliche Darstellungen einzieht.

Um 1850 hingegen, als man sich auf juristischer Seite von der Epoche Eichhorn und Savigny zu distanzieren begann, wurde ein Erzählverständnis vertreten, wonach faktuales Erzählen in der Jurisprudenz als Regelfall, fiktionales Erzählen hingegen als Abweichung galt. In diesem Sinn kritisierte der Jurist Carl Friedrich Gerber die Rechtsgeschichtsschreibung seines Kollegen Eichhorn und machte ihm die Narrativität seiner Darstellung zum Vorwurf: „In jenen Darstellungen Eichhorn's und seiner Nachfolger liegt Nichts, was einen specifisch juristischen Charakter an sich trüge; das Juristische liegt dabei nur im Stoffe, die Darstellung ist nur die eines Erzählers" (Gerber 1850, XXIV). Im Gegensatz dazu wurde in der deutschen Philologie das Erzählen von Literaturgeschichte zum künstlerischen Schöpfungsakt erhöht, z. B. durch Georg Gottfried Gervinus, Verfasser der *Geschichte der poetischen Nationalliteratur der Deutschen* (1835). Wie er in deren Einleitung notiert, wähnt er sich gar als Schöpfer einer neuen Wissenschaft, nämlich der Literaturgeschichte: „Wer das Verhältnis meiner Arbeit zu jeder existierenden Kunstgeschichte durchschaut, wird vielleicht urteilen, es sei fast eine ganz neue Wissenschaft, die ich mir erschaffen mußte" – und dabei ging er als genialischer Künstler zu Werke: Weil er „zugleich darstellen und in einem Geschichtswerke künstlerisch verfahren" wollte, musste er „seine kleine Schöpfung nach inneren Gesetzen gestalten" (Gervinus 1980, 184–186).

Für das einundzwanzigste Jahrhundert werden vergleichbare Wechselwirkungen zwischen literarischen und akademischen Schreibpraktiken konstatiert, so von Michael Stolleis, der in *Rechtsgeschichte schreiben. Rekonstruktion, Erzählung, Fiktion* die Narrativität der Rechtsgeschichtsschreibung im Anschluss an die Narrativitätstheorie von Hayden White diskutiert. Einleitend notiert er: „Die Wissenschaftsgeschichte beobachtet erzählend die Erzähler" (Stolleis 2008, 8). Woraufhin der Schritt in Richtung eines literarischen Erzählens von Rechtsgeschichte nicht weit ist: Da der Historiker „nur eine gelehrte und unter besonderen methodischen Regeln stehende Spezies der Gattung ‚Dichter/Schriftsteller'" sei, verliere der „Grenzbereich zwischen gesicherter und frei erfundener Dichtung seinen Schrecken" (33). Rechtshistorikern und Dichtern sei die sprachliche Erschaffung der Vergangenheit gemein, so Stolleis weiter. „Besonders deutlich wird der changierende Übergang der Gattungen im autobiografischen Roman" (34). Zwar will Stolleis die „Vermischung von Historiographie und Dichtung" (38) nicht auf die Spitze getrieben wissen. Dass er jedoch narrative Verfahren der fiktionalen Literatur in Analogie zur Rechtsgeschichtsschreibung sieht, zeugt von einem innovativen juristischen Umgang mit Erzähltexten, der die oben skizzierten Praxen der Rechtsgeschichtsschreibung neu aufleben lässt. Nicht zuletzt ist dies vor dem Hintergrund der anglo-amerikanischen Forschung zu sehen, wo Studien zu narratologischen Konzeptualisierungen des Rechts wie *courtroom narratives* prominent vertreten sind.

Zitierte Literatur

Amira, Karl von (1897) *Grundriss des Germanischen Rechts*. 2., verb. Aufl. Sonderabdruck aus der zweiten Auflage von Pauls *Grundriss der germanischen Philologie*. Strassburg: Truebner.

Asmuth, Bernhard (2007) „Charakter." *Reallexikon der deutschen Literaturwissenschaft*. Bd. 1: A–G. Hg. Harald Fricke und Klaus Weimar. Berlin/New York: De Gruyter. 297–299.

Blanckenburg, Friedrich von (1775) „Rezension zu J.W. Goethe Die Leiden des jungen Werthers." *Neue Bibliothek der schönen Wissenschaften und der freyen Künste*. Bd. 18. Leipzig. 46–95.

Blanckenburg, Friedrich von (1965) *Versuch über den Roman* [1774]. Mit einem Nachwort v. Eberhart Lämmert. Stuttgart: Metzler.

Bodmer, Johann Jakob, und Johann Jakob Breitinger (1891) *Die Discourse der Mahlern* [1721–1722]. 1. Theil. Hg. Theodor Vetter. Frauenfeld: Huber.

Fohrmann, Jürgen (1989) *Das Projekt der deutschen Literaturgeschichte. Entstehung und Scheitern einer nationalen Poesiegeschichtsschreibung zwischen Humanismus und Deutschem Kaiserreich*. Stuttgart: Metzler.

Eichhorn, Carl Friedrich (1808) *Deutsche Staats- und Rechtsgeschichte*. Göttingen: Vandenhoeck und Ruprecht.

Gerber, Carl Friedrich (1850) *System des Deutschen Privatrechts*. 2. verb. Aufl. Jena: Mauke.

Gervinus, Georg Gottfried (1980) „Geschichte der poetischen Nationalliteratur der Deutschen. Einleitung“ [1835]. *Eine Wissenschaft etabliert sich: 1810–1870.* Hg. Johannes Janota. Tübingen: Niemeyer. 172–188.

Goethe, Johann Wolfgang (1774) *Die Leiden des jungen Werthers.* Leipzig [München [u.a.]]: [Saur].

Goethe, Johann Wolfgang (1795/1796) *Wilhelm Meisters Lehrjahre. Ein Roman.* Berlin: Unger.

Goßens, Peter (2011) *Weltliteratur. Modelle transnationaler Literaturwahrnehmung im 19. Jahrhundert.* Stuttgart/Weimar: Metzler.

Grimm, Jacob (2005) Vorlesung über deutsche Literaturgeschichte („die Geschichte der deutschen Literatur von der ältesten bis zur neuesten Zeit“, nach studentischen Mitschriften). *Werke und Briefwechsel*, Teil: Materialien, Bd. 1. Hg. Matthias Janssen. Kassel/Berlin: Verlag der Brüder-Grimm-Gesellschaft.

Hall, Joseph (1608) *Characters of Vertues and Vices.* London: Printed by Melch. Bradwood for Eleazar Edgar and Samuel Macham.

Harth, Dietrich (1996) „Geschichtsschreibung.“ *Historisches Wörterbuch der Rhetorik.* Bd. 3: Eup–Hör. Hg. Gert Ueding. Tübingen: Niemeyer. 832–870.

Hugo, Gustav (1790) *Lehrbuch der Rechtsgeschichte bis auf unsre Zeiten.* Berlin: Mylius.

Hugo, Gustav (1799) *Lehrbuch der Geschichte des Römischen Rechts.* Berlin: Mylius.

Koberstein, August (1827) *Grundriß der Geschichte der deutschen National-Literatur.* Leipzig: Vogel.

Kondylis, Panajotis (2002) *Die Aufklärung im Rahmen des neuzeitlichen Rationalismus.* Hamburg: Meiner.

Koselleck, Reinhart (1985) *Vergangene Zukunft. Zur Semantik geschichtlicher Zeiten.* Frankfurt a. M.: Suhrkamp.

La Bruyère, Jean de (1692) *Caractères De Théophraste Traduits Du Grec* […] [1688]. Bruxelles: Leonard.

Lessing, Gotthold Ephraim (1973) „Hamburgische Dramaturgie.“ *Werke.* Bd. 4: Dramaturgische Schriften. Hg. Herbert G. Göpfert. Darmstadt: WBG. 229–720.

Lieb, Claudia, und Christoph Strosetzki (2013) (Hg.) *Philologie als Literatur- und Rechtswissenschaft. Germanistik und Romanistik 1730–1870.* Heidelberg: Winter.

Lieb, Claudia (2021) *Germanistiken. Zur Praxis von Literatur- und Rechtswissenschaft 1630–1900.* Berlin/Heidelberg: Metzler.

Meißner, August Gottlieb (1781–1788) *Alcibiades.* Leipzig: Breitkopf.

Meißner, August Gottlieb (1792) *Spartakus.* Berlin: Maurer.

Meißner, August Gottlieb (1798) *Epaminondas*. Prag: Barth.

Meißner, August Gottlieb (1799) *Julius Caesar*. Berlin: Frölich.

Moritz, Karl Philipp (1785–1790) *Anton Reiser. Ein psychologischer Roman*. Berlin: Maurer.

Möser, Justus (1842) *Patriotische Phantasien*. Hg. J. W. J. von Voigt. Berlin: Verlag der Nicolaischen Buchhandlung.

Rosenkranz, Karl (1830) *Geschichte der deutschen Poesie im Mittelalter*. Halle: Anton und Gelbcke.

Savigny, Friedrich Carl von (1840) *System des heutigen Römischen Rechts*. Bd. 1. Berlin: Veit.

Steinecke, Hartmut (1976) *Romantheorie und Romankritik in Deutschland. Die Entwicklung des Gattungsverständnisses von der Scott-Rezeption bis zum programmatischen Realismus*. Bd. 2. Stuttgart: Metzler.

Stolleis, Michael (2008) *Rechtsgeschichte schreiben. Rekonstruktion, Erzählung, Fiktion?* Basel: Schwabe.

Wagner-Egelhaaf, Martina (2013) „Einleitung: Was ist Auto(r)fiktion?" *Auto(r)fiktion. Literarische Verfahren der Selbstkonstruktion*. Hg. dies. Bielefeld: Aisthesis-Verlag. 7–21.

Weimar, Klaus (2003) *Geschichte der deutschen Literaturwissenschaft bis zum Ende des 19. Jahrhunderts*. Paderborn: Fink.

Wezel, Johann Carl (1780) *Herrmann und Ulrike. Ein komischer Roman*. Frankfurt a. M./Leipzig: o.V.

Wieland, Christoph Martin (1986) *Geschichte des Agathon* [1766/67]. Hg. Klaus Manger. Frankfurt a. M.: Deutscher Klassiker Verlag.

Wilda, Wilhelm Eduard (1842) *Geschichte des deutschen Strafrechts*. Bd. 1: Das Strafrecht der Germanen. Halle: Schwetschke.

Wolf, Friedrich August (1986) *Darstellung der Altertumswissenschaft nach Begriff, Umfang, Zweck und Wert* [1807]. Weinheim: Acta Humanoira.

Penal Theory and Practice as Plot Matrix: From Jeremy Bentham's Principles of Penal Law to Margaret Atwood's The Heart Goes Last

Claire Wrobel

Introduction

The interconnections between law and literature may be approached by exploring the polysemy of *plot*, well-known for being "one of the most elusive terms in narrative theory" (Dannenberg 2005, 435). The 'law' under scrutiny here is Jeremy Bentham's penal theory, with which Margaret Atwood's 2015 novel *The Heart Goes Last*, the representative of 'literature' in these pages, holds an intertextual dialogue. Rather than being a weakness, the polysemy of *plot* makes it possible to highlight the importance of space and theatricality within this dialogue.

When asked how she came to be the head of a sprawling surveillance system, Jocelyn, one of the protagonists, gives the following answer:

> I was an English major [...] It's a real help [...] It's where all the plots are. That's where you learn the twists and turns. I did my senior thesis on *Paradise Lost*. (Atwood 2015, 136–137)

What seems to be implied is that being familiar with the "twists and turns" common in storylines can help one anticipate the plots (in the sense of 'conspiracies') that surveilled subjects may foment, but also possibly that it helps one design successful plots in response. The term *plot* is used in both senses, that of a "series of events consisting of an outline of the action of a narrative or drama" and of a "secret plan to accomplish a hostile or illegal purpose" – the third and fourth meanings provided by the *American Heritage Dictionary*, which Peter Brooks refers to in *Reading for the Plot*. These two meanings build on the first two entries in the dictionary, namely plot as a "measured area of land" and as the "ground plan" or "diagram," and according to Brooks are connected to them by "a subterranean logic": "the idea of boundedness, demarcation, the drawing of lines to mark off and order" (Brooks 1984, 11–12).

This chapter first discusses the part played by plots in the two senses of storylines and conspiracies in Jeremy Bentham's penal theory, arguing that by trying to thwart, or even better, forestall, plots on the part of subjects intent on breaking the law, Bentham within his theory makes space for literary plots. This ambition to stop plots from being hatched was in fact firmly rooted in space, embodied in the architecture of his model prison, the Panopticon. The building was originally meant to be erected on a very specific plot of land, i.e. the Rootstein Hopkins Parade Ground in London. Instead, on the same area, the Millbank penitentiary was later built, ironically designed on principles at odds with Bentham's.[1] Moving from the spatial back to the metaphorical, we could say that the Panopticon also became the "*diagram* of a mechanism of power reduced to its ideal form" in Foucault's elaboration of its functions in *Discipline and Punish*, thereby illustrating the interplay between the four senses of *plot* highlighted above (Foucault 1995, 205, emphasis mine).

Margaret Atwood's *The Heart Goes Last* may be read as a response to a number of utilitarian tenets. The novel engages not only with Bentham's Panopticon but also more broadly with his penal theory and offers a critique of a carceral society to be experienced vicariously through focal characters by the readers of the text. Atwood appropriates the plot potential present in Bentham's theory for her own satirical ends. Taken together, the two parts of this paper suggest that penal theory produces plots both within theoretical and literary texts. In the latter case, the connection is not merely one of inspiration, but rather a creative engagement with theoretical and social tensions.

1. *Plots in Bentham's Penal Theory*

1.1. Plotting as a Historically and Spatially Anchored Practice

While there may be a tendency in narratology to think of plots in ahistorical terms, the first examples given by the *Oxford English Dictionary* all come from the early modern period, and more precisely the late sixteenth and early seventeenth centuries. It has been suggested that "concepts of narrative organization emerged from a sixteenth-century movement to impose geometric order upon the land" (Brückner & Poole 2002, 619[2]). Phenomena such as "the explosion of surveying manuals (guidebooks for charting the land)" and "the development of the idea of narrative plot (literal and figurative charts of a story line)" were "interconnected" (Brückner & Poole, 618). The "plat" [sic!] (a "representation of manorial properties that included both the graphic form of the map and the discursive description") was used for purposes of taxation, and was therefore linked to economic and social imperatives (Brückner & Poole, 635). Geodesy, the branch of mathematics dealing with the shape and area of the earth, helped foster "a cartographically and chorographically shaped consciousness of nation-

[1] For a presentation of the historical background and of a creative reappropriation of the plot of land, see Cottell & Mueller (2020).

[2] I would like to thank Peter Schneck from the University of Osnabrück for drawing my attention to this piece.

al power," through which the English "took effective visual and conceptual possession of the physical kingdom in which they lived" (Helgerson 1992, 108, 107). Taking possession of land through mapping is also at the core of the colonial enterprise, a point which must be borne in mind when examining Bentham's writings on the penal colony of New South Wales, to which his own Panopticon plan was supposed to be superior.

According to Brückner and Poole, the concept of *plat* was surrounded by a "profound sense of deception and corruption," thus providing the connection to the sense of the plot as an evil scheme (642). Malpractice on the part of surveyors could indeed ruin families and wreak havoc; on the theatrical stage, this corresponded with the figure of the mischievous plotter. Plot was confronted by Elizabethan and Jacobean authors as "a form which potentially subverts, corrupts, and distorts meaning," an approach which stands in sharp contrast with the nineteenth-century faith in plot as a touchstone for narrative truth and certainty (Brückner & Poole, 644). The subversiveness of plots is illustrated by the seemingly endless punning allowed by its polysemy, as evidenced by the passage from Thomas Middleton's play *A Game at Chess* (perf. 1624) with which Brückner and Poole open their article. In Bentham's penal theory, the very possibility of punning enabled by polysemy was to be done away with lexicographically, and usurpation of identity was to be made impossible by giving one and the same name to only one person. Bentham's theory can therefore be read as an attempt to stabilize the proliferation of meaning.

While Peter Brooks's study *Reading for the Plot* centers on nineteenth-century 'great' novels such as Stendhal's *Le Rouge et le Noir* or Dickens's *Great Expectations*, the literary form connected to plots in the early modern period was the theatre. At the time, *plot* began to signify "textual structures" that materialized in "the relatively new theatrical practice of creating a graphic schematic of a play" (Brückner & Poole, 635). This "schematic" was posted in the tiring house for the guidance of actors, but was also published and could therefore be brought to the playhouse and consulted during the play. The practice is represented in Middleton's *Women Beware Women* (1626). In this play, numerous schemes of revenge are performed on stage during a masque-like entertainment. This performance departs uncontrollably from the script it was supposed to follow, thus befuddling the Duke, who watches as part of a fictional audience and at whose wedding the masque is being performed. The theatrical dimension in relation to evil purposes is also a point which must be kept in mind for the analyses below. Both in Bentham's writings and Atwood's fiction inspections of penal institutions tend to turn into masquerades hiding sinister plots.

1.2. Law, Statistics and Space Control

Before turning to the issue of plots specifically, a few words are in order to discuss the sources that can be drawn upon for Jeremy Bentham's penal theory. Indeed, that theory should not be reduced to penal devices or inferred solely from the reformer's Panopticon writings.[3] These latter include the famous memoir but also two postscripts published in 1791 in which practical details of his scheme are worked out, as well as texts which compare the model prison with other systems such as the hulks, transportation, or the penitentiaries in North America. These comparative essays include – among other texts – early material on Bentham's engagement with the penal colony under the title "New Wales" (1791) as well as his three letters to Lord Pelham (1802), who was then Home Secretary; they are now available in the latest volume of the *Collected Works* put together by the Bentham Project at UCL, entitled *Panopticon versus New South Wales, and other Writings on Australia* (Bentham 2022). Although, due to the influence of Foucault's reading, the Panopticon may now only evoke an abstract mechanism, the original plan was not developed in isolation from the realities of eighteenth-century Britain and its colonies. Rather, the scheme was in direct competition with transportation to New South Wales. One of the reasons why the plan was dropped was the supposedly improved condition of the colony (Bentham 2022, 73). It should also be noted that penal reform was only one of the areas to which Bentham sought to apply his Panopticon scheme; he also developed variations of the schema for workhouses, schools and political institutions (Brunon-Ernst 2012, 19–21).

Beyond the Panopticon writings, Bentham's penal theory must be reconstructed from a number of additional texts. Published sources include his *Introduction to the Principles of Morals and Legislation* (finished in 1780 but not published until 1789), his *View of the Hard Labour Bill* (1778), and his address to the French on the question of capital punishment (1831). The latter two texts subsequently appeared in the fourth volume of John Bowring's edition of Bentham's *Complete Works* (1843). The Bowring edition also includes Bentham's *Principles of Penal Law*, which comprises three parts: "Political Remedies for the Evil of Offences"; "Rationale of Punishment," which consists in a survey of all forms of punishment and reaches the conclusion that the most acceptable is active or laborious imprisonment; and "Of Indirect Methods of Preventing Crimes." My chapter in this volume draws mainly on the Panopticon writings and on *Principles of Penal Law*.

Reforming prisons entailed mapping their locations in Britain, as well as charting the abuses they sheltered. Such topographical ambitions were illustrated, for instance, by John Howard's survey in his *State of the Prisons* (1777) or

[3] See Draper (2002).

James Neild's *Account of Persons confined for Debt in the various Prisons of England and Wales* (1800), complemented for the third edition in 1808 by the result of his investigations in Scotland. Bentham presents Neild as "a second Howard," whose mission was to "hunt out of their holes" tyrannical prison managers, although he also points out that Neild actually started his tour of British prisons before Howard (Bentham 2022, 286, 290). Locating places of detention was not as easy as it may seem today, since it was common for debtors to be detained in private houses. Neild also inspected hulks, i.e. ships which housed convicts and were used to relieve Britain's overflowing prisons; in his third letter to Lord Pelham Bentham described them as uninspectable black holes. In Bowring's introduction, the term *topography* is also used metaphorically to refer to penal science: the "Rationale of Punishment," as Bentham argues, "exhibits the topography" of the "department of Criminal Law," whereas former writings only provided "a general map" (Bentham 1843b, 390).

The circular shape of the Panopticon may be read as Bentham's own attempt to "impose geometric order upon the land" whether literal or figurative. Although Bentham does not produce a "plat" of the sort described in Brückner and Poole's article, he does include tables which testify to a will to present information in a visually graspable, synthetic form and, ultimately, to show that the Panopticon is superior to the other systems with which it is compared. Several tables offer an estimate of the expenses incurred by transportation and compare them to the Panopticon's relative frugality (Bentham 2022, 19, 139, 142–143, 145, 252–253). Other tables compile statistics about the convict population, among them on convict emigration, convict mortality on the voyage and on the settlement, the number of lawful and unlawful returns from New South Wales to Britain or the number of sick, invalid or dead convicts in the hulks (Bentham 2022, 118, 132–133, 284). For the sake of comparison, a table is also provided which lists the number of prisoners in the penitentiary of New York, contrasting the number of those who have been admitted with that of the discharged, whether by death, pardon, expiration of sentence or escape (Bentham 2022, 228).

In Bentham's endeavor to control the land, statistics, defined as "a science based on the collection and analysis of aggregate data via surveys," takes precedence over geographic mapping. His effort in "Pauper Management Improved" to compile numerical data in tables when assessing the number of paupers in English parishes is contemporary with the first use of statistics in Sir John Sinclair's *Statistical Accounts of Scotland* (1791–1799) (Arneil 2020, 744–745). As Arneil comments, "statistical analysis was born for the express purpose of serving internal improvement of both land and paupers – that is, domestic colonization" (Arneil 2020, 744–745). Just as in Bentham's pauper panopticons, such enterprises of domestic colonialism focused on land, and more precisely waste land, which was to be surveyed and seized so as to be made productive and profitable through agrarian work. In penal law and in the model prison, but also in actual places of confinement, space control was crucial for the prevention of fomenting plots.

1.3. Countering Plots in Penal Law and Penal Practice

In his survey of eighteenth-century English penal law, Bentham spotted loopholes which made the law vulnerable; such loopholes allowed criminals to hide in obscurity, taking advantage of the system's oversight and ambiguities. More precisely, Bentham sought to make abduction, usurpation and forgery impossible. In his desire to anticipate the last of these, he produced scenarios which were exploited to the full in literature, especially of the sensationalist kind.[4] In his discussion of the criminal opportunities opened up by the existence of namesakes, he contemplates an almost allegorical scenario in which confidence is betrayed, innocence is exposed to danger and crime is offered "security" (Bentham 1843c, 557). Property – like identity – needed to be firmly established by stabilizing written texts such as title-deeds (Bentham 1843c, 551). Bentham's solution was twofold: it consisted in creating centralized registers and making them public. To avoid usurpation of marital rights, for instance, he recommended transcribing the register of each parish into a more general one (1843c, 553). Similarly, in order to protect individuals from illegal detention, he suggested creating registers to keep a systematic record of places of confinement along with the grounds for detention for each person detained without their consent. These registers were to be "publicly exposed, or at least allowed to be freely consulted by every body [sic!]" (Bentham 1843a, 370). This faith in transparency and publicity as protection is directly challenged in Margaret Atwood's novel, as we will see below.

The same drive towards transparency and control is also embodied in Bentham's treatment of space, whether real or fictional. The plots which Bentham sought to prevent were mainly escapes on the part of detainees, but they also included abuses on the part of the authorities, which could be "the result of design or negligence" and were, for instance, covered up by the collusion between the prison manager and the inspectors (Bentham 1843f, 122). Indeed, Bentham stressed the fact that although "the interest of the delinquent" could rightly "in part be sacrificed to that of the rest of the community," it should not "be totally disregarded" (Bentham 1843b, 398). The solution to avoid conspiracies on the part of both prisoners and managers, was to ensure continuous lighting of the premises with the elimination of even the smallest recesses where plotting could take place. Plotters, in addition to dark corners, needed time, and they

[4] For a detailed analysis, see Wrobel (2020, 422–426).

could be deprived of this resource for plotting by continuous inspection.[5] After presenting the example of J. Murphy, a convict who by 1802 had managed to escape from Newgate, from the hulks (in Woolwich and Portsmouth) and from a bridewell, the reformer asks:

> How many times in the same period would this ingenious person have effected his escape from a prison on the Panopticon plan, out of an apartment exposed night and day to the view of several pairs of eyes, themselves unseen by him, and commanding the whole circle, without so much as a change of place? (2022, 234)

The inspections of hulks were ineffective because managers were notified in advance:

> [so that] every thing not fit to be seen might first be put out of sight as much as possible:—that part of the filth might be shoveled away:—that eatable food might for the moment take place of uneatable: that the plague of famine might for the time be stayed: that in the motley company there each person might have his part given him to act: that instructions might be given to one class, injunctions backed with menaces to another: that every mouth might have a padlock put to it: that a varnish of some sort or other might be put upon every object—that a mask of some sort or other might be put upon every face. (Bentham 2022, 287)

Here, the covering up of abuses is presented as a staging involving "part[s]" and "mask[s]," harking back to the link between plots and theatricality.

Bentham sought to counter such plots with his own narrative, which intended to take inmates from corruption to reformation. The link between narrative and architectural design in Bentham's time has long been established. In *Imagining the Penitentiary*, John Bender shows how realist novels highlight "the power of confinement to reshape personality" (1987, 1) and sees in the penitentiary prison the embodiment "of the underlying assumption that narrative processes can reproduce (re-present) human behaviour so as to re-create personality" (8–9). The means of reformation was "a programmatic course of events with the end of shaping personality according to controlled principles" (35). Ultimately, the penitentiary "tell[s] the story of the materially constructed self" (38). Similarly, in *The Fabrication of Virtue*, Robin Evans highlights "a profound belief in the transforming powers of architecture," which is allotted "the central task of fabricating normality" (1982, 5, 8). In addition to producing a narrative of reformation, the penitentiary was also "an architecture of inescapable relationships" (92) in which "relationships between the prisoners and the gaoler were *plotted*" (46, emphasis mine). The Panopticon was "an essay in the engineering of behaviour through the manipulation of architectural form" (222). The chapter entitled "Architecture against Communication" in Evans's book (318–345) shows the technical ingenuity deployed to prevent communication between prisoners and deprive them of the possibility to foment plots.

---

5 See Wrobel (2020, 421–422).

In addition to engaging with plots on several levels – as spaces to be controlled, schemes to be prevented, and narratives to be produced – Bentham's penal theory, including but not limited to the Panopticon, is both novel – in the sense of new – material, and material that is particularly suitable to novels, a fact which has not gone unnoticed by authors. The popularization of Bentham's scheme by Foucault means that there are now explicit references to the Panopticon in contemporary fiction as well as in literary criticism.[6] The example discussed in this chapter, Margaret Atwood's *The Heart Goes Last*, makes covert reference to Bentham's theory. The plot potential present in the Benthamite Panopticon model is appropriated for satirical purposes. Atwood targets some of Bentham's tenets but also what may be called the carceral society of North America.

2. *Carceral Society in Margaret Atwood's The Heart Goes Last*

2.1. Presentation of the Novel and Narratological Setup

In *The Heart Goes Last*, economic meltdown has struck the United States, and the North-East in particular: the rust belt has turned into a "rust bucket" (5). Stan and Charmaine, the "middle-of-the-road" protagonists (9), decide to join the Consilience/Positron project, a gated "twin town" in which complementarity between carceral and non-carceral space guarantees full employment for all and the disappearance of crime:

> [I]t occurred to the planners of Positron [...] that if prisons were scaled out and handled rationally, they would be win-win viable economic units. So many jobs would be spawned by them: construction jobs, maintenance jobs, cleaning jobs, guard jobs. Hospital jobs, uniform-sewing jobs, shoemaking jobs, jobs in agriculture, if there was a farm attached: an ever-flowing cornucopia of jobs. Medium-size towns with large penitentiaries could maintain themselves, and the people inside such towns could live in middle-class comfort. And if every citizen were either a guard or a prisoner, the result would be full employment: half would be prisoners, the other half would be engaged in the business of tending the prisoners one way or other. Or tending those who tended them. (Atwood 2015, 48–49)

Because it is "unrealistic to expect certified criminality from 50 per cent of the population," participants take turns (Atwood 2015, 49). Every other month, they leave Consilience to spend a month working inside Positron. Meanwhile, their homes will be occupied by their "alternates," who will leave them on "switchover day," when it is their turn to go back to prison. The project is led by Ed, whose use of TV screens and paternalistic attitude is reminiscent of Or-

[6] See Fludernik (2017).

well's Big Brother but who also runs the scheme as a CEO who is accountable to shareholders, with Jocelyn at the head of the surveillance system.

From a narratological point of view, the novel replicates the framework of *Nineteen Eighty-Four*, acknowledged by Atwood as a major influence.[7] To borrow Genette's terms, third-person heterodiegetic narration is combined with internal focalization. The difference to *Nineteen Eighty-Four* is that there are two focal characters (Stan and Charmaine) instead of one, and as a consequence the same events are sometimes shown from both perspectives, most notably the climactic scene in which Charmaine is required to execute Stan. (On the context see below.) This narratological setup ("heterodiegesis *with ontological difference* plus internal focalization") makes the reading of *The Heart Goes Last* as "claustrophobic" as that of *Nineteen Eighty-Four*, and enables readers to experience vicariously the story-world of the novel (Bode 2019, 26, original emphasis). In terms of levels of knowledge, there is a discrepancy between Stan and Charmaine on the one hand, and Jocelyn, the head of surveillance, on the other. Because she controls the surveillance system, including the central database, she is clearly superior, hence her ability to become a mastermind and set up successful plots.

In Bentham's *Principles of Penal Law*, the agents of the plots as well as their victims tend to remain ciphers. They are broad categories ("offenders", "ravishers"), generic terms ("the person", "a man") or allegories ("innocence", "crime"). From a grammatical point of view, crime features more prominently – through nouns and passive voices – than the criminal or the victim. Literature, through its instantiating power, offers another perspective by bringing to life fictional characters with their individual specificities and perceptions. Free indirect discourse, which is itself a form of internal focalization, opens up ironic perspectives. The narrator does not make his or her presence felt, but readers are clearly invited to distance themselves from the characters' thoughts and from how they read their environment as well as one another. For instance, while Charmaine, seen from the outside and especially through her husband's eyes, initially seems to be blindly taken in by the Consilience/Positron scheme, merely aspiring to play the role of a harmless housewife, the novel shows that her motivations and character are more complex. Although her husband believes she is the embodiment of "transparency, certainty, fidelity" and is utterly "predictable," she has quite a few surprises in store for him: she cheats on him, hides the fact that her position as "Chief Medications Administrator" means she is in charge of the "Special Procedure" by which people are put to death, and even brings herself to perform it on Stan when she is herself threatened with elimination (59, 90). Readers have access to the thoughts of Stan and Charmaine who, as noted above, are both focal characters. The gap

[7] See "George Orwell: Some Personal Connections" in Atwood (2011, 141–149).

between Charmaine's actual character and motivations as opposed to how they are perceived by Stan encourages readers to distance themselves from Stan's thoughts and to revise their earlier judgments on Charmaine.

2.2. The Novel's Intertextual References to Bentham's Theory

The Heart Goes Last does not refer to Bentham's theory explicitly but there are numerous intertextual links. First of all, the names Positron and Panopticon sound somewhat similar. The two prison schemes moreover share similar 'utopian' characteristics: their circularity, self-containment and relative self-sufficiency, the claim to solve social problems and the fact that life is highly regulated within an authoritarian organization. Additionally, both prison models potentially degenerate into dystopias. One need not limit consideration of the Panopticon to its carceral application. Bentham's pauper Panopticon, too, can be described as a utopia.[8] In Bentham's scheme, just as in Atwood's novel, the problems to be solved are crime and poverty. Analogously, the Positron project "offer[s] not only full employment but also protection from the dangerous elements that afflict so many at this time" (31) and it is supposed to have "[u]nemployment and crime solved in one fell swoop, with a new life for all those concerned" and "a future that will be more secure, more prosperous" (45). The Positron project's utopian intent is to spread to other areas and to bring "salvation, not only of the many regions that have been so hard-hit in recent times but eventually, if this model comes to be adopted at the highest levels, of the nation as a whole" (44).

The Consilience/Positron project is built on a specific plot of land, which has been devalued because it is located in the most hard-hit region of the United States. By the middle of the novel, nine more new towns built on similar lines have appeared, projecting a "reordering of civic life" onto disorderly social space (100). The spread is materialized in the map which ornaments Ed's office: "There's a map on the wall behind Ed's desk, with pins in it. Orange pins are the Positron Prisons that are going up. [...] Red pins are for the Ruby Slippers branches" (287). The scheme has become a profitable franchise in which, after Positron prisoners have been put to death, their bones, organs and DNA are sold to retirement homes which belong to the "Ruby slippers" branch mentioned above. The implementation of evil plots is once more indissociable from spatial considerations, as evidenced by the map.

8 See J. R. Poynter's remark that "[t]he Pauper Plan grew into a Utopia, and is not the least interesting of the species. If, in much of his work, Bentham preserved a delicate equilibrium between economic liberalism and public planning, in this scheme the planner ran riot" (Poynter 1969, 109, quoted in Arneil 2021, 3).

Consilience and Positron, like the Panopticon, are surveillance-intensive spaces, but Atwood's novel critically takes stock of the decentralization of the gaze in contemporary times. The watchtower is replaced by a combination of databases and elusive surveillance technologies such as biometric identification, facial-expression analyzers or GPS tracking. The walls, however, remain. Positron is indeed sealed off from Consilience, which is itself cut off from the outside world by a "shiny black-glass wall" (30). Within the wall, as in the Panopticon, surveillance is asymmetrical. As Stan puts it, "Because you can't see them doesn't mean they can't see you" (113), which may be read in correspondence with the panoptic economy of the gaze as highlighted by Foucault. Indeed, occupants know they may be watched at any time, but do not know when.[9]

The specificity of Atwood's novel is that it does not simply refer to the Panopticon and/or Foucault's elaboration of it, but seems to locate dystopia within the broader context of utilitarian theory. Indeed, the community is run according to a nightmarish version or dark parody of utilitarian principles. In his foundational *Introduction to the Principles of Morals and Legislation*, Bentham defined utility as "that property in any object whereby it tends to produce pleasure, good or happiness, or to prevent the happening of mischief, pain, evil, or unhappiness to the party whose interest is considered" (12). The object of all legislation – the greatest happiness of the greatest number – seems echoed in the Consilience/Positron motto of "maximum possible happiness" (50) and in Ed's new business scheme to turn people into sex slaves, meant to be sold beyond the walls of the twin city where it is being developed. The scheme consists in having customers designate the object of their desire, who will then be kidnapped and undergo brain surgery that will "wipe out [their] previous love object and imprint [them] with a different one," i.e. the customer. Ed describes the neurosurgery as "beneficial to all," i.e. to the person who will pay for the kidnapping and surgery as well as to the person who will undergo the surgery. He ends his speech by announcing "[t]he greatest possible happiness of the greatest possible number" (325–326). Finally, the insistence on the fact that people – and especially prisoners – have to become "productive members of society" may be read as an echo of Bentham's goal to turn inmates into industrious members of society. The idea is taken to macabre extremes when what the prisoners 'produce' is body parts and to do so they will have to be killed. Although Charmaine does not know what is done with the dead bodies, she believes that "whatever happens, it's bound to be useful" (87), which is perhaps an echo of Bentham's essay "Auto-Icon," the full title of which includes the words "Or Farther Uses of the Dead to the Living" (Bentham 2002).

9 See the development on panopticism in Miceli (2019).

Intertextual links can also be identified with Foucault's elaboration of Bentham's scheme, which he assimilated to a "laboratory" (Foucault 1995, 203, 204). Indeed, while the founders of the twin city claim that their endeavor is "an ultra, ultra important experiment" (44), this term is echoed with very different connotations in Stan's thoughts: "Panic of a rat in a cage, with ample food and drink and even sex, though with no way out and the suspicion that it's part of an experiment that is sure to be painful" (113). However, it is not so much a disciplinary society that Atwood is describing but a carceral one in which Positron is the heart of society, "the meaning of it all" (234). While in Foucault's account, the prison is only one example of the institutional manifestations of discipline meant to spread to the whole of society, in Atwood's novel, the prison retains a central place. It is arguably the purpose and guiding principle that gives "meaning" to the "outside world" (142). Stan believes that "citizens were always a bit like inmates and inmates were always a bit like citizens, so Consilience and Positron have only made it official." His next remark confirms the hypothesis of the intertextual link to utilitarian theory: "Anyway, the point is the greatest happiness all around" (180).

2.3. Exploiting the Narrative Potential of Bentham's Theory: Plots and Counterplots

In the self-contained world described in the novel, plots and counterplots feature prominently. The actual "bona fide criminals" (78), who used to live in the twin cities, had been preparing "an uprising against Management, with hostages taken and ears cut off." But, the novel tells us, "that plan was discovered in time, through a spy" (79), and the malefactors disposed of. Another plot-related aspect emerges when tension builds up as journalists try to "worm their way in" (246) to find out what is actually happening in the secret womb of Positron. These infiltrations from journalists lead to a spate of repressive measures, legitimated as necessary to "overcome the subversive elements" (246). In Ed's account, there is an outside in which "online radicals and malcontents [...] claim that Consilience/Positron is an infringement of individual liberties, an attempt at total social control, and insult to the human spirit" (46). Their campaign is described by central management as a sabotage attempt "under the pretense that transparency is a virtue and the people need to know" (147).

The managers of Positron intend to control what is said about their scheme on the outside:

> The whole town is under a bell jar: communications can be exchanged inside it, but no words get in or out except through approved gateways. No whines, no complaints, no tattling, no whistle-blowing. The overall message must be tightly controlled: the outside world must be assured that the Consilience/Positron twin city project is working. (62)

The image sent to the outside world, as in all propaganda, relies on theatricality, on the staging of an "ideal life," and, one suspects, some careful editing. Indeed, participants are informed that "[f]rom time to time a film crew may arrive to shoot some footage of the ideal life they will all be leading, to be shown outside Consilience" (52–53). This invokes the historical link between plots and the theater.

The main plot (as in *plotting*), and narrative focus is that elaborated by Jocelyn, one of the founders of the scheme. She turns against the utopia when she realizes it is in fact a death machine run for profit. Her plan (or counterplot) involves smuggling Stan out of Positron to enable him to leak a flash-drive containing damaging documents. Stan's death is carefully staged so he can disappear from the database, take on another identity and be transferred to Las Vegas. As for Charmaine, she has to play the part of the bereaved widow when she is the one who put him to death – or so she believes. In church, she wishes she could kneel and place her forehead on her hands "as if in despair" so that she could "just zone out, which would help her get through this bogus funeral," but she knows she has to "sit up straight and *act* noble" (256, emphasis mine). The language of theatricality pervades the whole ceremony around the empty coffin. There is thus a double staging: the scene during which Charmaine killed Stan, but in fact only put him in a comatose state; and the staged funeral with the accompanying story that presents Stan as a hero who died to save his fellow employees when an electrical fire started in the chicken facility where he worked. Charmaine must not know that her husband is actually alive, because her grief has to appear genuine: "We don't want her to act, they'd see through it: they have facial-expression analyzers" (163).

Because even Jocelyn is under surveillance, it is necessary to fool Ed and provide a convincing motive for why she would want to have Stan eliminated. The motive is produced by means of an elaborate comedy of errors focusing on adultery. All couples have "alternates" whom they are not supposed to meet, i.e. the people who live in their house when they are in prison and return everything when it is their turn to go to Positron. When Stan finds a love note signed by a mysterious "Jasmine," he believes the latter to be his wife's alternate. In fact, Jocelyn and her husband Phil are alternates of Charmaine and Stan. "Jasmine" is the pseudonym Charmaine uses to communicate with her lover, who is no other than Phil. Their affair is part of Jocelyn's plan, which she calls a "scenario" or "stunt" (161, 162). Their illicit encounters have been caught on video, and so have Jocelyn's "degrading and jealous attempts to re-enact that affair and punish Charmaine through [Stan]": "Why do you think we had to go through all that theatrical sex in front of the TV?", she asks Stan (161). She is convinced that "those who might have to be shown those videos will see why [she] might want to get rid of [Stan]" (162). Charmaine's rescue from Ed's schemes at the end of the novel is also realized by means of a performance, namely the staging of a show at a retirement home, in which Stan plays an active part.

Jocelyn's plot, with all its theatrical elements of love, lust, revenge and mistaken identities, is meant to reveal the dark truth of the Consilience/Positron project. At the same time, it is also an escape narrative of the kind that Bentham wanted to forestall in his model-prison. One could therefore argue that on yet another level, the novel calls into question the mechanisms which Bentham had designed so as to protect prisoners from abuses on the part of the authorities. The two most important of these guarantees were private management and transparency – clearly caricatured and thus undermined in Atwood's utopia.

2.4. Questioning Private Management and the Faith in Transparency

Bentham advocated private management because he thought it would better protect prisoners, on certain conditions. First, the governor's interests had to coincide with those of the prisoners in a symbiotic relationship. This is apparent when Bentham describes his Panopticon project. He was supposed to manage the project himself, in contrast with transportation to New South Wales: "In no point did my system rest itself upon cold forms. In body, in mind, in every way, if my patients suffered, I suffered with them. By every tie I could devise, my own fate had been bound up by me with theirs" (Bentham 2022, 82). Secondly, Bentham believed that private management would arouse more suspicion among the public and needed to be more critically scrutinized, a dimension which is often overlooked in discussions of panopticism. As Janet Semple explains, there were five levels of inspection within the Panopticon, the last one involving the opening of the whole panoptic structure to the public gaze, not just of inspectors but also of any casual visitor curious enough to take a look and for whom constant access to the central watchtower was guaranteed (Semple 1993, 140). In other words, the governor and wards, too, were to be put under inspection, and this was to offer a protection against abuses. In Bentham's words, "Jealousy is the life and soul of government. Transparency of management is certainly an immense security; but even transparency is of no avail without eyes to look at it" (Bentham 1843f, 130).

As Jocelyn in the novel notes, "once you've got a controlled population with a wall around it and no oversight, you can do anything you want" (157). The question is how to make oversight effective. Whenever the tightly sealed door of Consilience is opened to let outsiders in, the tour is carefully orchestrated. For instance, when Charmaine runs into Lucinda Quant, whom she recognizes as the presenter of *The Home Front*, a reality show about people being evicted, Ed explains: "We're giving her a quick tour of our wonderful project. She's considering a new show called *After the Home Front*, so she can tell the world about the wonderful solution we have here to the problems of homelessness and joblessness" (143). The tour is obviously not meant to be an inspection but part of the scheme's communication, or even propaganda, plan.[10]

Transparency in Benthamite theory takes the shape of registers, public inspections and, in his later writings, what he called the Tribunal of Public Opinion. Atwood's novel presents a particularly devastating effect of transparency when it transcribes the public debate – conducted in social media, talk shows and blogs – which follows the revelations leaked by Stan. Outrage bursts out about "prison abuse," "organ harvesting," the creation of sex slaves through neurosurgery and the "plans to suck the blood of babies" (Atwood 2015, 354). Questions about the failure of oversight arise:

> [T]he misappropriation of people's bodies, the violation of public trust, the destruction of human rights – how could such things have been allowed to happen? Where was the oversight? Which politicians bought into this warped scheme in a misguided attempt to create jobs and save money for the taxpayer? (354)

However, what happens after the revelations is not the triumph of truth and justice but rather an anticlimax which leaves central questions unanswered. Talk shows supposedly make it possible for "two sides" to express themselves:

> *Some say* those who got their organs harvested and may subsequently have been converted into chicken feed were criminals anyway, and they should have been gassed, and this was a real way for them to pay their debt to society and make reparation for the harm they'd caused, and anyway it wasn't as wasteful as just throwing them out once dead. *Others said* that was all very well in the early stages of Positron, but it was clear that after Management had gone through their stash of criminals and also realized what the going price was for livers and kidneys, they'd started in on the shoplifters and pot-smokers, and then they'd been snatching people off the street because money talks, and once it had started talking at Positron it wouldn't shut up. (354, emphasis mine)

In this passage, the mixture of direct and indirect discourse bluntly reveals the accepted dehumanization of prisoners: neither side seems to question the idea of using criminals' corpses for profit. Atwood's text therefore also highlights the uselessness of institutional transparency when confronted with a powerful bias against prisoners ranging from mere indifference to actual hostility.

Conclusion

Going back to the historical etymology of *plot* has made it possible for this chapter to highlight two key dimensions of the Panopticon: the centrality of space and the link to theatricality. These have been illustrated in various ways both in Bentham's writings and in Atwood's novel. Theatricality in this context

---

[10] For other examples of mock-inspections read in the light of panopticism, in respectively Ann Radcliffe's *A Sicilian Romance* (1790) and Wilkie Collins's *Armadale* (1864), see Wrobel (2010, § 42; 2020, 428–430).

is conceived as a suspicious practice, which is used as a strategy to hide an unpalatable reality, for instance during inspections which are just masquerades. In Bentham's penal theory, the plots to be nipped in the bud before they are even hatched are escape plans on the part of prisoners and their possible accomplices outside the prison, as well as abuses on the part of the authorities, i.e. governors and warders as well as inspectors. Bentham's model prison is supposed to be the place where a narrative of redemption unfolds for each individual. His solutions to protect prisoners included the institution of private management and the Panopticon's openness to the public, two provisions whose value is challenged in Atwood's novel.

The Heart Goes Last is deeply anchored in North American detention practices. At one point, Jocelyn provides Stan with a very short history of incarceration. This history starts with the reforming age to which Bentham belongs and which materialized in the United States in the Philadelphia and New York penitentiaries:

> Prisons used to be about punishment, and then reform and penitence, and then keeping dangerous offenders inside. Then, for quite a few decades, they were about crowd control – penning up the young, aggressive, marginalized guys to keep them off the streets. And then, when they started to be run as private businesses, they were about the profit margins for the prepackaged jail-meal suppliers, and the hired guards and so forth. (157)

In the evolution sketched here, the narrative of reformation has entirely disappeared. Before turning into a death machine, Positron, like many other American prisons, was used for the "warehous[ing]" of prisoners (137) and did not even pretend to try and make them fit to return to society.[11] Reference is also made to the "for profit hosting of recalcitrants from other states" in Louisiana (146). Atwood, in dystopian fashion, "takes the premise of for-profit prisons to monstrous, comic ends" (Mead § 47). Although the privatization of prisons, which began in the 1980s, is far from having spread to the whole carceral system (according to the Sentencing Project, in 2019 private prisons held 8% of the federal and state prison population[12]), they have come under heavy criticism.[13]

Atwood's novel shows what happens when private management is dissociated from the transparency advocated by Bentham. As Alford contends, prisons in contemporary America are not so much panopticons as "nonopticons" in that no one bothers to look at the prisoners beyond making sure that they have not escaped (Alford 2000, 131). Instead of discipline, one finds indifference on

[11] Fludernik (2019) gives Herivel & Wright (2003) as reference on the topic, among others.
[12] https://www.sentencingproject.org/publications/private-prisons-united-states/.
[13] The criticism, highlighting high rates of violence, has come from the Department of Justice itself. See the 2016 report by the Office of the Inspector General: *Review of Federal Bureau of Prisons' Monitoring of Contract Prisons*, available online.

the part of the authorities, and idleness among inmates. If civil society does not bother to look either, then prisons have indeed the potential to become laboratories where sinister plots based on the commodification of the human body can prosper. Atwood's novel, through its dialogue with both Bentham's theory (a fiction of its own kind as it was never put into practice in the manner the reformer envisaged) and with contemporary practice, draws our attention to the necessity of defining transparency – Bentham's main cure to stop plots in the sense of evil schemes – and its implementation within democratic society.

Works Cited

Alford, C. Fred (2000) "What Would It Matter if Everything Foucault Said about Prison Were Wrong? *Discipline and Punish* after Twenty Years." *Theory and Society* 29.1: 125–146.

Arneil, Barbara (2020) "Origins: Colonies and Statistics." *Canadian Journal of Political Science* 53.4: 735–754.

Arneil, Barbara (2021) "Jeremy Bentham: Pauperism, Colonialism, and Imperialism." *American Political Science Review* 115.4: 1–12.

Atwood, Margaret (2011) *In Other Worlds: SF and the Human Imagination*. London: Virago Press.

Atwood, Margaret (2015) *The Heart Goes Last*. New York: Anchor Books.

Bender, John (1987) *Imagining the Penitentiary: Fiction and the Architecture of the Mind in Eighteenth-Century England*. Chicago: Univ. of Chicago Press.

Bentham, Jeremy (1843a) "Political Remedies for the Evil of Offences." *Principles of Penal Law: The Works of Jeremy Bentham*. Ed. John Bowring. Edinburgh: William Tait. Vol. I, 367–387.

Bentham, Jeremy (1843b) "Rationale of Punishment." *Principles of Penal Law: The Works of Jeremy Bentham*. Ed. John Bowring. Edinburgh: William Tait. Vol. I, 388–532.

Bentham, Jeremy (1843c) "Of Indirect Means of Preventing Crimes." *Principles of Penal Law: The Works of Jeremy Bentham*. Ed. John Bowring. Edinburgh: William Tait. Vol. I, 533–580.

Bentham, Jeremy (1843d) "Panopticon; or, the Inspection-House." *The Works of Jeremy Bentham*. Ed. John Bowring. Edinburgh: William Tait. Vol. IV, 36–66.

Bentham, Jeremy (1843e) "Postscript I." *The Works of Jeremy Bentham*. Ed. John Bowring. Edinburgh: William Tait. Vol. IV, 67–121.

Bentham, Jeremy (1843f) "Postscript II." *The Works of Jeremy Bentham*. Ed. John Bowring. Edinburgh: William Tait. Vol. IV, 121–172.

Bentham, Jeremy (1996) *An Introduction to the Principles of Morals and Legislation*. Ed. J.H. Burns, H.L.A. Hart and F. Rosen (*Collected Works*). Oxford: Clarendon Press.

Bentham, Jeremy (2002) *Bentham's Auto-Icon and Related Writings*. Ed. James E. Crimmins. Bristol: Thoemmes Press.

Bentham, Jeremy (2010) "Pauper Management Improved." *Writings on the Poor Law*, vol. 2. Ed. Michael Quinn (*Collected Works*). Oxford: Clarendon Press.

Bentham, Jeremy (2022) *Panopticon Versus New South Wales and Other Writings on Australia*. Ed. Tim Causer and Philip Schofield (*Collected Works*). London: UCL Press.

Bode, Christoph (2019) "Totalitarianism by Consent: Orwell, Huxley, and Capitalism in the Stage of Corporate Surveillance." *Narrating Surveillance: Überwachen erzählen*. Ed. Betiel Wasihun. Baden-Baden: Ergon. 21–42.

Brooks, Peter (1984) *Reading for the Plot: Design and Intention in Narrative*. New York: A.A. Kropf.

Brückner, Martin, and Kristen Poole (2002) "The Plot Thickens: Surveying Manuals, Drama, and the Materiality of Narrative Form in Early Modern England." *ELH* 69.3: 617–648.

Brunon-Ernst, Anne (2012) *Beyond Foucault: New Perspectives on the Panopticon*. New York: Routledge.

Cottell, Fran, and Marianne Mueller (2020) "From Pain to Pleasure: Panopticon Dreams and Pentagon Petal." *Bentham and the Arts*. Ed. Anthony Julius, Malcolm Quinn and Philip Schofield. London: UCL Press. 244–269.

Dannenberg, Hilary P. (2005) "Plot." *Routledge Encyclopedia of Narrative Theory*. Ed. David Herman, Manfred Jahn and Marie-Laure Ryan. London: Routledge. 435–439.

Draper, Tony (2002) "An Introduction to Jeremy Bentham's Theory of Punishment." Web. *Journal of Bentham Studies* 5.

Evans, Robin (1982) *The Fabrication of Virtue: English Prison Architecture, 1750-1840*. Cambridge: Cambridge Univ. Press.

Fludernik, Monika (2017) "Panopticisms: From Fantasy to Metaphor and Reality." *Textual Practice* 31.1: 1–26.

Fludernik, Monika (2019) *Metaphors of Confinement: the Prison in Fact, Fiction and Fantasy*. Oxford: Oxford Univ. Press.

Foucault, Michel (1995) *Discipline and Punish; the Birth of the Prison* [1975]. Trans. Alan Sheridan. 2nd ed. New York: Vintage.

Helgerson, Richard (1992) *Forms of Nationhood: The Elizabethan Writing of England*. Chicago: Univ. of Chicago Press.

Herivel, Tara, and Paul Wright (2003) Ed. *Prison Nation: The Warehousing of America's Poor.* London: Routledge.

Mead, Rebecca (2017) "Margaret Atwood, the Prophet of Dystopia." Web. *The New Yorker*, 10 April.

Miceli, Barbara (2019) "Margaret Atwood's *The Heart Goes Last*: Panopticism, Discipline, Society, and Utopia." Web. *Metacritic Journal for Comparative Studies and Theory* 5.2.

Poynter, J. R. (1969) *Society and Pauperism*. Toronto: Univ. of Toronto Press.

Semple, Janet (1993) *Bentham's Prison: a Study of the Panopticon Penitentiary*. Oxford: Clarendon Press.

Sentencing Project (2021) "Private Prisons in the United States." Web. https://www.sentencingproject.org/publications/private-prisons-united-states/.

US Department of Justice (2016) *Review of Federal Bureau of Prisons' Monitoring of Contract Prisons*. Web. https://oig.justice.gov/reports/review-federal-bureau-prisons-monitoring-contract-prisons.

Wrobel, Claire (2010) "Gothique, réforme et panoptique." Web. *Revue d'Études Benthamiennes* 7.

Wrobel, Claire (2020) "At the Crossroads of Law and Literature; on the Role of Fiction in Jeremy Bentham's Penal Theory." *Law and Literature* 32.3: 415–435.

Mahatma Gandhi's Autobiographical Narration of the Law

Klaus Stierstorfer

Mahatma Gandhi (1869–1948) is back in the limelight. Helped not least by the many activities on his 150th anniversary in 2018, he is celebrated as a global icon of peaceful resistance and a politics without violence, but also as a major figure in the construction of Indian identity even today. Trained as a lawyer, he developed his life's philosophy and politics in the colonial and postcolonial geographic triangle formed by India, Britain and South Africa. The full complexity of this setup between East and West, tradition and modernity, and many further dilemmas to boot, is illustrated in the hesitant and ultimately highly sophisticated narrative of his autobiography. This text testifies to his life-long struggle to learn, understand and make use of or 'practice' the law; but his autobiographical narration and his concept of the law are also caught up in the (post)colonial East-West divide. The narrative thus has an unparadigmatic and uneasy fit with either side, a circumstance that might also lend the text its greatest interest today. This essay will discuss experiences with the law as Gandhi presents them in his autobiography.

1. *Gandhi's Unease with Genre*

From a narratological point of view, autobiographies are characterized by the fact that the narrator professes his identity with the author who is the subject of the narration; that is, the narrator narrates his or her own life. In Genette's terms, autobiography is the 'highest degree' of a homodiegetic narration, namely the autodiegetic; Stanzel calls the texttype "autobiographical first-person narration" and Cohn "self-narration" (Löschnigg 2019, 104). Autobiography sounds, at first glance, as the most unproblematic and straightforward case of narration, since what could potentially be closer and better known to the storyteller than the narrator her- or himself? And who could be better placed to tell that story as the narrating self? Troubles start, however, with the problem that, as Martin Löschnigg puts it, "there are no textual criteria which allow the reader to distinguish between 'fictional autobiography' of the *David Copperfield* (1849/50) type and the autobiography of a really existing (historical) person." Even Löschnigg's suggestion to use the paratextual "onomastic (non-)identity of author and narrator" (104) as a kind of fictionality/factuality criterion is not fool-proof: (non-)identity may be just as much a part of the fictional setup as are asseverations that a particular text is "the true story of" – a phrase which readers of eighteenth-century novels will be particularly familiar with. Much of this modality management between reality and fiction, of the big grey area in between and of the postmodern dissolution of the binary differentiation, happens in the writers' and readers' minds, as Philippe Lejeune has formalized it in the legal image of the "autobiographic pact" (Philippe Lejeune 1989).

Similarly, Monika Fludernik's (1996) description of the development of narrative is a caution against any intuitive simplification of autobiography's narrative setup, when she points out:

> First-person narrative of course relates back to narratives of personal experience, a model from oral storytelling that has developed into autobiographical proportions. Autobiography itself is actually a fairly late development, long preceded by the third-person form of the *Life*. This is not surprising, after all, since people may easily tell of their adventures, their particular experiences at one point or another, but to write one's own life requires a sustained Augustinian effort to construct from the random succession of remembered scenes (the material of narratives of personal experience) that well-structured tale with teleological shape. *Other* people's lives, paradoxically, are knowable and tellable much more easily, and therefore surface as a genre soon after prose takes over. (Fludernik 1996, 47)

Although Fludernik' underlying historical teleology from less to more well-structured narration is debatable, her point against any assumption of a privileged access to, and easier narration of, the subject presented in autobiographies is valid. This is why Fludernik's own narratological approach centred on the concept of "experientiality" has become widely accepted as a more viable approach to autobiographical narration (Löschnigg 2019, 106), as she assigns a "crucial role" to consciousness, which "both mediates narrativity and constitutes one of its signifiers" (Fludernik 1996, 374). As Martin Löschnigg has it, further recent narratological research on autobiography has foregrounded "the selective dynamics of memory" involved in the autobiographical narrative as well as its epistemological function. It is seen either from a constructivist angle as constituting an identity which, outside of the narrative, would not exist (Jerome Bruner and others), or, following Paul Ricoeur and Alasdair MacIntyre, as mirroring of an experience which in and of itself is already narratively structured.[1] With these complications in mind, it is unsurprising that scholarly interest in autobiography has risen in the recent context of postmodernism and poststructuralism with whose central issues and conundrums it seems to resonate particularly well.[2]

When he set out to write his autobiography, Gandhi was keenly aware of the narrative complexities that his venture entailed. In the introduction, Gandhi

---

1 See Löschnigg (2019, 107).

2 The most comprehensive scholarly consideration of autobiography to date has now been presented in De Gruyter's three-volume *Handbook of Autobiography/Autofiction* (2019) edited by Martina Wagner-Egelhaaf.

reports doubts about his writing an autobiography as advanced by one of his friends who had asked him:

> Writing an autobiography is a practice peculiar to the West. I know of nobody in the East having written one, except among those who have come under Western influence. And what will you write? Supposing you reject tomorrow the things you hold as principles today [...], is it not likely that the men who shape their conduct on the authority of your word, spoken or written, may be misled? (2018, 44–45)

This identification of autobiography as a specifically Western tradition is still underwritten in Georges Gusdorf's classic article "Conditions and Limits of Autobiography," first published in French in 1956, when he wrote with special reference to Gandhi:

> First of all it is necessary to point out that the genre of autobiography seems limited in time and space: it has not always existed, nor does it exist everywhere. [...] it would seem that autobiography is not to be found outside of our cultural area; one would say that it expresses a concern peculiar to Western man [sic!], a concern that has been of good use in his systematic conquest of the universe and that he has communicated to men [sic!] of other cultures; but those men will thereby have been annexed by a sort of intellectual colonizing to a mentality that was not of their own. When Gandhi tells his own story, he is using Western means to defend the East. [...] the concern which seems natural to us, to turn back on one's own past, to recollect one's own life in order to narrate it, is not at all universal. It asserts itself only in recent centuries and only on a small part of the map of the world. (1980 [1956], 28–29)

I have provided this extensive quotation, as Gusdorf's text is, of course, in itself a richly layered historical document which would merit, but cannot be given, extensive comment here, sandwiched as it is between an awakening postcolonial attitude on the one hand and what could be called a meta-colonial and gender-insensitive approach on the other. It is now received wisdom that, historically speaking, both Gandhi's friend and Gusdorf were patently wrong. As the respective surveys in vol. 2 of the De Gruyter *Handbook* amply document,[3] autobiographic writing has globally been a wide-spread practice of great historical depth. It is by no means restricted to the West, but manifests itself in most other parts of the world. Angelika Malinar (2019a) is surely right in specifically summarizing the Indian situation as follows:

> Autobiographical writing in India has a considerable classical and medieval as well as colonial modern past, and the trajectories linking it with the literature in the post-colonial period still need to be explored in greater detail. (982)

When taking up the doubts of his friend regarding the wisdom of his choice of genre, Gandhi probably did not have an awareness of the wider literary historical background; he will repeatedly confess in his life story that his upbringing had not made him a widely-read man to start with. But when we consider that he was writing in Gujarati, as Gandhi did, the innovative impact of the

[3] See the surveys for Asia and Africa in vol. 2 of the *Handbook*.

genre stands out. In his introduction to his edition of the *Autobiography* (2018), Tridip Suhrud points out that Gandhi had few precedents. The first of only two earlier autobiographies in Gujarati identified by Suhrud appeared in 1866 and composed by the journalist and historian Narmadashanker Lalshanker Dave (1833–1886). Dave explicitly states that, by means of his publication, he hoped "to institute the practice of writing autobiography which does not exist among us" (quoted in Suhrud 2018, 15), an intention Suhrud cast within a wider "impulse to modernize the literary culture" in mid- to late-nineteenth-century India.

Leaving aside for a moment the question of Gandhi's generic innovativeness, we also need to take into account his own justification in answer to his friend's doubts. He first of all seems to sidestep the issue when he writes: "But it is not my purpose to attempt a real autobiography (*ātmakathā*)," or, in Suhrud's translation, "But, do I intend to write an autobiography?" (45). Gandhi then explains: "I simply want to tell the story (*kathā*) of my numerous experiments with truth, and as my life consists of nothing but those experiments, it is true that the story will take the shape of an autobiography (*jīvanvṛttānt*)." (45) It has to be noted that the word Gandhi uses here in the first sentence in Gujarati is *ātmakathā*, "the story of a soul," as Suhrud points out, and that he contrasts it with *jīvanvṛttānt*, "chronicle of life or autobiography," regretting that this distinction gets blurred by the undifferentiated rendering of both terms as "autobiography" in the translation (17). The two terms are connected, as Malinar observes, by the concept of *kathā*, story; the text is the story of his experiments with truth with an emphasis on "a certain sequence and connectedness of the narrated events" (Malinar 2019b, 1710). This emphasis is further confirmed by Suhrud's observation that it is only the English title "An Autobiography or The Story of My Experiments with Truth" that puts the autobiography first, whereas the Gujarati original starts with the "Experiments" and has "An Autobiography" at the end of the title, thus originally foregrounding the story line of the experiments and adding the generic marker as a kind of afterthought.

But what does Gandhi's statement imply? First of all, this can, of course, be seen as a strategic move to assuage the apprehensions of a friend with evident traditionalist and anti-Western leanings. When we look more closely at the history of the genre of autobiography and what it had come to stand for in the Indian context at the time, Gandhi is also making a more sophisticated point which reveals his high sensitivity to generic meaning, to what Hayden White would call (after Louis Hjelmslev) the content of the form. Gandhi's subsequent apologetics show his keen awareness of the potential misconstrual that his autobiography might be read as an exercise in self-aggrandisement. This is why he emphasizes that it is not his politics and achievements he wants to narrate, but his spiritual quest:

> If the experiments are really spiritual, then there can be no room for self-praise. They only add to my humility. [...] What I want to achieve – what I have been striving and pining to achieve these thirty years – is self-realization, to see God face to face, to attain *moksha* [fn.: "freedom from birth and death"]. (2018, 45–46)

This is also why Gandhi distances himself from the title Mahatma which he had been assigned by that time: "Often the title [Mahatma] has deeply pained me; and there is not a moment I can recall when it may be said to have tickled me" (45). He does not write as the "Great Soul" or, in the European equivalent, "Saint" (Mahatma), but as a seeker after truth and his text is the story of this search.

How then does Gandhi describe this search? He integrates the motif of a spiritual quest for truth which he identifies with God (47), within a modern, scientific research narrative. The aim is *moksha*, a concept which unites the kenotic paradox of complete dissolution of the self with its fulfilment and plenitude. The way to reach this goal, which is yet unachieved at the time of writing the autobiography, is a serial narrative of scientific experiments of the self. With his spiritual quest motif, Gandhi harks back to an earlier tradition of autobiographies in the line of Augustine's *Confessiones*; in the Islamic tradition, to Muḥammad al-Ghazālī's eleventh/twelfth-century *Deliverance from Error and Attachment to the Lord of Might and Majesty*; or to later similar narratives like John Bunyan's *Pilgrim's Progress*. In these spiritual texts the focus was not on the individuality and personality of the narrated subject, but on the progressive insight into and recognition of the divine. Gandhi claims that the "passion for truth was innate in me" (66) and the narrative is, as Philipp Holden (2008) describes it, not so much the "'development,' characteristic of modern autobiography, in which the self is formed through interaction with the world," but of "what Weintraub calls 'unfolding' in which the life is seen as developing according to an overall principle" (75).[4]

In this sense, Gandhi does not step out of the long tradition of autobiographical writing, but is deeply immersed in its early, spiritual variant. As Bhattacharjee (2018) comments: "The spirit that Gandhi borrows from his Christian /Western predecessors is that truth is very much the higher-order or master narrative that *orders* the narrative of the self/soul." Except that the predecessors of such spiritual autobiography are by no means only Western or Christian, Bhattacharjee is right in identifying a master narrative coming from this older autobiographical tradition. And it is this master narrative that holds together the other, modern side of the story to be found in his concept of a series of experiments with truth. Here Gandhi resorts to the principle of modern science as he understood it, casting his life as a series of experiments based on testing and falsifying concepts, strategies and theories – in his case, the one grand master theory of the pursuit of Truth:

4 His Weintraub quotation is from: Weintraub (1975, 830, 832).

> Far be it from me to claim any degree of perfection for these experiments. I claim for them nothing more than does a scientist who, though he conducts his experiments with the utmost accuracy, forethought and minuteness, never claims any finality about his conclusions, but keeps an open mind regarding them. (Gandhi 2018, 47)

And for this purpose he chose the genre of autobiography:

> If I had only to discuss academic principles, I should clearly not attempt an autobiography. But my purpose [is] to give an account of various practical applications of these principles [...]. These will of course include experiments with non-violence, celibacy and other principles of conduct believed to be distinct from truth. But for me, truth is the sovereign principle, which includes numerous other principles. This truth is not only [...] the relative truth of our conception, but the Absolute Truth, the Eternal Principle, that is God. (47)

This is in a nutshell why Gandhi needs autonarration for his experiments: they are not purely academic or intellectual, not *in vitro*, but *in vita* so to speak. Gandhi here implements a basic narrative transformation, as described by Paul Ricoeur (1983–1985), when the abstract, timeless principle of truth is pulled into time and given human shape and experience through autobiographical narrative: "time becomes human time to the extent that it is organized after the manner of a narrative; narrative, in turn, is meaningful to the extent that it portrays the features of temporal experience" (I, 3).

Returning now to the question in how far Gandhi was innovative in his choice of genre, the answer is complex and could be summarized roughly as follows. Yes, he was innovative in taking up autobiography as a genre that was associated with modernity and Western culture by most of his contemporaries at the time. He had become acquainted with this genre through Western literature, since much of his initial studies, even of classic Indian texts, was through Western texts and translations. And no, he did not re-invent the genre or side-step its conventions as such, but reanimated an older model, harking back to well-established traditions going back to St. Augustine or Muḥammad al-Ghazālī. This model foregrounded not the individual as such but an idea, ideal or concept after which the individual was shown to be striving. The success of this narrative and of the autobiographer's life did not consist in the aim of creating a self-assured, distinctive individuality, but of being subservient to that higher principle, culminating in a emptying out of individuality towards that higher realm. Here, the individual does not construct, but deconstruct or 'de-narrate' its individuality; paradoxically she finds plenitude in the dissolution and integration into the higher ideal. Nor does Gandhi's autobiography follow the Bildungsroman pattern in which he, as the Mahatma, would authoritatively show the way, or at least one way, leading to perfection. This, he maintains, he cannot do as he does not feel he has reached that perfection himself. Modestly, though sincerely and accurately, he wants to present his own experiments in trying to achieve his spiritual aim, how to move towards it. The autobiography's main narrative attraction lies in the overriding master narrative of a quest for Truth which is, however, realised in the narrative practice in a chronologically ordered series of experiments.

2. *The Legal Narrative in the Autobiography*

As we have seen, Gandhi's quest for truth on the formal side needs the narrative of his experiments with truth to be converted into human time; arguably the same conversion is necessary on the content side. Gandhi does not answer the question "What is Truth" in the abstract – in fact he does not even claim to have found an abstract answer to the question. His approach is exploratory and discursive. In parallel with the translation of an abstract concept into a narrative, he uses his life's 'experiments' in various fields as a matter of content, as the material in which his explorations of truth have taken shape. Truth becomes the abstract principle which needs to be converted into narrative to become part of the human sphere and to be made accessible to human experience. Gandhi explicitly excludes politics from the focus of his autobiography, stating that "My experiments in the political field are now known, not only to India, but to a certain extent to the 'civilized' world. For me, they have not much value" (45). Instead, for him personally more importantly, the fields in which he has explored the enactment of the truth principle in his life were "non-violence, celibacy and other principles" (47). However, what Gandhi does not explicitly refer to, and what has remained almost inexplicably unnoticed by commentators on his autobiography, is his views on and practice of the law. This is all the more surprising since the law is one of the most important and pervasive themes of Gandhi's entire narrative, both on a theoretical as well as practical or experiential level. This legal thread in the autobiography will be unfurled in my essay.

Gandhi's father was, as his father before him, chief minister of the district Porbandar on the Kathiawar peninsula on the coast of today's Gujarat. Gandhi was born in Porbandar in 1869. His father later became Prime Minister in Rajkot and then in Wankaner (two other Gujarat principalities). As Gandhi reports, his father was also a "member of the Rajasthanik Court", which, he continues, "is now extinct, but in those days, it was a very influential body for settling disputes between the chiefs and their fellow clansmen" (54). The practice of law and political office clearly had been running in the Gandhi family for several generations. His father's engagement was with the kind of law and jurisdiction which relied on local traditions and practices. After his father's early death in 1884, a Brahmin friend of the family advised Gandhi that he should go to England for his studies. His father had intended for him to follow in his political footsteps, which the Brahmin doubted could be achieved by local education at the present time. Gandhi's original preference for the medical profession was opposed, as he relates, by both the Brahmin and his elder brother. The reasons for that opposition came from their wish to see Gandhi make his way to high office, and because his father would not have liked someone from their caste, the Vaishnavas, to have anything "to do with dissection of dead bodies." "Father intended you for the bar" (101), was his brother's summary conclusion, which young Gandhi dutifully obeyed, and here his legal career began.

From his family home, Gandhi set out to Porbandar to meet his uncle, who had followed his father as chief minister there. That uncle agreed neither with the brahmin's nor with the brother's arguments for the law and strictly argued against the young Gandhi's plans to become a lawyer. The autobiography quotes the uncle's remonstrance:

> When I meet these big barristers, I see no difference between their life and that of Europeans. They know no scruples regarding food. Cigars are never out of their mouths. They dress as shamelessly as Englishmen. All that would not be in keeping with our family tradition. (102–103)

In short, Gandhi's "going to England [...] was in his opinion an irreligious act" (103). This early doubt about the moral integrity of the legal profession and, from hindsight in the wider framework of his experiments in and pursuit of truth, was to remain with Gandhi throughout much of his early career as a lawyer; his troubled reflections about the law form a main theme in his autobiography. It should be noted, however, that the uncle's warnings did not affect the law as such. The law which Gandhi was to study in England prevailed, at least in the higher courts, during the British Raj in India. The uncle had no issue with British law but was apprehensive concerning the immoral Westernization he observes to go hand in hand with the legal profession at the time.

And indeed, Westernization is also what irked Gandhi most during his stay in England, as he outlines in Pt I, ch.15, entitled "Playing the English Gentleman" (119–124). He describes how well-meaning friends tried to persuade him to eat meat and how he attempted to "become polished," which included new and expensive sets of 'English' clothes, and "to take lessons in dancing, French and elocution" (122). Despite these influences, Gandhi never wavered from his strict vegetarianism and in fact found in that predilection a way of getting into contact with a part of British society which was critical of the standard British way of life in other respects as well. His other attempts at social adaptation which he had entered on to make up for his vegetarian 'crotchet', as it seemed to his friends, were short-lived: "This infatuation must have lasted about three months. The punctiliousness in dress persisted for years" (124). He quickly saw that such practices of "mimicry," in the terms Homi Bhabha (1994, 86 and passim), would still not put him on an equal standing with his English peers, and he decided to devote himself to what he had come for: the study of the law.

When Gandhi describes his legal training in England, there is no criticism of the legal system he was to master. His (probably justified) lack of enthusiasm is directed at the legal training as such, which can already be seen by its delayed place in his autobiographical narrative. In Pt. I, ch.12 he describes his departure to England "for being called to the bar" (107), but it is only in Pt. I, ch.24, "'Called' – But Then?", that he finally gets round to addressing his legal studies. His report is worth quoting at some length:

> There were two conditions which had to be fulfilled before a student was formally called to the bar: 'keeping terms' equivalent to about three years; and passing examinations. 'Keeping terms' meant eating one's terms, i.e. attending at least six out of about twenty-four dinners in term. […] The curriculum of study was easy, barristers being humorously known as 'dinner barristers'. Everyone knew that the examinations had practically no value. In my time there were two, one in Roman Law and the other in Common Law. There were regular textbooks prescribed for these examinations which could be taken in compartments, but scarcely anyone read them. […] Question papers were easy and examiners were generous. The percentage of passes in the Roman Law examination used to be 95 to 99 and those in the final examinations 75 or even more. (163–165)

These exams, Gandhi concludes, "could not be felt as a difficulty. But I succeeded in turning them into one" (166). Far from lowering his standards to the easy life of an English law student, he set out on a course of further readings, notably Roman Law, and that in Latin, which he had started to study in earnest at the University of London. He read "Broom's Common Law," "Snell's Equity," "White and Tudor's Leading Cases," "Williams' and Edward's Real Property" and "Goodeve's Personal Property." Gandhi was called to the bar in June 1891, enrolled in the High Court and immediately after took the next ship home. The surprising fact regarding this first phase of Gandhi's encounter with the law is that there is not a single word of criticism or even further reflection on the concept and underlying philosophy of the British law. The exclusive focus of Gandhi's autobiographical attention here is on the cultural context and on the quality of the course of studies of that legal entity.

This focus remains unchanged on his return to India, where he found that, despite all his very serious readings during his time in London, "It was easy to be called, but it was difficult to practice at the bar. I had read the laws, but not learnt how to practice law" (167). Trying to set up a legal practice in Bombay, he not only noticed that he did not know anything about Indian law (which he began to study), whether "Hindu or Mahomedan Law" (91): "This is how I began life. I found the barrister's profession a bad job – much show and little knowledge" (184). At this job he failed dramatically: when taking on a minor defence job in Court he could not find it in his heart to cross-examine the plaintiff's witnesses and had to leave the court in complete embarrassment and shame. He fled from Bombay back to Rajkot, where his brother gave him some legal office work, and he even considered abandoning the law completely and becoming a school teacher of English. It is quite possible that this failed barrister who was too diffident for the clamorous life at the bar and felt too principled to enforce the elbow-room he would have needed in an increasingly competitive field, would never have risen to prominence. What jerked Gandhi out of the dismal situation he encountered during in the two years after his return to India in 1891 was a chance opportunity that opened up to him in 1893 to go to South Africa and help with a lawsuit of an Indian firm there. Thus, his failing legal career jumpstarted his trajectory towards his mission as a political leader and national icon by means of what first appeared as a low-profile, run-of the-mill, temporary lawyer's job abroad. He had, to take up his own words, "read the laws" in Britain and India, but he only "learnt how to practice the law" in South Africa. What was the reason for this climactic turnaround?

To be more specific the turnaround came in two stages. A first step was taken through Gandhi's development of a mature attitude towards the law through his own legal practice in South Africa and his experiences there. This began with Gandhi's continuing struggle for his own way of truth and honesty against the impression, instilled in him early on during his studies in England, that "the lawyer's profession was a liar's profession" (561). Gandhi's counterstrategy was to stick to truth and honesty no matter what were the strategic requirements of a case: "I warned every new client at the outset that he should not expect me to take up a false case or to coach the witnesses" (562). He goes on to tell about his experience in a particularly complicated trial in South Africa, where his clients had made a mistake in a contentious accounting and Gandhi as junior counsel got his way to persuade the senior counsel and the clients to own up to that mistake in front of the Court. Gandhi presented the case and they won to Gandhi's huge relief:

> I was delighted. So were my client and senior counsel; and I was confirmed in my conviction that it was not impossible to practice law without compromising truth. (566)

Still, he was not entirely at ease, as he immediately adds a cautionary remark: "Let the reader, however, remember that even truthfulness in the practice of the profession cannot cure it of the fundamental defect that vitiates it" (566). That inbuilt defect of the law was, in Gandhi's view, systemic, as he writes earlier in the autobiography:

> I became disgusted with the profession. As lawyers the counsel on both sides were bound to take up points of law in support of their own clients. I also saw for the first time that the winning party never recovers all the costs incurred. (237)

Gandhi's conclusion was that the current practice of the law as a confrontation of two factions where he as lawyer was serving one of the sides for exorbitant remuneration (and possibly against his own moral judgement) could not satisfy him. In fact, he only discovers his true vocation as a lawyer in a case where he succeeds in bypassing legal procedure and bringing about an out of court settlement:

> My joy was boundless. I had learnt the true practice of law. I had learnt to find out the better side of human nature and to enter men's hearts. I realized that the true function of a lawyer was to unite parties riven asunder. (238)

His time in South Africa thus turned out to be a period of experience and maturation in his personal understanding of the law:

> The year's stay in Pretoria was a most valuable experience in my life. Here it was that I had opportunities of learning public work and acquired some measure of my capacity for it. Here it was that the religious spirit within me became a living force, and here too I acquired a true knowledge of legal practice. Here I learnt the things that a junior barrister learns in a senior barrister's chamber, and here I also gained confidence that I should not after all fail as a lawyer. (234)

In sum, the first stage of Gandhi's legal maturation meant that he was able to integrate his principle of truth in his legal practice. Where he had so far felt deep unease towards a profession whose essence he saw, both in Britain and in India, as a typically disingenuous court proceeding between two opponents where he was to take sides as a lawyer for the party who paid him, and not in accordance with truth, principle or justice. His policy of rejecting all cases where he felt that he would support an unjust cause and of throwing aside strategic subterfuges and lies even in court, could be seen as an impediment by some of his clients, but it allowed him to make peace with his work in the legal profession.

In addition to this, South Africa provided second inspiration for him beyond his private settlement with the dubious and potentially nefarious character of the legal profession. What he encountered in South Africa was a real need for the law to redress social injustice and discrimination. As a consequence, he increasingly came to see law as an important instrument in a wider, socio-political context. And whereas this social agenda had its first focus in the injustices he encountered in South Africa, it quickly transcended this geopolitical limitation. The following quotation from the autobiography shows him addressing all kinds of discrimination, including that of his Indian home culture:

> Some of the classes which render us the greatest social service, but which we Hindus have chosen to regard as 'untouchables', are relegated to remote quarters of a town or a village, called in Gujarati *dhedvado* [...]. Even so in Christian Europe the Jews were once 'untouchables', and the quarters that were assigned to them had the offensive name of 'ghettoes'. In a similar way today we have become the untouchables of South Africa. (452)

While his individual course of action consisted in employing his legal training to support his countrymen in the Indian diaspora in the law courts, the public and political instrument that he developed in response was *satyagraha*. The Gujarati and Hindi word which means 'holding on to truth' or 'firmness in a good cause' (see the entry in the *Oxford English Dictionary*), powerfully expressed not only a non-violent attitude, but also the readiness to suffer without any admixture of hatred or revenge. The report in his autobiography is brief, since he refers the reader to his book-length history of *Satyagraha in South Africa* (1928, esp. 302). It was during his South African years that Gandhi developed the concept. Satyagraha was the guiding principle of the resistance against racial discrimination against Indians in South Africa. Gandhi masterminded this movement, which culminated in the famous march of over 2000 Indians from Charlestown (Natal) over the border into the Transvaal. There followed a wave of imprisonment of the Satyagrahis whose numbers swamped the prisons of South Africa and could not be upheld for long. Hence Gandhi was able to strike a deal with the Union Government represented by General Smuts, which has gone down in history as the Smuts-Gandhi compromise. It brought significant relief to Indians in South Africa. Gandhi saw his mission accomplished and returned to India, taking with him the full treasure-trove of his social, legal and political experience from the diaspora.

What the first South African attempts at *satyagraha* already demonstrate, and which Gandhi's autobiographical report of its subsequent practice in India bears out, is the further profound change implied in Gandhi's understanding and practice of the law. First, he had discovered and then eschewed the disparity between private legal practice and what he saw as the desirable application of his truth principles. Now he reflects on the difference between the state's (that is: British-controlled) legislative and judiciary practices and his perception of a higher justice or truth. He thus reports that, when he went to Champaran in Bihar to support the indigo farm labourers against the zamindars and planters there,[5] he was served a notice from the Police Superindendent to leave the region as a precaution against public disorder. Gandhi disobeyed and was duly arrested and put on trial. Here the gap between the legal authority of the state and his own concept of lawfulness is spelled out most clearly for the first time:

> I have disregarded the order served upon me not for want of respect for lawful authority, but in obedience to the higher law of our being, the voice of conscience. (638)

And this tallies with his view of the trial: "According to the law, I was to be on my trial, but truly speaking Government was to be on its trial" (637). Gandhi concludes: "The country thus had its first direct object-lesson in Civil Disobedience" (468).

But the problem he now faced was to distinguish the occasions when it was acceptable to disobey the law and when it was not. His solution is summarized towards the end of the autobiography:

---

[5] On the indigo revolts and the final abolishment of the Tinkathia system there see Mishra (1978).

> A satyagrahi obeys the laws of society intelligently and of his own free will, because he considers it to be his sacred duty to do so. It is only when a person has thus obeyed the laws of society scrupulously that he is in a position to judge as to which particular rules are good and just and which unjust and iniquitous. Only then does the right accrue to him of the civil disobedience of certain laws in well-defined circumstances. (720)

He confesses:

> My error lay in my failure to observe the necessary limitation. I had called on people to launch upon civil disobedience before they had thus qualified themselves for it[.] (720–721)

But when confrontation occurred, Gandhi describes how law and justice began to elude the Government, which he had already put on trial in the quotation above, and how justice and lawfulness are now to be associated with the resistance movement:

> Thus, whilst this movement for the preservation of non-violence was making steady though slow progress on the one hand, Government's policy of lawless repression was in full career on the other, and was manifesting itself in the Punjab in all its nakedness. Leaders were put under arrest, martial law, which in other words meant no law, was proclaimed, special tribunals were set up. These tribunals were not courts of justice but instruments for carrying out the arbitrary will of an autocrat. Sentences were passed unwarranted by evidence and in flagrant violation of justice. (722)

It is with this stage of the independence movement in India that the autobiography ends: Gandhi has become a public figure and leader of the movement. This is the vantage point from which Gandhi is looking back on his life in his autobiography.

3. *Conclusion*

As Gandhi explains in the first lines of the "Introduction," he meant to set about writing his autobiography "four or five years ago" (43) but was interrupted because of the civil unrest in Bombay starting in November 1921. Gandhi was subsequently tried and imprisoned for sedition in 1922. He was urged to write his autobiography in prison but refused to do so. He was released in February 1924. He finally started on the autobiography in instalments, which he wrote for the journal *Navajivan* from November 1925 to February 1929. This was a time when Gandhi had become a public figure, had secured the support of Congress behind him and, as history shows, was ready to continue with his Satyagraha movement against British rule in India. By this time, the rule of law had been set aside by both sides: protests had turned violent, and the Amritsar/Jallianwala Bagh massacre (13 April 1919) had shown what atrocities the British were capable of. Courts were no longer dealing out justice (as Gandhi had observed in the quotation above) but merely served the interests of the colonial power. Indian society had lost its legal framework, a common understanding and practice of the law to which all members of society could defer. This was, obviously, a disastrous state of affairs in general, but more particularly so for Gandhi the lawyer, whose life-long pre-occupation had been with the law in its philosophical, practical and experiential dimensions. As he would have argued, if the State lost its function as an anchor for the law, an alternative was urgently needed; otherwise, there was a threat of fragmentation of the law in India, and ultimately of lawlessness.

Alongside all the speeches and activities he undertook at the time, Gandhi's most sustained and reflective answer to this crisis can be found in his autobiography. It is here that he offers a new anchor-point for the law which has to be founded on Truth. Although truth is for him an ultimately religious principle, he propounded it as a highly ecumenical concept. While he professed his preference for Hindu texts, notably the *Bhagvad Gita*, he paid his respects, in his autobiography and elsewhere, to Islam and Christianity (48). By locating the faculty to decide on truth in individual conscience (329), by stating that "the essence of religion is morality" (46) and by the humble gesture of a fellow-seeker for God, not a guru,[6] he moreover widened his appeal far beyond a narrowly religious focus. Gandhi was thus trying to find a new orientation of the legal system and legal practice in the face of the crisis of a failing state judiciary and legislative in India.

His answer to this crisis is a personal narrative which shows his life-long struggle with and explorations of the law. This story starts with his depressive early attempts in a profession he experienced as mercenary and disingenuous, never far from the dangers of moral corruption. It proceeds on to his introduction of the principle of truth in his personal legal work, and from there builds a legal foundation for his public and political principle of Satyagraha. Satyagraha, finally, respects existing laws but allows for a critical distance to state dominance of the law when the state was seen to fail its truth principle. From this perspective, the legal narrative running through Gandhi's *Autobiography* emerges as one of its major themes. In fact, he at one point describes himself, the author, as continually faced by a court of law where the chapters he has written are under "cross-examination" (442). Gandhi's legal preoccupations in this text clearly merit more scholarly attention than they have received so far. His choice was to turn his legal concerns into the narrative of an autobiography, a genre that would appear as a modern and innovative genre to many of his readers, but which also harkened back to a long-standing literary tradition present in many parts of the world and therefore appears entirely convincing. Both the choice of genre and of the legal issues he addresses with it go a long

[6] He writes in the Introduction: "I have not yet found Him [God], but I am seeing after Him" (47).

way, I would argue, to explain the book's continuing appeal and relevance today.

Works Cited

Bhabha, Homi K. (1994) *The Location of Culture.* London/New York: Routledge.

Bhattacharjee, Manash Firaq (2018) "Who Wrote Gandhi's Autobiography of Errors." *The Wire.* [5 August 2018.] Web. 12 March 2020: https://thewire.in/books/who-wrote-gandhis-autobiography-of-errors.

Fludernik, Monika (1996) *Towards a Natural Narratology.* London: Routledge.

Gandhi, M. K. (1928) *Satyagraha in South Africa.* Trans. Valji Govindji Desai. Ahmedabad: Navajivan Trust.

Gandhi, M. K. (2018) *An Autobiography, or The Story of My Experiments with Truth.* New Haven/London: Yale Univ. Press.

Gusdorf, Georges (1980) "Conditions and Limits of Autobiography." *Autobiography: Essays Theoretical and Critical.* [1956] Ed. and trans. James Olney. Princeton: Princeton Univ. Press. 28–48.

Holden, Philipp (2008) *Autobiography and Decolonization. Modernity, Masculinity, and the Nation-State.* Madison, Wis.: Univ. of Wisconsin Press.

Lejeune, Philippe (1989) "The Autobiographical Pact." *On Autobiography.* Ed. Paul John Eakin. Trans. Katherine M. Leary. Minneapolis: Univ. of Minneapolis Press. 3–30.

Löschnigg, Martin (2019) "Narratology." *Handbook of Autobiography/Autofiction.* Ed. Martina Wagner-Egelhaaf. Berlin/Boston: DeGruyter. 103–110.

Malinar, Angelika (2019a) "India." *Handbook of Autobiography/Autofiction.* Ed. Martina Wagner-Egelhaaf. Berlin/Boston: DeGruyter. 967–985.

Malinar, Angelika (2019b) "Mohandas Karamchand Gandhi: શત્યના પ્રયોગો અથવા આત્મકથા;सत्य के प्रयोग अथवा आत्मकथा (1925–1928) [An Autobiography or The Story of My Experiments With Truth]." *Handbook of Autobiography/Autofiction.* Ed. Martina Wagner-Egelhaaf. Berlin/Boston: DeGruyter. 1703–1718.

Mishra, Girish (1978) *Agrarian Problems of Permanent Settlement. A Case Study of Champaran.* New Delhi: People's Publishing House.

Ricoeur, Paul (1983–1985) *Time and Narrative.* Trans. By Kathleen McLaughlin and David Pellauer. Chicago/London: Univ. of Chicago Press.

Suhrud, Tridip (2018) "Introduction." *An Autobiography, or The Story of My Experiments with Truth.* M. K. Gandhi. New Haven/London: Yale Univ. Press.

Wagner-Egelhaaf, Martina (2019) Ed. *Handbook of Autobiography/Autofiction.* Berlin/Boston: De Gruyter.

Weintraub, Karl (1975) "Autobiography and Historical Consciousness." *Critical Inquiry* 1: 821–848.

Täter im Bild – Schweriner Kunstbetrachtung im Interdisziplinären Dialog

Ulrike Tabbert

1. *Einführung*

Dieser Beitrag stellt ein interdisziplinäres Projekt von Frau Dr. Katharina Schmidt-Uhl und der Verfasserin am Staatlichen Museum Schwerin[1] vor, in dessen Rahmen wir uns der Darstellung von Straftätern und Straftaten in Werken der bildenden Kunst sowohl aus kunst- und kulturwissenschaftlicher als auch aus strafrechtlicher und kriminologischer Sicht angenähert haben. Frau Uhl als Kunstwissenschaftlerin und Kuratorin hat sich erstmals im Jahr 2017 zusammen mit mir auf eine gemeinsame Reise durch die Kunstgeschichte anhand der in der ständigen Ausstellung des Museums gezeigten Werke (jedoch nicht mehr beschränkt hierauf) begeben. Hieraus ist die Idee entstanden, in der Kunst nach Darstellungen von Tätern und Straftaten zu suchen und zu erkunden, ob die kriminal- und rechtsgeschichtliche Entwicklung anhand der in verschiedenen Epochen entstandenen Kunstwerke nachvollzogen werden kann. Im ersten Teil dieses Aufsatzes stelle ich die Projektidee sowie die Entwicklung unserer Vortragsreihe vor, welche in der Publikation unseres Buches *Täter im Bild* (Uhl & Tabbert 2020) mündete.

Nach einer kurzen Einführung zur Strafnorm des § 201a StGB (Verletzung des höchstpersönlichen Lebensbereichs durch Bildaufnahmen) behandelt dieser Beitrag zudem die Phänomene des Voyeurismus und die anhaltende Faszination von Straftaten und erwähnt vorhandene Schemata in der Wahrnehmung des Devianten, welche gerade dort Bedeutung erlangen, wo der/die RezipientIn Lücken in der erzählten Geschichte wahrnimmt.

Der zweite Teil des Aufsatzes (vornehmlich im Abschnitt 6) wird am Beispiel von Marcel Duchamps (1887–1968) Arbeit *Étant donnés: 1° la chute d'eau / 2° le gaz d'éclairage* [Gegeben sei: 1. der Wasserfall, 2. das Leuchtgas] (2009) das Thema des Voyeurismus aufgreifen. Den Künstler Duchamp und speziell dieses Werk habe ich gewählt, da Duchamp als der Wegbereiter der modernen Kunst, insbesondere der Konzeptkunst, im Gegensatz zu der von ihm als retinal bezeichneten Malerei gilt. Das Staatliche Museum Schwerin besitzt 91 seiner Kunstwerke, das Schweriner Duchamp Forschungszentrum widmet sich der Erforschung von Duchamps Œuvre.

---

1 https://www.museum-schwerin.de/.

Dieser Aufsatz mit dem Bericht zum Schweriner Projekt ist eine Fortschreibung der ursprünglichen Projektidee mit einem primären Fokus auf der strafrechtlich/kriminologischen Annäherung an Kunst.

2. *Vorstellung des Projekts*

Im Rahmen unseres Projekts haben wir in den Jahren 2017 bis 2020 drei Vorträge in der *Rendezvous*-Reihe des Museums gehalten und zudem das erwähnte Buch *Täter im Bild* im Auftrag des Museums geschrieben. Der Kontakt zu Frau Uhl kam über den Verein der Freunde des Staatlichen Museums Schwerin e.V.[2] zustande, dessen Mitglied die Verfasserin ist. Ziel dieses Vereins ist die vornehmlich finanzielle Unterstützung der Arbeit des Museums, darunter des am Museum ansässigen Duchamp Forschungszentrums[3], welches regelmäßig Forschungsstipendien an NachwuchswissenschaftlerInnen vergibt; die wissenschaftlichen Arbeiten zum Œuvre von Marcel Duchamp werden in den beiden das Forschungszentrum begleitenden Schriftenreihen *Poeisis* und *Lecture Notes* publiziert.

Die Schweriner Sammlung Marcel Duchamp, eines der Sammlungsschwerpunkte des Staatlichen Museums Schwerin, besteht aus 91 Werken dieses französisch-amerikanischen Objektkünstlers und „Wegbereiter[s] der Konzeptkunst" (Holzhey & Röder 2021), welche weltweit als Leihgaben zu Ausstellungen reisen und gegenwärtig u.a. im Kaiser Wilhelm Museum in Kleefeld in der Ausstellung *Beuys & Duchamp: Artists of the Future*[4] gezeigt werden. Ich erwähne Duchamp und die Verbindung zum Schweriner Museum hier, weil ich im Abschnitt 6 dieses Aufsatzes auf ein Werk Duchamps näher eingehen werde.

Am Rande der von Frau Uhl als Kunstwissenschaftlerin im Rahmen ihres Volontariats am Schweriner Museum geleiteten Führungen durch von ihr co-kuratierte Ausstellungen entstand die Idee, die Schnittstelle zwischen Kunstbetrachtung, Kunstgeschichte, Strafrecht und Kriminologie anhand der in der ständigen Ausstellung des Museums gezeigten Werke und der darin enthaltenen Darstellungen von Straftätern oder Opfern von Straftaten auszuloten. Bei näherer Betrachtung der in der ständigen Ausstellung gezeigten Werke wurden wir schnell fündig, denn nicht selten sind die bspw. von Renaissance-Malern wie Peter Paul Rubens gewählten biblischen Motive *de facto* Darstellungen von Straftaten, wie z.B. die Inzest-Geschichte von Lot und seinen Töchtern, oder

---

2 https://freunde-des-museums.de/.

3 https://www.museum-schwerin.de/sammlung/forschung/duchamp-forschungszentrum/. Ich bedanke mich an dieser Stelle bei Frau Dr. Kornelia Röder für den mir gewährten Zugang zur Bibliothek des Duchamp Forschungszentrums. Die vornehmlich im Abschnitt 6 dieses Aufsatzes verwendete Literatur entstammt der dortigen Bibliothek.

4 https://kunstmuseenkrefeld.de/de/Exhibitions/2021/Beuys-Duchamp-Kuenstler-Der-Zukunft.

Darstellungen von Strafgefangenen, wie z.B. das Werk *Befreiung Petri* aus dem Gefängnis (Hendrick ter Brugghen) oder *Josef im Gefängnis deutet die Träume* (Werkstatt Ferdinand Bal). Alle drei, hier lediglich beispielhaft erwähnten und im Buch *Täter im Bild* näher besprochenen Werke finden die Museumsbesucher im Großen Saal im Obergeschoss, wo üblicherweise der Rundgang durch die Sammlung beginnt. Für uns war es verblüffend, auf welche Vielzahl von Werken mit Bezug zu unserem Thema wir stießen. Der uns vom Museum dankenswerterweise gewährte Zugang zum Sammlungsarchiv förderte weitere relevante Werke zutage.

Ziel eines jeden unserer Vorträge und unseres Buches war es, den Besuchern und Lesern zum einen den Schweriner Sammlungsbestand durch Abwandlung des üblicherweise bei Führungen gewählten konservativ-kunsthistorischen Ansatzes näherzubringen. Zudem ermöglichten uns die ausgewählten Werke, kriminologische Theorien, wie bspw. den positivistischen Ansatz des Cesare Lombroso[5], oder strafrechtliche Themen, wie bspw. anhand des Porträts der Giftmörderin Gesche Gottfried die Frage von Schuldfähigkeit bei psychischen Erkrankungen, zu erörtern. Wir haben festgestellt, dass gesellschaftliche Wandlungen immer auch einen Wandel in der Einstellung und Behandlung von Straftaten und Straftätern bedingen und dies anhand der Kunstwerke aus den verschiedenen Epochen nachvollzogen werden kann.

In unserem ersten Vortrag im Jahr 2017, welcher vom Journalisten Frank Pergande für das *Frankfurter Allgemeine Magazin* (Juli 2017) begleitet wurde, haben wir die Besucher auf einen Spaziergang durch die Ausstellungsräume eingeladen und anhand der besprochenen Werke aus unterschiedlichen Epochen erläutert, wie sich die Einstellung zu Straftaten im Lauf der Geschichte gewandelt hat. In der Zeit vor Beginn der Aufklärung im 18. Jahrhundert waren die Strafen zumeist drakonisch. Wie am Beispiel der bereits erwähnten Darstellungen von biblischen (Gefängnis)Szenen (*Befreiung Petri* aus dem Jahr 1629) zu sehen, kam es zu jener Zeit lediglich auf das „Wegsperren", oft unter lebensfeindlichen Bedingungen an, während heute unterschiedliche Ansätze zum Zweck des Strafens (Strafzwecktheorien) nebeneinander existieren und diskutiert werden. Vorherrschend in der Rechtsprechung und dort vorgegeben durch das Bundesverfassungsgericht ist die sogenannte Vereinigungstheorie[6], welche „die Grundideen von Gerechtigkeit, Sühne, General- und Individualprävention sowie Resozialisierung vereint" (Uhl & Tabbert 2020, 15). Hierbei steht der Strafzweck der Vergeltung zur Wiederherstellung von Gerechtigkeit sowie der Versöhnung des Täters mit der Rechtsordnung gleichberechtigt neben dem Gedanken der abschreckenden Funktion von Strafe sowie dem Bestreben, das

---

[5] Lombroso unternahm den Versuch, durch Vermessung menschlicher Schädel zu erklären, warum jemand zum Straftäter wird (Lombroso 2006).

[6] Siehe hierzu Bundesverfassungsgericht, Urteil vom 21. Juni 1977 – 1 BvL 14/76 – BVerfGE 45, 187–271.

Vertrauen der Allgemeinheit in die Rechtsordnung zu stärken (Uhl & Tabbert 2020, 15). Zur Zeit der Entstehung von ter Brugghen's Gemälde *Befreiung Petri* lebten die Menschen in einer Gesellschaftsordnung, in der die oft Unfreien oder Abhängigen sich zum Selbsterhalt und aus Furcht vor Übergriffen unter den Schutz von Feudalfürsten stellten und dafür im Gegenzug diesen Autoritäten gehorchten und Abgaben entrichten mussten. Dieser „Vertrag“ zugunsten des Souveräns wurde von Thomas Hobbes (1588–1679) theoretisch aufgearbeitet (Vertragstheorie) und bereitete den Weg hin zum aufgeklärten Absolutismus. Cesare Beccaria (1738–1794) entwickelte diese Theorie fort und wandelte sie zur „sozialen Vertragstheorie“. Beccaria gilt als Strafrechtsreformer und gleichzeitig als Begründer der klassischen Kriminologie im Zeitalter der Aufklärung. Sein 1764 erschienenes Werk *Dei delitti e delle pene* [Von den Verbrechen und von den Strafen] setzt drakonischen Strafen ein Ende, indem er argumentiert, dass die Strafe der Verfehlung angemessen sein soll, und dass nur die Strafe verhängt werden soll, welche zur Aufrechterhaltung der Ordnung erforderlich ist.

In unseren Vorträgen ebenso wie in unserer Publikation haben wir die weitere Entwicklung der verschiedenen kriminologischen Ansätze zur Erklärung des Phänomens „Straftat“ über die Jahrhunderte ebenso in den Blick genommen wie den Wandel des Strafrechts in der Bundesrepublik Deutschland, so bspw. die erst im Jahr 1977 eingeführte Strafbarkeit von Vergewaltigung in der Ehe oder die Abschaffung des abwertend so bezeichneten „Schwulenparagraphen“ § 175 StGB, wonach noch bis in das Jahr 1994 sexuelle Handlungen zwischen gleichgeschlechtlichen Personen (zuletzt nur noch sexuelle Handlungen mit männlichen Jugendlichen unter 18 Jahren) unter Strafe gestellt waren.

3. *Schutz des höchstpersönlichen Lebensbereichs durch Strafgesetzgebung*

Eine im Jahr 2004 eingeführte und seither bereits zwei Mal (erstmals 2015 im Zusammenhang mit dem Fall des damaligen Bundestagsabgeordneten Sebastian Edathy und nachfolgend im Jahr 2021) geänderte Strafnorm ist § 201a StGB (Verletzung des höchstpersönlichen Lebensbereichs und von Persönlichkeitsrechten durch Bildaufnahmen), landläufig auch als „Gafferparagraph“ bezeichnet, welche in der Begründung zum ursprünglichen Gesetzesentwurf[7] dem Schutz des „höchstpersönlichen Lebens- und Geheimbereichs [...] gegen unbefugte Bildaufnahmen“ dient und mit der letzten Änderung (gültig seit 01. Januar 2021) nunmehr auch die Anfertigung und Verbreitung von grob

[7] BT-Drucks. 15/2466, 1.

anstößigen Bildaufnahmen von Verstorbenen unter Strafe stellt[8]. Eine andere Strafnorm (§ 184k StGB, gültig seit 01. Januar 2021) stellt das sogenannte *Upskirting* oder *Downblousing*[9] unter Strafe. Insbesondere die Neufassung der Strafnorm des § 201a StGB wird als eine Erweiterung des „Schutzes des ‚Rechts am eigenen Bild' als besondere Ausprägung des Allgemeinen Persönlichkeitsrechts" (Leipold et al. 2020) angesehen. Das vom Bundesverfassungsgericht in ständiger Rechtsprechung aus Artikel 2 Absatz 1 in Verbindung mit Artikel 1 Absatz 1 GG hergeleitete allgemeine Persönlichkeitsrecht ist grundsätzlich bereits durch die Strafnormen der §§ 185–187 (14. Abschnitt, Beleidigungstatbestände) und §§ 201–203 (15. Abschnitt) StGB geschützt. Zusätzlich schützt die Vorschrift des § 33 KunstUrhG (in Verbindung mit §§ 22, 23 KunstUrhG) das Recht am eigenen Bild, welche jedoch lediglich auf das Verbreiten oder öffentliche zur Schau Stellen von Bildnissen ohne Einwilligung des Abgebildeten abstellt. Die Strafnorm des § 201a StGB führt den Rechtsbegriff des „höchstpersönlichen Lebensbereiches" ein und schließt damit vor dem Hintergrund der sich fortentwickelnden technischen Möglichkeiten eine Gesetzeslücke und passt zudem das Recht am eigenen Bild dem bis dahin weitreichenderen Schutz des gesprochenen Wortes durch unbefugte Tonaufnahmen (geregelt in § 201 StGB) an.

Diese kurz skizzierten Gesetzesentwicklungen können durchaus als Ausfluss einer Haltungsänderung in der Gesellschaft gewertet werden, was sich im Fall des § 201a StGB bereits aus dem Umstand herleiten lässt, dass nach verschiedenen Initiativen in der 14. und 15. Legislaturperiode des Deutschen Bundestages der Gesetzesentwurf schließlich von Bundestagsabgeordneten der Fraktionen der CDU/CSU, Bündnis 90/Die Grünen und der FDP und mithin fraktionsübergreifend eingebracht wurde[10].

Es ist bereits angesprochen worden, dass das Strafrecht kein unveränderliches Regelwerk, sondern ständigem gesellschaftlichen Wandel unterworfen ist und daher auch immer neu die Frage beantworten muss, welches Verhalten in der Gesellschaft als strafbar und welches zwar als moralisch verwerflich, jedoch legal angesehen wird. Im Fall des § 201a StGB bietet sich die Abgrenzung zum nicht unter Strafe stehenden Voyeurismus (definiert als „unerwünschte Beobachtung durch andere" (Leipold et al. 2020)) ebenso an wie die Abgrenzung zum bußgeldbewehrten „Gaffen" mit daraus resultierenden Behinderungen von Rettungskräften, welches rechtlich in verschiedenen Straf- und Bußgeldtatbeständen (letztgenannte sühnen sogenanntes Verwaltungsunrecht) geregelt ist.

---

8 BT-Drucks. 19/17795, 1.

9 Unbemerkt gefertigte Aufnahmen von Intimbereichen anderer Personen in der Öffentlichkeit.

10 BT-Drucks. 15/2466, 1, siehe auch Kächele (2007).

4. *Voyeurismus*

Der Voyeurismus entstammt einer zutiefst menschlichen Neugier. Die Wahrnehmung des Anderen oder „das Erscheinen eines Menschen in *meinem* Universum" ist Sartre (1994, 461–462, Hervorhebung im Original) zufolge ein „Element der Desintegration". Sartre (1994, 467) führt als Beispiel für eine voyeuristische Handlung den Blick durch ein Schlüsselloch an, welcher für die nachfolgende Besprechung der Arbeit von Duchamp noch eine signifikante Bedeutung erhalten wird. Als Motive für einen solchen Blick durch ein Schlüsselloch nennt Sartre Eifersucht, Neugier und Verdorbenheit, mithin alles niedere Motivlagen.

Schwering (2015, 135) merkt in diesem Zusammenhang an, dass der „Beobachter am Schlüsselloch frei" sei, da er „ohne Hemmungen" agiere. Der Freiheitsbegriff, durchaus positiv konnotiert, muss jedoch dort seine Begrenzung finden, wo Persönlichkeitsrechte anderer tangiert sind.

Dennoch kann Voyeurismus, die Beobachtung des anderen, durchaus auch aufgrund berechtigter Motive erfolgen, bspw. ermöglicht durch die vom Utilitaristen Jeremy Bentham (1995) vorgeschlagene und u.a. von Michel Foucault (2008, 900–902) aufgegriffene Gefängnisarchitektur des Panopticons, mit relativ wenig Personal eine größere Zahl von Gefangenen zu überwachen.

Die Neugier auf das (selbst unbeobachtete) Beobachten des anderen wird bspw. im Fall von „portrayals of crime" durch „voyeuristic glimpses of rare and bizarre acts" ermöglicht, denn Straftaten sind von Natur aus „private, secretive, and hidden, surreptitiously committed and studiously concealed" (Surette 2009, 240). Nun beschränkt sich indes der Voyeurismus nicht auf das Interesse an Straftaten, sondern umfasst natürlich auch die Beobachtung von nicht strafrelevanten, aber durchaus zutiefst privaten Vorgängen; die Grenze zwischen beiden ist oft eine Frage der Perspektive, wie am Beispiel von Duchamps Werk *Étant donnés* zu besprechen sein wird.

5. *Straftat als Narrativ*

Bevor ich das zu besprechende Werk Duchamps vorstelle, sei mir der Exkurs erlaubt, dass eine Straftat durchaus als ein Narrativ, eine Geschichte, verstanden werden kann. Zwar ist die Straftat im Moment ihrer Begehung eine Handlung, welche aktiv durchgeführt wird (in Abgrenzung zu Unterlassungsdelikten). Jedoch ist ihre rekapitulierende Darstellung im nachfolgenden Strafprozess durch die verschiedenen Prozessbeteiligten (die Angeklagten in der Einlassung zur Sache, ggf. die Verteidigung bei Abgabe einer Verteidigererklärung, die Staatsanwaltschaft in der Anklageschrift, das Tatopfer und Augenzeugen in deren Vernehmungen, das Gericht in der mündlichen Urteilsbegründung sowie in den schriftlichen Urteilsgründen) eine subjektive Erzählung dessen, was passiert ist. Diese Erzählung (oder Narrativ) erfüllt die Kriterien von Narrativität. Als Definition für diesen Begriff greife ich zur Vereinfachung auf Fluderniks *Glossary* (2013, 176) zurück, wonach Narrativität traditionell „handlungsbezogen definiert [wird], [...], als Anwesenheit von mindestens zwei Handlungen oder Ereignissen in zeitlicher Abfolge, die aufeinander bezogen sind". Zwar ist die eigentliche Tathandlung, z.B. das Abschlagen des Kopfes des Holofernes durch Judith in der biblischen Geschichte aus dem Buch Judith, die eigentliche Straftat, jedoch vorbereitet durch die „Vorgeschichte", welche zu dieser grausamen Tat führt und heute für die Strafrechtspflege von Bedeutung wäre (z.B. für eine etwaige Rechtfertigung der Tat durch Notwehr/Nothilfe oder aber im Rahmen der Strafzumessung). Darstellungen von Straftaten in der bildenden Kunst, besprochen bspw. am Werk *Judith und Holofernes* von Franz von Stuck in dem von uns verfassten Buch (Uhl & Tabbert 2020, 30–32), sind zwar Momentaufnahmen (Judith wird mit dem Schwert in der Hand stehend neben dem schlafenden Holofernes gezeigt), jedoch kommt es dem Künstler ebenfalls auf das Erzählen einer Geschichte an, von welcher oft der dramatischste Moment herausgegriffen und dargestellt wird. Der im Gemälde nicht gezeigte Teil der Geschichte wird vom Künstler als den BetrachterInnen bekannt vorausgesetzt, anders jedoch im noch zu besprechenden Werk von Duchamp im Abschnitt 6.

Damit ermöglichen solche bildlichen Darstellungen durchaus voyeuristisches Beobachten. Ein Beispiel, wo dies bereits bei physischer Annäherung an das Kunstwerk deutlichst zum Ausdruck kommt, ist Marcel Duchamps Arbeit *Étant donnés: 1° la chute d'eau / 2° le gaz d'éclairage*, dauerhaft ausgestellt im Philadelphia Museum of Art, Philadelphia, USA. In dem nun folgenden Abschnitt dieses Aufsatzes werde ich zunächst den Künstler und die Arbeit vorstellen und abschließend den Bogen zurück zum Projekt von Frau Uhl und mir und zum Staatlichen Museum in Schwerin schlagen.

6. Étant donnés *von Marcel Duchamp*

Marcel Duchamp, geboren und verstorben in Frankreich, hat viele Jahre seines Lebens in den USA gewirkt. Er hat wie kaum ein anderer Künstler den modernen Kunstbegriff initiiert und geprägt. Unvergessen ist das Einbringen eines im Sanitätsgeschäft erworbenen Urinals (signiert mit „R. Mutt", Werktitel *Fountain*, im Original nicht mehr vorhanden) in die Schau der Society of Independent Artists im Grand Central Palace in New York im Jahr 1917. Der Beitrag wurde auf Beschluss der Gesellschaftsmitglieder nicht zur Ausstellung zugelassen. Das Werk wurde jedoch kurze Zeit später in der Galerie von Alfred Stieglitz ausgestellt und Fotos von dieser Ausstellung, veröffentlicht in der Dada-Zeitschrift *The Blind Man*, zeigten letztlich *Fountain* einem größeren Publikum. Mit derartigen Readymades[11] war die Definitionshoheit darüber, was Kunst ist, dem Künstler überlassen, was das Verständnis von Kunst zu Beginn des 20. Jahrhunderts radikal veränderte und Molderings (2012, 7) zu der Aussage verleitet, dass „[k]aum ein Œuvre der bildenden Kunst des vergangenen Jahrhunderts [...] heute so isoliert" dastehe wie das von Duchamp.

Duchamp hatte bereits 1913 mit einem ausgestellten Fahrradrad (das Original ist verloren, die früheste Replik wird im New Yorker Museum of Modern Arts gezeigt) und 1914 mit einem handelsüblichen Flaschentrockner, welchen er signierte (beide abgebildet im Werkverzeichnis von Schwarz 2000, 364–365), gezeigt, dass der Künstler letztlich bestimmt, was Kunst ist. Duchamp löste damit „die Malerei von ihrer Stofflichkeit" (Röder 2019, 38), nicht zuletzt auch durch den Einsatz von Sprache, welche bspw. eine „Spannung" zwischen den titelgebenden Worten und Bildern auslöst (Gold 1958, 69) oder als Kommentar in Karikaturen „weit über das Dargestellte hinaus" verweist und auf diese Weise „neue Sinnzusammenhänge" und mithin „neue geistige Bedeutungsebenen" eröffnet (Röder 2019, 38).

Ebenfalls bedeutsam für die nachfolgende Besprechung von *Étant donnés* ist der von Duchamp entwickelte „prozesshafte Kunstbegriff", wonach „der Betrachter seine Fragen, seine Ideen, seine Gedanken in den Prozess der Aneignung einbringt" und mithin „die Rezeption selbst zum lebendigen Vorgang" wird (Röder 2019, 36). Duchamp hat sich diesem Begriff genähert, indem er in seinem Werk *Akt, eine Treppe herabsteigend, Nummer 1–3* (Schwarz 2000, 317–319) das Phänomen der physischen Bewegung (beim die Treppe Herabsteigen) in den Blick genommen und „Bewegung als adäquaten Ausdruck von physikalischer Transformation" (Röder 2019, 38) anerkannt hat. Jedoch auch andere Transformationsvorgänge wie der Wechsel zwischen Aggregatzuständen bspw. von Flüssigkeiten zu Gasen (dargestellt im *Großen Glas*, Originaltitel: *The Bride Stripped Bare by Her Bachelors, Even*, 1915–1923) oder Duchamps eigene Transformation in die Kunstfigur *Rrose Sélavy* (beide abgebildet in Schwarz 2000, 361, 692–693) sind Zeugnisse der Umfänglichkeit von seinem Interesse an Transformation.

Wenn man sich im Museum in Philadelphia dem Kunstwerk *Étant donnés* nähert, „geht der Betrachter zuerst in einen leeren Raum, wo er durch zwei kleine Löcher, die in eine alte, massive Eichentüre eingelassen sind, schauen muss, um etwas zu sehen" (Banz 2013, 91–92). Sodann sieht man durch ein größeres Loch in einer Backsteinmauer, ähnlich einer „Camera obscura" (Molderings 2012, 37), eine vollständig unbekleidete weibliche Figur in Form einer lebensgroßen Puppe auf einem Tableau liegen, welche in der linken Hand eine glimmende Öllampe hält und auf Reisig und herabgefallene Blätter gebettet scheint. Die gespreizten Beine eröffnen den Blick auf die (rasierte und augen-

[11] Ein Alltagsgegenstand wird durch den „Akt der Auswahl, des Signierens und des Ausstellens" zu einem Kunstwerk, erklärt Röder (2019, 39).

scheinlich verstümmelte) Vulva. Der Kopf der Figur ist nicht zu erkennen. An der gegenüberliegenden Wand findet sich die Abbildung einer Landschaft mit Wasserfall, betrieben von einem versteckt verbauten Motor. Ein möglicher Hinweis darauf, dass die dargestellte Person noch lebt, ist das aktive Halten der Lampe. Duchamp hat eine detaillierte Aufbauanleitung zu diesem Werk mit Detailfotos hinterlassen (Duchamp et al. 2009); ein Foto des Werkes, wie es sich den BetrachterInnen beim Blick durch eines der beiden Löcher in der Eichentür darbietet, findet sich im umfassenden Werkverzeichnis von Schwarz (2000, 437). Dieses Werk schuf der Künstler während eines Zeitraums von 20 Jahren (1946–1966), einer Zeit, in der er sich aus der Kunstwelt zurückgezogen hatte und dem Schachspielen nachging (Molderings 2012, 33). Der Umstand, dass er an diesem Werk arbeitete, war nur wenigen Vertrauten bekannt. Nach Fertigstellung verkaufte er das Werk an die *Cassandra Foundation* seines Freundes William N. Copley und verband dies mit der Auflage, das Werk nach seinem Tod dem Philadelphia Museum of Art zu stiften, wo es in räumlicher Nähe zum *Großen Glas* ausgestellt werden sollte, und erstmals im Juni 1969 der Öffentlichkeit präsentiert wurde (Molderings 2012, 34).

Bereits der Aufbau des Kunstwerkes, mit welchem Duchamp die „Ready-made-Ära“ „zu Ende gehen lässt“ (Wall 2013, 86), fordert die BetrachterInnen heraus und versetzt sie gleich von Anfang an in die Rolle von Voyeuren, welche Beobachtungen durch ein „Schlüsselloch“ tätigen. Ganz so „frei“ wie Schwering (2015, 135) bei „echtem“ Schlüssellochvoyeurismus annimmt, ist der/die BetrachterIn in diesem musealen Kontext indes nicht, denn der/die „VoyeurIn“ ist jederzeit gewahr, während der eigenen Kunstbetrachtung selbst durch andere MuseumsbesucherInnen, welche oftmals anstehen, um ihrerseits die Arbeit ansehen zu können, beobachtet zu werden. Dies führt zu einem ambivalenten Kunsterlebnis: Einerseits indiziert die durch die Anordnung des Werks hinter einer marode anmutenden Tür, zu welcher man in einem separaten, nicht erleuchteten Bereich des Ausstellungsraumes gelangt, Verborgenheit oder Heimlichkeit. Zum anderen ist sich der/die BesucherIn aufgrund der weltweiten Bekanntheit dieses Werkes und dem damit einhergehenden Besucherinteresse selbst der ständigen Beobachtung beim Betrachten gewiss, welches zumindest das Element der Heimlichkeit nahezu negiert. Jasper Johns (1980, 276) hat dieses Werk als „the strangest work of art any museum has ever had in it“ bezeichnet.

Mit großer Sicherheit würde ein aus der BetrachterInnenperspektive gefertigtes Foto einer solchen Situation, sollte sie echt sein und außerhalb des musealen Kontextes, den Straftatbestand des § 201a StGB erfüllen[12], schon allein aufgrund der damit erfolgten Abbildung des unverstellten Blicks auf die intimsten Geschlechtsteile der liegenden Frau. Was *Étant donnés*, gesehen

[12] Hier bleibt bewusst außer Acht, dass sich ein solch hypothetischer Vorgang in einer anderen Jurisdiktion ereignen würde.

in der Zeit seiner Entstehung, als kulturkritisch erscheinen lässt, ist nicht zuletzt Duchamps Auffassung, dass „der Umgang mit Kunst im Zeitalter der Unterhaltungsindustrie in erster Linie von der Schaulust diktiert wird“ (Molderings 2012, 38). Dieses Werk nimmt damit explizit den Voyeurismus, auch und gerade bei der Kunstbetrachtung, kritisch in den Blick, doch verharrt hierbei nicht, sondern widmet sich zudem der Anziehungskraft von zur Schau gestellter Sexualität, getreu dem noch heute gültigen Werbemantra „sex sells“. Jedoch geht die kunstwissenschaftliche Bedeutung des Werkes weit über dessen kulturkritischen Aspekt hinaus. Duchamp mit seiner Abneigung gegenüber der klassischen Malerei (Molderings 2012, 39) ist mit diesem Werk dennoch „in die Tradition der Kunstgeschichte“ zurückgekehrt und hat dabei „nicht nur versucht [...], die Retina mit den grauen Zellen zu verbinden, sondern auch durch Auseinandersetzung mit bestimmten Bildtraditionen zu neuen Formulierungen zu gelangen“ (Banz 2013, 90–91). Wie Molderings (2012, 39) ausführt, ist *Étant donnés* ein „gegenständliches, illusionistisches Bühnenbild, das nach den Regeln der klassischen zentralperspektivischen Projektionsmethode für einen festen Betrachterstandpunkt konstruiert wurde“ und damit dem klassischen Bildaufbau in der Malerei entspricht. Zwar handelt es sich bei dem gezeigten Torso um zusammengesetzte Bruchstücke aus, wenn man so will, Ready-mades, dennoch erscheint der/dem BetrachterIn der Körper komplett, was durch beim Betrachten ablaufende kognitive Prozesse anhand von vorhandenem schematischem Wissen zum Aussehen eines Frauenkörpers ermöglicht wird.

7. *Diskussion und Ausblick*

Abschließend sei mir gestattet, den Bezug von *Étant donnés* zum Staatlichen Museum Schwerin und unserem Museumsprojekt kurz zu umreißen. Es drängt sich im Licht der bisherigen Ausführungen geradezu auf, dass *Étant donnés* bei der/dem BetrachterIn „die Vorstellung hervorruft, dass hinter der Mauer ein Verbrechen begangen wurde. Assoziationen an den Tod stellen sich ein, an einen Sexualmord oder eine Hexenverbrennung“ (Molderings 2012, 37), letzteres bezogen auf den früher üblicherweise für Scheiterhaufen verwendeten Reisig. Wie erwähnt, weckt die in der Hand gehaltene Lampe jedoch den gegenläufigen Eindruck, dass die Frauenfigur noch leben könnte, was Molderings (2012, 38) zur Verwendung des Begriffs einer „sexuellen Liveshow“ durch den im musealen Kontext und damit in der Öffentlichkeit hervorgerufenen „pornographischen Blick auf den zur Schau gestellten nackten Frauenkörper“ veranlasste. Die/der BetrachterIn ist folglich hin- und hergerissen zwischen Abscheu bei der Beobachtung eines vermeintlichen Schauplatzes eines (Sexual)Mordes einerseits und lustbetonter Vulgarität einer sich sexuell darbietenden Frauenfigur. Möglicherweise ist es legitim zu behaupten, dass dieser Wechsel zwischen möglichen Szenarien oder Narrativen ebenso einen Transformationsvorgang im der/dem BetrachterIn auslösen kann wie der bereits erwähnte Wechsel zwischen der Rolle des Beobachters und des gleichzeitig Beobachteten. Molderings (2012, 121) spricht von „Sehen und Erkennen", welches für Duchamp „immer nur lebendig ist im Verhältnis zu sich selbst" und erlaubt mir den Verweis auf einen Aspekt, den Gregoriou (2011, 6) im Zusammenhang mit Serienmorden erwähnt, nämlich „how crime is ‚imagined'". Diese Imagination, welche nicht zuletzt auch das lediglich phantasierte, weil unbekannte „Vortatgeschehen" umfasst und im Fall von *Étant donnés* letztlich unaufgeklärt und ambivalent bleibt, macht deutlich, dass der bis in die heutige Zeit fortbestehenden Schaulust aus rechtlicher Sicht Grenzen gesetzt werden müssen. Zwar steht Voyeurismus in Deutschland nicht unter Strafe, jedoch legen die im Abschnitt 3 angerissenen jüngsten Verschärfungen von Strafnormen zum Schutz von Persönlichkeitsrechten nahe, dass derzeit ein Wertewandel zu beobachten ist und als Ausfluss dessen der Schutz durch das Gesetz immer umfassender wird. Duchamps letztes Werk ist insofern eine willkommene Gelegenheit, die Schnittstelle zwischen Kunstwissenschaft und Strafrecht sowie die vielfältigen Bezüge zwischen beiden Disziplinen auch zukünftig weiter auszuloten und möglicherweise als zusätzlichen, interdisziplinären Aspekt in die Forschungsarbeit am Duchamp Forschungszentrum in Schwerin einzubringen. In der Sammlung Marcel Duchamp am Staatlichen Museum Schwerin befindet sich die mit der Inventar-Nummer 18701 Gr B[13] versehene *Grüne Box* aus dem Jahr 1934, welche Aufzeichnungen zu den später bei *Étant donnés* verbauten Schlüsselelementen, dem Wasserfall sowie dem Gas, enthält (Taylor 2009, 23), womit sich zum Ende dieses Aufsatzes der Bogen zurück nach Schwerin schließen lässt. *Étant donnés* ist die Coda zu einem Narrativ, welches unerzählt bleibt und vielleicht gerade hierdurch fasziniert.

Zitierte Literatur

Banz, Stefan (2013) „Étant Donnés: Ein Nachwort." *Marcel Duchamp: Étant Donnés.* Hg. Jeff Wall. Nürnberg: Verlag für Moderne Kunst Nürnberg GmbH. 90–97.

Beccaria, Cesare (2005 [1764]) *Von den Verbrechen und von den Strafen* (Dei delitti e delle pene). Aus dem Italienischen von Thomas Vornbaum. Berlin: BWV Berliner Wissenschafts-Verlag.

Bentham, Jeremy (1995). *The Panopticon Writings*. Ed. Miran Božovič. London: Verso.

[13] https://www.museum-schwerin.de/export/sites/museum/.galleries/dokumente/Inventarliste_Duchamp.pdf.

Duchamp, Marcel, Michael R. Taylor und P. Andrew Lins (2009) *Étant Donnés: Manual of Instructions / Marcel Duchamp*. Philadelphia: Philadelphia Museum of Art.

Fludernik, Monika (2013) *Erzähltheorie: Eine Einführung*. Darmstadt: WBG.

Foucault, Michel (2008) *Die Hauptwerke*. Frankfurt a. M.: Suhrkamp Verlag.

Gold (1958) „Interview mit Marcel Duchamp." Übersetzt und annotiert von Serge Stauffer. *Marcel Duchamp. Interviews und Statements*. Hg. Graphische Sammlung Staatsgalerie Stuttgart durch Ulrike Gauss. 69.

Gregoriou, Christiana (2011) *Language, Ideology and Identity in Serial Killer Narratives*. London: Routledge.

Holzhey, Magdalena und Kornelia Röder (2021) *Website zur Ausstellung Beuys & Duchamp: Künstler der Zukunft, 8. Oktober 2021 bis 16. Januar 2022 im Kaiser Wilhelm Museum in Kleefeld*. DOI: https://Kunstmuseenkrefeld.De/De/Exhibitions/2021/Beuys-Duchamp-Kuenstler-Der-Zukunft.

Johns, Jasper (1980) zitiert in Calvin Tomkins (2005) *Off the Wall: A Portrait of Robert Rauschenberg*. London: Picador.

Kächele, Andreas (2007) *Der Strafrechtliche Schutz vor Unbefugten Bildaufnahmen (§ 201a StGB)*. Band 513. Baden-Baden: Nomos.

Leipold, Klaus, Mark Alexander Zöller und Michael Tsambikakis (2020) *Anwaltkommentar StGB*. 3. Auflage. Heidelberg: Müller.

Lombroso, Cesare (2006) *Criminal Man*. Durham: Duke Univ. Press.

Molderings, Herbert (2012) *Die Nackte Wahrheit: Zum Spätwerk von Marcel Duchamp*. München: Carl Hanser Verlag.

Pergande, Frank (Juli 2017) „Kunst als Krimi: Die Schweriner Oberamtsanwältin Ulrike Tabbert geht auf Tätersuche ins Museum." *Frankfurter Allgemeine Magazin*. 36–37.

Röder, Kornelia (2019) „Marcel Duchamp: Transformation Als Künstlerisches Konzept." *Marcel Duchamp: Das Unmögliche Sehen*. Hg. Gerhard Graulich, Kornelia Röder und Patricia Dick. Dresden: Sandstein Verlag. 34–55.

Sartre, Jean-Paul (1994) „Das Sein und Das Nichts. Versuch einer Phänomenologischen Ontologie [1943]." Übersetzt von Hans Schöneberg und Traugott König. *Gesammelte Werke. Philosophische Schriften I*. Hg. Jean-Paul Sartre. Paris: Rowohlt.

Schwarz, Arturo (2000) *The Complete Works of Marcel Duchamp*. New York: Delano Greenidge Editions.

Schwering, Gregor (2015) „‚Über das Auge triumphiert der Blick': Perspektiven des Voyeurismus." *Big Brother: Beobachtungen (Masse und Medium)*. Hg. Friedrich Balke, Gregor Schwering und Urs Stäheli. Bielefeld: transcript. 129–150.

Surette, Ray (2009) *The Entertainment Media and the Social Construction of Crime and Justice*. Crime and Media Band 2. Hg. Yvonne Jewkes. London: Sage Publications.

Taylor, Michael R. (2009) (Hg.) *Marcel Duchamp: Étant Donnés.* Philadelphia: Philadelphia Museum of Art in association with Yale Univ. Press.

Uhl, Katharina and Ulrike Tabbert (2020) *Täter im Bild: Betrachtungen zwischen Kunstgeschichte und Kriminologie*. Wien: VfmK Verlag für moderne Kunst GmbH.

Wall, Jeff. „Étant Donnés." *Marcel Duchamp: Étant Donnés*. Hg. ders. Nürnberg: Verlag für Moderne Kunst Nürnberg GmbH. 65–89.

Onlineressourcen

https://freunde-des-museums.de/.

https://kunstmuseenkrefeld.de/de/Exhibitions/2021/Beuys-Duchamp-Kuenstler-Der-Zukunft.

https://www.museum-schwerin.de/.

https://www.museum-schwerin.de/export/sites/museum/.galleries/dokumente/Inventarliste_Duchamp.pdf.

https://www.museum-schwerin.de/sammlung/forschung/duchamp-forschungszentrum/.

Abkürzungsverzeichnis

BGBl.	Bundesgesetzblatt
BT-Drucks.	Bundestags-Drucksache
BVerfGE	Entscheidungen des Bundesverfassungsgerichts
BvL	Normenkontrollverfahren, die nach Art. 100 Abs. 1 GG auf die Vorlage eines Gerichts erfolgen (sog. konkrete Normenkontrolle)
GG	Grundgesetz für die Bundesrepublik Deutschland in der im Bundesgesetzblatt Teil III, Gliederungsnummer 100-1, veröffentlichten bereinigten Fassung, das zuletzt durch Artikel 1 u. 2 Satz 2 des Gesetzes vom 29. September 2020 (BGBl. I S. 2048) geändert worden ist

KunstUrhG	Gesetz betreffend das Urheberrecht an Werken der bildenden Künste und der Photographie in der im Bundesgesetzblatt Teil III, Gliederungsnummer 440-3, veröffentlichten bereinigten Fassung, das zuletzt durch Artikel 3 § 31 des Gesetzes vom 16. Februar 2001 (BGBl. I S. 266) geändert worden ist; Kurzform: Kunsturheberrechtsgesetz
StGB	Strafgesetzbuch (Deutschland) in der Fassung der Bekanntmachung vom 13. November 1998 (BGBl. I S. 3322), das zuletzt durch Artikel 2 des Gesetzes vom 22. November 2021 geändert worden ist

Autorenverzeichnis

Ruth Blufarb ist Referentin beim Bundesbeauftragten für den Datenschutz und die Informationsfreiheit in Berlin. Ihre Forschungsinteressen liegen insbesondere im Bereich von "Law as Literature" und "Law and Narrative" aus rechtswissenschaftlicher Perspektive. Sie ist Autorin von *Geschichten im Recht - Übertragbarkeit von "Law as Narrative" auf die deutsche Rechtsordnung* (2017).

***Ruth Blufarb** works in the team of the German Federal Commissioner for Data Protection and Freedom of Information in Berlin. Her research interests focus on Law as Literature and Law and Narrative from a legal perspective. She is the author of the monograph* Geschichten im Recht – Übertragbarkeit von "Law as Narrative" auf die deutsche Rechtsordnung ('Narratives in Law – The Possibility of Adopting Law as Narrative for German Law', 2017).

Monika Fludernik ist Professorin für englische Literatur an der Universität Freiburg im Breisgau. Ihre Forschungsschwerpunkte liegen in den Bereichen Erzählforschung, linguistische Analysen von Literatur, postkoloniale Literatur(theorie), Law and Literature sowie Ästhetik des 18. Jahrhunderts. Sie war ab 2012 Sprecherin des von der DFG geförderten Graduiertenkollegs "Faktuales und fiktionales Erzählen" (GRK 1767), das im März 2022 endete. Fludernik ist Trägerin des Landesforschungspreises Baden-Württemberg. Ihre Publikationen inkludieren die erzähltheoretischen Bücher *Towards a 'Natural' Narratology* (1996) und *Erzähltheorie: Eine Einführung* (^{4}2013) sowie die für Law and Literature relevante Studie *Metaphors of Confinement: The Prison in Fact, Fiction and Fantasy* (2019). Sie hat zahlreiche Sammelbände herausgegeben, u.a. *In the Grip of the Law* (mit Greta Olson; 2004), *Narrative Factuality: A Handbook* (mit Marie-Laure Ryan, 2019) und *Being Untruthful: Lying, Fiction, and the Non-Factual* (mit Stephan Packard, 2021).

***Monika Fludernik** is Professor of English Literature at the University of Freiburg/ Germany. Until recently she was the director of the graduate school Factual and Fictional Narration (GRK 1767). Her major research interests include narratology, linguistic approaches to literature, especially metaphor studies, 'Law and Literature,' postcolonial studies and eighteenth-century aesthetics. She is the author of, among others, the award-winning* Towards a 'Natural' Narratology *(1996),* An Introduction to Narratology *(2009, German ^{4}2013) and* Metaphors of Confinement: The Prison in Fact, Fiction and Fantasy *(2019). Among her several (co-)edited volumes are* In the Grip of the Law *(with Greta Olson, 2004),* Narrative Factuality: A Handbook *(with Marie-Laure Ryan, 2019) and* Being Untruthful: Lying, Fiction, and the Non-Factual *(with Stephan Packard, 2021).*

Jeanne Gaakeer erwarb Abschlüsse in englischer Literaturwissenschaft, holländischem Recht und Philosophie. Sie ist Professorin für Rechtswissenschaft: Hermeneutische und Narratologische Grundlagen an der Erasmus-Rechtsfakultät Rotterdam in den Niederlanden. Sie arbeitet auch als höhere Richterin am Berufungsgericht für Kriminalfälle in Den Haag. Ihr Forschungsschwerpunkt liegt in der philosophisch-rechtlichen Hermeneutik, der Narratologie und im Bereich Recht und Literatur / Recht und Geisteswissenschaften sowie in ihrer praktischen Anwendung. Gemeinsam mit Greta Olson (Gießen) ist sie die Gründerin des European Network for Law and Literature (www.eurnll.org). Im Jahr 2013 erhielt Jeanne Gaakeer den J. B. White Preis, der von der Association for the Study of Law, Culture and Humanities verliehen wird. Unter ihren Publikationen befinden sich folgende für diesen Sammelband einschlägige Beiträge: "Judicial Narration as Explanation of Facts and Circumstances," in *Narratives in the Criminal Process*, hg. F. H. Pedersen et al. (2021); "'Select Before you Collect': Uses and Abuses of Profiling and Data Mining in Law and Literature," *Pólemos*, vol. 14 (2020); *Judging from Experience. Law, Praxis, Humanities* (2019); "Fuss about a Footnote, or the Struggle for (the) Law in German Legal Theory," in *As You Law it – Negotiating Shakespeare*, hg. D. Carpi and F. Ost (2018); "Reality, Veracity and Probability in Law and Literature," in *Le droit malgré tout*, hg. Y. Cartuyvels et al. (2018).

***Jeanne Gaakeer** holds degrees in English literature, Dutch law and philosophy. She is Professor of Jurisprudence: Hermeneutical and Narrative Foundations, at Erasmus School of Law, Rotterdam, the Netherlands. She serves as a senior justice in the criminal law section of the Court of Appeal in The Hague, the Netherlands. The focus of her research is on legal-philosophical hermeneutics, narratology, and* Law and Literature//Law and the Humanities *and their relevance to legal practice. With Greta Olson (Giessen University, Germany), she co-founded the European Network for Law and Literature (www.eurnll.org). She is the 2013 recipient of the J.B. White Award bestowed by the Association for the Study of Law, Culture and Humanities. Her recent publications in English include: "Judicial Narration as Explanation of Facts and Circumstances," in: F. H. Pedersen et al. (Ed.),* Narratives in the Criminal Process *(2021); "'Select before you collect': uses and abuses of profiling and data mining in law and literature,"* Pólemos, *vol. 14, (2020);* Judging from Experience. Law, Praxis, Humanities *(2019); "Fuss about a Footnote, or the Struggle for (the) Law in German legal theory," in D. Carpi and F. Ost (Ed.),* As You Law it – Negotiating Shakespeare, *(2018); "Reality, Veracity and Probability in Law and Literature," in Y. Cartuyvels et al. (Ed.),* Le droit malgré tout *(2018).*

Dominique Hipp ist wissenschaftliche Mitarbeiterin und Referentin am Deutschen Historischen Museum Berlin sowie Mitglied des DFG-Netzwerkes *Emanzipation nach der Emanzipation. Jüdische Geschichte, Literatur und Philosophie von 1900 bis heute*. Ihre Forschungsinteressen liegen im Bereich postmigrantischer, queerer und deutsch-jüdischer (Gegenwarts-)Literatur, der Interrelation von Geschichte und Literatur und nicht-fiktionalem Erzählen. Sie ist u.a. Autorin folgender Forschungsbeiträge: *Von NS-Konzentrationslagern erzählen. Angeklagte vor Gericht über Dachau, Mauthausen, Neuengamme und Ravensbrück* (2020), "Die Normalität der Täter? NS-Täter bei Littell, Amis und Jelinek" in einer Aufsatzsammlung zu gegenwärtigen literarischen Reflexionen über den Holocaust (2018), "One Hundred Years of Evil – mockumentary als kontrafaktische Erzählung und kritischer Kommentar zur Erinnerung an die Geschichte des Nationalsozialismus" in einem Band zu kontrafaktischen Darstellungen des Nationalsozialismus (2019) sowie "Staatsbürgerschaft. Eine Geschichte der Emotionen" (im Druck).

Dominique Hipp *studied German literature and history in Freiburg. She currently works as a consultant at the German Historical Museum. She is the member of a research network funded by the German Research Foundation on 'Emancipation after Emancipation: Jewish History, Literature and Philosophy from 1900 to the Present'. She also works as a director of the cultural meeting centre at the monastery of Speinshart. Dr. Hipp's research focuses on postmigrant, queer and German Jewish German contemporary literature, on history and literature and on non-fictional narratives. She is the author of the monograph* Von NS-Konzentrationslagern erzählen *('Telling about NS Concentration Camps: Defendants in Trials about Dachau, Mauthausen, Neuengamme and Ravensbrück'; 2020) and of essays on 'The Normality of Perpetrators: Littell, Amis und Jelinek' (2018), on the genre of the mockumentary and the history of National Socialism (2019) and 'Nationality: A History of Emotions' (in print).*

Claudia Lieb ist Privatdozentin für Neuere deutsche Literatur am Germanistischen Institut der Universität Münster und wissenschaftliche Mitarbeiterin am Käte Hamburger Kolleg Münster „Einheit und Vielfalt im Recht". Ihre Forschungsschwerpunkte umfassen Recht und Literatur, Geschichte der Germanistik, Romantik, Literarische Moderne sowie Literaturausstellungen. Zu ihren Publikationen zählen die Monographien *Germanistiken: Zur Praxis von Literatur- und Rechtswissenschaft 1630 bis 1900* (2022) und *Crash: Der Unfall der Moderne* (2009), der Sammelband *Philologie als Literatur- und Rechtswissenschaft: Germanistik und Romanistik 1730-1870*, hg. mit Christoph Strosetzki (2013) und die Anthologie *Romantik. Das große Lesebuch*, hg. mit Detlef Kremer (2010). Derzeit ediert sie als Mitherausgeberin das Handbuch Literatur & Recht in der Reihe Handbücher zur kulturwissenschaftlichen Philologie (De Gruyter, erscheint voraussichtlich 2022).

Claudia Lieb *habilitated in the area of modern German literature at the German Department of the University of Münster and is a research associate at the Käte Hamburger Kolleg Münster "Unity and Diversity in Law"* (Einheit und Vielfalt im

Recht). *Her areas of research include Law and Literature studies, history of German studies, Romantic literature and the literature of Modernism and literary exhibitions. Her publications include the monographs* Germanistiken: Zur Praxis von Literatur- und Rechtswissenschaft 1630 bis 1900 *(2022), which focuses on the history of German studies and German legal studies between 1630 and 1900; and* Crash: Der Unfall der Moderne *(2009), a study on the concept of accident invented in modernity. She has edited the volume* Philologie als Literatur- und Rechtswissenschaft: Germanistik und Romanistik 1730-1870 *('Philology as Literary Discpline and as an Area of Legal Studies in German and Romance Studies', with Christoph Strosetzki, 2013) and an anthology of Romantic literature (with Detlef Kremer, 2010). She is currently co-editor of the handbook 'Literature and Law' in the De Gruyter series 'Handbooks of Philology and Cultural Studies' (in preparation).*

Hans Jochen Lind unterrichtet Deutsche Literatur, Theaterstudien und Medienwissenschaften an der Universität Yale in den USA sowie an der Universität Wien. Seit 2003 ist er auch als Rechtsanwalt tätig. In 2004-2005 war er als Fulbright Stipendiat und Giamatti-Fellow an der Universität Yale. In der Folge übernahm er die Koordination der Arbeitsgruppe 'Fiktionalität – Interdisziplinäre Ansätze: Recht – Literatur – Naturwissenschaften' des Yale Whitney Humanities Center (2010-2013). In seinem Rechtsreferendariat war er u.a. als Mitarbeiter der fünften Berufungskammer unter dem Vorsitzenden Richter Basel zugeordnet.

Hans Jochen Lind *teaches German Literature, Theatre Studies and Media Studies at Yale University/USA and at the University of Vienna/Austria. Since 2003 he has also worked as an attorney-at-law. He was a Fulbright Scholar (2004–2005) and a Giamatti-Fellow at Yale University (2005–2006) and later acted as coordinator of the Yale Whitney Humanities Center's working group "Fictionality – Interdisciplinary Approaches. Law – Literature – Science" (2010–2013). Legal clerking included the 5th Civil Chamber of Appeal (Law Clerk to Presiding Judge Basel). Publications include* Fictional Discourse and the Law *(Routledge, 2020).*

Arild Linneberg ist emeritierter Universitätsprofessor für Komparatistik an der Universität Bergen in Norwegen. Zwischen 2013 und 2018 war er der Vorsteher des Zentrums für Geisteswissenschaftliche Rechtsstudien und leitete das Forschungsprojekt 'Die Dramaturgie von Justizirrtümern: Über die Konstruktion falscher oder fiktiver Geschichten im Gericht' (2009-2013). Darüber hinaus fungierte er als Principal Investigator im Projekt 'Narratologie von Kriminalfällen' (2016-2020) und stand der Forschungsgruppe 'Rhetorik, Literatur und Recht' (2009-2022) vor. Seine Forschungsschwerpunkte inkludieren Law and Humanities, Kritische Theorie, Ästhetik und Rhetorik. Er ist Autor und Herausgeber von mehr als dreißig Werken, meist in norwegischer Sprache, u.a.

eine Geschichte der norwegischen Literaturkritik zwischen 1848 und 1870 (*Norsk litteraturkritikks historie*); eine Studie über Adornos ästhetische Theorie (1999); Essays über Literatur und Krieg (2001); Reden über Literatur und Recht (2008); sowie eine Studie zur Rhetorik des Justizirrtums (*Justismordets retorikk*; mit Johan Dragvoll et al., 2014). Linneberg hat darüber hinaus wichtige Werke von Theodor Adorno übersetzt (*Ästhetische Theorie*, *Minima Moralia*, *Noten zur Literatur*) sowie zentrale Schriften von Walter Benjamin (*Ausgewählte Schriften* in zwei Bänden, *Das Passagenwerk*; zusammen mit Janne Sund). Darüber hinaus liegen auch Übersetzungen von Werken Siegfried Kracauers (*Das Ornament der Masse*; *Strassen in Berlin und anderswo*) und Hannah Arendts (*The Origins of Totalitarianism*) vor.

***Arild Linneberg** is Professor emeritus of Comparative Literature at the University of Bergen/Norway. He was the director of the Centre for Humanistic Legal Studies (2013–2018), leader of the research project "The Dramaturgy of Miscarriages of Justice. On the Construction of false or fictitious Stories in Court" (2009–2013) and PI on the project, "A Narratology of Criminal Cases" (2016–2020), and leader of the research group "Rhetoric, Literature and Law" (2009–2022). His research interests include law and the humanities, critical theory, aesthetics and rhetoric. He has authored and edited some 30 books, mainly in Norwegian language, such as:* The History of Literary Criticism in Norway 1848–1870 *(1992),* A Rough Guide to Theodor W. Adornos Aesthetic Theory *(1999),* Thirteen melancholic Essays on Literature and War *(2001),* Twelve and a half Speeches on Literature and Law *(2008),* The Rhetoric of Miscarriages of Justice *(co-writer, 2014), and he has translated main works of Theodor W. Adorno (*Ästhetische Theorie; Minima Moralia; Noten zur Literatur*), and together with Janne Sund: Walter Benjamin (*Ausgewählte Schriften in zwei Bänden, Das Passagenwerk*), Siegfried Kracauer (*Das Ornament der Masse *und* Straßen in Berlin und anderswo*) and Hannah Arendt (*The Origins of Totalitarianism*).*

Frode Helmich Pedersen lehrt als associate professor (Førsteamanuensis) nordische Literaturen an der Universität Bergen und arbeitet auch als Literaturkritiker für die norwegische Zeitung *Morgenbladet*. Er war der Leiter des Forschungsprojekts "Narratologie von Kriminalfällen" (2016-2020). Seine vorrangigen Forschungsinteressen liegen im Bereich Narratologie, Law and Literature, Literaturkritik und der norwegischen Literatur des 19. Jahrhunderts. Er hat mehrere Studien in norwegischer Sprache verfasst und ist Mitherausgeber des Sammelbandes *Narrative in the Criminal Process* (2021).

***Frode Helmich Pedersen** is Associate Professor of Nordic Literature at the University of Bergen and literary critic in the Norwegian paper* Morgenbladet. *He was the principal investigator of the research project "A Narratology of Criminal Cases" (2016–2020). His major research interests include narratology, "Law and literature," literary* *criticism and Norwegian literature of the 19th century. He is the author of several books in Norwegian and co-editor of the volume* Narrative in the Criminal Process *(2021).*

Frank L. Schäfer ist Professor für Deutsche Rechtsgeschichte und Bürgerliches Recht sowie Direktor der Germanistischen Abteilung des Instituts für Rechtsgeschichte und geschichtliche Rechtsvergleichung an der Universität Freiburg. Zu seinen Forschungsinteressen zählen Bürgerliches Recht (Schuld- und Sachenrecht) sowie die Grundlagen des Rechts (besonders Deutsche Rechtsgeschichte, Privatrechtsgeschichte und Wissenschaftsgeschichte). Neben zahlreichen Beiträgen zum Privatrecht hat er Abhandlungen zur Geschichte der juristischen Germanistik publiziert, u.a. die Monographie *Juristische Germanistik: Eine Geschichte der Wissenschaft vom einheimischen Privatrecht* (2008).

***Frank L. Schäfer** is Professor of German Legal History and Civil Law and Director of the German Section of the Institute for Legal History and Comparative Legal History at the University of Freiburg. His research interests include civil law (law of obligations and property law) and the foundations of law (especially German legal history, history of private law and history of legal scholarship). In addition to numerous contributions on the subject of private law, he has published work on the history of German legal history as an academic subject, for instance* Juristische Germanistik: Eine Geschichte der Wissenschaft vom einheimischen Privatrecht *(2008).*

Robert Spoo hat die Professur Chapman Distinguished Professorship an der Rechtsfakultät der Universität Tulsa inne. Darüber hinaus war er in seinem ersten Karriereweg für viele Jahre habilitiertes Mitglied des Englischen Seminars der Universität Tulsa und Herausgeber des *James Joyce Quarterly*. Robert Spoo erhielt vor kurzem ein Guggenheim Foundation Fellowship sowie ein Law and Public Affairs (LAPA) Fellowship der Universität Princeton. Seine Forschungsgebiete inkludieren Autoren der literarischen Moderne, Fragen des Urheberrechts, informeller Normen und der Theorie der Gemeinfreiheit (*public domain*). Unter seinen Publikationen befinden sich folgende Studien und Sammelbände: *Modernism and the Law* (2018); *Without Copyrights: Piracy, Publishing, and the Public Domain* (2013); *Ezra and Dorothy Pound: Letters in Captivity, 1945–1946* (mit Omar Pound, 1999); *James Joyce and the Language of History: Dedalus's Nightmare* (1994) sowie and *Ezra Pound and Margaret Cravens: A Tragic Friendship, 1910–1912* (mit Omar Pound, 1988). Neuere Beiträge sind erschienen in der *Stanford Law Review*; der *UCLA Law Review*; in *Law & Literature*; *Cardozo Arts & Entertainment Law Journal*; *Journal of Modern Literature* und dem *James Joyce Quarterly*. Er ist Mitherausgeber der Reihe Law & Literature bei der Oxford University Press.

***Robert Spoo** is Chapman Distinguished Professor at The University of Tulsa College of Law. He has also been the editor of the* James Joyce Quarterly *and a tenured member of the English Department at the University of Tulsa. His research interests include modern authors, copyright law, informal norms, and theories of the public domain. His books and editions include* Modernism and the Law *(2018),* Without Copyrights: Piracy, Publishing, and the Public Domain *(2013),* Ezra and Dorothy Pound: Letters in Captivity, 1945–1946 *(co-edited, 1999),* James Joyce and the Language of History: Dedalus's Nightmare *(1994), and* Ezra Pound and Margaret Cravens: A Tragic Friendship, 1910–1912 *(co-edited, 1988). His recent articles have appeared in the* Stanford Law Review, UCLA Law Review, Law & Literature, Cardozo Arts & Entertainment Law Journal, Journal of Modern Literature, *and* James Joyce Quarterly. *He is co-editor of the Law & Literature series with Oxford University Press, and is the recent recipient of a Guggenheim Foundation Fellowship and of a Law and Public Affairs (LAPA) Fellowship from Princeton University.*

Peter Schneck ist Professor für Amerikanistik und Geschäftsführender Direktor des Instituts für Anglistik und Amerikanistik in Osnabrück. Er ist Leiter eines Teilprojekts des SFB 1385 mit dem Titel "Literature as Property between Law and Culture" ('Literatur als Eigentum im Spannungsfeld zwischen Recht und Kultur'), das so wie der SFB 1385 ("Recht und Literatur") an der Universität Münster von der DFG gefördert wird. Seine Forschungsschwerpunkte liegen im Bereich Law and Literature, Eigentum und Eigentumsrecht, Medienkulturwissenschaft, kognitive Ästhetik und Literaturwissenschaft. Unter seinen Publikationen befinden sich die Bände *Rhetoric and Evidence: Legal Conflict and Literary Representation in US-American Culture* ('Rhetorik und Beweisführung: Die Konflikthaftigkeit des US-amerikanischen Rechts und ihre literarische Darstellung', 2011); *We the People? The US and the Question of Rights* (hg. mit Irina Brittner und Sabine Meyer; 2020) sowie *Terrorism, Media, and the Ethics of Fiction* (hg. mit Philipp Schweighauser, 2010). Zahlreiche Artikel befassen sich u.a. mit Themen wie Kreativität, Kunstgeschichte, kognitiver Literaturtheorie, Literatursoziologie und Migration(sliteratur). Im Jahr 2009 gründete er das Osnabrücker Sommerseminar zur kulturwissenschaftlichen Erforschung von Recht (OSI, Osnabrück Summer Institute for the Cultural Study of the Law).

***Peter Schneck** is Professor of American Studies and currently chair of the Department of English and American Studies at Osnabrück University/Germany. He is currently leading a research group on 'Literature as property between Law and Culture' as part of the Collaborative Research Cluster on "Law and Literature" hosted at the University of Münster/Germany and funded by the German Research Foundation (SFB 1385 "Recht und Literatur"). His research interests include cultural legal studies, 'Law and Literature,' property and ownership, visual and media cultures, cognitive aesthetics and literary studies. Publications include* Evidence and Rhetoric: Legal

Conflict and Literary Representation in US-American Culture *(2011)*, The US and the Question of Rights *(co-edited, 2020)*, Terrorism, Media, and the Ethics of Fiction *(co-edited, 2010) as well as articles on creativity, art history, cognitive literary studies, literary sociology, and migration and literature. He is the founder of the Osnabrück Summer Institute for the Cultural Study of the Law (OSI, since 2009).*

Klaus Stierstorfer Ist Professor für anglistische Literaturwissenschaft an der Universität Münster. Seit 2019 ist er Sprecher des Sonderforschungsbereichs (SFB 1385) "Recht und Literatur" an der Universität Münster. Seit 2017 leitet er das von der Volkswagenstiftung geförderte Projekt 'Literarische Modellierung und die Energiewende'. Von 2013-2018 war er der Sprecher des Graduiertenkollegs (GRK 1886) "Literarische Form". Seine Forschungsschwerpunkte inkludieren die Bereiche Law and Literature, Literaturtheorie, Literaturgeschichte und Diasporastudien. Er hat extensiv publiziert, besonders zum Drama des 19. Jahrhunderts, zu Fragen der Literaturgeschichte und zu den Literaturen in englischer Sprache. Er ist der Herausgeber der Reihe *Grundthemen der Literaturwissenschaft* (Basic Topics in Literary Studies), die vom De Gruyter Verlag herausgegeben wird, momentan 13 Bände umfasst und in Kürze abgeschlossen sein wird. Im Jahr 2006 erschienen auch sechs Bände der von ihm als Reihenherausgeber betreuten Reihe *Women Writing Home, 1700-1920* (London: Pickering & Chatto).

***Klaus Stierstorfer** is Professor of English Literature at the University of Münster, Germany. He is the spokesperson of the Collaborative Research Centre 1385 "Law and Literature" (since 2019) funded by the German Research Foundation. He is also the director of the project "Literary Modelling and Energy Transition" (since 2017, funded by the Volkswagen Foundation). He was spokesperson of the Research Training Group "Literary Form" (2013–2018). His main research interests include law and literature, literary theory, literary history, and diaspora studies. He has published widely on English literature, especially on nineteenth-century British drama, on literary history and on the wider field of literature in English, as in his series edition of* Women Writing Home, *6 vols (London: Pickering and Chatto, 2006). He is series editor of* Grundthemen der Literaturwissenschaft, *13 vols (Berlin, De Gruyter), a series about to completed.*

Ulrike Tabbert ist Oberamtsanwältin bei der deutschen Staatsanwaltschaft Schwerin. Sie hat auch den Posten einer Gastdozentin am Institut für Sprache und Linguistik der Universität Huddersfield in Großbritannien inne, wo sie im Fach Linguistik promovierte. Ihre Forschung befasst sich mit der Darstellung von Verbrechen, Straftätern und Opfern in einer Palette verschiedener Textgattungen. Sie ist die Autorin der Monographien *Crime and Corpus* (2015) und *Language and Crime* (2016) sowie Mitherausgeberin des bei Cambridge University Press im Druck befindlichen Bandes *The Linguistics of Crime: A Linguistic Contribution to the Study of Crime* (2022).

***Ulrike Tabbert** is a Senior Public Prosecutor (Oberamtsanwältin) at a German prosecution office and a Visiting Research Fellow in Language and Linguistics at the University of Huddersfield, UK. She holds a PhD in linguistics from Huddersfield and researches the construction of crime, criminals and victims across a variety of text types. Among her publications are her monographs* Crime and Corpus *(2015) and* Language and Crime *(2016). She is co-editor with John Douthwaite of the volume* The Linguistics of Crime: A Linguistic Contribution to the Study of Crime *(in print, 2022).*

Claire Wrobel ist Professorin (*maître de conférence*) für englische Literaturwissenschaft an der Universität Paris-Panthéon-Assas (Paris 2) und Mitglied des Forschungsnetzwerks VALE (Voix Anglophones, Littérature et Esthétique – Sorbonne Université/France). Ihr Forschungsschwerpunkte liegen auf der Philosophie von Jeremy Bentham (1748-1832) und seiner Rezeption, auf Fragen von Recht und Literatur sowie auf Überwachung in der anglophonen Literatur und Gesellschaft. Sie hat sich auch mit dem Schauerroman und postmodernen Transpositionen solcher Romane und ihrer Motive im Werk von Gegenwartsautorinnen wie Rachel Cusk und Jeanette Winterson befasst. Sie ist Autorin einer französischsprachigen Monographie über den Schauerroman (*roman noir*) und seine Thematisierung von Strafrechtsreform und Überwachung in England im 18. und 19. Jahrhundert sowie eines Buches zum Schauerroman und dem Panoptikon (*Gothique et panoptique*, im Druck, 2022). Mit Michel Houdiard zusammen hat sie den Sammelband *The Dark Sides of the Law: Perspectives on Law, Literature, and Justice in Common Law Countries* (2019) herausgegeben. Aktuell arbeitet sie an einem Sonderheft der Zeitschrift *Revue d'Etudes Benthamiennes* zum Thema Literatur und Panoptizismus und ist Mitherausgeberin einer Sonderausgabe von *Sillages Critiques* über britische Dystopien seit Orwells Roman *1984*.

***Claire Wrobel** is Associate Professor in English at the University Paris-Panthéon-Assas/France and a member of VALE (Voix Anglophones, Littérature et Esthétique – Sorbonne Université/France). Her research interests include the thought of Jeremy Bentham (1748–1832) and its reception, 'Law and Literature', surveillance and/in Anglophone literature. She is a specialist of canonic Gothic literature but has also published articles on rewritings of Gothic tropes by contemporary authors such as Rachel Cusk or Jeanette Winterson. She is the author of* Roman noir, réforme et surveillance en Angleterre (1764–1842)*;* Gothique et panoptique *(2022). She has co-edited* The Dark Sides of the Law: Perspectives on Law, Literature, and Justice in Common Law Countries *(2019). She is currently editing a special issue of the*

Revue d'Etudes Benthamiennes *on literature and panopticism, and co-editing a special issue of* Sillages Critiques *on British dystopias since* Nineteen Eighty-Four.

FSC
www.fsc.org
MIX
Papier | Fördert
gute Waldnutzung
FSC® C083411

Kolibri 360 GmbH
Ferdinand-Jühlke-Straße 7
99095 Erfurt, Deutschland
produktsicherheit@kolibri360.de